P9-DMF-561

WHITE ENSIGN

THE
BRITISH NAVY AT WAR
1939-1945

By the Same Author

THE WAR AT SEA
H.M.S. WARSPITE
THE SECRET CAPTURE

White Ensign

THE
BRITISH NAVY AT WAR
1939-1945

CAPTAIN S. W. ROSKILL
D.S.C., R.N. (RETD.)

UNITED STATES NAVAL INSTITUTE
ANNAPOLIS, MARYLAND

Published simultaneously in the British Commonwealth
by William Collins Sons & Co., Ltd. under the title
The Navy at War 1939-1945
Library of Congress Catalog Card No. 60-15791
© Captain S. W. Roskill, 1960
Printed in Great Britain
Collins Clear-Type Press : London and Glasgow

This book is dedicated to the Officers and Men of the British Maritime Services who fought on, above or beneath the seas in the Second World War

CONTENTS

7

Contents

LIST OF ILLUSTRATIONS

9

List of Illustrations

NOTE:

All but three of the illustrations are reproduced by kind permission of the Imperial War Museum. The three exceptions are:

(1) *The bottom photograph facing p. 281 which belongs to Captain H. J. Reinicke of the German Navy.*
(2) *The bottom photograph facing p. 321 which is the property of Herr Franz Selinger.*
(3) *The top photograph facing p. 441, the copyright of which belongs to the U.S. Coast Guard Service.*

LIST OF MAPS

List of Maps

AUTHOR'S PREFACE

THIS SHORT account of the British effort in the war at sea 1939-45 owes its origin in the first place to the desire of my friends at the United States Naval Institute to include such a volume in their series which deals with the last war from the point of view of all the major participants. Having had a long and intimate association with the United States Navy, starting in London in 1940 while America was yet at peace, and continuing during my service at sea in the Pacific from 1941 to 1943 and in the British naval mission in Washington during the last eighteen months of the war, I was very happy that a book from my pen should be published in the U.S.A. Moreover, I was aware that the Naval Institute had already published volumes about the war by German, Italian and French authors; and as in some respects those writers seemed to me to have shown a rather unhistorical approach to events with which I was familiar, I felt that an unbiased account of the policies, purposes, successes and failures of the British sea services might help to preserve the balance of the Naval Institute's series. Though I readily admit that I feel proud of the tale of endurance in face of disaster, of patience in adversity, and of persistence in the pursuit of victory here recounted I have none the less tried to present it with honesty towards our own mistakes and with fairness towards our late enemies.

It was Mr. Mark Bonham Carter of Collins & Co. who suggested that a book such as I had in mind would also meet a need in my own country, by making available to a wider public than would be reached by my four-volume official history both the broad outline of the greatest maritime war in which Britain has ever been engaged, and the lessons to be derived from study of those events. It was, however, not until I had sketched the book in outline that I realised that to produce it in a form suitable to both British and American readers presented some rather difficult problems—particularly with regard to the last four years of the war, when the Royal and United States Navies worked and fought alongside each other in every theatre all over the world. Thus it was plainly redundant to give American readers even a bare outline of their own Navy's contribution; yet after the United States entered the war there was no aspect of the struggle at sea which was unaffected by that service's actions and outlook. To British readers on the other hand, the omission of some account both of the impact of American strategy and policies on our own affairs, and of the United States Navy's participation in joint operations, would have given a highly misleading impression of the manner in which victory was won. Furthermore, it has always seemed to me that the strategy employed in the Pacific, and the tactics of the American-fought battles in that vast theatre, provide a fascinating study and suggest some of the most important lessons of the whole war; and I have sometimes felt that they have received too little attention from my countrymen.

I therefore came to the conclusion that, even at the risk of including some material which my American readers might think superfluous, I had to give a sufficient account of the great campaigns and battles in the Pacific to place those events in proper perspective, and to bring out the influence which they had on British strategy and dispositions. Though it is justifiable that the White Ensign ships and aircraft should occupy the central position on my stage, I have here tried to do justice to the work of their colleagues flying the Stars and Stripes; and when the purposes of the two maritime Allies diverged I have, while generally taking my stand from the British point of view, endeavoured to present the case with fairness towards those who saw things differently. Nor would I wish to place excessive emphasis on British-American differences, as has been done in some volumes of war memoirs and autobiographies: for the most outstanding feature of the war was not the occasional disagreements but the degree of intimacy and understanding, and the mutual confidence developed between the two nations' maritime services; and placed alongside that great accomplishment the differences fade almost into insignificance.

I would thank both my British and American publishers for their patience in waiting for this volume while I was still engaged on completing the official histories, and for giving me much wise guidance and some valuable criticisms. Commander Geoffrey Hare, D.S.C., R.N., has, as so often, given me invaluable help in checking facts and figures and in preparing the maps, all of which have been

skilfully drawn by Mr. Charles Green; while the devotion of my
secretary, Miss Edith V. Eales, in deciphering my manuscript and
amending it to suit all my whims and fancies has been beyond praise.
I am also very grateful to Mrs. Trevor Napier for allowing me to
quote from her husband's wartime letters, and to Captain J. S. S.
Litchfield, O.B.E., M.P., R.N., for allowing me to make use of a
letter about his experiences in the Arctic convoy PQ 17. Finally, I
would thank Her Majesty's Stationery Office for permission to
include copyright material contained in my official history, and the
Imperial War Museum for permission to reproduce illustrations.

S. W. ROSKILL

Blounce,
South Warnborough,
Basingstoke, Hants.
July 1960.

" This power [i.e. sea power] feels and is moved by many interests ; it has a great history in the past, it is making a great and yet more wonderful history in the present."

A. T. Mahan *The Influence of Sea Power on the French Revolution and Empire* (Sampson Low, Marston & Co.), 14th Ed., Vol. II, p. 373.

CHAPTER I

THE SHIPS AND THE MEN

" Men make the city and not walls or ships without men in
them."

Thucydides VII, 7.7. (Nikias's speech to the
Athenians at Syracuse.)

MARITIME POWER is the means whereby we control the sea for
our own purposes and deny such control to the enemy. It is
a complex phenomenon depending on a wide range of human
factors, such as experience of the element on which it works, and
of material resources such as the ships and aircraft which apply it;
but it is safe to say that no factor is more influential than the quality
and training of the men who handle and fight the instruments—
whether they swim, float or fly—by which it is applied. Although
it is undoubtedly true that without secure and efficient bases (whether
mobile or static), and without adequate sea transport to support and
sustain the active fleets, maritime power cannot be effectively
wielded, in the final issue—and notwithstanding the vast changes
which technological progress has wrought during the past two or
three decades—it is on the men that the decision of life and death
for countries and their causes will largely depend. Thus it will be
logical at the outset of our story to survey briefly the state of the
Royal Navy's personnel in 1939, and then to summarise the types
and condition of the ships and aircraft provided for the service of
the sea.

Before the war, and for many years previously, the British Navy
had been wholly manned not only by volunteers, but by volunteers
who had engaged themselves to serve for what by more recent
standards can only be regarded as very long terms. Training began
at early ages—at 13 for most officers and about 16 for the majority
of the men; the officers looked for a life's career in the service, while
the men signed initially a twelve-year engagement which counted

from the age of 18, when they had completed their shore training. After their first period of service the men could re-engage for a further 10 years, thus qualifying for a pension; and a great many of the best of them did so. The men in their second term of service were mostly Chief or Petty Officers, or at least Leading Rates, and their value was immense. They were not only masters of their special crafts—which might be those of the seaman, signalman, engineer, electrical or many other branches—but they were deeply imbued with the traditions of the service, and with knowledge of the element on which they had passed the greater part of their lives. They were indeed the direct descendants of the men of the eighteenth or early nineteenth centuries, of whom it was said that their " blood was Stockholm tar, and their every finger a marlinespike"; and their influence on the younger entries was profound. Yet in the newer branches—wireless telegraphy, electrical engineering and so on—the influence of technological advance was already making itself felt, a higher standard of education was being demanded, and a difference of outlook was becoming perceptible. It was, however, remarkable that the practitioners of the new arts had been so smoothly assimilated with the older school that a warship's company remained an integrated, composite whole, with men who could sail a cutter in a gale of wind or splice a 6-inch wire living and working happily alongside others whose skill in maintaining fire control or radio equipment, or in operating immensely powerful machines, was a closed mystery to the older seamen. Pride of ship and of service was the common bond between them; and that pride, though rarely expressed, could be felt very strongly at all times. It was indeed the catalyst which fused the many different human elements into the homogeneous whole of a warship's company; and it undoubtedly owed a great deal to the early entry of officers and men, to the long apprenticeships they served, and to the age-old traditions which inspired them.

The numerical strength of the permanent Royal Navy has, considering its world-wide influence, always been remarkably small. On 1st January, 1939, it consisted of under 10,000 officers—the great majority of whom were of course in the lower ranks—and about 109,000 men. To those should be added 12,400 officers and men of the Royal Marines, who in those days manned a quarter of the armaments of all the larger ships and, in addition, maintained their ancient function of instant readiness to provide landing parties wherever and whenever they might be needed. The active service officers and men of the Navy and Marines were, however, barely sufficient to man those ships which were kept in more or less permanent commission. To man the Reserve Fleet, composed of the older ships which had undergone little or no modernisation during the long period of financial stringency between the wars, it was necessary to recall reservists to the colours. These comprised about 73,000 more officers and men of various qualifications. Some were pensioners, or men in the Royal Fleet Reserve who had completed their 12-year engagement but had not renewed it; others were Merchant Navy men who had joined the Royal Naval Reserve and had undergone a certain amount of naval training; and not the least important were the 6,000 Royal Naval Volunteer Reservists. These last were amateurs, who of their own volition had devoted their spare time to training for the sea service; and their jealously guarded amateur status enabled them to bring to the Navy an unrivalled enthusiasm, for which they were greatly respected by their professional brethren. Such, then, were the reserves which the Admiralty could rapidly call on in emergency—to bring the total strength of the service up to some 200,000. Some reservists had been recalled at the time of the crisis with Italy over the Abyssinian adventure of 1935, and again three years later when Hitler's rapacious designs on Czecho-Slovakia brought Britain to the brink of war; and those test mobilisations proved valuable rehearsals for the clash with the dictators which the Royal Navy had increasingly regarded as inevitable. Thus no surprise was felt when, in mid-June, 1939, the Reserve Fleet was manned, and in the following August full mobilisation was ordered.

As the war progressed and more and more ships, some of them of entirely new design and functions, entered the naval service the original reserves had to be supplemented by a very large intake of officers and men from a wide variety of sources. It was in the R.N.V.R. that the expansion was much the greatest, and that reserve finally reached a total of 48,000 officers and 5,000 ratings. Young men from all over the Empire came to Britain to join the Royal Navy: many of them gained commissions in the R.N.V.R., and not a few rose to command destroyers, submarines and smaller vessels such as combined operations craft. The contribution of the

R.N.V.R. to the rapidly expanded Fleet Air Arm was particularly great, and before many years had passed some of its squadrons were commanded by officers from that branch of the reserves. At its peak in mid-1944 the personnel of the Royal Navy totalled 863,500 officers and men, including 73,500 of the Women's Royal Naval Service (" Wrens "), whose remarkable keenness and versatility quickly won the confidence and affection of the entire regular service. Though the majority of the new men were recruited under the National Service Acts for " hostilities only," it was the comparatively small body of regulars and the original reserves who held the ring while expansion was in progress, and simultaneously undertook the training of the vast influx of men from civilian life.

Let us now look at the ships available to Britain, and how they were disposed as the lights began to go out all over Europe in that fateful summer. Her main maritime strength was concentrated in home waters and in the Mediterranean. The Home Fleet, under Admiral Sir Charles Forbes, consisted of five battleships, two battle cruisers, two aircraft carriers, three squadrons totalling fifteen cruisers, two flotillas each of eight or nine destroyers and about a score of submarines. Its main base was at Scapa Flow in the Orkneys; but that great anchorage, which had served us so well in the previous war, was in no fit state to receive the fleet when it moved north at the end of August, 1939. This state of affairs derived from a complex series of causes, including the demilitarisation of the base at the end of the earlier struggle, and the late date (April, 1938) at which the decision had been taken that Rosyth on the Firth of Forth could not meet the needs of the fleet in the event of a new clash with Germany. The failure to push ahead rapidly with the strengthening of the defences of Scapa, once the decision had been taken to base the fleet there, meant however that Admiral Forbes was deprived of virtually all security for his ships while in harbour; and he very soon had to abandon his chosen base. We shall return to that matter later. Apart from the main Home Fleet, considerable naval strength was disposed in the English Channel (two battleships, two aircraft carriers, three cruisers and a destroyer flotilla), and in the Humber River on the east coast (two cruisers and a destroyer flotilla); while escort forces were allocated to the Plymouth command for duty in the Western Approaches to the British Isles, and to Portsmouth and Dover to guard our Channel traffic; and

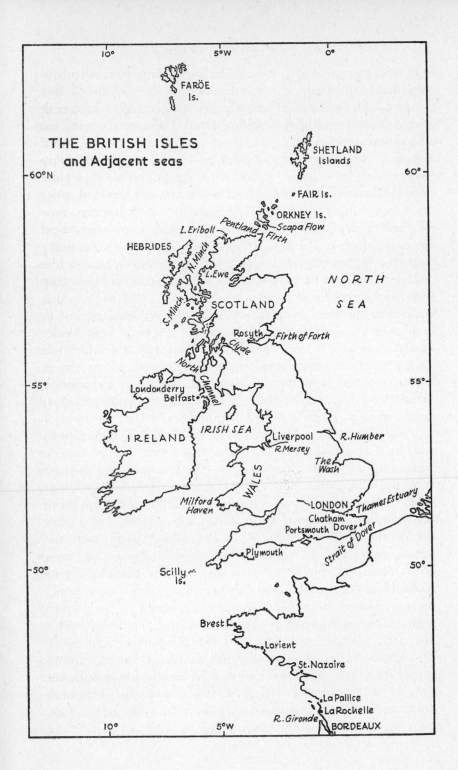

THE BRITISH ISLES
and Adjacent seas

FARÖE Is.

SHETLAND Islands

FAIR Is.

ORKNEY Is.
Scapa Flow

L. Eriboll
Pentland Firth

HEBRIDES

N. Minch

L. Ewe

SCOTLAND

NORTH SEA

S. Minch

Rosyth
Firth of Forth

Clyde

North Channel

Londonderry
Belfast

IRELAND

IRISH SEA

Liverpool
R. Mersey

R. Humber

The Wash

WALES

Milford Haven

LONDON
Thames Estuary

Chatham
Portsmouth Dover

Strait of Dover

Plymouth

Scilly Is.

Brest

Lorient

St. Nazaire

La Pallice
La Rochelle
R. Gironde
BORDEAUX

10°   5°W   0°

60°N   60°

55°   55°

50°   50°

10°   5°W

minesweepers were sent to all the more important naval and commercial ports around our coasts.[1]

In the Mediterranean Fleet, which was based on Alexandria (by virtue of the Anglo-Egyptian treaty of 1936) because its normal base at Malta was considered too vulnerable to Italian air attack, Admiral Sir Andrew Cunningham had three battleships, one aircraft carrier, two cruiser squadrons (six ships), four flotillas of destroyers and one of submarines. It is no exaggeration to say that this fleet was at the time the finest naval force in the world; for it comprised many of our best ships, and they had been trained by Cunningham and his predecessors to the highest pitch of fighting efficiency. But, as with the Home Fleet, its work was greatly handicapped by the inadequacies of the base organisation, which had been extemporised somewhat hurriedly in Egypt.

Farther overseas—in China, the East and West Indies, and the south Atlantic—were squadrons of cruisers and escort vessels whose chief duty was the defence of trade in the waters for which they were each responsible; while ships belonging to the small navies of the Commonwealth of Australia, Canada and New Zealand (comprising cruisers and destroyers) were very soon to come from their home waters to join our fleets in the main theatres of war.

What of the ships themselves which comprised the fleets and squadrons summarised above? It is undeniable that in 1939 the position of the Royal Navy was immensely stronger in the quality of its men than in the matter of giving them modern ships to fight with. Not until 1937 had a reluctant government voted funds even for a modest measure of rearmament, and for the previous two decades the Admiralty had waged an unceasing struggle to prevent our entire Navy declining into obsolescence. In part, this state of affairs arose through the confidence placed by politicians in the naval limitation agreements of the early 1920s, and in part through the age-old unwillingness to provide funds for the fighting services until a threat becomes so plain that no alternative remains open to our rulers. But the aggregate effects of the parsimonious policies of the inter-war years were extremely serious. Of Britain's fifteen capital ships only two (the *Nelson* and *Rodney*) had been built since the end of the previous struggle, and modernisation work on the remainder had only proceeded very slowly. True, by 1939 four

[1] See Map p. 23.

new battleships (the *King George V* class) were building; but none of them would enter service for another eighteen months. Of the six aircraft carriers in service, one was a very small ship, four were conversions from battleship or battle-cruiser hulls, and only one (the *Ark Royal*) was new and had been specifically designed as a carrier. Six new fleet carriers of 23,000 tons, capable of operating 35-55 aircraft, had been laid down since 1937; but, as with the new battleships, none could be ready to join the fleet for many months after the outbreak of war. In cruisers, and still more in destroyers, the situation was a good deal better; for of 25 large and 38 small cruisers (including Dominion ships and 6 old cruisers converted to anti-aircraft escorts) all but 21 had been completed between the wars, and 19 more were on the stocks in 1939, and for the previous ten years the Admiralty had managed to obtain approval to include a complete flotilla of destroyers in each year's naval programme. Thus of 168 destroyers available for service, about two-thirds were relatively modern ships. Finally, most of the 69 submarines had also been built comparatively recently.

Because the great majority of the modern destroyers would be required to work with the main fleets separate provision had to be made to meet the very large demands for anti-submarine and anti-aircraft convoy escorts. This urgent problem was tackled energetically—once steps to rearm the fleet had received government approval in 1937; and it was tackled from several directions. Firstly, the Admiralty converted the 6 old cruisers already mentioned and 15 destroyers of 1914-18 war design to anti-aircraft escorts; secondly, they ordered more escort vessels of the generic type known as sloops, which displaced 1,000-1,250 tons and, although slow, were blessed with comparatively long sea-keeping endurance. By 1939 there were 53 of these useful vessels in service. Thirdly, an entirely new design of small and fast destroyer (900 tons and 32 knots) with dual purpose gun armaments but no torpedo tubes was introduced. Twenty of these " Hunt " class ships were on the stocks on the outbreak of war, and another 66 were included in the first two naval building programmes to be approved thereafter. Though their short endurance proved a considerable handicap, they performed excellent service in the narrow seas and on the coastal shipping routes. Lastly, a completely new type of small long-endurance escort vessel, designed on the lines of the whale-catcher and called corvettes, was produced. In 1939 and '40 a total of 141 of these vessels was authorised, and although their small size and liveliness in a seaway taxed their crews severely, they soon proved their value on the ocean routes. Unhappily their top speed (15 knots) was too slow to enable them to overtake a surfaced submarine.

From the foregoing brief summary of the escort vessels in service and building it will be seen that the gravest deficiency lay in the shortage of fast, long-endurance ships capable of making the Atlantic crossing without refuelling, and able to catch and destroy a U-boat whether it was surfaced or submerged. Modern destroyers would meet the need best, but such ships take a long time to build; and the rearmament programmes were started too late to enable that deficiency to be made good before war broke out. Until the frigates of the 1941 and later programmes, many of which were built in America under Lend-Lease, began to enter service, we thus suffered from an acute and chronic shortage of fast, long-range escorts.

It will be appropriate to mention here one other deficiency from which the Royal Navy suffered in 1939. In spite of the frequency with which, during the past three centuries, we had been called on to carry military expeditions overseas and to land them on a hostile coast, the importance of "combined operations" as a means of exploiting the benefits derived from maritime power seems to have been almost completely ignored between the wars. Very little training was carried out in such highly specialised tasks, no common doctrine had been developed between the services, and in 1939 we had only just begun to construct a few of the special types of craft needed for such operations. In part this undoubtedly arose through the misleading claims made by the extreme protagonists of air power, to the effect that the new instruments of war had made sea-borne landings impossibly hazardous; but in part it was also derived from neglect of the abundant experiences available in history. It thus happened that we had to relearn all the old lessons from the beginning, and by a costly process of trial and error. But Mr. Churchill fully realised the importance of combined operations, and after July, 1940, when he set up a special directorate to develop weapons and train men, progress was on the whole rapid; for in the Royal Marines (which are controlled by the Admiralty) we possessed a corps whose tradition accorded with the needs.

As to the equipment of our ships, the guns, torpedoes and fire control instruments provided for surface action were—except in the case of the older vessels—well designed and of good performance; but in anti-aircraft defence the situation was much less satisfactory, since our guns and control arrangements were both inferior to those fitted in certain foreign navies—notably those of Germany and America; and for close-range work we soon came to rely largely on weapons of Swiss and Swedish design. The "Asdic" anti-submarine detection equipment fitted in all our flotilla vessels was, on the other hand, a great advance on the hydrophone listening apparatus of the 1914-18 war; but its fine performance in the hands of skilled operators did cause the Naval Staff to believe that the submarine menace had to a great extent been overcome, and so to underestimate the consequences of a renewal of the *guerre de course* by underwater raiders. In 1939 very few ships were as yet fitted with any form of radar, and the sets were only capable of giving distant warning of the presence of an enemy. But in the Admiralty the immense potentialities of the new device which the scientists had put into the hands of our sailors was fully recognised, and as soon as it became possible to produce sets which worked on short (50 and 10 centimetre) wavelengths arrangements were made to produce the instruments and to fit them in ships as fast as possible. It is no exaggeration to say that in radar development Britain led the world—to the great benefit later on of our American ally.

Turning from the surface fleet to naval air developments we came face to face with what has since been widely recognised as a grave error of policy for which the Royal Navy itself cannot escape a share of the blame. At the end of the 1914-18 war naval aviation was a vigorous, if youthful branch of the British sea services, whose value was certainly recognised among far-seeing officers; but it had so far made little impression on the ranks of orthodoxy, which still pinned their faith on the heavy gun as the ultimate arbiter of defeat or victory at sea. In consequence in 1918 no less than 2,500 naval aircraft and 55,000 men were transferred from the Navy, with scarcely a murmur of protest, to the newly-formed Royal Air Force. Nearly twenty years were to pass before the Admiralty regained full control of naval aviation; and during the greater part of those two decades the young Fleet Air Arm was ruled by a complicated compromise arrangement made between the Admiralty and Air Ministry, which only worked at all thanks to the fundamental goodwill and common sense that prevailed in both services. Its most serious consequences were, firstly, the frustrating effect that it had on the development of aircraft specifically designed for offensive and defensive work from carriers; for while the Admiralty stated the specifications and had to provide the funds, the responsibility for design and production rested with the Air Ministry. Secondly, it delayed the formation of a strong and experienced corps of naval aviators until it was almost too late. From 1918 until 1937 the Admiralty was thus in the anomalous position of being responsible for the design and construction of aircraft carriers, but was dependent on another department for the aircraft which would work from them, and on another service to provide a proportion of the aircrews who flew on and off their decks. Development of the carriers themselves thus proceeded steadily, from the conversions of the early 1920s to the *Ark Royal* (completed in 1938), and so to the *Illustrious* and *Implacable* fleet carriers of the 1936-1939 programmes; but the Air Ministry, itself long subject to even tighter financial stringency than the Admiralty, could hardly be expected to develop and produce naval bombers, torpedo-bombers and fighters at the highest priority, what time it was having the greatest difficulty in meeting its own requirements for shore-based aircraft. The result was that the standard naval aircraft of 1939 (such as the Swordfish torpedo-bomber-reconnaissance biplane, the Skua fighter-dive-bomber, and the Roc and Sea Gladiator fighters) were none of them machines of the quality which the few but splendidly keen naval pilots and observers needed; and until modern American aircraft, such as the Grumman Martlet and Avenger became available under Lend-Lease, the Royal Navy had to make do with a succession of adaptations from land aircraft such as the Seafire (which was a converted Spitfire), or with types which had been developed for its own purposes but at such a low priority that they were obsolescent even before they entered service.

As to the duties to be carried out by naval aircraft, reconnaissance for the fleet was placed first, attack on retiring enemy surface forces (with the object of enabling our heavy ships to bring them to action) came second, protection of the fleet against submarine and air attacks third, and gunfire spotting in ship to ship actions or shore bombardments last. No mention, it will be observed, was made of the need to provide aircraft for defence of shipping or small carriers to work with mercantile convoys.

Looking back to-day the most astonishing thing about British naval aviation in the last war is not that it occasionally failed to meet the heavy demands made on it, but that the carriers and their aircrews accomplished so much with the inadequate types of aircraft which they had to use.

Nor in 1939 was the situation regarding the provision of shore-based aircraft to co-operate with our surface fleets and squadrons one whit more satisfactory than the supply of modern aircraft for the Fleet Air Arm. This was a constitutional responsibility of Coastal Command of the Royal Air Force; but not until 1936 did it gain independent status under its own Commander-in-Chief, and throughout the preceding years it had always been the Cinderella of its own service. None the less, 1937 produced important decisions defining the status and duties of Coastal Command, as well as plans for its expansion; and as those decisions, though modified as experience was gained, governed co-operation between our naval and air forces throughout the war, we should look at them a little more closely. It was, firstly, established that Coastal Command would be responsible for trade protection, reconnaissance work, and co-operation with the Royal Navy; and, secondly, that its aircraft would not be diverted to other purposes without Admiralty agreement. The most surprising omission from the duties allocated to Coastal Command was the function of attacking enemy warships and supply vessels. We shall see later, as our story unfolds, how this became one of its most important activities; but the failure to appreciate the Command's offensive potentialities before the war certainly contributed to the very long delay in equipping it with a properly organised striking force.

As to the strength to be provided to Coastal Command, the 1937 agreement established that 291 aircraft were to be allocated to the home station, mainly for convoy escort duties and for reconnaissance over the North Sea, and 48 at convoy assembly points abroad; but we knew that under the current expansion programme less than two-thirds of the required total would be available by the spring of 1939. Nor was the situation satisfactory regarding the types of aircraft then in service; for the replacement of the slow and obsolete Anson by Lockheed Hudsons purchased in America had not gone very far, and few of the modern Sunderland flying boats were as yet in service.

Perhaps the most important decision regarding sea-air co-operation taken before the war was the establishment of Area Combined Headquarters (A.C.H.Q.s) adjacent to the naval bases of Plymouth, Chatham and Rosyth. In those headquarters all three services were represented, but their main function was to exercise joint control of the Navy's and Coastal Command's forces; for the three Groups of the latter command (Nos. 15, 16 and 18) responsible for providing air co-operation in our home waters covered the same areas as the relevant naval commands. By controlling both sea and air forces from the same centre it was possible not only to arrange for the efficient hour to hour direction of all maritime forces, but to create an intimate understanding between the two services concerned. This system reached the peak of its success in the Atlantic Battle, which was fought mainly from a new headquarters for the Western Approaches Command and No. 15 Group which was established at Liverpool in 1941; but as the war progressed the same principles were introduced on all foreign stations.

So much for the maritime strength available to Britain shortly before the war. We must now look briefly at the organisation, which had grown up in the Admiralty during the preceding three centuries, by which it was controlled. The British Admiralty differed from the other service departments in being an operational as well as an administrative headquarters. This meant that all naval operations were centrally controlled from Whitehall, and that the Admiralty held the right to send orders to any fleet or squadron, or to individual ships, when judged necessary—even over the heads of the Commanders-in-Chief. This unique arrangement dates only from the 1914-18 war, when developments in the field of naval intelligence were held to justify it. The dangers and the possibilities of confusion inherent in it will easily be appreciated; but the centralised collection, evaluation and dissemination of intelligence was held to be sufficiently important to justify acceptance of the risks. Nor is there the slightest doubt that the work of the Admiralty's Operational Intelligence Centre (O.I.C.) was outstandingly successful right through the war—especially in dealing with the U-boat threat. The United States Navy, whose representatives were shown our methods in 1940, later paid us the compliment of modelling its parallel organisation on similar lines. Whether the need for a centralised intelligence organisation justifies, let alone necessitates, centralised operational control is, of course, quite another matter. Certainly the U.S. Navy never found it necessary. But there is little doubt that, during the first two years of the war, the Admiralty intervened in the day to day conduct of operations to a quite unjustifiable extent; nor that on several occasions their signals caused confusion, and on one occasion brought about a disaster of some magnitude.[1]

The excessive interventions of the early months derived in large measure from the character and personality of the remarkable man who, on the day that war was declared, returned to the Admiralty as First Lord after an interval of nearly a quarter of a century. Mr. Churchill's appointment was certainly warmly welcomed throughout the Navy—not only for his outstanding record during the long years of his exclusion from office, nor yet for his utter integrity and his colourful personality; but because, as the whole world was soon to find out, there was a magnetism in his character, a single-minded devotion in his patriotism, and a dynamic force in his energy which made it difficult—and sometimes dangerous—to resist his forcefully presented arguments. No doubt the arrival of a tornado in any government department is in large measure a healthy barometric phenomenon; for it blows the accumulated cobwebs and dust of ages out of the windows, disperses inertia, and stimulates everyone to greater efforts. But in Churchill's case a price had to be paid for this refreshing gale; and part of the price was that, as he himself has described[2], he found the Operational Intelligence Centre (or rather the streamlined duplication of it called the First Lord's War Room) an irresistible attraction; and once inside its map-hung walls the temptation to send signals could too seldom be repressed. But the whole blame for such practices cannot be laid at Churchill's door; for he left the Admiralty to become Prime Minister in May, 1940, and the interventions did not cease with his translation to the

---

[1] To convoy PQ.17 in the Arctic in July, 1942. See pp. 204-9.

[2] See *The World Crisis*, Vol II (Thornton Butterworth, 1923) pp. 126-7: ". . . The Admiralty is not merely an administrative Department, but is actually carrying on the war, and . . . orders are being issued constantly from this office to ships and squadrons in immediate contact with the enemy" (W. S. Churchill, 1st Lord, to H. H. Asquith, Prime Minister, 22nd January, 1915). Also p. 132 " There can be few purely mental experiences more charged with cold excitement than to follow, almost from minute to minute, the phases of a great naval action from the silent rooms of the Admiralty."

highest office in the land. The First Sea Lord himself, Admiral of the Fleet Sir Dudley Pound, probably initiated some of them even while Churchill was First Lord; and he was undoubtedly responsible for the continuation of the interventions after that time. None the less, we should remember that the tremendous strains and stresses of the first few years of war were chiefly carried, as far as the Navy was concerned, by Admiral Pound; that the fleet of which he was the service head rose to every demand made on it, and that he won and retained Mr. Churchill's complete confidence and even his affection—in spite of having to head him off from some of his more dangerous projects. Though this last may be a somewhat negative accomplishment, with a leader such as Churchill it was an extraordinarily difficult one; for apart from his active interest in day-to-day operations he was always full of ideas regarding the future conduct of the war. In the Admiralty he at once made his presence felt in every field—tactical, technical and strategic; and if the Naval Staff sometimes found him a difficult master to serve, he inspired everyone with something of his own burning patriotism and vitality. But the settlement of disagreements with him and his advisers largely fell, as was inevitable, on Admiral Pound.

Perhaps the most remarkable accomplishment of the Admiralty during the first anxious months of the war was that, in spite of all the new demands being made on the Naval Staff and supply departments, and the constant stream of minutes, directives, urgings, protests and objurgations which emanated from the First Lord's room, the less spectacular but more essential problems of maintaining our world-wide maritime control were successfully met. Convoys were organised and escorted homeward and outward, the main fleets swept the seas for which they were responsible, the reconnaissance aircraft peered into the mists probing for signs of enemy activity, while the minesweepers searched the shallows for hidden perils. We must now look briefly at the plans and policies which made all that possible.

CHAPTER II

MARITIME PLANS AND POLICY, 1939

" The Royal Navy of England hath ever been its greatest
defence and ornament; it is its ancient and natural strength—
the floating bulwark of our island."

Sir William Blackstone, *Commentaries* 1765-
1769, Vol. I, Book I, Chapter XIII.

THE BRITISH naval war plans were based on a conflict in alliance
with France against both the European Axis powers. Responsibility for the Atlantic and North Sea would rest mainly with the
Royal Navy, though the French would make important contribu-
tions to convoy work on the southerly routes and to the pursuit of
enemy raiders in the broad spaces of the Atlantic. The Mediterranean
theatre was to be divided between France and Britain, with the
former responsible for the western and the latter for the eastern
basin; but a force comprising some of the older French battleships
and some modern cruisers would come to Alexandria to work under
Admiral Cunningham's command. The Italian Navy was something of an unknown quantity—for we had never fought against it;
but we were apprehensive of the power of the numerous bombers
of the Regia Aeronautica, and of the 105 submarines which the
Regia Marina possessed. The decision was therefore taken to close
the Mediterranean to mercantile traffic, and to divert all shipping
bound for the Middle East to the long haul (11,000 miles) round
the Cape of Good Hope. This at once produced the need to create
fuelling and repair bases on the African coasts, where very little
existed by way of naval shore installations. Freetown in the colony
of Sierra Leone thus at once assumed great importance, and the
commercial ports of Cape Town, Durban and Mombasa had to
prepare to deal with a vastly increased traffic, and to meet the needs
of the naval escorts.

As long as the British Mediterranean Fleet had the co-operation

and support of its French allies there was every reason to believe that it could deal adequately with the surface ships of the Italian Navy; but the possibility that it might have to face the same enemies alone was never envisaged in the pre-war plans. They did, however, take account of the increasingly unfriendly attitude of Japan; but recognised that, if that country joined its European Axis partners, only by leaving the whole Mediterranean to the French could we provide a balanced fleet to fight in the Pacific. We then had hopes that such a fleet would reach Singapore ninety days after orders for the move had been given. Little did we foresee that, when the need actually arose, we would not only have no French ally to share the burden in Mediterranean and Atlantic waters, but would already have suffered such heavy losses that the possibility of sending a proper fleet east had vanished.

The German surface ships, though greatly outnumbered by those forming our Home Fleet, were viewed with some apprehension; for they were all modern vessels (we having generously deprived the Germans of all their older units in 1918); and we knew that the so-called pocket-battleships, with their powerful armaments and very long endurance, had been specially designed for commerce raiding. Though we were aware that the battle cruisers *Scharnhorst* and *Gneisenau* were among the most powerful warships afloat, and that the heavy cruiser *Hipper* would soon be joined by four sister ships, we did not know that all major warships built by the Germans after the pocket-battleships greatly exceeded their published displacements—which were supposed to conform to treaty limitations. While we recognised that only a concentration of our heavy cruisers could fight a pocket-battleship with some prospects of success, we were unaware that the *Hipper* and her sisters greatly outclassed any cruiser we had afloat, or that the two German battle cruisers, though less heavily armed than our capital ships, were so well protected and possessed such a good turn of speed that they were extremely formidable adversaries.

The Admiralty regarded the major German warships as the most serious threat to our shipping. " Nothing would paralyse our supply system and seaborne trade so successfully," wrote the First Sea Lord shortly before the war, "as attack by surface raiders." Thus in home waters our plans were based primarily on the need to detect the departure of such raiders, and to bring them to action as quickly as

possible. Hence arose the priority given to the North Sea air reconnaissance mentioned in the last chapter; while the cruisers of the Home Fleet were to patrol on a line drawn between the Shetland Islands and Norway with the same object.

In the light of what we now know it does seem surprising that the submarine threat should have been regarded as less dangerous than the surface raiders, and that the effect of air attacks on merchant-men and of mines laid in our coastal channels and estuaries should have been considerably underestimated; for we had assessed German U-boat strength (56 boats, of which about half were ocean-going and half coastal types) almost correctly, and we knew that the Luftwaffe was a very formidable force. Several factors contributed to the misjudgment over the U-boat threat. In the first place, though we had little faith in German respect for treaties, we did not believe that they would again wage unrestricted warfare with submarines—because of the risk of antagonising neutral countries, and especially the United States. Secondly, we had great confidence in our Asdic submarine detection equipment, which was, in fact, a very marked advance on anything we had used in the earlier struggle against the U-boats. It thus happened that, before the war, there was considerable discussion regarding the desirability of order-ing merchant ships into convoy. The Air Staff for a long time opposed the measure, on the grounds that ships concentrated into convoys would present easier targets to enemy aircraft; and the old arguments about delays to shipping and congestion in ports—all of which had been discredited during the earlier struggle—were also resurrected. Happily at the end of 1937 the Admiralty and Air Ministry reached an agreement, which was in fact a victory for those who favoured convoy, and the Navy was then able to press ahead with the measures necessary for it to be promptly introduced on many routes if war broke out. By 1939 the necessary staff had been sent to all major commercial ports abroad, and the intricate world-wide organisation needed to gather ships into convoy had been established by the Admiralty and Ministry of Shipping. On 26th August, 1939, as the clouds gathering over Europe darkened, the Admiralty assumed control of all merchant shipping, and within the next month escorted convoys were sailing on our east coast between the Thames and Firth of Forth, outward and homeward between Britain and Gibraltar, and homeward from Halifax across the north Atlantic and from Sierra Leone in West Africa. The promptness with which these measures were put in hand was a fine tribute to the care with which the pre-war plans had been cast. Thus was the ancient strategic principle that escort of convoy provides the best means not only of protecting merchant shipping, but of counter-attacking commerce raiders, both reaffirmed and rapidly vindicated. Unfortunately, if inevitably, the movements of Britain's 3,000 merchant ships were so far-spread and so complex, and our shortage of flotilla vessels was so acute, that it was impossible for all ships to be sailed in escorted convoys—even during the final stages homeward across the Atlantic. The faster ships (over 15 knots) and also those which could not keep up with a 9-knot convoy were therefore generally routed independently; and it was among them, and especially among the slow independents, that the U-boats generally claimed their victims. Furthermore, the effectiveness of the convoy strategy was all too soon vitiated by a school of thought— supported, regrettably, by some senior naval officers—which believed that patrolling the sea approaches to Britain and hunting for the enemy in the ocean spaces were more likely to produce successful counter-attacks than convoy and escort. We will return to that subject later.

Although our initial strategy was bound to be defensive, the Admiralty emphasised in the war plans that senior officers should lose no opportunity for local and tactical offensives by "bringing the enemy to action wherever and whenever his forces can be met." But the only offensive measure instituted immediately was the blockade of Germany and Italy. While the Home Fleet "closed the North Sea to all movements of enemy shipping and exercised contraband control of neutral shipping," the Mediterranean Fleet was "to isolate Italy from all sea communication with countries outside the Mediterranean." In fact, German merchant shipping was, almost immediately, swept off the surface of the oceans; for very few ships succeeded in running the gauntlet of our blockading forces, and after the first few weeks it was only in the Baltic that the enemy could sail his merchantmen comparatively freely. A trickle of German ships, or of neutrals in their service, crept up and down the Norwegian coast, and between the ports of the southern North Sea; but we soon took steps to stop, or at least reduce that traffic as well. None the less, we were well aware that, in the geographical and political circumstances of 1939, we could not make the blockade of Germany anything like complete. Italy, the weaker partner of the Axis, was likely to allow cargoes destined for Germany to pass through her ports; and as we were anxious to keep the Italians neutral we were unwilling to apply the full rigours of our contraband control to her shipping. Secondly, after the pact signed between Germany and Russia in Moscow in August, 1939, we were fully aware that the latter country could and would supply Germany with many of the goods and raw materials which she could no longer obtain from overseas. Experience was indeed soon to show that on this and on other important issues—such as giving assistance to German commerce raiders—Russian policy was by no means friendly towards the western Allies.

Control of contraband cargoes carried in neutral bottoms was exercised by intercepting ships at sea and sending them into the bases established for the purpose in the Orkneys, in the anchorage in the English Channel called the Downs, and at Malta, Haifa, Aden, Gibraltar and other ports in the overseas Empire. But, as always, interference by a belligerent with neutral shipping, though a well-recognised and perfectly legitimate right, aroused protests from the countries concerned; and on several occasions the Admiralty judged it wise to mitigate the full stringency of its measures. The United States kept itself free from such undesirable entanglements by declaring, on 7th November, 1939, that the waters enclosing the French and British coasts were a war zone into which American shipping was prohibited from entering. This was unquestionably an unfavourable move from the Allies' point of view; but the cold wind from Washington was tempered by the almost simultaneous repeal of the Neutrality Act, thus enabling the Allies to buy war stores in America—so long as they could pay for them and carry them across the Atlantic in their own ships. This "Cash and Carry" order was the first of a number of legislative or administrative acts by which the United States President and Government, at first cautiously but soon with increasing confidence, made their weight and strength felt in favour of the Allies.

The blockade of Germany was mainly enforced by the warships of the Northern Patrol, which kept a continuous watch on the waters between the Shetland Islands and Iceland. At first we used converted fishing trawlers and some of our older cruisers for the purpose; but the stormy seas of those high latitudes soon found weak places in the latter, and they were gradually replaced by newer ships or by armed merchant cruisers. These latter were converted passenger liners, of which the Admiralty had requisitioned fifty. They were needed, for lack of anything better, to strengthen our exiguous cruiser strength on the ocean routes, as well as in the far north; but only obsolete armaments were available for them, and they were very vulnerable to both underwater and surface attack. Many were lost before, in 1942, most of the survivors were transferred to service as troopships.

Before leaving the British naval war plans mention must be made of our defensive and offensive minelaying. In the former category must be placed the Dover Barrage which was laid, with French assistance, very soon after the outbreak of war, and successfully closed the Dover Straits to passage by U-boats; and the East Coast Barrier, which was designed to prevent enemy incursions on to the long coastal route by which all shipping coming round the north of Scotland had to approach the Thames ports. By way of offensive minelaying we promulgated an extensive "declared area" in the Heligoland Bight, to catch enemy surface ships or submarines entering or leaving their North Sea ports; but very few mines were actually laid in those waters during the early months. The reader should remark that all these minelaying operations were planned and carried out strictly in accordance with International Law, which forbade the laying of mines broadcast. The Germans, however, very soon showed that they entertained no such scruples; for both their submarines and aircraft began to lay mines quite indiscriminately.

While the Home Fleet at once took up its initial tasks of watching the northern exits to the Atlantic, covering the weak ships of the Northern Patrol and the convoys coming across the North Sea from Norway, and enforcing the blockade, the Mediterranean Fleet could only wait upon the attitude of Italy; but as soon as it was clear that Mussolini intended to continue sitting on the fence a limited re-opening of through traffic to Suez was ordered, and many of Admiral Cunningham's ships were temporarily removed for service in more active theatres. Meanwhile, far overseas the foreign commands were patrolling the focal areas of shipping and seeking intelligence of the surface raiders which soon revealed their presence.

In fact, the Germans had started their preliminary movements well before war was declared. Between 19th and 31st August, 1939, every ocean-going U-boat which was fit for sea sailed for the Atlantic, while the coastal boats patrolled in the North Sea and prepared to lay mines off our ports and bases. By the end of the month, out of an operational strength of 56 U-boats no less than 39 were on their war stations. The enemy's orders were, however, that they were to adhere to the international treaties governing attacks on merchantmen; and that probably reduced the impact of their initial offensive. Hitler's ruling had no altruistic purpose behind it: he was merely anxious to avoid giving offence to neutrals. We shall, however, see shortly how very rapid was the German progress towards what was virtually "unrestricted U-boat warfare" —even though they carefully avoided use of an expression which aroused unpleasant recollections of the acts which brought the United States into the Kaiser's war in 1917.

As to the German surface fleet, on 21st and 24th August the pocket-battleships *Graf Spee* and *Deutschland* sailed to take up waiting positions in the Atlantic; and the Germans had also made very careful plans to fit out specially selected merchantmen as disguised raiders. The first of these put to sea in February, 1940, and we shall encounter the ten which were actually completed later in our story.

CHAPTER III

NO "PHONEY WAR"

September, 1939–April, 1940

<hr>

" This priceless heritage [of sea power], born out of our insular state, has been handed down and cultivated through the ages."

Lord Beatty. From his address on election as Lord Rector of Edinburgh University, 28th October, 1920.

IN BRITAIN the winter of 1939–40 was referred to as the "phoney" or "twilight" war; because the great armies facing each other on the continent sparred without coming to grips, and the hail of bombs which we had expected to fall on our cities did not materialise. But for the Royal Navy the period was anything but "phoney," since from the very first day its ships were working at full stretch, contacts with the enemy were frequent, and considerable losses were suffered. Moreover, the turn of the year brought an exceptionally severe spell of wintry weather, and for weeks on end conditions in the English Channel and North Sea, let alone in the high latitudes where the Home Fleet cruised and searched, resembled those with which we were to become familiar later in the Arctic Ocean.

The first responsibility placed on the southerly squadrons and commands was to carry and escort the British Expeditionary Force to France. The movements had been carefully planned well before the outbreak of hostilities, and from the early days of September a continuous stream of transports and supply ships moved across the narrow seas. By June, 1940, half a million men and 89,000 vehicles had made the crossing in one direction or the other, and not a man or a gun had been lost. We expected the chief danger to the cross-Channel convoys to come from the U-boats; but in fact only one ever passed through the Dover Straits safely, and in October, 1939, when the last of the 3,600 mines was laid in the barrage mentioned earlier, three underwater enemies were destroyed. Thereafter the Germans abandoned the attempt to attack our Channel shipping and to reach the Western Approaches by the shortest route. Instead they sent all their Atlantic U-boats in and out by the much longer passage round the north of Scotland.

Nor did the U-boats sent to lie in wait off the Home Fleet's main base do any better than their colleagues in the south; for they scored no successes, and the fleet's destroyers accounted for several of them in northern waters and the Western Approaches in September and October. It is, however, certain that the immunity of some of the ships attacked owed a good deal to the inefficiency of the German magnetic torpedo pistol, regarding which U-boat captains soon began to complain bitterly; but we did not know at the time that, for instance, the narrow escape of the fleet carrier *Ark Royal* when U.39 attacked her on 14th September was probably attributable to that cause. The early successes in the anti-submarine war were, however, certainly heartening to the hard-run destroyers. Unfortunately those successes were largely offset by U.29 sinking the fleet carrier *Courageous* (22,500 tons, 48 aircraft), which she encountered by chance in the Western Approaches three days after the *Ark Royal's* escape. The *Courageous* was at the time employed on submarine hunting, with only a small screening force; and it certainly seems surprising that so valuable a ship should have been used in that manner. It is likely that it arose from pressure in high places, and especially from the First Lord, to take the "offensive" against the U-boats, rather than devote our maximum effort to the defensive strategy of convoy and escort.[1] Although the disaster caused the immediate withdrawal of fleet carriers from U-boat hunting, this was by no means the last occasion on which the old fallacy regarding the alleged superiority of seeking for enemies in the ocean spaces instead of convoying shipping with the greatest possible strength, and so forcing the enemy to reveal his presence within range of immediate counter-attack, reared its hoary head in

[1] See for example W. S. Churchill, *The Second World War*, Vol. 1, pp. 362-3. " I always sought to rupture this defensive obsession by searching for forms of counter-offensive. . . . I could not rest content with the policy of ' Convoy and Blockade.' " Also his minutes of 9th and 20th November, 1939, to the First Sea Lord (*Ibid.* pp. 589-90) regarding "independent flotillas" sweeping the Western Approaches.

British circles. Half a century previously Mahan had condemned it;[1] and after World War I both Admiral Beatty and Admiral Sims, U.S.N., went on record with similar opinions based on their recent experiences;[2] yet in 1939 the whole massive weight of historical evidence was again ignored.

To protect shipping in the Western Approaches we needed to base our ships and aircraft as far to the west as possible, and it was now that we felt very grievously the lack of the bases in Eire (Berehaven in the south and Lough Swilly in the north), which had served us so well in the previous struggle. It now seems almost incredible that, as recently as 1938, we had voluntarily surrendered our right to make use of those bases, and without any conditions regarding their re-occupation in the event of war. Nor, when negotiations were opened in 1939, would the government of Eire do anything to mitigate the consequences of our disinterested but short-sighted act. The only substitutes for the abandoned bases were Belfast and Londonderry in loyal Ulster; but they were both considerably farther from the waters where the escorts had to work, and neither of them was adequately equipped to serve as a base. As long as our ships had to start out from the Clyde, Liverpool, Milford Haven and Plymouth, and had to turn for home while they still had an adequate margin of fuel, we could only escort the convoys out to the meridian of 15 degrees west (about 200 miles to the west of Ireland), or in the case of south-bound shipping, to the 47th parallel (about the middle of the Bay of Biscay); and this was very soon shown to be inadequate. With the development of the advanced bases in Ulster the north Atlantic zone of escort could be extended slightly, but as late as April, 1941, it reached only as far as the meridian of 19 degrees west. At the principal overseas assembly ports (Halifax, Gibraltar and Freetown) small local forces —from the Canadian Navy in the case of Halifax—accompanied the homeward convoys for the first few hundred miles of their journeys; but after they had broken off only an ocean escort, perhaps

---

[1] See *The Influence of Sea Power on the French Revolution and Empire* (1892), Vol. II, p. 217. "In fact . . . the result of the convoy system, in this and other instances, warrants the inference that, when properly systematised and applied, it will have more success . . . than hunting for individual marauders—a process which, even when most thoroughly planned, still resembles looking for a needle in a haystack."

[2] See W. S. Chalmers, *The Life and Letters of David, Earl Beatty*, pp. 295 and App. VI and W. S. Sims *The Victory at Sea*, pp. 136-7, 141 and App. V for the views of the British and American fleet commanders in the 1914-18 war on this matter.

a battleship or cruiser but more commonly an armed merchant cruiser, would be present during the long mid-ocean passage. Troop convoys were, however, always given special protection, and before the end of 1939 the First Canadian Division had crossed the Atlantic safely. They were the first of the stream of fighting men from the New World who came, finally in a flood, to support a cause in which they believed—and in all too many cases to leave their bones in remote Europe or Africa. Nor were the Canadians the only Commonwealth troops to be brought, often over great distances, to the active war theatres. Very soon Indian Army contingents were sailing from Bombay, escorted by the East Indies squadron's cruisers, for the Middle East; while many of the finest British passenger ships, including the monster liner *Queen Mary*, and later the *Queen Elizabeth*, brought the Australians and New Zealanders from their home countries to Egypt. During the first six months of the war the movements of British and Empire troops was, in fact, almost world-wide; and the first convoys carrying the men were everywhere followed by slower convoys carrying their vehicles, ammunition and supplies. Because the movements were kept very secret, and still more because there was virtually no interference from the enemy, this accomplishment has attracted little attention. Yet the quiet efficiency with which it was carried out provides a wonderful example of the functioning of maritime power. The troop transports merely slipped quietly out to sea one silent dawn, to arrive safely at their destinations many days, or even weeks later. Yet it was the cruisers which accompanied them, supported by the main fleets in the background, which made their unhindered passages possible; and it was the Admiralty's world-wide shipping control organisation which not only kept a close, if distant, watch on their progress, but ensured that fuel, water and stores were available at each port of call.

The mercantile convoys suffered little harm during the early months; but we have already remarked how it was unavoidable that many ships should still be sailing independently, and it was among them that the U-boats generally claimed their victims. U.30 sank the liner *Athenia*, without warning and with heavy loss of life, on the very day that war was declared—in direct contravention of Hitler's orders. Although it may be the case that her captain (Lemp) mistook her for an armed merchant cruiser, post-war investigation makes it seem more probable that he had misread his orders and believed such attacks to be permitted by his government; but however that may be, the Germans certainly went to great lengths, including the destruction of the relevant pages of the U-boat's log, to hush up the truth, and it was not until after the war, when most of the German naval records came into our hands, that we found out the whole story.

In view of the statements made in justification of Lemp's action, and indeed in excuse for the entire U-boat campaign against merchant shipping by certain ex-enemy apologists in recent years,[1] it may be justifiable to remind the reader of how the matter stood in the eyes of the law in 1939. As recently as November, 1936, Hitler's representatives had signed the London Protocol, and towards the end of the same year Germany had joined with other powers in denouncing submarine war on merchant shipping in accordance with that agreement.[2] In British circles, which could hardly ignore Hitler's earlier record in the matter of unilateral abrogation of international treaties, the new German avowals seem to have been viewed with some cynicism; for in 1938 the Admiralty openly published its instructions to Masters of merchant ships in the event of war.[3] These orders dealt entirely with defence of shipping, and included a statement of the Admiralty's intention to fit merchantmen with defensive armaments. Since the war German writers have argued that these instructions provided a valid excuse for U-boats to attack without warning; yet at the time when the British policy was announced there was no whisper of a suggestion from Germany that it might cause them to reconsider the pledges given under the London Protocol, let alone that they regarded it as releasing them from that agreement. It is indeed quite plain that the excuse is entirely of post-war fabrication. It is true that Britain—and later the United States—ultimately made attacks on merchantmen in a manner which was indistinguishable from the German; but we for our part only lifted the pre-war restrictions on such methods of warfare very slowly and cautiously, and as late as 1941 unrestricted attacks were only permitted in certain declared areas. Our unwillingness to descend to reprisals could hardly be better shown than by

[1] See Karl Dönitz, *Ten Years and Twenty Days*, Ch. VI (Eng. Ed. Weidenfeld and Nicolson, 1959).

[2] See Oppenheim, *International Law*, 7th Ed., Vol. II (1952), p. 491.

[3] In *Defence of Merchant Shipping*, Part I, an unclassified document.

the fact that on 12th December, over three months after the sinking of the *Athenia*, the British submarine *Salmon* forbore to attack the 52,000 ton German liner *Bremen* which she intercepted off the Norwegian coast on her way home from New York via Murmansk.

Though there was a good deal of justifiable anger over Lemp's action it did have one favourable result for Britain; for it convinced us that the enemy had begun unrestricted U-boat warfare, and therefore eliminated the last doubts regarding the need to introduce convoy.

In spite of the initial advantage gained by the enemy through having sent every possible U-boat to sea well before war was declared, the broad trend of the first seven months of the campaign (September, 1939, to March, 1940) was by no means unfavourable to the Allies. Merchant ship losses totalled 222 ships of 764,766 tons —little more than 100,000 tons per month; and no less than 18 U-boats—more than a third of the entire operational strength available at the beginning—were destroyed by one means or another. Furthermore, new U-boats were still only completing very slowly, because Hitler had not yet given their construction high priority. Thus with only 11 new boats commissioned in those seven months Dönitz had not even replaced his losses; and we (though we did not know it) were sinking them faster than they were being built.

It was during this period that we first came to appreciate the potential value of shore-based reconnaissance aircraft in anti-submarine warfare; for Coastal Command's North Sea patrols frequently sighted U-boats on passage to or from the Atlantic by the northern route. In November, 1939, a new directive was therefore issued giving attacks on U-boats a priority equal to the aircrafts' reconnaissance function; and that directive was an important first milestone set up on the road which we were to travel all too slowly towards achieving full co-ordination of our sea and air forces in the Atlantic battle. Unfortunately Coastal Command crews had received no training at all in anti-submarine warfare; and the belief that to destroy a U-boat from the air was a comparatively easy matter was all too widely held. This and the fact that our anti-submarine bombs were completely useless prevented any results being accomplished for a very long time. The first joint success achieved by sea and air forces did not occur until 30th January, 1940, when two escort vessels and a Sunderland flying-boat shared in the destruction of U.55 in the Western Approaches; and many more months were to elapse before there was any repetition. Although conclusive evidence of the ineffectiveness of our anti-submarine bombs very soon became available from the (fortunately negative) results of attacks by friendly aircraft on our own submarines, the change to depth charges was extraordinarily slow to come about. It is an involved story, in which sheer prejudice in favour of the bomb and against the use of naval weapons certainly played a big part; but the result was that the spring of 1940 had come before depth charges were first issued to Coastal Command, and another year elapsed before charges which had been satisfactorily modified for use by aircraft came into general service. It seems true to say that the long delay in giving the Coastal Command aircrews an effective A/S weapon was part of the price we had to pay for the divided control of maritime aircraft.

If the struggle with the U-boats went reasonably well for the Allies during the first seven months, in two other forms of attack on shipping the Germans certainly had the better of it; for we were much less well prepared to deal with bombing attacks and with the magnetic mines than we were to face the U-boat threat. When in October, 1939, the Luftwaffe started to bomb ships plying up and down the long and vulnerable east coast convoy route, we had not achieved any satisfactory arrangement for the provision of fighter protection for them; and Fighter Command, whose main responsibility was the air defence of British cities, was reluctant to extend its cover to the coastal convoys. Not until February, 1940, were satisfactory arrangements made for daily covering sweeps by single-seater fighters, and it was the following May before Fighter Command accepted responsibility for countering air attacks within forty miles of the coast. The Admiralty also experienced the greatest difficulty in finding any A-A. guns for the merchantmen; for although the need had been foreseen before the war, and we had even ordered 20 m.m. Oerlikon guns from Switzerland, the demand for weapons had suddenly become astronomical, and far outstripped the supply. Resort was had to all sorts of emergency measures, and many ingenious—if not very effective—devices were produced in substitution for the guns that did not exist. Rockets trailing a wire were shot up in the path of approaching aircraft, compressed air mortars lobbed Mills hand grenades at the Luftwaffe, and we even gave ships totally innocuous fireworks with which to frighten the Stukas. Yet in the sum, and with a good deal of help from army gunners, the extemporised measures did tide us over a difficult crisis, and gradually better weapons became available to replace the improvisations. By March, 1941, the Admiralty's Defensively Equipped Merchant Ship (D.E.M.S.) organisation had not only fitted 3,434 ships with anti-submarine guns, but had found one or more close-range anti-aircraft weapons for 4,431 British and Allied ships; and the energetic steps taken to train the merchant seamen in their use were beginning to bear fruit. In the first winter of the war, however, such a satisfactory state of affairs seemed infinitely remote. Luckily the German attacks, though trying to the crews of unarmed vessels, were not at first very accurate. Not until December, 1939, did we lose any ships, and between that month and the end of March, 1940, our losses to air attacks amounted to only 30 small ships (36,189 tons in all).

Disturbing though the bombing attacks were, the mines laid by surface ships, U-boats and aircraft presented by far the greater threat during those early months; and there the Germans undoubtedly scored a tactical and technical success. Very early in the war sinkings off the east coast raised suspicions that they were using "influence type" ground mines, and by mid-September we had definite confirmation of the fact. This knowledge caused some consternation, for although we ourselves had actually made and laid a few magnetic mines in 1918, twenty years later we had not developed a satisfactory means of sweeping them; and the entire British minesweeping service was fitted only to deal with moored contact mines. Luckily in November a German mine was dropped on land, and a very gallant officer (Lieut.-Commander J. G. D. Ouvry) dissected it at no small risk to himself. This gave us firm knowledge of the type of mine we had to deal with, and we were at once able to press ahead with the design and production of an efficient magnetic sweep. Yet November, 1939, was a very anxious month, for the enemy almost succeeded in stopping the east coast traffic. At one time only a single channel into the Thames was open, and we lost 27 ships (120,958 tons) on mines during the month. While awaiting the arrival of the new sweep many extemporised measures were adopted, and together they just succeeded in keeping the east coast traffic moving. Though losses continued on a considerable scale in the New Year, and in the first seven months of the war no less than 128 ships totalling 429,899 tons fell victims to mines, we never again had to face as serious a crisis as that of the first autumn. Thus began the battle of wits between the German mine designers and the British sweep designers, which was to last right to the end of the war, and was to produce many ingenious variations on the original themes. The introduction of influence mines, and their use in conjunction with variable delay mechanisms and anti-sweeping devices had far-reaching results on naval warfare; for they added vastly to the work of the sweepers, and gave that branch of the naval service a greater importance than ever before. Channels could not be declared clear until they had been swept again and again for different types of mine; and the sweepers never knew when some new bit of devilry might not blow them sky high. To go out day after day and night after night actually seeking the hidden perils demanded great persistence and a particularly cold-blooded form of gallantry; yet because the work was generally unspectacular it has received scant recognition.

We must now turn to the doings of the main Home Fleet, which we left just after Admiral Forbes had taken up his war station at Scapa at the end of August. The Commander-in-Chief did not lose a day in making the influence of his fleet felt in the North Sea. Immediately war was declared he carried out a succession of sweeps across to the Norwegian coast with his battle squadron, while other units patrolled the northern passages, through which enemy raiders would have to pass to reach the open Atlantic;[1] but this conventional exercise of maritime power produced no contacts with enemy surface forces. On the first day of the war, however, a reconnaissance aircraft reported that German warships were putting to sea from Wilhelmshaven. The Royal Air Force was anxious to put its theories about the deadly effect of bombing attacks on warships to the test, and sent out a striking force of 54 bombers; but they failed to find the targets. Next day Bomber Command made an attempt to attack the enemy ships lying in Schillig Roads off Wilhelmshaven and in Brunsbüttel at the western end of the Kiel Canal. This time

[1] These were the Fair Island Channel, the Faeroes—Iceland passage, and the Denmark Strait between Iceland and Greenland. See Map. p. 23.

the bombers, led by a naval observer, found the targets, and actually hit the pocket-battleship *Scheer* with three or four bombs; but none of them exploded. No enemy ships suffered more than superficial damage, and one-fifth of the striking force of 29 bombers was lost. The failure of these raids was a sharp rejoinder to those who had so confidently predicted that air-power had made large surface warships obsolete. Luckily the Germans did very little, if at all better in their early attacks on the Home Fleet ships. The Admiralty was, however, apprehensive of the possible effects of a heavy bombing raid on the fleet while in Scapa Flow, which was very ill-defended; and they accepted greatly exaggerated estimates of the Luftwaffe's strength. For this reason on 7th September they told Forbes to shift to a secret temporary base on the west of Scotland, and by the 12th many of his ships had transferred to Loch Ewe;[1] but that anchorage was even less well defended than Scapa, nor was its use kept secret for long. There next ensued a long discussion on the future main base for the fleet, for it was Forbes's earnest wish to get back to Scapa as soon as possible, and Loch Ewe was too exposed for comfort; but the defences of Scapa could not be made satisfactory overnight, and he had finally to agree to using the Clyde until his chosen base had been made more secure. This, however, had the result that his fleet was several hundred miles farther away from the northern waters which it had to control, and where it might be needed at any moment.

In October reinforcements, some of them from the Mediterranean Station, reached Admiral Forbes; but they were more than offset by the need to detach a substantial number of ships to the central and south Atlantic; for early in October we obtained definite evidence that one pocket-battleship was at large in the ocean, and on the 21st the arrival in the Orkneys of survivors from a Norwegian ship proved that there were two powerful raiders—actually the *Graf Spee* and *Deutschland*—at sea.[2] We shall return to their adventures shortly.

On 8th October the battle cruiser *Gneisenau*, the light cruiser

[1] See Map p. 23.

[2] The pocket-battleship *Deutschland* was renamed *Lützow* in November, 1939, because Hitler feared that the loss of a ship bearing the name of the Fatherland might have serious effects on morale. She appears later in this narrative as the *Lützow*, but must not be confused with the heavy cruiser which originally bore that name. The cruiser *Lützow* was handed over to the Russians in April, 1940, as part of the price exacted by Stalin for the Russo-German agreement of August, 1939.

Köln and a number of destroyers made a brief sortie into the North Sea; and as soon as Forbes learnt that they were out he took his main force to a position north-east of the Shetlands, whence he could cover the passages to the Atlantic. His adversaries, however, reversed course after dark and returned to Kiel, and by the 11th Forbes's ships were mostly back in Loch Ewe. The battleship *Royal Oak*, however, which had been detached to guard the Fair Island Channel,[1] anchored in Scapa after this operation; and it thus came to pass that it was she who paid the price for the insecurity of the base. On the night of 13th-14th while the northern lights flickered in the sky U.47, commanded by Gunther Prien, penetrated through a narrow, tide-swept and incompletely blocked passage between two islands into the anchorage; and in the early hours of 14th he sent the battleship to the bottom with three torpedo hits. He then withdrew safely by the way he had come. The disaster, in which 833 lives were lost, was a severe shock to Britain; but it did have the salutary result of hastening measures to bring the defences of Scapa up to an adequate standard. On the German side every credit must be given for the careful planning which lay behind Prien's success, and for the audacity with which he carried out the operation.[2]

Within three days of the sinking of the *Royal Oak* the first air attacks took place on Scapa and on Rosyth in the Firth of Forth, but in far less strength than we had anticipated. Insignificant military damage was done by the score of bombers which attacked the former base, and only slight damage to warships in the latter. The results strengthened Admiral Forbes's belief that we only had to provide reasonable defences to enable the fleet to make undisturbed use of its chosen base; but he himself and all his main force were far away, covering the Northern Patrol cruisers, when these events took place. November saw further sweeps by the fleet for such purposes as covering the passage of the convoys coming across the North Sea from Bergen; but on the afternoon of 23rd, just after Forbes had returned to the Clyde, he picked up an "Immediate"

---

[1] See Map p. 23.

[2] The story that Prien's success owed a great deal to a German spy who, in the guise of a watchmaker, had taken up residence in Kirkwall, the capital of the Orkneys, has appeared several times since the war (e.g. Kurt Singer *Spione und Verräter des Zweiten Weltkrieges*, Falken Verlag, 1946). Careful investigation in contemporary German records proves, however, that the watchmaker is a wholly mythological character.

signal from the Armed Merchant Cruiser *Rawalpindi* reporting that she had an enemy battle cruiser—shortly afterwards amended to a pocket-battleship—in sight. The whole Home Fleet at once raised steam for full speed, and within a few hours was heading out to sea, some ships making for the position of the A.M.C.'s enemy report, while others steamed north-east to the "intercepting position" between the Shetland Islands and Norway through which the enemy would have to pass on his return journey.[1]

Actually, it was the battle cruisers *Scharnhorst* and *Gneisenau* which had attacked the *Rawalpindi* (Captain E. C. Kennedy). They had sailed from Wilhelmshaven on the afternoon of 21st November under Admiral Marschall, passed undetected to the north of the Shetlands and Faeroes, and sighted their first quarry as dusk was falling two days later. A brief and very one-sided action followed, in which the old converted liner fought to the end. The cruiser *Newcastle*, which was next to the *Rawalpindi* on the Northern Patrol, picked up her enemy reports, closed the position at high speed, and actually sighted the battle cruisers; but they withdrew promptly to the east, and the *Newcastle* failed to keep in touch. Admiral Marschall now acted with great circumspection, and disappeared into the northern mists until the weather was suitable for his break back to Germany. In the early hours of 26th he came south, and actually passed through the cruiser and destroyer patrol lines which Forbes had established off Norway. He sighted, but was not sighted by one of the patrolling ships, and reached Wilhelmshaven safely next day, while our main fleet was still waiting hopefully not far to the west of the track he had actually followed.

In German circles there was a good deal of jubilation over the results of this foray; but in fact Marschall did not carry out his full plan, which was to make a feint out into the Atlantic to dislocate our shipping movements; and the actual achievements of two of the most powerful warships afloat were not really very impressive. On our side the operation underlined the fact that little reliance could be placed on the North Sea air patrols, and that the enemy's intelligence was greatly superior to our own. What we did not know was that this was due to the German cryptographers having broken our naval cipher. Radar was, of course, in its infancy at the time, and very few of our ships had any set all; but we realised

[1] See Map p. 23.

the immense part it could play in searches such as followed the sinking of the *Rawalpindi*, and the Admiralty was doing everything in its power to expedite its installation. It was, of course, discouraging that the enemy slipped through the meshes of the net Forbes had drawn across his return track; but the extreme caution displayed by Marschall at least showed that, although the barrier of our sea power across the North Sea was not, and was not expected to be impenetrable, it did make attempts to strike at our Atlantic shipping both difficult and dangerous. The operation had one unfortunate aftermath, for as Forbes's flagship the *Nelson* was re-entering Loch Ewe on 4th December she detonated one of the magnetic mines which a U-boat had laid a few weeks earlier. The battleship was considerably damaged, and had to come south to dock. Happily more reinforcements, including the famous *Warspite* —Cunningham's flagship from the Mediterranean—were already on their way to join the Home Fleet.

We saw earlier how, before the end of October, we knew that two pocket-battleships were loose on the trade routes, and it is to the measures taken to catch them that we must now turn. On 5th October the Admiralty, in conjunction with the French Navy, formed no less than eight Atlantic "hunting groups" of aircraft carriers and cruisers for the purpose. Three of them were placed under the orders of the Commander-in-Chief, South Atlantic, whose headquarters were at Freetown in Sierra Leone, and it is with Group G (the heavy cruisers *Exeter* and *Cumberland*, joined later by the light cruisers *Ajax* and *Achilles*—the latter belonging to the New Zealand Navy) that we here are principally concerned; for that group was responsible for the waters off the east coast of South America.

The *Graf Spee* sank her first ship off Pernambuco on 30th September, and in the following month found four more victims in mid-Atlantic. She then disappeared from our ken for more than a fortnight, to turn up again in the Mozambique Channel, where she sank a small tanker on 15th November. Meanwhile, in October the *Deutschland* had attacked two ships in the north Atlantic; but not until the 21st were we certain that they had not fallen to the ship which had been raiding the more southerly routes. From mid-November until 2nd December no whisper of the *Graf Spee's* movements reached the Admiralty; for she was then actually doubling back round the Cape of Good Hope. Then came another distress message from a ship attacked in the raider's earlier South Atlantic hunting ground. This was 3,000 miles away from the focal area for shipping off the River Plate; but Commodore H. Harwood, senior officer of Group G, had always believed that the raider would sooner or later be attracted by the rich traffic off that estuary. He calculated that she could reach the waters for which he was responsible by 12th December, and ordered his forces to concentrate. The *Exeter* therefore came north from the Falkland Islands, and by the early hours of the 12th she and the *Achilles* had joined Harwood's *Ajax* at a rendezvous 150 miles east of the River Plate. The *Graf Spee* sank two more ships in mid-ocean, and then steered straight for the river mouth off which Harwood's ships were patrolling. At 6.08 a.m. on 13th December, exactly 24 hours after his concentration had been completed, the *Ajax* reported smoke to the north-west. The Commodore ordered Captain F. S. Bell of the *Exeter* to investigate, and eight minutes later he signalled " I think it is a pocket-battleship."

The three British cruisers, which between them mounted six 8-inch and sixteen 6-inch guns, now closed at high speed, and were soon in action with their formidable adversary, who mounted six 11-inch and eight 5.9-inch guns. Moreover, the *Graf Spee* was so heavily protected that only the *Exeter's* 8-inch shells were at all likely to do her serious injury. Harwood, however, had long visualised just such an action as this, and so clearly did Captains W. E. Parry of the *Achilles* and C. H. L. Woodhouse of the *Ajax* understand his tactical intentions that very few signals were necessary. While the *Exeter* turned west to engage the German ship to starboard, the two light cruisers held on to the north-east to open fire from the other direction.[1] This forced Captain Langsdorff of the *Graf Spee* either to divide his main armament or leave one of the British divisions unfired at. He first chose the former alternative; but having mis-identified the two small cruisers as destroyers, he soon switched all his 11-inch guns on to the *Exeter*. The German gunnery was very accurate, and indeed remained formidably so throughout the fight. The *Exeter* was soon heavily hit, but Captain Bell held on towards the enemy, and fired his torpedoes—though to no purpose. Langsdorff undoubtedly now had a great opportunity

[1] See Map p. 54.

53

to finish off the *Exeter*, for by 6.50 she had only one turret left in action and was seriously on fire; but he allowed the chance to slip through his fingers—probably because he was receiving the concentrated fire of the light cruisers at the time. Soon after 6.30 he made smoke and turned to the west, thus allowing the *Exeter* to haul off to the south-east to effect repairs.

The second phase of the action now began, with the two light cruisers pursuing and harrying the pocket-battleship from the north,

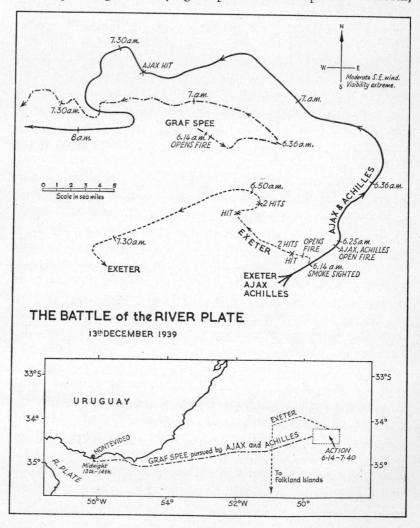

THE BATTLE of the RIVER PLATE

13th DECEMBER 1939

while she steered towards the South American coast. At 7.25 the *Ajax* received an 11-inch hit which put both her after turrets out of action, and again Langsdorff had a chance to settle the issue; for the armaments remaining to his adversaries were now little superior to his own secondary weapons. Harwood therefore made smoke and turned to the east; but when the German ship did not press her advantage he very soon resumed the pursuit. In the final phase, which lasted from 8 a.m. until after dark had fallen, the two cruisers shadowed their adversary as he steered towards Montevideo; while the German turned periodically to fire a few 11-inch salvos at them. By midnight it was obvious that Langsdorff intended to enter harbour, and Harwood therefore called off the pursuit and started to patrol the entrance to the estuary. But his position was unenviable; for both his ships had suffered damage—the *Ajax* the more seriously —and he could hardly hope to stop the pocket-battleship if she made a determined bid to regain the open sea. Moreover, the nearest reinforcement, the heavy cruiser *Cumberland*, was at Port Stanley in the Falkland Islands, and could not join him until the evening of 14th; and all other British ships were thousands of miles away.

A good deal of uncertainty still surrounds the question of how much damage the *Graf Spee* had actually sustained before she entered harbour. We did not believe that the cruisers' gunfire could have injured her appreciably; but the Germans told the Uruguayan authorities that she had received some 70 hits, and they sought and received permission to extend her stay in port for 72 hours beyond the one day permitted by International Law in order to effect repairs.[1] During the interval the Admiralty was rushing powerful reinforcements to the scene, and also conducting a game of bluff to convince the Germans that a much stronger force was waiting outside than was actually the case. Our real purpose was to hold the *Graf Spee* in harbour until the *Ark Royal* and *Renown* had arrived from the north; and to accomplish that the Admiralty sailed British merchantmen at intervals, and asked the Uruguayan government to give them each a day's clear start. Langsdorff was meanwhile communicating with Berlin, to whom he reported the supposed

---

[1] Michael Powell, who investigated the story of the *Graf Spee* very closely after the war, states in "*Graf Spee*" (Hodder and Stoughton, 1956, p. 173) that the Germans reported "65 hits on the superstructure alone" to the Uruguayan authorities. It seems very unlikely that the Germans would deliberately have exaggerated the damage she had suffered.

strength of the concentration waiting just out of sight; and on the evening of the 16th he was told to scuttle his ship rather than allow her to be interned. Twenty-four hours later he weighed anchor and steamed down-river with a German merchantman in attendance. At 7.56 p.m. on the 17th December the crowds massed on the waterfront of Montevideo were amazed to see a series of violent explosions in the distance. They marked the grave of one of Hitler's finest warships. Three hours later Harwood led the *Ajax, Achilles* and *Cumberland*, which were the only British ships actually patrolling the estuary, past the blazing wreck and into Montevideo; and on the 20th Captain Langsdorff shot himself, leaving behind a letter in justification of his actions. If his tactical conduct in battle is open to criticism, and his subsequent actions be held to indicate a lack of resolution, he should be remembered as a humane and generous enemy; for not a single British life was lost through his actions against merchantmen.

So ended the first challenge to British control of the ocean routes; since far away in the north the *Deutschland* was recalled to Germany after sinking only two ships. She broke back successfully by way of the Denmark Strait, eluded our Northern Patrol and reached Kiel undetected on 15th November. As the *Graf Spee's* total score was only 9 ships totalling some 50,000 tons the warship raiders had so far hardly justified themselves.

Compared with many sea fights which took place later in the war the Battle of the River Plate was a small affair; but success or failure in maritime war does not depend on the size and number of the ships engaged, and it has often happened in history that quite small battles have had extraordinarily far-reaching influence. It is undoubtedly true that the fight off the River Plate comes within that category. Not only did the success project a strong ray of light through the gloom of a winter which, for the British people, was singularly depressing; but it reaffirmed to the whole world that the Royal Navy would again, as so often in the past, give a very decisive answer to any challenge to its maritime control—once it could come to grips with the enemy. The very remoteness of the battle from the British Isles enhanced that impression; for if three cruisers could harry a pocket-battleship to its death over 6,000 miles away what, asked the man in the street, had he to fear in our home waters where our main strength was concentrated? It is certainly the case that, after

Destroyer depth-charging a U-boat

Dunkirk

The end of the *Graf Spee*, 17th December, 1939

13th December, 1939, the British people faced the future more confidently; and it is probably true to say that neutral—and especially American—opinion was a good deal impressed.

After the destruction of the *Graf Spee* the Admiralty organised widespread searches for her supply ship, the tanker *Altmark*, from which the raider had several times refuelled during her cruise, and to which she had to our knowledge transferred several hundreds of British Merchant Navy prisoners. But the tanker did not actually start homeward from the South Atlantic until late in January, 1940, and, taking advantage of a spell of very bad weather, she passed through the Iceland-Faeroes passage undetected, to arrive safely at Trondheim in Norway on 14th February. But we had received warning of her movement down the Norwegian coast, and Admiral Forbes at once ordered light forces which were already at sea to intercept the tanker. In the early hours of the 16th they sighted the *Altmark*, which had an escort of two small Norwegian destroyers. An order to the tanker to stop was ignored, the Norwegian ships frustrated our attempts to board her, and she took refuge in a narrow fiord north of the Naze—the south-western tip of Norway. Captain P. L. Vian in the destroyer *Cossack* followed her in, and demanded the release of the prisoners—which the senior officer of the Norwegian escort refused on the grounds that the *Altmark* had already been searched at Bergen, was unarmed and was making a legitimate use of his country's territorial waters. Faced by such a plainly delicate situation Captain Vian withdrew from the fiord to report by radio to the Admiralty. There the First Lord, Mr. Churchill, took the matter in hand personally; and it was mainly thanks to his resolution that Vian was told to offer to escort the *Altmark* back to Bergen jointly with the Norwegian warships, and —should they refuse that proposal—to board her and release the prisoners. At 10 p.m. that evening Vian took the *Cossack* into the fiord again, and made his compromise proposal to the Norwegian senior officer. When he refused to co-operate Vian laid his ship alongside the tanker, and a boarding party leapt on board just as Nelson's seamen would have done. The Germans offered little resistance, the ship was found to be armed, and 299 prisoners were quickly released from her holds. The *Cossack* then set course for Rosyth, covered by heavy ships of the Home Fleet.

The British action was, perhaps, more than a technical infringement of Norwegian neutrality; but the tacit acceptance by the Norwegians of such use of their waters, combined with the plainly perfunctory manner in which they had "searched" the *Altmark*, provided ample justification for what was done. Though the German propaganda machine promptly filled the ether with execrations of Britain's treatment of a neutral country, to the world at large it seemed that what we had done was, in ethical terms, impeccable; the joyous cry of the prisoners as the *Cossack's* boarders released them—" The Navy is here "—was a splendid tonic to a nation which had long since tired of irresolution towards the machinations of the dictators.

During the first three months of 1940 the German main units only offered one tentative and ineffective challenge to the Home Fleet's control of the North Sea and Atlantic passages. Constantly covered by Admiral Forbes's remote and rarely seen ships the convoys steamed steadily to and from British ports with little interruption; while all the time the grip of our blockade was tightened. Very few German ships succeeded in breaking through our patrols from the outer oceans, and more and more neutrals were coming voluntarily into our contraband control stations to get their cargoes cleared. Meanwhile, the Home Fleet's submarines, which were not yet allowed to interfere with enemy merchant ships except in accordance with International Law, patrolled off the German bases in the hope of getting in attacks on his surface warships or U-boats. Inevitably the chances which came their way were few, but in December, 1939, the *Salmon* made a remarkably successful patrol in which she sank U.36 and also torpedoed the light cruisers *Leipzig* and *Nürnberg*, while they were covering a destroyer force bound on a minelaying foray to our east coast. Her success in an anti-submarine role was the first of a long series which emphasised the importance of that aspect of submarine warfare; for in the final count no less than 39 German and Italian U-boats were victims of Allied submarines. Early in January, 1940, however, the Home Fleet submarines sustained an unpleasant reverse, when three of their number were lost in quick succession in the Heligoland Bight; and in the following April they suffered an even worse shock when the large minelayer *Seal* (submerged displacement 2,150 tons) was disabled by German mines in the Kattegat. After a harrowing ordeal she struggled to the surface only to be captured and towed into harbour by German anti-submarine craft. British submarines were not then fitted with scuttling charges; but one may feel that the chief responsibility for the disaster lay with those who sent such a large and unhandy vessel to work in shallow, heavily mined and constantly patrolled waters, rather than with her crew—who did their utmost to extricate their ship from an impossible predicament. Apart from two coastal craft which the Germans captured later, and several vessels which were salved after we had abandoned certain foreign bases—particularly in the Far East early in 1942—she was the only British warship to fall into enemy hands.

As the days began to lengthen with the passing of the first winter of the war, the generally favourable trends of the first few months appeared to be slowly gaining ground. With the convoy system becoming ever more widely applied there was no sign of the U-boats gaining the upper hand; the new " LL Sweeps " had entered service, and were achieving such prompt results that there was every reason to believe that the magnetic mine would soon be mastered; and better fighter protection had taken most of the sting out of the Luftwaffe's attacks on our coastal shipping. Meanwhile, we had turned to the offensive in the minelaying campaign, though at first in a small way. While our destroyers were laying mines in the swept channels leading to the enemy's North Sea bases, the Royal Air Force was preparing to sow mines in more distant waters. Initially Coastal and Bomber Command aircraft and the Fleet Air Arm all took part in this campaign; but gradually the entire responsibility was placed on Bomber Command. We need here only note that it was another contribution of air power to the war at sea which had not been envisaged in the pre-war plans.

In the winter of 1939-40 the Baltic was frozen for an unusually long period, and the carriage of Swedish iron ore to German ports suffered correspondingly. This greatly enhanced the importance of the alternative route for such traffic, from Narvik in north Norway to the ports on the German North Sea coast; and the Admiralty became increasingly anxious to extend its blockade to the ships using that route. The difficulty was that for almost the whole journey down the Norwegian coast it was possible for ships to remain in territorial waters by using the narrow passages between the offshore islands and the mainland known as the Inner Leads. To us it seemed intolerable that by keeping to that "covered way," as Mr. Churchill called it, German and neutral ships could evade our contraband control; and the First Lord strongly favoured forcing them out into the open sea by mining the Leads. However, it was March, 1940, before Mr. Chamberlain's cabinet would agree to such a proposal. The final decision was that mines (or dummy mines) were to be laid simultaneously at three points on 8th April, while a force from the Home Fleet covered the minelayers against Norwegian interference. We were, of course, aware that the German government was watching such developments with anxiety, and we expected a strong reaction to our minelaying operation. To forestall an enemy attempt to retaliate by seizing Norwegian ports we had therefore prepared a plan to occupy Stavanger, Bergen, Trondheim and Narvik as soon as any such enemy intention became clear; but the War Cabinet declined to make the first move, and that was bound to leave the initiative in German hands. By 6th April strong indications of unusual enemy activity, especially in the Baltic ports, were reaching London; but the Admiralty seems to have had its attention concentrated on the likelihood of an attempted breakout into the Atlantic, and the German plans and intentions were completely misinterpreted. On 5th April the minelayers sailed for Norway as intended, and the battle cruiser *Renown* and four destroyers went across to cover them. The lays were successfully completed on the 8th, but by that time events had begun to move very fast in the North Sea, and the first major clash with the German Navy and Air Force was pending. Yet for all the earlier indications that something unusual was afoot in the enemy's camp, no special precautions, such as bringing the Home Fleet to immediate readiness, were ordered from London. Indeed as late as the afternoon of the 7th the Admiralty sent Admiral Forbes what was virtually a correct account of German intentions, but added the unfortunate remark that "all these reports are of doubtful value and may well be only a further move in the war of nerves." None the less, air reports of the northward movement of enemy warships from the Heligoland Bight caused Forbes to raise steam for full speed, and at 8.15 p.m. on the 7th his main forces left Scapa and Rosyth and steered to the north-east. But it was actually by then too late for the Home Fleet to frustrate the German plan to occupy Denmark and Norway with lightning speed; for virtually their whole Navy was already on the move with the intention of seizing five key ports in Norway, from Oslo in the south to Narvik on the edge of the Arctic circle. The German plan, if it was ruthless in conception, was carried out with skill and determination; and in spite of all our preparations to meet that very eventuality we were caught completely by surprise.

CHAPTER IV

DEFEAT ON LAND : WITHDRAWAL BY SEA

April–June, 1940

" In the wreck of the continent, and the disappointment of our
hopes there, what has been the security of this country but its
naval preponderance ? "

William Pitt. From a speech in the House
of Commons, 2nd February, 1801.

W HILE THE main body of the Home Fleet was hurrying from
Scapa to the north-east on the 7th-8th April with the object of
reaching the position from which it could best deal with an Atlantic
breakout, the Germans successfully gained sufficient local command
in the southern North Sea to carry out their plan to invade Norway.
Only in Oslo fiord, where coastal batteries sank the heavy cruiser
Blücher, did they suffer anything approaching a check.[1] Even at
Narvik in the far north, where the risks to the invading forces were
by far the greatest, ten large German destroyers entered the long
approach through Vestfiord undetected—for the Admiralty had
signalled to the destroyers patrolling the newly laid minefield to join
the *Renown* out to sea. The Germans easily overwhelmed the
Norwegian defenders of Narvik, and successfully landed their 2,000
troops. The first contact between the British and German navies
actually came about accidentally; for the destroyer *Glowworm*, one
of the *Renown's* screen, had parted company to search for a man she
had lost overboard, and at 9 a.m. on 8th April she suddenly
encountered the heavy cruiser *Hipper* and her escort of four
destroyers. This was the German group bound for Trondheim with
1,700 troops on board. The *Glowworm* soon received fatal damage,
but in a truly heroic ending she managed to ram the *Hipper*, and

[1] See Map p. 64.

damaged her seriously. Few of the British destroyer's company survived.

When Admiral Forbes intercepted the *Glowworm's* enemy report he sent the battle cruiser *Repulse* and some lighter forces to her assistance, while the *Renown* set course to cut the enemy off if he was bound for Vestfiord. By this time (noon on 8th April) a full gale was blowing from the north-west, and the main fleet had to ease down for the sake of the destroyers. That evening Forbes ordered the *Repulse* and her detachment to reinforce the *Renown* off Vestfiord, while he himself turned south with two battleships, a cruiser and his destroyer screen. But before the reinforcements had joined her the *Renown* encountered a quite different enemy from the *Hipper's* group; for shortly after 3.30 a.m. on the 9th she suddenly sighted the battle cruisers *Scharnhorst* and *Gneisenau*, which were actually on their way to the far north with the object of drawing off the main British forces from the central North Sea. The German ships turned away at high speed, and a running fight took place in a very rough sea and intermittent snow squalls. Although the British battle cruiser only mounted six 15-inch guns, as against the two German ships' twelve 11-inch, and was far less well protected and considerably slower than her adversaries, she obtained three heavy shell hits on the *Gneisenau*, and did her considerable damage; but by 6.30 a.m. the German battle cruisers had outdistanced her, and disappeared in the mist and snow squalls. The *Renown*, which was practically undamaged, then proceeded to patrol off Vestfiord.

Meanwhile a flood of reports was reaching London from our own ships and from the Norwegian ports where the Germans had landed. The Admiralty, without waiting to see how the situation was developing, ordered every possible ship to join Admiral Forbes; and included in them were the four cruisers which had already embarked troops at Rosyth in case they should be needed to occupy key points in Norway.[1] By thus precipitately jettisoning the plan which we had prepared to deal with the eventuality which had now actually risen, we deprived ourselves of the only military force available to make a quick landing in the invaded country. Small wonder that, with a stream of urgent, and sometimes contradictory orders, some of which bore the unmistakable imprint of the First

[1] See p. 60.

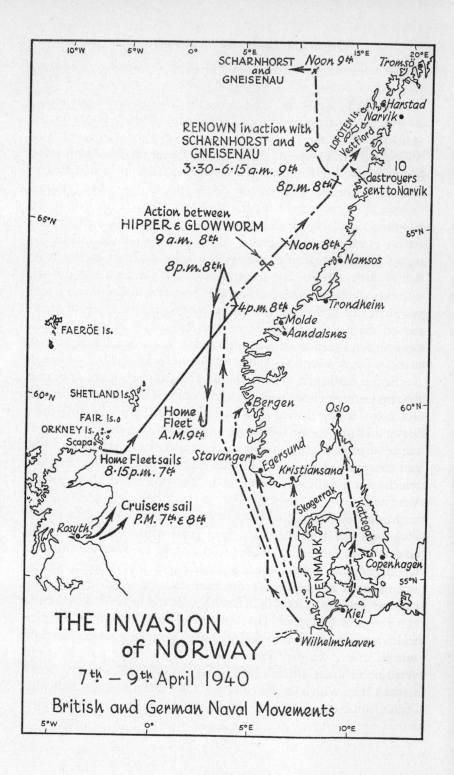

THE INVASION
of NORWAY
7th – 9th April 1940
British and German Naval Movements

Lord's language, emanating from London, Admiral Forbes should have been faced by an extremely confused situation. On the evening of 8th April, however, the Admiralty told him to regard the interception of the *Scharnhorst* and *Gneisenau* on their return journey as his primary object, and he therefore held on to the south during the night. Early next morning Forbes signalled to the Admiralty proposing an attack on Bergen, and he had actually detached four cruisers and seven destroyers for the purpose when the Admiralty cancelled his plan. Even to-day it is difficult to explain why this was done; and the fact that the attack would probably have caught the German invasion squadron in harbour makes it appear the more regrettable. The cancelled plan was, however, revived by the Admiralty itself a short while later—though in a different form, using torpedo-bombers from the carrier *Furious*. But she had been rushed out from the Clyde to join the Home Fleet, and had not been allowed time to fly on her complement of fighters from a shore station. Thus she could contribute nothing to the protection of herself or the fleet.

During the 9th the Luftwaffe attacked the main fleet heavily, and this convinced the Commander-in-Chief that to send the fighterless carrier within range of shore-based aircraft would be suicidal for her. However, that same day news of a welcome success reached London; for the submarine *Truant* torpedoed the light cruiser *Karlsruhe* in the Kattegat, and damaged her so severely that her own escort had to sink her; and more good news was soon to follow. Early on the 10th fifteen Fleet Air Arm Skuas, flying to the extreme limit of their range from the Orkneys, dive-bombed and sank the light cruiser *Königsberg* in Bergen. This was the first major warship on either side to be sunk by air attack; and the success was a fine feather in the cap of the naval aviators who accomplished it. But the rest of the German Bergen group (the *Köln*, *Bremse* and some smaller vessels) got away safely.

Forbes had meanwhile taken his main body farther west, to meet the *Warspite* and *Furious* to the north of the Shetlands, and to send some of his cruisers and destroyers into Scapa to refuel. He then steered north-east again with the object of using his carrier aircraft to attack Trondheim, and to cover a convoy of 37 merchantmen which, thanks entirely to the initiative of Captain J. S. Pinkney, the Master of one of the ships who was acting as Convoy Commodore, had got to sea from Bergen just before German forces arrived there. The whole convoy reached British ports safely, from under the very noses of the enemy.

We must now return to the far north to recount what happened off Vestfiord since we left the *Renown* and *Repulse* patrolling the entrance after the former's fight with the German battle cruisers early on the 9th. Rumours of an enemy force off Narvik reached the fleet flagship that same day, and Forbes therefore told the senior officer of the 2nd Destroyer Flotilla (Captain B. A. W. Warburton-Lee) to go up the fiord with the object of preventing a landing. He took with him the five available destroyers of his own flotilla (the *Hardy*, *Hotspur*, *Havock*, *Hunter* and *Hostile*, ships of 1,340 tons mounting four 4.7-inch guns and eight torpedo tubes[1]); and although he learnt from the Norwegian lighthouse keepers at the entrance that a greatly superior German force (actually ten destroyers of 1,625 tons, each mounting five 5-inch guns and eight torpedo tubes) had passed up the fiord that morning, he signalled "intend attacking at dawn high water." After an exceedingly difficult passage, made in continuous snowstorms, Warburton-Lee arrived off Narvik at 4 a.m. on the 10th, forced his way into the harbour, quickly sank two of his totally surprised enemies, and damaged three others. But five of the German destroyers were lying unnoticed in adjacent fiords, and these suddenly appeared just when the *Hardy* and her consorts were about to withdraw. They caught Warburton-Lee's ships between two fires and turned the tables on him. The *Hunter* was sunk, the *Hardy* disabled and driven ashore with the flotilla commander among those killed, and the *Hotspur* was badly damaged. But the Germans did not press home their advantage, and the three surviving British ships made their way safely down the fiord, sinking a German ship which was carrying the Narvik force's ammunition on the way. The First Battle of Narvik thus ended with honours about even; but the Admiralty was understandably anxious to finish off the surviving enemies, and on the 13th they sent up the battleship *Warspite* and nine fresh destroyers to accomplish that purpose. While the battleship's 15-inch salvos reverberated from the cliffs the destroyers searched every nook and cranny for enemies. In this action, the Second Battle of Narvik, eight large destroyers and a U-boat were lost to the Germans—the U-boat

[1] The flotilla leader *Hardy* was slightly larger, and mounted five 4.7-inch guns.

being bombed and sunk by the *Warspite's* catapult aircraft; and as a result their troops ashore at Narvik found themselves suddenly deprived of all naval support and in a very exposed state. Unhappily, we had no military force available to seize the chance of assaulting the place before the defenders had recovered from the shock sustained on 13th April.

Thus ended the first phase of the Norwegian campaign. The Germans had, by ruthless opportunism combined with the acceptance of substantial risks, achieved both strategic and tactical surprise; and they had made a good start towards accomplishing their purpose of occupying the whole country. In the second phase, which opened with the departure of the first troop convoy from the Clyde on 11th April, the Royal Navy was faced with the task of carrying several hastily organised military expeditions overseas, and of securing their supplies in waters where the enemy held command of the air; for it was impossible for the Royal Air Force to set up fighter bases in the invaded country at short notice, and shore-based aircraft sent out from Britain could only give brief and intermittent cover. We were thus forced to use carrier-borne fighters as substitutes; and they were ill-suited to deal with the modern German bombers, such as the Ju.88. It was now that the Royal Navy first learnt that it could not adequately command overseas coastal waters while lacking efficient fighter cover. But the attempt had none the less to be made; for the British and French governments had pledged themselves to give all possible support to the slender Norwegian land forces.

Some of the troopships in the first convoy from Britain were diverted while on passage to Narvik in order to make a landing at the tiny port of Namsos, north of Trondheim; for a plan had been made in London to try and seize Trondheim, which was the key to control of central and southern Norway. A few days later warships took across some 700 seamen and marines and landed them at the small ports of Aandalsnes and Molde, south of Trondheim.[1] Reinforcements for both the northern and southern landings followed in the cruisers and smaller warships of the Home Fleet; but the Luftwaffe very soon destroyed the ports of disembarkation.

[1] See Map p. 64.

It thus happened that although the naval side of the plan was successfully executed, once the troops had landed they found themselves beset by serious difficulties. Nor was an attempt to establish a temporary base for R.A.F. fighters on a frozen lake successful; for although the fleet carrier *Glorious*, recently recalled from the Mediterranean, carried them across and flew them off safely, they were all quickly destroyed by the German bombers. While the land operations were thus faring ill, a proposal for a frontal attack on Trondheim by the Home Fleet was personally urged on Admiral Forbes by Mr. Churchill. After a great deal of coming and going between London and the fleet flagship, Forbes agreed to carry troops across for such a purpose in his warships, but refused to employ troopships. Time was, however, very short, and the rehearsals for the landing, which the Commander-in-Chief rightly regarded as essential, could not be fitted in by 22nd-23rd April, the date selected for the attack. It was therefore with some relief that, on the 19th, Forbes learnt that the plan had been dropped; for he knew that, with combined operations in progress in north Norway as well as around Trondheim, he already had more than enough on his hands; and the frontal attack in face of strong enemy air power was bound to be expensive. Nor were his problems reduced by the constant reduction of his fleet which the increasingly threatening attitude of Italy now made necessary; for the Admiralty realised that the time had come when Admiral Cunningham's strength had to be rebuilt.

Before the end of April it was recognised in London that the landings against Trondheim could not succeed, and on 28th Forbes was told to re-embark all the troops as soon as possible. He therefore sent back his cruisers and destroyers; and they in a series of very skilful and daring night operations, extricated almost all the 11,000 troops who had been landed, and also took off the Norwegian Royal Family, the government, and the country's gold reserves. Two destroyers (one of them French) were sunk by bombing during the process.

Meanwhile the forces sent across to recapture Narvik had arrived in Vestfiord, and had established a temporary base at Harstad. Admiral of the Fleet Lord Cork and Orrery, a very senior officer, had been chosen by Mr. Churchill to command the naval side, and a few weeks later he was placed in supreme command of the whole expedition. But the difficulties of the undertaking were serious, and were undoubtedly underestimated in London; for the country was still under deep snow, the troop transports had not been "tactically loaded" to make quick disembarkation possible, and we possessed very few of the special craft needed for an assault landing. Moreover, the German bombers were paying increasing attention to the anchorages used by our warships and supply vessels, and losses began to mount. After warship bombardments had failed to induce the German garrison to surrender, landings were successfully made at the head of the fiord on 8th May; but it was still very difficult for the troops to make progress towards their objective. Meanwhile we were making frantic efforts to construct airfields on the high ground overlooking Vestfiord, and by 23rd May the carriers *Furious* and *Glorious* had brought across and flown ashore the first R.A.F. fighters; but by that time the situation in Norway was plainly becoming critical, for German forces were steadily forcing their way north, and subsidiary landings to the south of Vestfiord had failed to stop them. Narvik was finally captured on 28th May; but by that time the campaign in north Europe had become so critical that the War Cabinet decided that we could not possibly hold a base in Norway, and ordered the evacuation of all the 25,000 men so recently carried there.

The homeward movements began early in June, when a succession of troop and supply convoys started to leave Vestfiord, while the *Ark Royal* and *Glorious* provided fighter cover. By 8th June the last British ships had sailed, and the R.A.F. fighters from the shore air-fields had flown their Hurricanes safely on to the carriers' decks. But quite unknown to us, the *Scharnhorst*, *Gneisenau* and *Hipper* had left Kiel on the 4th under Admiral Marschall with the object of attacking our shipping at Harstad—for the Germans were unaware that we were in process of evacuating our forces. Four days later they encountered and sank a tanker and an empty troopship which were on passage home from Vestfiord; and they successfully jammed the troopship's distress message, which would otherwise have warned all our ships that an enemy squadron was on the prowl. By a stroke of extraordinarily bad luck, at 4 p.m. that evening, the 8th June, the German battle cruisers sighted the *Glorious*, which had with her only two destroyers—the *Acasta* and *Ardent*. The carrier had on board half a dozen Swordfish, but for reasons which will never be explained, she was not using them to fly patrols for her own protection. It thus happened that she was caught entirely by surprise, and although her crew made desperate efforts to arm the Swordfish with torpedoes and fly them off, she was overwhelmed by the German ships' gunfire before it could be accomplished. The two British destroyers tried most valiantly to shield the carrier with smoke; but were themselves soon sunk. The *Acasta* did, however, manage to hit the *Scharnhorst* with a torpedo while almost in her death throes; and that hit inflicted such damage that Admiral Marschall broke off the operation and set course for Trondheim, whither the *Hipper* had been detached earlier in the day. Only 46 of the 1,561 officers and men in the three sunk warships survived; but it seems certain that the *Acasta's* torpedo hit saved our weakly escorted troop and store convoys, several of which were within striking distance of Admiral Marschall—had he carried out the orders signalled to him from the German shore headquarters to continue the search for our convoys.

Not until the following morning did any news of these desperate actions reach Admiral Forbes; for the *Glorious's* main radio was destroyed by one of the first hits, and the enemy report she sent on a weak auxiliary set was picked up only by the cruiser *Devonshire*. As she was carrying the King and government of Norway from Tromsö to England she did not break wireless silence to repeat it. In fact only one battleship was covering the convoys at the time; for Forbes's two battle cruisers were pursuing a false scent towards Iceland, and anxiety about the exposed condition of the Northern Patrols had caused him to retain some forces at Scapa; but in retrospect it does seem that so large a movement should have been better protected. Although all the 25,000 troops from Vestfiord and most of their equipment reached British ports safely, we certainly had a narrow escape from a bigger disaster than the loss of the *Glorious*; and the events of 7th-9th June once again underlined the unreliability of our North Sea reconnaissance patrols and the superiority of the enemy's intelligence.

So ended the Norwegian campaign. For the Royal Navy, it had been a gruelling ordeal, since for more than two months the Home Fleet ships, and especially the cruisers and destroyers, had been forced to work in waters where the Luftwaffe held almost undisputed command of the air. The captain of one of our destroyers summed up the experiences of the campaign very graphically in a letter to a friend. "It is," he wrote, "very far from being a triumph of air over sea. In spite of the total absence of air cover, short nights and perfect weather, I do not think any essential sea or landing operation has not come off. And escort vessels, solitary and stationary in fiords, have been constantly maintained. But of course you can't go on for ever in what amounts to enemy coastal waters if he has *all* the air; and the wretched and undefended troops can't go on at all."[1]

Though the Royal and Merchant Navies had indeed successfully carried across all the troops and supplies ordered to Norway, and had brought home the expeditionary forces almost intact, their losses had been heavy. Those of the Royal Navy included a fleet carrier and two cruisers, as well as many small warships; while eight large merchantmen, including two troopships and two tankers, were lost through one cause or another. But it was the hard-run destroyers which suffered the most heavily of all; for nine of them were sunk, and twelve damaged. And it was those ships which were needed so urgently to meet the crisis which had meanwhile blown up in western Europe: since the struggle for control of the narrow seas in the south had begun with Hitler's attack on Holland and Belgium on 10th May—nearly a month before the withdrawal from north Norway. Though the German Navy had also suffered severely, the loss of the *Blücher*, *Königsberg*, *Karlsruhe* and ten destroyers, and the damage sustained by the *Lützow*, *Hipper* and both battle cruisers was perhaps a reasonable price to pay for the strategic advantages gained. For the enemy was now able to base his surface ships and U-boats about 1,000 miles nearer to our Atlantic convoy routes, and had completely outflanked the invisible but none the less real barrier which our sea power had established on the line between the Shetland Islands and south Norway. There was no alternative but to withdraw the barrier farther to the west; and although its southern hinge in the Orkneys still held, it was essential to find a new northern hinge on which to hang it. Only the Danish dependency of Iceland could meet that need, and the recent German rape of Denmark provided valid grounds for us to occupy it. On 10th May, the day that Hitler struck at Holland, Home Fleet cruisers

[1] Lieut.-Commander Trevor Napier of H.M.S. *Jackal* to Sir George Barnes, 28th April, 1940.

accordingly carried a Royal Marine advance guard from the Clyde to Reykjavik, while a smaller detachment landed and took possession of the Danish Faeroe Islands.[1] A week later an infantry brigade followed to Iceland, and in July Canadian reinforcements took over responsibility for its defence. Steps were at once taken to open a naval base at Hvalfiord, just north of Reykjavik, and to construct airfields for use by Coastal Command. We also started to lay an immense minefield between the Orkneys and Iceland, with the object of strengthening our hold on that passage; but it soon proved to be a singularly unprofitable undertaking. Thus began a new phase in the struggle for control of the Atlantic routes, with our maritime barrier forced westwards but still holding; and in the new phase Iceland was to play a most important part. But before telling that part of our story we must turn from the far north to the narrow seas.

Soon after the outbreak of war the Naval Staff had prepared plans to meet the very circumstances which arose suddenly, but not unexpectedly, in north-western Europe in May, 1940. They included arrangements for the withdrawal of all shipping from the Low Countries, the blocking of the principal ports and the demolition of their facilities, the destruction of important stores such as oil fuel, and the removal of gold and diamonds; for we realised that, even with the British and French armies advancing to their support, Holland and Belgium were unlikely to be able to offer prolonged resistance. But these plans, and the many additional demands on the fleet which always arise in an emergency, necessitated the immediate reinforcement of the Nore and Dover commands in the south at the expense of the Home Fleet. This, combined with the need to return to Admiral Cunningham the ships recently recalled from the Mediterranean, already mentioned, reduced Forbes's strength to a dangerously low level. It was lucky that the losses and damage inflicted on the German Navy in the Norwegian campaign—which were actually considerably heavier than we believed at the time— precluded any new forays being immediately made against our Atlantic shipping. Many cruisers and destroyers were thus detached from Scapa to work under Admiral Sir Reginald Drax (C.-in-C., Nore) and Vice-Admiral B. H. Ramsay (Flag Officer, Dover); and as soon as the Germans attacked the Low Countries the destroyers

[1] See Map p. 91.

took across naval and military parties to Ijmuiden, Hook of Holland, Flushing and Antwerp. Within two days so serious had the situation become in Holland that the blocking and demolition operations were put in hand. The withdrawal of the Queen and Royal Family soon followed; and by the 15th, when Dutch resistance ended, most of the shipping had been cleared, and the gold reserves and diamonds (for Amsterdam was the centre of the world's diamond cutting industry) had been removed. Similar needs next arose in the Belgian ports, and large numbers of merchantmen, barges and tugs were successfully removed from Antwerp; but the King of Belgium and his government would not leave their country to continue the fight. For a fortnight the destroyers worked with scarcely a break off the Dutch and Belgian coasts. There seemed no limit to the variety of the tasks which fell to them—embarking and landing troops, bombarding shore targets, rescuing Allied missions and foreign personages, towing, screening and repelling the increasingly frequent air attacks were all among them. So far their losses had not been unreasonably high; but as the German armies swept westwards into France and then turned north to cut off the British Expeditionary Force from its Channel bases, the demands grew heavier, and so did the losses. On 20th May two battalions of Guardsmen were rushed across in destroyers to hold up the German advance along the coast at Boulogne. Three days later they had to be extricated under heavy air and artillery bombardments; and it was again the destroyers that did it. In Boulogne harbour, while actually embarking the troops, they fought a series of very unusual close-range actions with German tanks which had broken into the town; but over 4,000 soldiers were brought away safely. Meanwhile an emergency force of Riflemen had been carried across to hold Calais; but when their situation became impossible the Cabinet forbade evacuation "for the sake of Allied solidarity," and the garrison was ordered to fight to the last—even though Admiral Ramsay had actually organised the ships and craft to rescue them.

Meanwhile the British Army was becoming more and more compressed within a narrow perimeter inland of Dunkirk, and it had become plain that if any of its men were to see their homeland again not a day must be lost. The Admiralty and Admiral Ramsay had already taken emergency steps to collect the ships needed for the rescue attempt; and although almost everything had to be

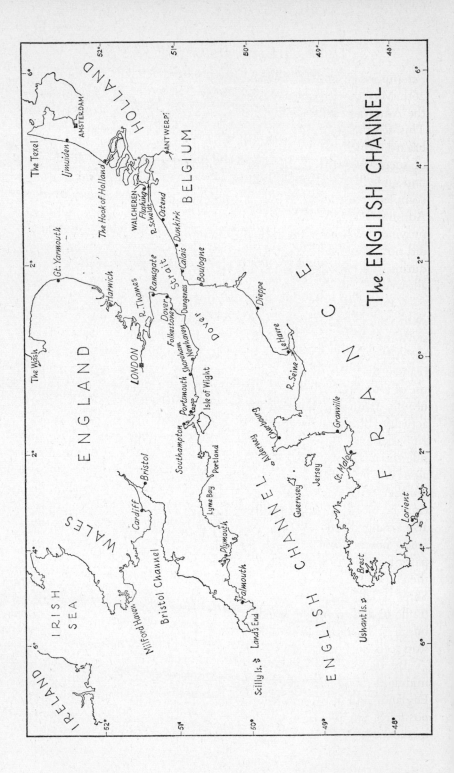

The ENGLISH CHANNEL

extemporised, and no formal orders were ever issued, by Sunday 26th May the Royal Navy was ready. At 6.57 p.m. that evening the Admiralty sent a laconic order to "begin operation Dynamo." This set the stage for an operation of immense complexity and hazard, which has no parallel in modern war, and whose prospects of success seemed at the time, highly dubious; for the Germans undoubtedly possessed such superiority on land and in the air that complete frustration of our purpose appeared all too easy. Yet Admiral Ramsay and the crews of the scores of ships and craft moving towards Dover in increasing numbers never hesitated. We did not, however, expect to be able to lift more than 45,000 men during the two days which seemed all that we were likely to be allowed.

Captain W. G. Tennant had already gone across to Dunkirk with a small staff to organise the evacuation on the far side, and the outward movement of ships from Dover had actually started before the Admiralty sent the executive order. Ramsay and Tennant both realised that, to lift large numbers of men quickly, we had to make use of Dunkirk harbour; but its piers and quays had already suffered heavily from bombing, and only by using the long east mole— actually a breakwater—for berthing ships was there any hope of rapid embarkation. Luckily Tennant found that the depth of water alongside the mole would allow ships of the size we were using to berth alongside it; and it was from that improvised pier that the greatest number of men were rescued. Because the harbour might at any time be blocked, or put totally out of action by bombing, Tennant also arranged for men to be lifted by boat from the long stretch of sandy beaches which stretch for miles to the east of Dunkirk, and part of which lay within the ever-narrowing British perimeter. Here the chief difficulty was that the sea bed shelved only very gradually. Ships would therefore have to lie a long way off-shore, and boat traffic to and from the beaches was bound to be a desperately slow business. Moreover, only a slight swell was needed to put a complete stop to boat work.

By the evening of the first day (midnight 26th/27th May to midnight 27th/28th) only 7,669 men had been taken across to England, and prospects for the future looked about as black as possible. On the 28th supplies of food, water, ammunition and medical stores, all urgently needed by the hard-pressed Army, were

carried across; conditions in the harbour improved, and a steady
stream of destroyers and personnel ships moved to and from the east
mole, while Fighter Command aircraft kept watch overhead. The
fleet at Admiral Ramsay's disposal was increasing with the passage
of every hour, and a miscellaneous collection of minesweepers,
drifters, coasting steamers, Dutch "schuyts" and smaller craft worked
off the beaches all day. The total landed in England rose to 17,804
men—more than double the first day's accomplishment. Up to this
time the evacuation fleet had not suffered unduly heavily, but
Wednesday, 29th May, told a very different tale. Three destroyers
were sunk,[1] and seven others received such serious damage—mostly
from bombs—that they had to be withdrawn; four of the personnel
vessels, whose large carrying capacity made them particularly
valuable, were also sunk; and nearly a score of miscellaneous vessels
fell victims to torpedoes, bombs or mines. None the less 47,310
soldiers, of whom 13,752 were lifted off the beaches, reached Britain
during the twenty-four hours. But the Admiralty feared that, if we
went on losing destroyers at the rate suffered on this day, the Navy
might soon be crippled for lack of them; and they therefore ordered
the withdrawal of the large, modern ships. But the fifteen then
remaining to Ramsay soon proved insufficient to enable him to
carry on, and most of the withdrawn ships had to be sent back to
him next day. Meanwhile everything possible was being done to
improve the shore organisation on the other side; for we found that
rapid embarkation depended largely on having naval parties available
to marshal the soldiers to the right points, and arrange for the proper
number of craft to be there ready to take them on board. We also
found it essential to establish emergency wireless stations, so that
Admiral Ramsay could communicate direct with the port and beach
parties. It is interesting to see in these hastily extemporised arrangements of May, 1940, the origin of the highly specialised Naval
Beach Commandos, who contributed so much to the success of the
great combined operations of later years.

Admiral Ramsay's flotillas had meanwhile swept and marked
three routes between Dover and Dunkirk; but the shortest one
(39 miles) had come under heavy artillery fire where it passed close

---

[1] Until recently we believed that the torpedoes fired at ships taking part in the evacuation
all came from E-boats, but scrutiny of German records has proved that U.62 was present on
29th May, and it was undoubtedly she who sank either the destroyer *Grafton* or the *Wakeful*.

off the French coast, and the evacuation traffic therefore had to be diverted to a much longer route (87 miles) to the north-east. This, however, delayed the movements excessively, and on the 29th Ramsay therefore switched all ships to a central route which was only 55 miles long. Luckily the Germans did not discover the change for three days.

Many factors contributed to the great accomplishments of Thursday, 30th May, when we rescued 53,823 men, nearly 30,000 of whom were lifted off the beaches; and these encouraging figures made Ramsay decide to press ahead with the evacuation "with the utmost vigour," with the object of reducing the land forces to a small rearguard by 1st June. The last day of May, however, saw an unpleasant swell breaking on the beaches. For a time boat-work was impossible; and German bombing and artillery fire had become so intense that large ships could not use the port. During the forenoon it seemed that a serious crisis had arisen; but then the swell moderated, the enemy's fire decreased, and the little ships seized their chance with both hands. The day which had begun so discouragingly ended with an astonishing feat; for 68,014 men were brought home—the zenith of the whole operation. Now the Army contracted its perimeter still farther, and the most easterly beaches were abandoned.

The 1st June started badly with heavy bombing attacks on Dunkirk port and on the off-shore fleet; and, as on 29th May, it was the destroyers and personnel vessels which suffered the most heavily. Four of the former (one of them a French ship) and one of the latter were sunk, and although other ships always went promptly to the assistance of any stricken vessel, it was inevitable that, with as many as 1,000 soldiers crammed on board a destroyer, casualties should have been heavy. None the less the total disembarked in England was 64,429—nearly as many as on the previous day. Ramsay now planned to complete the withdrawal next night (1st/2nd June); for the last beaches in British hands and the off-shore shipping were being heavily shelled. But it soon became plain that this plan could not be fulfilled; for we would not abandon the French troops who were holding the final perimeter, and through whom our own men had withdrawn to the beaches. On the other hand, Ramsay had, if possible, to avoid a repetition of the previous day's losses of destroyers and personnel vessels. He therefore decided to lift as many men as possible in a single night operation, and as dusk fell on 1st June he sent across every ship which could be made fit for sea. Between midnight on 1st/2nd June and the following midnight, by which time "Dynamo" had been running for a full week, 26,256 soldiers were rescued; and late on the evening of 2nd news reached Dover that, except for the wounded, whose evacuation had been prevented by continuous and callous German attacks on fully illuminated hospital ships, the whole of the British Expeditionary Force had reached England.

It now remained to try to bring across all the French troops who could be extricated. The first night operation having been so successful Ramsay decided to repeat it; but insufficient French troops arrived to fill all the ships sent across, and although 26,746 men, nearly all of them French, landed in England on 2nd/3rd June, more could have been lifted had they arrived in time. None the less Ramsay refused to abandon his purpose—so long as a chance to bring off the French rearguard remained. Though he knew that the crews of his fleet had about reached the limit of human endurance, he also knew that they would rise to a call for one more effort. But the night of 3rd/4th June must, he decided, see the last attempt. We believed that about 30,000 men remained in the shrunken perimeter, and the ships available at Dover were just adequate to lift that total—provided that they arrived promptly. Only 9 of the 41 destroyers originally allocated to "Dynamo," and 5 of the 45 personnel vessels, now remained; but at 10.15 p.m. on the 3rd they and about a score of smaller ships started across. By 3.30 a.m. on the 4th they had taken off 26,175 men, mostly from the east and west moles of the harbour; and a few hours after the last ship had left Dunkirk crammed with about 3,000 soldiers the Admiralty signalled that operation "Dynamo" had been completed.

Starting with the modest hope of rescuing 45,000 men, it finally achieved the astonishing figure of 338,226 saved from the enemy's clutches—308,888 of them in British ships and most of the rest in French ships. Of these totals the destroyers and personnel vessels brought back by far the greatest proportion; and it was they who suffered the most severely. "Dynamo" cost the Royal Navy six destroyers sunk and nineteen seriously damaged. Nine personnel vessels were also lost, and eight others suffered such injuries that they had to be withdrawn. In Britain the sense of relief was profound;

for although we knew that we had suffered a crushing defeat on land the "nine days' wonder" had saved us from the humiliation of surrender on an unprecedented scale.

Meanwhile the rest of the free world had been watching these events with bated breath and, initially, with little hope for Britain. Hitler's armies had recently overrun Poland, Denmark, Norway, Holland and Belgium, and had crushed their peoples into submission in a few days. France, the world saw, was rapidly going the same way. How, then, asked the foreigner, could the British Army survive? Happily the British government and people knew the answer to that question—almost instinctively—and the enemy did not. The success of "Dynamo" owed an enormous debt to many causes and people; to Admiral Ramsay's leadership and determination, to the soldiers who fought so stubbornly to hold the perimeter, and then patiently waited their turn to embark; to the fighter pilots who fought in, and sometimes cleared the sky over Dunkirk; and to the weather, which was almost miraculously favourable. But there was one factor without which the operation could certainly never have been undertaken, let alone have succeeded; and that was sea power. Once again, as so often in the past, the Royal Navy and its comrades of the Merchant Navy, had shown that by their skill and resolution, by their training and their intimate understanding of the element on which they worked, they could and would deny a continental enemy the fruits of his victories on land. The recognition of that fact, which slowly dawned in the minds of the people of the free world as each day passed without a hint of the British Army succumbing to disaster, created a profound impression—especially in the United States; for it brought the hope, and finally the belief, that tyranny would not ultimately prevail. Operation "Dynamo" thus cast a ray of light like a sunbeam through the gloom of the preceding months, warming the spirit of mankind, and filling it with a new determination to resist evil without counting the cost, and to accept the sacrifices which would inevitably be demanded. And in America the new policy of giving help to hard-pressed Britain gained strength; for there was now some confidence that the help would not be thrown away. In June, 1940, however, the British people had no time to indulge in abstract theorising; for as the month advanced the disaster to the French armies deepened into a cataclysm involving the whole nation, and the British navies therefore quietly turned their attention to rescuing all that they could from the wreckage of a continent.

Between the end of "Dynamo" on 4th June and the 25th of the same month British ships carried out a whole series of further evacuations. They started in mid-channel at Havre, moved west to the Gulf of St. Malo, the Channel Islands and Cherbourg, then rounded Ushant to Brest, reached down the French Biscay coast to St. Nazaire and La Pallice, and finally used Bayonne and St. Jean de Luz just short of the Spanish frontier.[1] In only one instance did the Navy fail in its purpose to any considerable extent; and that was when the rescue of the 51st (Highland) Division, which had been trapped with its back to the sea at St. Valéry between Dieppe and Havre, was frustrated by fog and by the premature surrender of the French commander. From every other port to which our ships were sent, including many on the French Mediterranean coast, they returned with British and Allied soldiers, or with civilians who had good reason to flee before the Germanic hordes. These operations were collectively known as "Aerial," and in the sum resulted in 191,870 more fighting men and between 30 and 40,000 civilians reaching Britain in safety. Nor was the price paid by the navies at all heavy; for only at St. Nazaire, where we lost the big troopship *Lancastria* with 3,000 men on board, did the enemy react at all effectively. Because "Dynamo" so caught the free world's imagination, "Aerial" attracted little attention; but in some ways it was an even more convincing demonstration of the effectiveness of sea power.

There was one important purpose, however, in which we largely failed at this time; and that was in our endeavour to persuade the French Navy to sail to British ports to continue the struggle alongside us. Though most of its modern ships got away from their stricken country in time to avoid capture, they sailed to North Africa. Only two old battleships, four destroyers, seven submarines and a number of minesweepers came to Britain. This was not only a severe disappointment to the Royal Navy, but a cause of great anxiety to the British government, of which Churchill had become Prime Minister on 11th May; for we simply could not afford to risk Germany gaining possession of a great part of the French fleet, we did not consider it secure from seizure while it remained in Oran

[1] See Map p. 23.

and Dakar, and we felt a good deal of mistrust towards Admiral Darlan, the head of the French Navy, who possessed immense influence over his service, but had remained in conquered France and was plainly subject to German pressure. Such was the background to the violent action ordered by the British government against its former Ally in the dark days of June, 1940.

CHAPTER V

BACKS TO THE SEA WALL

June–December, 1940

" But the most remarkable feature of the time was the flame which burst forth and spread its light over the whole of Britain. It was not merely the flame of patriotism . . . it appeared to be fed and rendered intense by a passionate hatred of Napoleon personally."

Sir Henry Bunbury, *Narratives of Passages in the War with France,* 1799-1810 (1854).

THE FAILURE of the expeditions to Norway, the overrunning by the Germans of Holland, Belgium and France, and the declaration of war by Italy on 10th June, 1940, had transformed the strategic situation in Europe in a manner so wholly unfavourable for Britain that most continental observers—and not a few in America—considered that her hour had come. The British people, however, inspired by Churchill's leadership, thought quite otherwise; for in disaster they had, as so often before in their history, not only closed their ranks in new-found unity of purpose, but had rediscovered those qualities of stubborn resolution which, though often dormant, never lie far beneath the surface of their character. They knew that their homeland was bound to be subjected to heavy bombing, that the threat of invasion was very real, and that the danger to their Atlantic lifeline was now far more acute. But they had deep faith in the Navy—that "sure shield" which had saved them so often from the trampling heel of continental conquerors; they knew that the English Channel presented a far more formidable obstacle to an invasion fleet than a river crossing; they despised Mussolini and his bombastic colleagues, and felt sure that Cunningham's Mediterranean fleet, even if greatly outnumbered, would give a very good account of itself; and they were, for the first time for many years, confident in the leadership of the government which the crisis had brought into power. In all those respects their judgment was very soon shown to be well-founded.

Of all the difficult problems which beset Mr. Churchill's War Cabinet and the Admiralty at the beginning of June the replacement of lost French maritime power in the western Mediterranean, and the measures needed to prevent the Axis powers gaining the use of the important French warships lying in African ports, were regarded as the most urgent. Thanks, however, to the superiority of the Home Fleet over the German Navy, the first of the two requirements could be met comparatively easily; and before the end of the month a powerful squadron had assembled at Gibraltar under Vice-Admiral Sir James Somerville. For reasons which even now remain obscure, it was called "Force H"; and it consisted initially of the fleet carrier *Ark Royal*, the battle cruiser *Hood*, two battleships and a small number of cruisers and destroyers. At Gibraltar it was ideally placed to exert its influence in many different directions. A few hours' steaming to the east would make its presence felt in the Mediterranean; by steering west it could cover the important trade route from Freetown, Sierra Leone; it could lunge out into the wide Atlantic if a threat developed in the northern waters of that ocean; and it could easily reinforce Admiral Forbes's Home Fleet, or be reinforced by it. No better example of the importance of defended naval bases, and of the flexibility of maritime power, can be found in all the annals of history than in the rapid creation of Force H at Gibraltar in June, 1940.

While Somerville's new command was assembling the Admiralty was also urgently considering whether Admiral Cunningham could maintain his position in the eastern basin of the Mediterranean, or whether his fleet should withdraw—partly to Gibraltar and partly through the Suez Canal to the Red Sea and Indian Ocean. The chief danger did not arise through any inability to deal with the Italian Navy, but because the Army of the Nile was so enormously outnumbered by the Italians in Libya that it might not be able to protect the base at Alexandria. If the Italians overran the Nile delta the fleet's position would become perilous in the extreme. When, however, the First Sea Lord (Admiral of the Fleet Sir Dudley Pound) asked Admiral Cunningham for his views on the tentative proposal to withdraw, the latter's reaction was to express his "earnest hope that such a decision would never have to be taken"; and within a few days of receiving this vigorous rejoinder the proposal was dropped.

Force H was only a few days old when there fell to Somerville what Churchill called "one of the most disagreeable and difficult tasks that a British Admiral has ever been faced with";[1] for he was ordered to proceed in full strength to Oran and offer Admiral Gensoul, who was in command of the French fleet, four alternative courses. If he refused either to join our forces, or to sail with reduced crews to a British port or to the French West Indies, or to scuttle his ships within six hours, Somerville was to try to get them demilitarised to our satisfaction where they lay; but if all those proposals were rejected he was to use force and destroy the Oran squadron. Early on 3rd July an emissary was sent into the port to put the peaceable alternatives to Gensoul; but he refused to discuss them. The exchange of documents which followed produced no solution, and the French Admiral undoubtedly exacerbated the rising tension by signalling to his government that he had been presented with an ultimatum to "sink his ships within six hours or we will use force." His failure to mention any of the other alternatives offered to him, combined with an increase of pressure on Somerville, who in the afternoon was told from London "to settle matters quickly or he would have reinforcements to deal with," made inevitable the tragedy that quickly followed. Just before 6 p.m. Somerville opened fire. The battleship *Bretagne* blew up, the *Dunkerque* and *Provence* and a number of lesser ships were seriously damaged, and 1,297 French lives were lost; but the battle cruiser *Strasbourg* and five destroyers, though attacked by the *Ark Royal's* torpedo-bombers, broke out of the harbour and reached Toulon safely.

The necessity for this violent action by the Royal Navy against its former Ally has been hotly debated ever since that fateful day. What can be said with confidence is that the three British flag officers involved in it—Admiral Sir Dudley North on shore at Gibraltar, Admiral Cunningham at Alexandria, and Admiral Somerville himself—all viewed the government's orders with something approaching horror; and all three believed that, given time for negotiation, a peaceful solution could have been found. Admiral North indeed expressed such a view to the Admiralty in writing,

[1] W. S. Churchill, *The Second World War*, Vol. II (Cassell Ed.) p. 209.

and that report provides the background to what became a *cause célèbre* in British naval and political circles after the war; for in the following October, after the failure at Dakar shortly to be recounted he was relieved of his command.[1]

Oran was not the only overseas base where French warships were lying in July, 1940, and where a solution to the vexed question of their future had therefore to be sought. At Alexandria was Admiral Godfroy's squadron consisting of the battleship *Lorraine*, three fine 8-inch cruisers, one 6-inch cruiser, and a number of lesser warships, which had come to the eastern Mediterranean before the fall of France to work under Admiral Cunningham; in the West African ports of Casablanca and Dakar were the new battleships *Jean Bart* and *Richelieu*, recently arrived from Brest, and a considerable number of lesser warships; while two cruisers and an aircraft carrier were in French West Indian ports. As soon as the Franco-German armistice was signed Admiral Cunningham took up the question of the future of Godfroy's squadron with its commander, and after long and patient negotiations a personal agreement for their peaceful demilitarisation at Alexandria was signed between the two officers on 4th July. This was a personal triumph for Cunningham, since the violent action at Oran had produced understandably strong feelings among the French crews; and at one moment the Admiralty—probably under pressure from the Prime Minister—very nearly destroyed the possibility of a peaceful solution by an ill-timed message, which Cunningham wisely disregarded. Over the future of the new and powerful *Richelieu* at Dakar, however, the British Government was not prepared to take any chances, and on 8th July an attempt was made to immobilise her without causing heavy loss of life. A fast motor-boat from the light fleet carrier *Hermes* first penetrated the defences, and dropped depth charges under the battleship's stern, with the object of damaging her rudder and propellers; but the charges failed to explode in the shallow water. Then torpedo-bombers from the same carrier attacked, and succeeded in inflicting some damage. The battleship was not, however, completely put out of action; and, as we shall see shortly, the attacks of 8th July did not mark the end of the

---

[1] Not until 23rd May, 1957, when Mr. MacMillan as Prime Minister investigated the matter, was Admiral North publicly acquitted of any dereliction of duty while serving as Flag Officer, North Atlantic, in 1940.

attempts to deal with her. The French ships in the West Indies, which had on board a considerable quantity of bullion and a large number of aircraft purchased on French account in America, were finally kept immobilised by diplomatic pressure combined with the denial of oil supplies. In sum it may be said that, where violent measures were taken against French ships to secure British ends, they accomplished no more than partial success, and aroused passionate hatred in French breasts; where negotiation was employed it was successful; and where no measures were taken—as against the large number of ships in Algiers and Toulon—the French honoured their undertaking that none of them should fall into German or Italian hands. Perhaps the best justification for the use of force was that to the British people, and also to the neutral nations, including America, it did emphasise the determination of Churchill's leadership; and as Britain was at the time faced with the most serious of all the many invasion threats with which her long history is punctuated, and every ounce of her own resolution was needed, the psychological effect of her leaders' firmness of purpose must not be dismissed as insignificant.

Measures to meet the invasion threat were actually put in hand before the withdrawal from Europe was completed; for there could be no mistaking the purpose for which the German armies were massing along the French coast. The Admiralty actually issued its plans and intentions on 28th May. They stressed the importance of attacking the invasion fleet from the sea and air before it sailed, and of gaining the earliest possible knowledge of its intended departure. If, however, our reconnaissance and intelligence services failed to give adequate warning, the fullest possible weight was to be thrown into "attack at the point of arrival." Though the Admiralty expected the enemy to cross by the shortest route (near to the Straits of Dover) they considered that diversions and subsidiary landings would probably take place at other points; and the whole coast from the Wash to Newhaven therefore had to be guarded.[1] The principal striking force, composed of four destroyer flotillas with cruiser support, was to be stationed in or near the Thames estuary; and commanders of bases on the east coast and in the Channel were to organise other similar forces. Escort vessels, principally from the Western Approaches, were to be taken off convoy duty to strengthen the

[1] See Map p. 74.

southern commands, and large numbers of small vessels were requisitioned to establish continuous off-shore patrols. These latter measures aroused strong protests from Admiral Forbes, the Commander-in-Chief, Home Fleet, who held that, as long as the Royal Air Force remained undefeated and our naval supremacy unimpaired, the enemy could not launch a large expedition against England with any prospect of success; and that if he attempted to do so we were bound to gain sufficient warning to enable our forces to move to the danger spot in good time, and with the virtual certainty of inflicting a crushing defeat. Thus the dispersal of many of his ships on purely defensive duties and the grave weakening of our Atlantic escorts were, in Forbes's opinion, strategically unsound. He considered that the correct strategy was to keep our main strength based at Scapa, whence Ireland as well as the southern coast of England could be covered; to conduct offensive sweeps in the North Sea to impress upon the enemy the extent of our control of those waters, and to continue to employ all the light forces we could spare on Atlantic escort duties. Although such a strategy had behind it the authority of centuries of experience, it was rejected both by the naval authorities in the southern commands and by the British government. To-day, however, it seems plain that Forbes's contemporary views were entirely sound; but their rejection in the summer of 1940 resulted in the greatly weakened Home Fleet having to play a passive role, what time our losses in the Western Approaches rose alarmingly. By August it was plain that many of the flotilla vessels must return to escort duty. It should not, of course, be thought that the cruisers and destroyers in the south waited idly in port during those critical months. They carried out many sweeps in the narrow seas, and bombarded the ports where invasion craft were assembling; but German records do not indicate that either the air or naval bombardments inflicted appreciable damage. In the enemy's camp Admiral Raeder and the German naval staff had few illusions regarding the difficulty and danger of carrying a large army across stormy, tide-swept waters over which they did not possess adequate maritime control; but the German army cast its plans in reckless disregard—or total ignorance—of such factors. They seem to have anticipated no greater difficulties than were involved in a river crossing, and it was nearly the end of August before they were even persuaded to modify their demand for 13 assault divisions to be

landed on a " broad front," covering 200 miles between Lyme Bay
and Ramsgate, and to substitute a substantially weaker assault on a
" narrow front " between Folkestone and Newhaven in the Dover
Straits.[1] Even so, the Germans never came near to resolving the
difficulties of transporting large numbers of soldiers and great
quantities of equipment across those deceptively narrow waters. To
give but one example of the lack of realism which characterised their
plans, the proposal to tow river barges across the Channel at a speed
of three knots seems quite derisory. Admiral Raeder, however,
dared not enlarge upon the futility of the plan to Hitler and his
military advisers. He could only seek to modify it by persuasion,
and welcome postponement when it came. It was actually Göring
who presented him with the avenue of escape which he desired;
for when the commander of the Luftwaffe boasted that he would
subdue Britain by air power alone, Raeder was only too glad to
watch the attempt. By the time that the great air battles of August
and September had ended in the Luftwaffe's defeat by Fighter
Command, the season was too far advanced to enable the attempt
to be launched; and on 17th September Hitler postponed it
indefinitely. We who lived through those anxious days may
reasonably regret that the expedition never sailed; for, had it done
so, it is virtually certain that it would have resulted in a British
victory comparable for its decisiveness to Barfleur or Quiberon
Bay; and it can hardly be doubted that such a victory would have
altered the entire course of the war. It is indeed plain to-day that,
of all the factors which contributed to the failure of Hitler's
grandiose invasion plans, none was greater than the lack of adequate
instruments of sea power and of a proper understanding of their
use on the German side. Britain, on the other hand, not only
possessed the necessary ships and craft, but they were manned by
devoted crews who were imbued with a traditional and burning
desire to come to grips with the enemy invasion fleet. Finally, we
may remark how the events of the summer of 1940 emphasised once
again what Louis XIV and XV of France, Napoleon, the Kaiser and
many other continental would-be conquerors of Britain had learnt
in turn—namely, that an overseas expedition cannot be launched
with any prospect of success without first defeating the other side's

[1] For a full exposition of the German high command's vacillations the reader is referred
to Ronald Wheatley, *Operation Sea Lion* (Oxford, 1958).

maritime forces, and so gaining control of the waters across which the expedition has to pass. The British destroyer captain quoted in an earlier context summed up the issues and the principles involved very succinctly in a letter to a friend. " If you haven't got command of the sea," he wrote, " your expedition must have long preparation and a short passage. . . . I shall not go near his ruddy warships . . . unless they get in my way· nor shall I waste my time crumpling my bows on any old barge. When I have expended my very considerable stock of ammunition and my torpedoes I am by no means at the end of my resources for this sort of thing. . . . And their task is a great many times more difficult than ours."[1] As there were about half a hundred British destroyers ready to hand, and all were imbued with the spirit of the writer of that letter, the reluctance of the Germans to hazard their troops on the short sea crossing can readily be understood.

We have already remarked on the great strategic changes which were brought about by the German occupation of the entire French sea coast in June, 1940. From the Admiralty's point of view the most urgent needs were to recast our convoy organisation to bring all Atlantic shipping in by the North Channel, instead of by routes passing south of Ireland;[2] to organise new convoys passing round the north of Scotland to and from the ports on the east coast, and to start running heavily protected convoys of small ships up and down the English Channel. These changes greatly increased the importance of the Clyde and Mersey ports on the west coast, because only essential shipping could now use the harbours facing the North Sea and occupied France. The coastal convoys were, of course, very exposed to attack by U-boats, fast surface vessels and aircraft; and the shallow waters through which they had to steam were all too easily infested with mines. Thus the expansion of our minesweeping force continued to demand a very high priority, and by the summer of 1940 it had grown to some 700 vessels, over half of which were fitted to sweep "influence" type as well as moored mines. Flotillas of sweepers were based on each important commercial harbour, to keep the entrance channels clear; while others toiled continually, by night as well as by day, in the off-shore approaches. Apart from the inevitable dangers involved in seeking for the hidden devices,

[1] Lieut.-Commander T. M. Napier of H.M.S. *Jackal* to Sir George Barnes, 4th July, 1940.
[2] See Maps pp. 23 and 91.

the sweepers were constantly attacked by enemy bombers and fighters; and the losses they suffered from one or other cause were not light. None the less there was never any shortage of the sturdy, hard-bitten fishermen who provided a large proportion of the crews; and now that minesweepers were being built all over the Empire on Admiralty account, the shortage of ships from which we had suffered in the early days was being rapidly overcome. During the whole of 1940, and in spite of the many urgent problems which beset the Admiralty and our maritime commands, losses on mines reached no more than 201 merchantmen of just over half a million tons.

The east coast convoys, which ran on a two-day cycle between the Thames and Firth of Forth, were by this time well established, and fighter aircraft flown from bases along the landward flank of their route were keeping the German bombers well in check; but in the summer the problem of fighter protection became acute in the English Channel, where the convoys were very exposed to attack from nearby air bases in France. In July losses became so severe that the Admiralty actually stopped the Channel convoys for a short time; but by making the passage of each one into a combined air and naval operation the difficulties were overcome, and by the autumn they were again sailing regularly in both directions.

It was in the Atlantic that the most serious difficulties arose during the second half of 1940. Across the northern waters of that ocean came the "fast" (9-10 knot) HX convoys from Halifax, and the "slow" ($7\frac{1}{2}$-8 knot) SC convoys from Sydney, Cape Breton Island;[1] while the slow SL convoys came up from the south on their long 19-day passages from Freetown, Sierra Leone. All of these, and the corresponding outward convoys, now had to be routed as far as possible from the enemy's newly-won U-boat and air bases, thus greatly increasing the length of their passages; and the approach to our home ports through the North Channel to the Irish Sea had become the artery on which the flow of the nation's life-blood entirely depended. Thus it was mainly in the north-west approaches to the British Isles that our sea and air escorts came to grips with the U-boats and the long-range bombers in the first of the many deadly struggles which together came to be called the Battle of the Atlantic.

It has already been suggested that, by depleting our escorts to

[1]See Map p. 91.

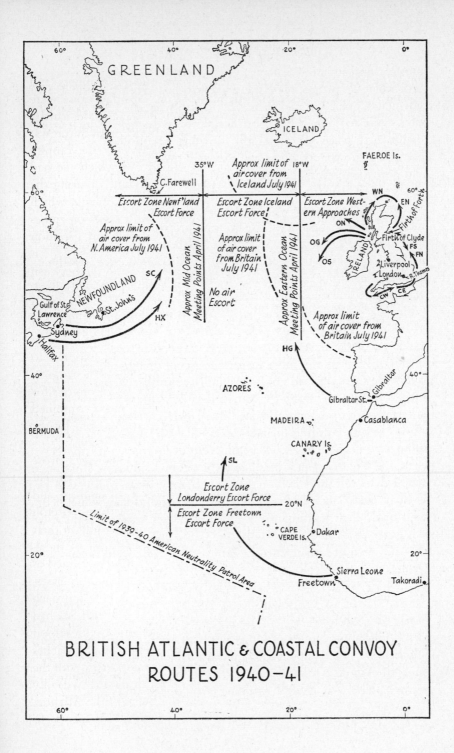

GREENLAND

ICELAND

FAEROE Is.

35°W   *Approx limit of air cover from Iceland July 1941*   18°W

C.Farewell

WN

EN

Escort Zone Newf'land Escort Force   *Escort Zone Iceland Escort Force*   *Escort Zone West-ern Approaches*

ON

Approx limit of air cover from N. America July 1941   *Approx Mid Ocean Meeting Points April 1941*   *Approx limit of air cover from Britain July 1941*   *Approx Eastern Ocean Meeting Points April 1941*   OG   Firth of Forth

Firth of Clyde   FS

FN

OS

SC   IRELAND   Liverpool

NEWFOUNDLAND   *No air Escort*   London   R.Thames

Gulf of St. Lawrence   St. John's   HX   CW   CE

Sydney

Halifax

Approx limit of air cover from Britain July 1941

HG

40°   AZORES   Gibraltar   40°

BERMUDA   MADEIRA   Gibraltar St.

Casablanca

CANARY Is.

SL

Escort Zone Londonderry Escort Force   20°N

Escort Zone Freetown Escort Force   CAPE VERDE Is.   Dakar

Limit of 1939-40 American Neutrality Patrol Area

20°   Sierra Leone   20°

Freetown   Takoradi

BRITISH ATLANTIC & COASTAL CONVOY
ROUTES 1940-41

provide anti-invasion patrols we presented the Germans with an avoidable advantage; but there were other errors on the British side which helped to make this period into what the U-boat captains later came to look back upon nostalgically as the "happy time." In the first place we were still devoting a considerable effort to patrolling the waters where we expected the U-boats to lie in wait, and also to hunting for them in the open ocean; and there is no doubt at all that the employment of the greatest possible strength on convoy escort duty would have been both more economical and more effective.[1] Secondly, we were unprepared to meet the tactics now used by U-boat captains, who had begun to attack in "wolf-packs" by night, while operating on the surface like torpedo-boats. In these conditions our underwater detecting equipment (the Asdic) was useless; and the escort vessels—none of which were yet equipped with radar—thus had to fall back on sighting their quarry visually. Moreover, most of the vessels allocated to Atlantic convoy duty, and in particular the new corvettes, were too slow to catch a surfaced U-boat. Perhaps the most surprising aspect of our unpreparedness is that the Germans had not only employed similar tactics with great success during the 1914-18 war, but had made no secret of their intention to do so again. In fact, in 1939 Dönitz himself published a book strongly urging the advantages of such tactics;[2] yet our anti-submarine crews had all been trained to deal only with submerged enemies. Thus new methods had to be devised, and new equipment supplied to the ships before they could cope successfully with the U-boat "aces" such as Prien, Kretschmer, Endras and Frauenheim, who made their names famous at this time. In these circumstances it is easily to be understood why the comparatively few U-boats at sea—never more than fifteen—for a time achieved outstanding results.

In June, 1940, when the invasion precautions had reduced our escorts almost to vanishing point, the U-boats sank 58 ships of nearly 300,000 tons—by far the highest losses so far inflicted; and in the following month sinkings were little fewer. It was on 15th July that we finally closed the approach route south of Ireland; and on 17th August Hitler declared a total blockade of Britain, and warned that even neutral shipping would be sunk at sight. All

[1] See pp. 41-2.
[2] See Karl Dönitz, *Die U-bootswaffe* (E. S. Mittler, Berlin, 1939), p. 39.

pretence that the campaign against British shipping was being conducted in accordance with international law was thus discarded. The U-boats from western France were now working as far out into the ocean as 25° West—nearly 500 miles beyond the range to which we could escort most convoys; while the long-range bombers, against which we had as yet few defences, ranged far and wide over the convoy routes, and added appreciably to the toll exacted by the U-boats. In August losses continued on about the same scale; nor did the gradual return of flotilla vessels which had repaired damage sustained in the fighting in the narrow seas, or been released from anti-invasion duties, bring quick relief. September was a worse month than August, and in October several ill-defended convoys were almost massacred by U-boat packs. To give but two examples of the heavy casualties suffered, between the 18th and 20th of that month convoys SC 7 and HX 71 had 17 and 14 ships sunk respectively. Moreover, other U-boats had meanwhile appeared in the focus of our southern traffic off Freetown where they found many ill-defended targets. Our total losses in October reached 103 ships of 443,000 tons, about two-thirds of which were attributable to the U-boats. It was plain that if sinkings continued on such a scale our lifeline would soon be cut.

Happily several circumstances combined to bring some easement of the situation during the closing months of 1940. The agreement whereby 50 old American destroyers were transferred to Britain in exchange for the lease of bases in the western hemisphere was ratified on 2nd September, and the ships were quickly brought into service with British crews. Though totally unmodernised, equipped with obsolete weapons, and by no means free from mechanical defects, we were in no position to look what amounted to a gift horse in the mouth; and the four-funnel ex-American ships soon became a familiar sight on the convoy routes. Secondly, our own new destroyers, sloops and corvettes were beginning to enter service in some numbers, thus enabling the numerical strength of the escort groups slowly to be increased. Thirdly, the Germans had given U-boat construction so low a priority that, after fifteen months of war, they had not even replaced the 31 boats they had lost; and by the end of 1940 their operational strength had actually declined to an all-time low figure of twenty-two boats. The slowness with which Hitler's government accepted the need for a large

U-boat building programme undoubtedly eased Britain's peril. But perhaps the greatest gains arose, not through German errors but from British efforts to improve the organisation and training of our escort vessels. In the first place the need to establish permanent escort groups was now accepted as essential to tactical efficiency. The fact that the groups consisted of many different classes of ship—destroyers, sloops, corvettes and trawlers—was a small disadvantage compared with the benefits derived from a high degree of mutual understanding. Henceforth every effort was made not to break up a group, even if it had to go to sea substantially below its proper strength. Secondly, new training bases were established to give anti-submarine vessels an adequate period to work up fighting efficiency; and thirdly, co-operation between the surface ships of the Western Approaches command and the maritime aircraft of the R.A.F.'s Coastal Command was steadily improving. The foundations of the great structure of sea-air co-operation, which was to make the decisive contribution to victory in the Atlantic Battle, were laid in 1940.

But the U-boats and bombers working against the North Atlantic convoys were by no means the only weapons used by the enemy against our shipping at this time, and we must now take a glance at events in the outer oceans. One of the many anxieties which beset the British government and Admiralty after the fall of France was whether Spain would yield to German pressure, and allow passage to Hitler's forces to attack Gibraltar—a base which we could ill afford to lose. As the only possible alternative to Gibraltar lay in gaining possession of the Spanish or Portuguese Atlantic Islands (Madeira, the Canary Islands, the Cape Verde Islands and the Azores), preparations were made to occupy some or all of them if the Germans overran Spain and Portugal or prevailed upon General Franco to declare war on Britain. In fact, we now know that the Spanish Government successfully resisted all Hitler's threats and blandishments, and the danger to Gibraltar was thus never as acute as we imagined; but in 1940 this could not have been known in London, and an expedition was organised and for many months kept ready to sail for the islands at short notice. As in the case of Iceland, which we had occupied in the previous May,[1] it was only our sea power which could have enabled us to find a reasonable

[1] See pp. 71-2.

alternative to Gibraltar—should that base be lost or rendered useless to us.

The German battle cruisers *Scharnhorst* and *Gneisenau* and the heavy cruiser *Hipper*, whom we last encountered during the raid against the ships returning from Narvik at the end of the Norwegian campaign,[1] remained in Trondheim until the *Scharnhorst* had effected temporary repairs to the damage received by the torpedo fired by the *Acasta* in defence of the *Glorious* on 8th June. On 20th of that month the two battle cruisers put to sea to return to Germany, but the *Gneisenau* was promptly torpedoed by the submarine *Clyde*, which was patrolling off the Norwegian coast, and put back into port. Her sister ship, however, successfully ran the gauntlet of our submarine and air patrols, and reached Kiel safely on the 23rd. A month later the *Gneisenau* and several lesser warships also returned to Germany, where both battle cruisers docked to repair their battle damage. Only the *Hipper* showed activity in July and August, when she made an abortive foray into Arctic waters. There now followed a lull of about three months, during which nearly all the large German surface ships were in their home waters. Though R.A.F. bombers made numerous attacks on Kiel and Wilhelmshaven they failed to inflict any serious damage on them.

While preparing its major warships for further forays against our ocean shipping the German Navy did not, however, leave the Atlantic battleground entirely to the U-boats and bombers. Ever since the early days of the war carefully selected merchantmen had been secretly converting to armed raiders, and by the middle of 1940 the first five (the *Atlantis, Orion, Widder, Thor* and *Pinguin*) were all at sea; and before the end of the year they had been joined by two others (the *Komet* and *Kormoran*). The disguised raiders were formidable ships, armed with six to eight modern guns and torpedo tubes; and in most cases they carried one or two aircraft for reconnaissance purposes. The Germans not only provided them with very careful aids to disguise, but arranged secret rendezvous in remote parts of the ocean, where they could refuel and replenish from supply ships with little fear of interruption. They all employed similar tactics, attacking only single merchantmen, whom they either lured within range by simulating friendliness or sprang upon suddenly by night. As soon as one zone had become dangerous to

[1] See pp. 69-70.

them they changed their disguise and shifted to a new cruising ground. From the British point of view they presented a very difficult problem; for they were exceedingly hard to locate, and only a cruiser was sufficiently well armed to deal with them. Though the central and south Atlantic long remained their favourite hunting ground, several appeared in the Indian Ocean, and even farther afield, in 1940. Thus the *Komet* reached the Pacific by making, with the assistance of Russian ice-breakers, a remarkable passage along the north coast of Siberia.

It was the middle of July, 1940, before the Admiralty gained firm intelligence of the presence of disguised raiders, and on 28th of that month there took place in the south Atlantic the first of a series of unsatisfactory actions between them and British Armed Merchant Cruisers. The ill-equipped A.M.C. *Alcantara* was quite outclassed by the raider *Thor*, and received serious damage herself without inflicting any on her adversary. On 1st December the same raider fought a second action in the same waters with another weakly-armed converted liner, the *Carnarvon Castle*, and with similar results. It was plain that none of the fifty liners which the Admiralty had fitted with a few obsolete guns and commissioned as Armed Merchant Cruisers was capable of dealing with the well-armed and highly efficient German raiders; but we could afford very few proper cruisers for the outer oceans, and the few ships of that class which could be spared from the main theatres were nearly always needed for such purposes as escorting the troop convoys on the long route to the Middle East by way of the Cape of Good Hope. The counter-measures adopted were therefore, firstly to put as much shipping as possible into convoy; secondly, to patrol the focal waters through which our most important traffic had to pass; and thirdly to strike at the enemy's supply system by discovering his secret fuelling rendezvous. In time all these measures were to yield the desired results; but they were unlikely to do so quickly, and the first six months of ocean raiding were thus wholly favourable to the enemy. Quite apart from the delays and dislocation caused by the presence, or suspected presence, of disguised raiders, in 1940 they sank between them 54 merchantmen of 370,000 tons. Though this was less than we lost from air attacks or mines in the same period, and only about one-eighth of the losses inflicted by the U-boats, the cumulative effect of the frequent and widespread appearances of these elusive enemies was far greater than the actual tonnage sunk by them. It is fair to mention here that, with one conspicuous exception, the captains of the German disguised raiders conducted their operations, which were a perfectly legitimate form of warfare, with due regard to international law. The exception was von Ruckteschell, who commanded first the *Widder* and later the *Michel*; and his ruthless methods so far transgressed the accepted codes that he was ultimately brought to trial as a war criminal.

But the disguised raiders were not the only surface ships to engage in the *guerre de course* against our shipping during the latter part of 1940; for they were soon joined by several far more dangerous colleagues. The *Scheer* and *Hipper* were the first major German warships to leave their home waters after the lull in surface ship activity which followed on the losses and damage suffered in the Norwegian campaign. The former sailed at the end of October, 1940, and the latter in early December; and they both passed undetected into the Atlantic by way of the Denmark Strait between Iceland and Greenland. The first intimation that a pocket-battleship was once again loose on our most important trade route came on 5th November, when the *Scheer* suddenly attacked the homeward-bound Convoy HX 84, whose 37 merchantmen were at the time only escorted by an Armed Merchant Cruiser, the *Jervis Bay*. Her Captain, E. S. F. Fegen, however, unhesitatingly engaged his formidable adversary, and although the results of the unequal contest were a foregone conclusion, his gallant sacrifice gained time for the convoy to scatter, and only five merchantmen were sunk. The Admiralty at once sent out strong forces to cover other convoys which were at sea; but the *Scheer* made herself scarce, and by the end of the year she had reached the latitude of Cape Town without doing any more damage. The *Hipper* had meanwhile been seeking to emulate her colleague's success on the northern route; but she found no victims at all. On Christmas Eve, however, she made contact with the large and valuable troop convoy WS 5A far to the west of Cape Finisterre, and attacked at first light on Christmas Day. But the troopships were, in accordance with the Admiralty's invariable policy, strongly escorted; and the German cruiser was driven off without having done any damage. On 27th December she reached Brest, after a cruise which had yielded only very small results; but her arrival in western France inaugurated a long period during which German surface warships endeavoured to exploit the excellent strategic situation of the French naval base, close on the flank of our main north-south convoy route. They constituted a threat which we could not afford to ignore, and it will be told later how we were forced to maintain strong surface ship and submarine patrols off the base, what time the Royal Air Force bombers did their utmost to put the enemy warships out of action.

So ended a year which, for the Admiralty and all the naval commands, had produced one crisis after another. Not for one day was the pressure on the Home Fleet relaxed. Starting with the Norwegian campaign, for which it had supplied almost all the supporting warships and carrier aircraft, there had followed the hard fighting in the narrow seas of midsummer, culminating in Dunkirk and the total withdrawal from Europe. Then the chief focus of the maritime war shifted to the Atlantic, where we had to deal not only with the rising onslaught by German U-boats and bombers, but with the warship and disguised raiders. It was Home Fleet battleships and cruisers which constantly endeavoured to cover the northern passages out into the ocean; and the same fleet provided the ocean escorts for the vital Middle East troop convoys during the first two thousand miles of their long journeys. Force H at Gibraltar was formed from the ships detached from the same fleet; and, as we shall see in the next chapter, the declaration of war by Italy necessitated strong reinforcements being sent from Scapa Flow to Admiral Cunningham. On top of those unceasing demands came the constant need to keep our coastal waters clear of mines, and to escort our local convoys to their destinations; and all the time our naval operations were grievously handicapped by the insecurity of our bases, and by the superiority of German intelligence. The former was, of course, mainly attributable to the governmental parsimony of the pre-war years; but it was not until after the war that we discovered the full extent to which the Germans had broken our naval ciphers. In August, 1940, however, we realised that they must have been compromised; and the Germans later admitted that the changes which the Admiralty then instituted deprived them of their best source of intelligence.

Although throughout this anxious period our strategy was of necessity defensive, Admiral Forbes had constantly endeavoured to collect sufficient strength to make offensive sweeps in the North Sea and off Norway; but the heavy calls which constantly poured in on him greatly reduced the number of occasions on which he could carry out such purposes. None the less we may remark how subordinate commanders invariably seized any opportunity for the local or tactical offensive which presented itself, thus fulfilling one of the cardinal requirements of a strategically defensive period. The River Plate battle, the two clashes in Narvik fiord, the pursuit of the German battle cruisers, and many lesser fights had shown that, once an enemy was sighted, there would be no hesitancy over engaging him—regardless of the odds.

To carry the responsibilities of high command at the beginning of a war must, at least in democratically governed countries, always be a situation of doubtful good fortune; for it is then that difficulties and neglects, for which the commander was in no way responsible, first become apparent. Admiral Sir Charles Forbes was no exception to that rule; and although to-day his strategic views and purposes —notably over the defeat of the German invasion plans—appear to have been absolutely sound, and he was able to meet every really important need placed upon his shoulders, he did find it necessary to resist certain demands (for the frontal assault on Trondheim for instance) which he considered dangerous and unreasonable. These latter occasions, perhaps inevitably, brought him into conflict with the Admiralty and with Mr. Churchill. Possibly, therefore, it was no great surprise to him to be told in the last month of the year that he was to be succeeded by Admiral Sir John Tovey; but his steady hands on the reins controlling our maritime power during the first fifteen months of the war certainly helped greatly to overcome the succession of crises which smote his country; and he was able to turn over a stronger and more experienced fleet to his successor than he himself had enjoyed during the greater part of his time as Commander-in-Chief.

CHAPTER VI

THE STRUGGLE FOR THE MIDDLE EAST

June–December, 1940

"Laurels grow in the Bay of Biscay—I hope a bed of them
may be found in the Mediterranean."

Nelson to Sir Gilbert Elliott, 4th August,
1794.

B Y THE Anglo-Egyptian treaty of 1936 Britain gained the use of
Alexandria as a naval base, and also the right to station troops
in Egypt. The strategic purposes of this diplomatic agreement were
the safeguarding of the Suez Canal and the maintenance of British
control over the land approaches to the oilfields of Iraq and Persia.
The presence of our forces in the mandated territory of Palestine,
with its valuable secondary base and oil pipe line terminal at Haifa,
and the rights obtained by our treaties with Jordan and Iraq, further
strengthened British influence; while the island of Cyprus, though
it possessed no harbours suitable for use by large ships, was excellently
placed to command the trade routes of the Levant. There our ancient
and traditional friendship with Greece, and recently much improved
relations with Turkey, added further support to the carefully planned
structure of diplomatic and strategic influence over the whole vast
area generally referred to as the Middle East. About 800 miles west
of Alexandria lay the island of Malta, with its superb harbours and
well-equipped dockyard, in a position from which the Sicilian
channel and "the Narrows" of the Mediterranean could be commanded;[1] while about 1,000 miles farther west the historic fortress
of Gibraltar stood guard over the only sea entry from the Atlantic.

Unfortunately the foundations of our policy to limit, and if
need be defeat, the aggressively expansionist tendencies of Fascist

[1] See Map pp. 112-13.

Italy were gravely vitiated by the British government having accepted the Army and Air Force view that Malta could not be defended against Italian air power, and by the numerical superiority of the Italian land and air forces in Libya and Abyssinia. The weakness of the Army and R.A.F. in the Middle East stemmed chiefly from the need to give France the greatest possible support in western Europe. Nor could it be rectified quickly after the fall of France; for the safeguarding of the British Isles themselves then demanded first priority for men and equipment, in order to meet the German invasion threat.

The decision not to defend Malta greatly enhanced the importance of Alexandria, to which a large proportion of the Mediterranean Fleet's supporting, or "logistic" organisation had actually been transferred before war broke out. But the new base was far from satisfactory, for it was ill-defended against every form of attack, and its facilities for the repair of ships were quite inadequate. Some of the risks entailed by having to use a poorly equipped base could be spread by creating smaller establishments at Port Said and Haifa; but they were considerably farther from the waters of the central Mediterranean, where the fleet was certain to be needed; they had at the beginning even fewer defences than Alexandria, and they were not suitable for use by big ships.

There was never any doubt about the strategy which our maritime forces in the Mediterranean, under Sir Andrew Cunningham, would adopt in the event of war with Italy. Their purposes would be to deny command of the central basin to the enemy, in order to make it impossible for him to supply his land and air forces in North Africa, and to gain a secure hold on the routes by which our own Army of the Nile had to be supplied. Nor did the Commander-in-Chief, a man of great determination who was gifted with the genius of leadership and imbued with the fighting tradition handed down from Blake and Hawke to Nelson himself, leave anyone in doubt that he would endeavour to accomplish those objects by seeking action with and defeating the main enemy fleet. This, however, was never likely to be an easy accomplishment, since geography had given the Italians an extremely well-placed strategic position, equipped with plentiful naval and air bases, from which to contest our purposes. Moreover, whereas enemy bases in southern Italy and Sicily were little more than 300 miles from the ports of entry for supplies in North Africa (Tripoli and Benghazi), Alexandria was at least double that distance from the sea routes which the Italians were certain to use.[1] Thus by choosing their moments skilfully the enemy could pass his convoys across before we could reach them; and it was always a simple matter for any force which we might threaten to run for safety under the guns of one or other of the many ports and bases which were ready to hand on the Italian mainland or in Africa. Hence geographical circumstances greatly reduced the prospects of either catching the supply convoys, or of forcing a fleet action on a probably reluctant enemy—unless we could exploit Malta's commanding position in "the Narrows" of the Mediterranean.

There were, moreover, other aspects of the strategic situation in the Middle East which were unfavourable to the British. Not only were our land and air forces greatly outnumbered, but they were hemmed in on the south flank by the strong Italian contingents in Eritrea and Abyssinia, and by the large armies in Libya to the west.[2] Though it was true that our control of the Suez Canal made it impossible for the Italians to reinforce and supply their East African forces by water, our own supply route up the Red Sea was by no means secure; for the Italians had considerable naval forces, including eight submarines, based on Massawa on its flank, and our convoys were also very exposed to air attack during almost the whole of their voyages between Aden and Suez.

The narrowness of the sea passages in the central Mediterranean and Red Sea, around which the struggle for the Middle East was bound to centre, and the dominant position of Sicily and Malta in the one case and of Aden and Massawa in the other, made it certain that air power would exert a very great influence on the campaigns. We could hardly have foreseen that the threat presented by the Regia Aeronautica would to a considerable extent prove illusory, nor that the full impact of the struggle for control of the air over the narrow passages would not be felt until the arrival of the Luftwaffe. Thus knowledge of our numerical inferiority in the air, as well as on the ground and in some respects at sea, was not the least of the worries which beset our Middle East commanders.

We saw earlier how the Mediterranean Fleet was deprived of much of its strength to reinforce the Home Fleet at the time of the

[1] See Map pp. 112-13. [2] See Maps pp. 112-13 and 153.

Norwegian campaign, while others of Admiral Cunningham's ships were sent to hunt for German commerce raiders in the South Atlantic and Indian Ocean.[1] As soon as it became clear that the total collapse of France was a distinct possibility, and that such an event might well be regarded by Mussolini as the opportunity for which he had been waiting, the Admiralty began to order ships back to the Mediterranean. Some came from home waters, others from the East and West Indies, and yet others from far away China and Australia. It was a classic example of a maritime concentration;[2] and it was carried out so quietly that few except those in high places even knew what was in train. By the middle of May, 1940, Alexandria harbour was once again filled with light-grey warships of all classes, Admiral Cunningham's fleet had been restored to approximately the strength originally planned for him, and he himself had rehoisted his flag in the famous battleship *Warspite*; but he was still markedly inferior to the Italians in cruisers and destroyers, and far weaker in submarines. Only in the possession of one, and later two aircraft carriers, did he possess any material advantage over his probable enemies.

At the same time as the major concentration in Alexandria was taking place, a lesser one was in progress in the Red Sea, which then formed part of the East Indies command. On 24th May all shipping proceeding in either direction between Aden and Suez was ordered into convoy, and the necessary escort vessels were assembled at one or other end of the 1,000-mile route. Meanwhile events in western Europe had moved from bad to worse, and the loss of all French assistance in the war at sea had plainly become imminent. The measures taken by the Admiralty to meet that situation, by the creation of Admiral Somerville's Force H at Gibraltar, have already been described.[3]

On 10th June, the eve of Italy's declaration of war, Admiral Cunningham wrote to the First Sea Lord, " I feel that the only way we can make the Italians think a bit . . . is to move a strong portion of the fleet into the central Mediterranean"; and he promptly proceeded to put that challenge into effect. Apart from the old light cruiser *Calypso* being sunk by an Italian submarine no action took

---

[1] See pp. 49 and 52.

[2] cf. Mahan, *Sea Power in its Relation to the War of* 1812; " Not by rambling operations or naval duels are wars decided, but by force massed and handled in skilful combination."

[3] See p. 83.

place on this occasion; nor did the fleet receive the attentions of the Regia Aeronautica which it had expected. But the moral effect of the sweep by strong British forces into waters which the Italians had to control if they were to prosecute an effective strategy must have been considerable. Moreover, the experiences of that operation probably strengthened Cunningham in his strong opposition to the Admiralty's tentative proposal, made on 17th June, that we should withdraw from the eastern basin. " I feel," wrote the Commander-in-Chief to Admiral Pound, " that we can keep the Italians pretty well engaged."

By 4th July Cunningham had achieved his purpose of im-mobilising the French squadron in Alexandria without resort to force,[1] and was ready to repeat his challenge by taking virtually his whole strength within sight of the south coast of Italy. Organised into three forces, the leading one consisting of five cruisers, the centre one of the fleet flagship and her destroyer screen, and the rear one of two older battleships, the carrier *Eagle* and ten destroyers, the fleet sailed from Alexandria on 7th July. A subsidiary purpose of the operation was to cover the passage of two convoys carrying urgently needed stores and men from Malta to Alexandria. Early next day one of our submarines stationed on a patrol line in the central basin reported a powerful enemy squadron, including two battleships, on a southerly course about midway between Taranto and Benghazi.[2] That same day, the 8th, and throughout the next five days, the Italian Air Force made very persistent, and sometimes unpleasantly accurate high-level attacks on the fleet; but although the Italians claimed to have inflicted much damage, the only ship actually hit was one of the cruisers of the van force. Meanwhile our reconnaissance aircraft were carefully watching the main enemy force, and when it was reported to be steering east Cunningham concluded, correctly, that it must be covering the passage of a convoy to Benghazi. He therefore increased speed, altered course to place himself between the enemy and his base at Taranto, and postponed the departure of the convoys from Malta.

At daylight on 9th Cunningham had reached a position some 60 miles off the south-west corner of Greece; and he knew that his adversary, with two battleships, sixteen cruisers (six of which

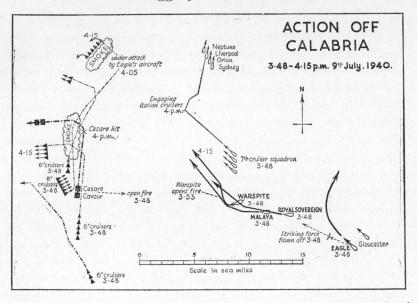

ACTION OFF CALABRIA
3·48–4·15 p.m. 9ᵗʰ July. 1940.

had 8-inch guns) and 32 destroyers was about 150 miles ahead of him. The urgent need was to slow down the enemy heavy ships, but a striking force from the *Eagle* failed to find them. The cruisers under Vice-Admiral J. C. Tovey had, however, pressed ahead; and the *Warspite*, which was some five knots faster than the other two battleships, was coming up to support them. At 2.47 p.m. the *Orion* on the cruiser line sighted the enemy battle squadron, and hopes of a general action rose in the British fleet. Half an hour later, when the western horizon appeared alive with enemy warships, the Italians opened fire on Admiral Tovey's cruisers, whose position was for a time unenviable. At 3.26, however, the *Warspite* came within range, and her 15-inch salvos caused the Italian cruisers to withdraw under cover of smoke. A short lull ensued until 3.50, when the *Warspite* sighted the enemy battleships, and quickly obtained an unmistakable hit on one of them—actually the *Giulio Cesare*, which suffered considerable damage and had her speed reduced. She and her sister ship the *Cavour* turned away drastically and were soon lost to sight in the smoke. There now followed a period of confused fighting between both sides' cruisers and light forces; but the Italian ships, dodging in and out of the smoke, were difficult targets, and little damage was done. By 5 p.m. all firing had ceased, and our aircraft reported the enemy to be retiring at high speed towards the Messina Straits. The Regia Aeronautica now added to the confusion of the enemy's precipitate withdrawal by bombing their own ships—and the angry signals evoked by this unfriendly action provided much amusement in the British fleet.

Cunningham pursued the enemy to within fifty miles of the Calabrian coast and then, seeing no chance of renewing the engagement, turned south towards Malta, where his destroyers refuelled. Meanwhile, the convoys had sailed to the east, and early on 11th the main body of the fleet followed them. The Italians now renewed their bombing attacks; but no ships were even damaged, and between 13th and 15th July all our forces and the convoys arrived safely in Alexandria.

This "Action off Calabria," as it came to be called, had far more important consequences than the material damage inflicted on the greatly superior enemy; for it established the moral ascendancy over the Italian Navy which was to become such a marked feature of the next year of the struggle for control of the Mediterranean; and it showed that we had less to fear from the enemy's bombing than some had anticipated. Little more than a week later, to be precise on 19th July, the lessons of the first brush were driven home when the Australian-manned light cruiser *Sydney* and five destroyers encountered two Italian light cruisers off the north coast of Crete and, after a running fight, sank the *Bartolomeo Colleoni*.

Meanwhile, in London discussions had been taking place regarding the urgent need to strengthen the fighter defences of Malta, where there were at the time precisely three of the obsolescent Gladiators—nicknamed " Faith," " Hope " and " Charity." Though the pre-war view that Malta was indefensible was thus revised at a very early stage in the hostilities, it was now no easy matter to put the new policy into effect. With France mostly occupied by the Germans it was impossible to fly out air reinforcements overland, and the only way of getting them to Malta quickly was therefore to send them out from Britain in an aircraft carrier, from which they would be flown off when she had reached a point within the fighters' range of the island. The Admiralty accordingly made the old carrier *Argus* available, and early in August she successfully despatched twelve Hurricanes to Malta from a position south-west of Sardinia. This was the first of a long series of hazardous and costly operations carried out for the same purpose; and the basic reason why they were necessary lies in our pre-war failure to provide for the proper defence of a vital overseas base.

Between August, 1940, and the end of the year the Admiralty managed, in spite of the manifold demands which pressed on them from all sides, to send Admiral Cunningham substantial further reinforcements of all classes of ship. They all passed safely through the Mediterreanean from Gibraltar, accompanied for the first part of their journey by Force H, and being met by Admiral Cunningham's fleet in the central basin. The opportunities which such operations afforded to run more supplies and men into Malta were invariably seized; and so the prospects of the island fortress being able to withstand a long siege gradually improved.

Of the reinforcements which reached Cunningham at this time none was more welcome than the new fleet carrier *Illustrious,* whose comparatively large aircraft complement (35–40) made her a very valuable addition to his striking power; while her armoured flight deck, which was a new feature in ships of her class, reduced the dangers of the Italian bombing attacks which were bound to be a feature of all incursions into the central Mediterranean. Moreover, her arrival enabled Cunningham to carry out a long-cherished plan to attack the Italian heavy warships in their base at Taranto; but before describing that operation we must glance briefly at a combined operation which had been planned at home, and in which Mr. Churchill had shown strong interest.

A glance at a map of the south Atlantic will make obvious the strategic importance of the French base at Dakar in Senegal,[1] whence the main north-south Atlantic shipping route, along which all our reinforcements for the Middle East had to pass, could be seriously threatened. Although it is now plain that there was in fact never any serious likelihood of the Germans gaining possession of the base, or of the Vichy Government granting them the use of it, the possibility of the enemy establishing himself in such a commanding position appeared alarming in London. This, and the acceptance of totally incorrect intelligence regarding the likelihood of de Gaulle's Free French forces being welcomed in Senegal, led to the preparation of an expedition whose object it was to install his régime there—if possible without bloodshed. The plan was approved at the end of August; but in spite of reliable information to the effect that de

[1] See Map p. 91.

Gaulle would certainly be resisted reaching London a few days later the decision was not reconsidered. The expedition, which included about 7,000 troops, two-thirds of which were British, sailed on 31st August, and strong naval forces from the Home Fleet and from Force H at Gibraltar were ordered to escort and support it.

On 11th September, when the troop convoys were some 300 miles north-west of Dakar, Gibraltar reported that three French cruisers and three large destroyers from Toulon had passed out of the Mediterranean; and this introduced an unforeseen complication into a plan which was already replete with difficult political implications. The Admiralty later held Admiral Sir Dudley North, the Flag Officer, North Atlantic, responsible for allowing the French squadron to pass through the Straits unmolested, and relieved him of his command; but an impartial review of the orders previously sent to him, which were by no means free from ambiguities, shows that his belief that he was not required to stop French ships proceeding to their colonial ports in West Africa was certainly reasonable. Moreover, he certainly did not possess the strength with which to enforce such a purpose; and we now know that the Germans had only allowed the Toulon squadron to sail on condition that it resisted any British attempt to deny it passage. In the end the Admiralty itself sent the *Renown* from Gibraltar in pursuit of the French ships; but it was by that time too late to prevent them reaching Dakar on 14th September.

In London the changed circumstances brought about by these confused events produced second thoughts, and the government proposed to cancel the operation; but the naval commander, Vice-Admiral J. H. D. Cunningham, and his military colleague both considered that their forces were adequate to meet all eventualities and, fully supported by de Gaulle, they urged that they should proceed with the plan. On 18th the British government authorised the men on the spot "to do what they thought best to give effect to the original purpose of the expedition."

By 20th September our forces had assembled at Freetown, and within the next few days the convoys sailed north again, with the intention of carrying out the attack on the 23rd. At dawn on the chosen day, however, a dense mist veiled the scene, adding physical obscurity to the many political and military uncertainties which were already influencing the operation. The first attempts to gain a foothold ashore by peaceful means were met by force, and failed completely. Then French warships tried to leave harbour, and our own were soon involved in a general engagement with them and with the coast defences. A breakdown of communications and the thickening mist frustrated the intended landing by de Gaulle's troops to the east of the town, and the day ended with nothing accomplished on our side but the French garrison thoroughly alerted. Nor did the broadcasting of an ultimatum late that evening produce any result other than an unqualified rejection by the shore authorities.

Next morning, the 24th, the warships moved closer inshore and opened fire on the harbour, where the battleship *Richelieu* and two of the cruisers from Toulon were lying; but the defenders laid a dense smoke screen across the entrance, and the return fire of the coast defence guns and the *Richelieu* was more effective than that of the bombarding ships, some of which suffered damage. Nor were the *Ark Royal's* aircraft any more successful than the heavy warships in subduing the defences. Thus passed a second day without any progress being made towards achieving the object of the expedition. That evening the commanders decided to renew the attempt to put the French warships out of action next day, and then to land British troops; but the third bombardment merely reproduced the pattern of the earlier ones and, after the battleship *Resolution* had been torpedoed and seriously damaged by a French submarine, at noon on 25th the commanders decided to call off the assault and withdraw to Freetown. Their decision crossed with orders from London to the same effect.

So ended a combined operation whose conception had been based on a misreading of the political situation in Senegal, and which had been handicapped in execution by the restrictions imposed on the use of force and by the total loss of surprise. All that we had accomplished was to add fuel to the flames of antagonism in Vichy France—and especially in the French Navy—and to get several valuable warships damaged. In retrospect it is plain that, until much clearer signs had been received that the Germans might gain the use of Dakar, the situation in West Africa was best left alone. Furthermore, even if the British government's initial anxiety on that score was justified—which now appears doubtful—an operation which was bound to require the diversion of substantial forces, and at a time when they could ill be spared, should hardly have been undertaken on such flimsy intelligence. In sum the expedition against Dakar provides a good example of the need for a nation blessed with the mobility conferred by maritime power to be constantly on its guard against dissipating its resources on secondary purposes.

A few days after we had admitted failure in West Africa news reached London from the Mediterranean which opened up new strategic possibilities, but at the same time posed a whole series of fresh problems; for on 28th October the Italians invaded Greece. Though we could spare very little for our new Ally from our slender resources in the Middle East, the Italian aggression did bring our fleet the benefit of the fine harbour of Suda Bay, on the north coast of Crete, as an advanced base. Admiral Cunningham at once set about creating the necessary organisation there, but once again we found ourselves unable to provide adequate defences; and an ill-defended base too often becomes a trap for the ships using it.

Early in November more reinforcements came out to Admiral Cunningham, and after meeting them in the central basin, and seizing the opportunity once again to strengthen the Malta defences, he was ready to strike at Taranto, where we knew that no less than six battleships, including the new *Vittorio Veneto* and *Littorio*, as well as several heavy cruisers, were concentrated. The plan was to attack on a moonlight night with two waves of torpedo-carrying Swordfish flown off from the *Illustrious* and *Eagle*; but defects caused by earlier near-miss bombs prevented the *Eagle* taking part, and five of her torpedo-bombers were therefore transferred to the modern carrier. During the main attack other aircraft were to drop flares to illuminate the scene, while bombing attacks were to be made against ships in the inner harbour, with the object of diverting attention from the torpedo striking force. Reconnaissance planes from Malta took a series of excellent photographs of the enemy anchorage, and after they had been flown to the *Illustrious* on 11th November the air crews were very precisely briefed regarding the positions of the targets. Admiral Cunningham then decided to attack that very night.

Shortly before 9 p.m. the first wave of 12 Swordfish, led by Lieutenant-Commander K. Williamson, took off from the *Illustrious* in a position 170 miles south-east of Taranto. The second wave, which various mishaps had reduced to 8 aircraft, followed about an hour later under Lieutenant-Commander J. W. Hale. At about

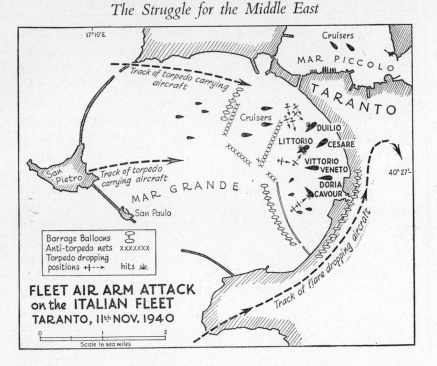

17°10'E

Track of torpedo carrying
aircraft

Cruisers

MAR PICCOLO

TARANTO

DUILIO
LITTORIO
CESARE
VITTORIO
VENETO
DORIA
CAVOUR

40° 27'

San
Pietro

Track of torpedo
carrying aircraft

MAR GRANDE

San Paulo

Barrage Balloons
Anti-torpedo nets   xxxxxxx
Torpedo dropping
positions +|--->   hits ↯

Track of flare dropping aircraft

**FLEET AIR ARM ATTACK
on the ITALIAN FLEET**
TARANTO, 11th NOV. 1940

0   1   2
Scale in sea miles

11 p.m. the flare- and bomb-droppers broke away from the torpedo
planes of the first wave to carry out their individual tasks, and the
latter dived down almost to sea level to penetrate through the
balloon barrage and make their attacks in sub-flights of three.
Though the enemy was alert, and anti-aircraft fire was heavy, the
moon and the flares together provided perfect illumination, and the
Italian battleships were clearly silhouetted against the western sky.
The *Cavour* was hit by one torpedo and the *Littorio* by two.[1] Then
the second wave arrived and, in spite of its reduced strength, one of
its torpedoes struck the *Duilio* and two more hit the *Littorio*; but
one of the latter did not, unfortunately, explode. The striking
forces, each of which had lost only one aircraft, then returned to
the carrier well satisfied with what they had achieved; and their
satisfaction was enhanced when the photographs taken next day
showed that all three of the battleships they had hit had sunk at their
moorings. Though the *Littorio* and *Duilio* were later raised and
repaired, they were out of action for five and six months respectively;
and the *Cavour* never went to sea again. The bombing attacks on the

[1] See Map above

III

THE
MEDITERRANEAN
THEATRE

DALMATIA

Split

ATIC

ri

Brindisi

Taranto

ABRIA

ina

se

ALBANIA

Salonika

CORFU

GREECE

Dardanelles

CEPHALONIA

Athens

PIRAEUS

SAMOS

Kalamata

LEROS

COS

C. MATAPAN

THE DODECANESE

RHODES

Suda Bay

CRETE

R. Danube

BLACK SEA

ASIA MINOR

CYPRUS

Beirut

SYRIA

Haifa

Derna

Tobruk

ULF of SIRTE

Benghazi

Alexandria

Port Said

CYRENAICA

El Alamein

SUEZ CANAL

Cairo

Suez

IA

BYA

cruisers in the inner harbour were less successful, partly because the only two bombs that hit failed to explode. None the less, the success of the operation was very striking, particularly when the small number of aircraft taking part is remembered; and the Fleet Air Arm crews unquestionably restored the balance of power in battleships, just when it was swinging strongly in the Italian favour. Lastly, the attack on Taranto wholly vindicated those who had pinned their faith to the carrier-borne strike plane as the most potent maritime weapon of the new era; and Cunningham was guilty of no exaggeration when he described the operation by which half the Italian battle fleet had been put out of action as an unprecedented example of economy of force. Nor, as we shall see in due course, were the lessons of Taranto lost on the Japanese.

The favourable experiences of the first months of the war against Italy caused the British government and Admiralty to consider running a fast convoy straight through to Malta and Alexandria with urgently needed men and supplies. Three merchantmen accordingly passed through the Straits of Gibraltar on the night of 24th-25th November, and headed to the east with Admiral Somerville's Force H in close attendance. Meanwhile, a detachment from Admiral Cunningham's fleet was steering west from Alexandria, with the object of meeting the convoy to the south of Sardinia. This overt challenge to Italian claims to control the central basin produced, however, a strong reaction; for early on 27th reconnaissance aircraft from the *Ark Royal* sighted a far superior force of battleships and cruisers off Sardinia. Somerville at once sent his five cruisers under Rear-Admiral L. E. Holland ahead to accept the challenge, while the *Renown* moved up to support them and the *Ark Royal* prepared her air striking forces. Early in the afternoon action was joined between the opposing cruisers, but the Italian ships soon retired on their battle squadron. At 1 p.m. Admiral Holland sighted the *Vittorio Veneto* and *Cesare*, which opened fire on his cruisers. He withdrew temporarily on the *Renown*, but when he saw the Italian battleships turn away to the north-east he resumed the pursuit.

Meanwhile eleven torpedo-bombers from the *Ark Royal* attacked the *Veneto*, but failed to hit her. The chase had, however, drawn Somerville's forces far from the convoy, which was their primary responsibility, and uncomfortably close to the enemy's air bases.

He therefore decided to return to his charges, and to send the torpedo-bombers to make a second attempt against the Italian heavy ships. Unfortunately this also failed to inflict damage. We had, in fact, known that the rapid expansion of the Fleet Air Arm had resulted in the *Ark Royal* having an unduly high proportion of inexperienced aircrews, and that the pressure under which Force H had been working had stultified all attempts to carry out the necessary training; but the failure of the air strikes was none the less disappointing. It underlined the importance of reaching a high standard of training before crews were committed to such tactically difficult operations as torpedo attacks on fast-moving ships.

During the surface action the detachment from Alexandria had met Force H, and by 5 p.m. all our forces were back in station to cover the convoy during the passage of "the Narrows." Though the *Ark Royal* was heavily bombed that afternoon she suffered no damage, and the movements thereafter proceeded according to plan. Two merchantmen discharged their supplies in Malta, while the third one, and the warships in which some 1,400 soldiers and airmen had been embarked, all reached Alexandria safely.

Though the operation had been completely successful, Somerville was criticised in London for not continuing the pursuit of the Italian fleet, and the Admiralty had actually set up a Board of Inquiry at Gibraltar before he returned to that base. Happily the Board, once possessed of all the facts, fully supported the Admiral's actions; but the Admiralty's very unusual measure, with its implication that they had less than complete confidence in the commander of one of our principal fleets, left an unpleasant after-taste.

The submarine war against merchant shipping had been in progress since the earliest days of the Mediterranean war, and both sides suffered some losses. The chief cause of our troubles was that the old and large boats which formed Cunningham's 1st Submarine Flotilla were unsuitable to work in those waters. Though they sank twelve merchantmen (about 45,000 tons) in the first six months, no less than ten of the flotilla had failed to return from patrols by the end of the year. The importance of the submarine in the struggle for control of the Mediterranean was, however, fully realised in London, and the formation of a new flotilla at Gibraltar and the arrival in Malta of the first of the much smaller and newer boats, which were later to form the famous 10th Flotilla, made it plain that the pressure on the Italian supply shipping sailing to North Africa would be increased.

The Italian losses of submarines in the first six months were even heavier than our own, amounting to fourteen in the Mediterranean and twenty in all waters. Several of their losses arose through the attempt to dispute our control of the vital Red Sea route. On 19th June the little trawler *Moonstone* captured the *Galileo Galilei* intact, and towed her triumphantly into Aden; and her success gained us intelligence which led directly to the sinking of two other enemies. Nor were the Italian surface and air forces any more successful than their submarines in hindering the passage of our convoys to Suez, which suffered only insignificant losses. Though the threat to our Red Sea shipping was not completely eliminated until our armies had completed their triumphant campaign in East Africa in March, 1941, it never proved as dangerous as we had feared.

As 1940 drew to a close it was plain that our cause had prospered in the Middle East to an extent which even the most optimistic would, six months earlier, have deemed highly improbable. We had entirely recovered from the effects of the withdrawal of French maritime power; in their several engagements with the Italian fleet Admirals Cunningham and Somerville had established a plain ascendancy; Malta had several times been reinforced and revictualled, and was in far better shape to resist a siege; our naval forces and aircraft had taken a heavy toll of Italian supply shipping (82 ships of nearly 190,000 tons in all); in East Africa great victories were being gained on land, and General Wavell had just struck and shattered the Italian army in Libya. It was becoming plain that the collapse of the weaker partner of the Axis was by no means improbable; but that possibility was equally obvious to the Germans, who realised that only by sending substantial reinforcements could they hope to stave off the total defeat of their ally. Such was the background to the dispatch of a strong detachment of the Luftwaffe to Sicily early in January, 1941, followed by the German invasion of Greece and the successful transfer of Rommel's Afrika Korps to support the Italians in Libya in March. Those events were to have a tremendous impact on the whole Middle East theatre; but before we recount the story of the trials and triumphs of the Mediterranean Fleet in 1941, we must return to the struggle in the Atlantic and the outer oceans.

CHAPTER VII

THE CHALLENGE ON THE OCEANS

January–December, 1941

" Now for the Services of the Sea, they are innumerable . . .
it is an open field for Merchandise in Peace, a pitched field for
the most dreadful fights of Warre."

Purchas, His Pilgrimes (1625).

AT THE beginning of 1941 the " happy time " enjoyed by the
U-boats against our ill-protected convoys in the Western
Approaches was still in full swing; and we were also suffering
substantial losses from air attacks on our coastal shipping, and from
mines laid in the off-shore swept channels. German aircraft and
E-boats (motor torpedo-boats[1]) were now laying acoustic as well
as magnetic and moored mines; but the designers of our counter-
measures were keeping well abreast of each new development, and
the acoustic mine never caused us anything like as much trouble as
the early magnetic varieties.

Though the German mines were a constant cause of anxiety, and
of delays to shipping, it was actually the bombers which caused us
the heavier losses during the first half of 1941; and in April, when
they sank 116 ships (323,000 tons), they actually accomplished their
highest figure of the whole war. Many of these losses were inflicted
by long-range aircraft flying from French or Norwegian bases to
seek their targets to the west of Ireland; but a substantial proportion
of the sinkings was still taking place in our coastal waters, where
we were still woefully ill-equipped to deal with this form of attack.
The basic needs were plain—to supply A-A guns to the merchantmen
themselves, and to arrange for protection by shore-based fighters

---

[1] The Royal Navy referred to all German fast coastal craft as E-boats. In the German
Navy, however, they were divided into many categories, and the motor torpedo-boats were
known as S-boats.

when close to the coast and by ship-borne fighters when beyond the range of the former; but it was easier to assess the needs than to meet them. The Admiralty was, however, doing everything possible to remedy the weapon shortage, and was also fitting merchantmen with catapults from which a single Hurricane fighter could be launched.[1] This, however, could only be a makeshift substitute for the proper escort carriers which we lacked. The conversion of the first ships to that function was, however, in hand; but none would be ready to enter the fray until nearly the end of 1941. At least as important as these steps were the increased attention given by Fighter Command to the defence of our mercantile ports in the west, to which Mr. Churchill gave "absolute priority" in February, and the improved co-ordination between the Navy and the R.A.F. authorities responsible for the defence of shipping within forty miles of the coast. In the latter case the need for the ships themselves to call for protection by fighters was now accepted by the R.A.F.; but there was a marked reluctance in Fighter Command to allow the convoy escorts to communicate direct with the aircraft when they arrived on the scene. Now that radar sets were beginning to be fitted in the escort vessels this was a plain necessity—since, left to themselves, the fighters often failed to sight the bombers which were threatening the merchantmen; but it was the middle of the year before agreement on the matter was reached. Such were the hesitant beginnings of " Fighter Direction " from warships, which was later to become the normal practice in all theatres, and for which duty specially designed ships were finally provided. As our defences against day air attacks improved, the Germans switched to night sorties, thus producing new problems for the sea and air convoy escorts. Indeed the defence of shipping against night air attacks was not satisfactorily solved until much later.

To deal with the enemy E-boats, which were excellently designed craft, we needed fast motor gunboats (M.G.B.s); since the slow motor launches (M.L.s), which were all that we had to begin with, were incapable of catching and fighting such adversaries. Conversion of faster vessels into M.G.B.s had however been put in hand, and in March, 1941, the first of them entered service. Meanwhile

---

[1] These ships were of two classes:

    (a) Fighter-Catapult (F.C.) ships, which were naval-manned and flew the White Ensign.

    (b) Catapult-Aircraft Merchantmen (C.A.M.s), which carried normal cargoes and flew the Red Ensign.

improved motor torpedo-boats (M.T.B.s) were being built to undertake forays into the enemy's inshore waters; and the offensive-defensive campaign for the control of coastal communications, in which we were finally to deploy hundreds of vessels, thus began to take shape. The light craft employed were given the collective title of Coastal Forces, and gradually special bases were created for them around our coasts. Though the bases themselves were commanded by Royal Navy Captains, who were responsible for the operations of all the craft stationed in them, the flotillas themselves, and also the individual craft, were generally commanded by young Volunteer Reserve officers; and their originality of thought and adventurous temperaments quickly proved them to be admirably suited to this fast-moving type of warfare.

While, therefore, the first six months of 1941 produced many problems for those responsible for the defence of our coastal shipping we managed to keep the traffic moving, in spite of all that the German bombers, minelayers and E-boats could do. Though 16½ million tons of shipping sailed safely up or down the east coast route in that period we were still far from gaining a firm mastery over all the various forms of attack; but at least the necessary defensive measures were now clearly recognised by the two services concerned, and steps had been taken to remedy the deficiencies in material and the false premises on which the service staffs had, in some respects, based their plans.

Although the defence of our own inshore traffic still absorbed a large share of our naval and air effort, the Admiralty and Air Ministry were by this time able to devote greater attention to the attack on the enemy's coastal shipping, and it is to that campaign that we must next briefly turn. It was prosecuted by a very wide variety of warships and aircraft; and the Royal Navy and Royal Air Force gradually established an intimate collaboration for this purpose, as in the Atlantic battle. The work of the Coastal Force craft has already been mentioned, but the Home Fleet's submarines also patrolled extensively off Norway and in the Bay of Biscay, and exacted a steady toll. Naval aircraft from the carriers also took a hand by striking at ships in Norwegian ports or moving along the coastal routes; but it was on Coastal Command of the Royal Air Force that the lion's share of the direct bombing attacks on enemy merchant shipping fell. As, however, a properly equipped air striking force was very slow to arrive, it was a long time before Coastal Command was able to develop its full potentialities. As to air minelaying, we have already seen how Bomber Command finally took over the whole responsibility, while the Admiralty supplied the mines and decided where they were to be laid. This aspect of the maritime air offensive soon began to achieve remarkable results; for not only did air-laid mines sink or damage many more enemy ships than direct bombing attacks, but the successes were achieved at far smaller cost to ourselves.[1]

Air minelaying, direct air attacks on the enemy's shipping, and forays by our light naval craft into his coastal waters did not, however, mark the limit of our offensive measures at this time. The landing of small bodies of highly trained troops to raid particularly important objectives on the enemy's coasts had for many centuries been a traditional way of exploiting the benefits of British sea power; and with the formation of the specialised Commandos, and the gradual production of craft designed for combined operations, the War Cabinet decided to revive this ancient strategy in modernised form. On 1st March, accordingly, a force sailed from Scapa with two Commandos embarked, and raided the Lofoten Islands at the entrance to Vestfiord in north Norway. The attack took place on the 4th in ideal weather, and was a complete success. All the shore targets were destroyed, a 10,000-ton German fish factory ship was sunk, and the Commandos came away with a satisfactory haul of German prisoners and accompanied by hundreds of Norwegian volunteers for service against the common enemy. In this raid we may find the genesis of the great combined operations of the later years of the war.

Though the defence of our coastal shipping and the attacks on the enemy's absorbed a great deal of our effort at this time, and was to continue to do so right to the end of the war, it was on the vital North Atlantic theatre that our main attention always remained concentrated. There the depredations of the U-boats, the bombers, and the German surface raiders caused us grave anxiety during the early months of 1941; for our losses of merchant ships continued

---

[1] During the entire war Coastal Command sank in the Home Theatre 366 enemy ships totalling about half a million tons by direct attacks, and damaged 134 others; but 856 aircraft were lost in the process. Mines laid by the R.A.F., on the other hand, accounted for 762 ships (738,000 tons) sunk and also 17 U-boats; and aircraft losses on minelaying sorties amounted only to 533.

at a far greater rate than the sunken tonnage could be replaced. With the first signs of spring the expected renewal of the U-boat offensive took place, and in March they sank 41 ships totalling 243,000 tons— a far higher figure than that achieved in the preceding two months, when the wintry weather had somewhat curtailed the enemy's activities. On 6th March the Prime Minister issued his famous " Battle of the Atlantic Directive," ordering the offensive to be taken against the U-boats and bombers "wherever and whenever we can," and giving absolute priority to the measures needed to foster that purpose. But it was in fact not by bombing the U-boats in their bases, as Mr. Churchill had urged, that we scored some outstanding successes in that same month; rather was it the strategy of convoy and escort which produced the desired result.

During heavy attacks on convoy OB 293 on 17th March the corvettes *Arbutus* and *Camellia* and the destroyer *Wolverine* sank U.70 and U.47; and the latter was commanded by Prien of Scapa Flow fame.[1] Ten days later the destroyers *Walker* and *Vanoc* disposed of U.99 and U.100 while defending convoy HX 112, and so eliminated two more famous "aces"—Kretschmer, who was captured, and Schepke who, like Prien, was killed. Before the end of the month the trawler *Visenda* sank U.551, and the Germans thus lost not only one-fifth of their operational U-boat fleet, but the elimination of the "aces" marked the end of the first phase of the long struggle. Never again were such great successes to be achieved by individual U-boat commanders, and with the disappearance of the "aces" the battle moved into a new phase—of prolonged, hardhitting actions between our escorts and the "wolf-packs," in which no quarter was given and none was expected by either side.

To turn temporarily to the more distant oceans, at the beginning of 1941 the pocket-battleship *Scheer* was in the South Atlantic, and was refitting herself at a secret rendezvous where she had met two disguised raiders; and no less than six of the latter class of ship were loose on the trade routes of the southern hemisphere. We knew that the battle cruisers *Scharnhorst* and *Gneisenau* had nearly completed repairing the damage suffered in the Norwegian campaign,[2] and that the heavy cruiser *Hipper*, which had reached Brest at the end of 1940 after her first raiding foray, was probably also fit for sea.

[1] See p. 50.　　　　[2] See p. 71.

Though we were unaware that three more disguised raiders were nearly ready to leave Germany, there were plentiful signs that the renewal of the onslaught on our shipping by surface warships was imminent. Furthermore, the new and very formidable battleship *Bismarck* was running trials in the Baltic, and it would not be long before she too was ready to join in the *guerre de course*. Nor was the Admiralty's anxiety lessened by the fact that recent experience had made it uncomfortably plain that our hold on the Denmark Strait between Iceland and Greenland was not nearly tight enough to prevent enemy warships breaking out into the Atlantic by that route —provided that they chose their moment skilfully.

Ever since the *Scheer's* attack on the Atlantic convoy HX 84 in November, 1940,[1] the Admiralty had been detaching battleships and cruisers from the Home Fleet to guard our ocean convoys during the most dangerous part of their journeys; and experience was now to show how fortunate it was that we possessed some reserve of heavy-gun ships to carry out this duty.

The *Scharnhorst* and *Gneisenau* left Kiel under Admiral Lütjens on 23rd January, 1941, and passed to the north of the Shetlands, with the intention of breaking out through the Iceland-Faeroes passage; but the Admiralty was forewarned of the movement, and Admiral Tovey, now Commander-in-Chief, Home Fleet, had disposed strong forces to the south of Iceland, whence they could guard both the northern passages to the Atlantic. Early on 28th, in very bad visibility, the cruiser *Naiad* briefly sighted the enemy ships; but they turned away at once at high speed to lose themselves in the northern mists. On 4th February Lütjens made a second attempt, and this time he got through the Denmark Strait undetected. Four days later the German battle cruisers sighted a Halifax convoy (HX 106); but as soon as they saw that the old battleship *Ramillies* formed part of the escort they hauled off without attacking.

Meanwhile the *Hipper* had left Brest on 1st February and, after refuelling at an ocean rendezvous, she encountered on the 12th a group of 19 unescorted merchantmen (described as convoy SLS 64) which were homeward-bound from Sierra Leone. Though she obtained seven easy victims from that group, she returned immediately to Brest, and her brief foray merely confirmed the view that, because of their short endurance and their liability to develop

[1] See p. 97.

mechanical defects, the German heavy cruisers were of little use as commerce raiders.

During the *Hipper's* short excursion on to the Sierra Leone route, and while the *Scharnhorst* and *Gneisenau* were at large in the North Atlantic, far away to the south the pocket-battleship *Scheer* had rounded the Cape of Good Hope early in February; and she soon made her presence felt in the Indian Ocean by sinking several ships to the north of Madagascar. There she was sighted by the cruiser *Glasgow's* aircraft on 22nd February, and the Admiralty at once ordered the nearest warships to concentrate against her. Unfortunately the *Glasgow* failed to keep in touch and, having shaken off the pursuit, the pocket-battleship returned to the south Atlantic, whence she set course for home. She passed through the Denmark Strait undetected on 27th March—chiefly because the Home Fleet was then engaged in the search for Lütjens's ships—and reached Kiel safely on 1st April. Her cruise had lasted five months, but she only sank 16 merchantmen (99,000 tons) and the A.M.C. *Jervis Bay*.[1] Her presence on the ocean route had, however, caused considerable dislocation to our convoys, and we had been forced to divert many warships to search for her and to protect our shipping. So it always is with commerce raiders which, in Mahan's words, "scatter that they may see and seize more prey."[2]

The Germans had cleverly timed the *Scheer's* homeward passage so as to distract our attention from the search for the *Scharnhorst* and *Gneisenau*; and when the *Ramillies* reported that an enemy warship had approached her convoy on 8th February, the Admiralty assumed that it was the *Scheer* and not one of the battle cruisers. Actually after that abortive attempt Lütjens took his ships farther west, with the object of seeking less well protected targets in the waters off Newfoundland. There, on 22nd February, they sank five vessels from a recently dispersed outward convoy, after which Lütjens moved to a fuelling rendezvous farther south before making a lunge at the Sierra Leone route. On 8th March an aircraft from the battleship *Malaya*, which was escorting the homeward convoy SL 67, sighted the battle cruisers about 350 miles north of the Cape Verde Islands. Lütjens, however, again declined to attack a convoy escorted by a single battleship and, after refuelling once more, he

[1] See p. 97.
[2] *The Influence of Sea Power on History* (Sampon, Low Marston & Co., 1890), p. 31.

returned to the waters where he had achieved his only success. This time he had even better luck, for on 15th and 16th March he encountered many ships from dispersed convoys, and sank or captured no less than 16 of them. But his presence had now been accurately reported in waters which could more easily be scoured by our heavy ships than those off West Africa, and the Admiralty had in fact moved strong detachments from the Home Fleet against him. Lütjens therefore set course for Brest; but he was not yet clear of all dangers, for the Admiralty had anticipated such a move, and had called Force H north from Gibraltar to intercept him. Late on 20th March reconnaissance aircraft from the carrier *Ark Royal* sighted the German ships while they were still far out in the Atlantic; but the carrier herself was 160 miles away at the time, and as evening was drawing on it was impossible to send a striking force immediately. Low visibility frustrated night shadowing, and next day the weather was no better; but it was only by a narrow margin that Lütjens escaped a heavy attack by carrier-borne aircraft. He reached Brest on 22nd March and Admiral Tovey at once disposed his forces to blockade the port—very much as Cornwallis had blockaded Gantéaume's Brest squadron in the Trafalgar campaign—while the Royal Air Force made repeated endeavours to put the ships out of action by bombing. Though these two powerful ships had been at large for almost exactly two months they had only sunk or captured 22 ships (115,600 tons); and luck, which can never be wholly absent from operations of war, seems to have favoured them on several occasions when they were nearly brought to action. Nor were the two battle cruisers ever again employed on commerce raiding; for the *Gneisenau* was severely damaged by an air torpedo while in Brest on 6th April, and received no less than four bomb hits a few days later; while the *Scharnhorst* also suffered severely at the hands of the R.A.F. later in the year.

While the German warships were thus causing us considerable trouble and dislocation on the vital Atlantic routes, the disguised raiders were continuing their depredations much farther afield. By the clever use of secret rendezvous they were able to keep themselves supplied with fuel and stores; and they even refitted themselves at remote anchorages such as Kerguelen Island in the southern Indian Ocean, or in the Japanese-mandated islands of the Pacific. Since the war German apologists have protested against the help afforded to Britain by the United States while still neutral; but they have conveniently forgotten that their raiders and U-boats received repeated help from Russia, Spain and Japan while those countries were also neutral. To give a few examples of how it was not only the United States that acted in an "un-neutral" manner: Russia, as already told, helped the raider *Komet* to reach the Pacific by the Arctic route in the summer of 1940,[1] Spain permitted the tanker *Winnetou* to use the Canary Islands as a base from which to fuel U-boats, while Japan allowed the raider *Orion* to refit in the Mariana Islands, and so greatly prolong her cruise, in 1941. Though this help from neutral nations was certainly far less important to Germany than American aid was to Britain, the principle involved was the same. Nor can any belligerent reasonably be expected to eschew such help as she can obtain from neutral countries.[2]

The first six months of 1941 brought considerable successes to the German disguised raiders, and on 4th April the *Thor* drove home the earlier lessons regarding the inadequacies of our A.M.C.s[3] by surprising and sinking the *Voltaire* in the central Atlantic. Though several of these redoubtable enemies had narrow escapes from interception, not until 5th May, when the cruiser *Cornwall* sank the *Pinguin* in the Indian Ocean, did we succeed in catching one of them. Between them they sank 38 merchantmen (191,000 tons) during the first six months of 1941, to which the warship raiders added a further 37 ships (188,000 tons). After the middle of that year, however, neither class of raider caused us serious losses; for by putting as much shipping as possible into convoy, and by catching and sinking the supply vessels on which they depended, we gradually restricted their operations, and finally frustrated them altogether. As in so many other aspects of trade defence convoy proved far more effective than patrolling the focal areas and hunting in the ocean spaces for these elusive enemies—for the simple reason that, when far from home and only able to repair quite minor damage themselves, no raider, be she warship or disguised merchantman, dared to become seriously involved with the convoy escorts.

To return to the U-boats, in April the merchant shipping sunk

[1] See p. 96.
[2] On the subject of German resentfulness towards America see Karl Dönitz *Ten Years and Twenty Days* (English ed. Weidenfeld & Nicolson, 1959).
[3] See p. 96.

by them rose to nearly ¼ million tons; and in the following months, by which time about two score U-boats were fully operational and the number completed had passed the hundred mark, it was a good deal higher. Another ominous sign was that in May it became apparent that these enemies were reaching out beyond 35° West— the limit of longitude to which our escorts could reach even by sending groups south from Iceland to cover the mid-ocean section of the Atlantic route. Losses were swollen by the arrival of six U-boats off Freetown, where shipping was only lightly protected; and the Admiralty had to divert as much traffic as possible from the new danger area, and also strengthen the sea and air escorts based in West Africa. But the main battleground was still in the North Atlantic, and especially in the waters to the south of Iceland. Early in May convoy OB 318 suffered a fairly heavy attack, losing five ships; but on the 9th, two days after Captain A. J. Baker-Cresswell's 7th Escort Group from Iceland had taken over the convoy from the original escorts, we scored a very important success. The corvette *Aubrietia* blew U.110 to the surface, her crew abandoned ship precipitately, and a boarding party from the destroyer *Bulldog*, the senior officer's ship, captured the U-boat intact. They ransacked the prize, removed material of priceless value to our intelligence organisation, and then started to tow the U-boat towards Iceland. The coup was the more valuable because the prisoners were put below so quickly that they remained in complete ignorance of the fact that their ship had been captured.[1] Though she was lost next day, when heavy weather frustrated the towing operation; the success of the 7th Escort Group was one of the outstanding achievements of the whole war. Moreover, U.110's captain was Lemp, who had achieved notoriety by sinking the *Athenia* on the day war was declared;[2] and his death diminished still further the rapidly thinning ranks of Dönitz's favourite "aces." A fortnight later convoy HX 126 was attacked by a wolf-pack in 40° West, and lost heavily—partly because the Commodore dispersed the convoy prematurely. This battle led, however, to the immediate introduction of continuous escort right across the Atlantic for homeward-bound convoys. The Admiralty had long

[1] For a full account of the passage of convoy OB 318 and the capture of U.110 see Roskill, *The Secret Capture* (Collins, 1959).
[2] See pp. 43-4.

been planning to introduce this plainly desirable measure; but shortage of escort vessels had so far made it impossible to fulfil. By May, 1941, however, with the help of the Canadian Navy a new advanced base was established at St. John's, Newfoundland, and a new escort force was formed to work from it. Convoy HX 129, which sailed on 27th May, was the first to be given continuous escort by Canadian or British groups throughout the homeward passage; but it was July before we could introduce similar arrangements on the Sierra Leone route, or give the outward-bound North Atlantic convoys continuous escort. These changes, though they greatly strengthened our shipping defence, complicated the operational problems involved; for the staff of the Commander-in-Chief, Western Approaches, who, under the Admiralty, still bore the whole responsibility for the Atlantic battle, had to make very careful arrangements to ensure that each successive escort group would arrive at the proper rendezvous at the right time and with full tanks, notwithstanding delays which might have resulted from bad weather or been caused by diversions from the route originally ordered. Air cover and escort for the convoys were improving at the same time; but Coastal Command still suffered from lack of long-range aircraft and of a really effective anti-submarine weapon. None the less the U-boats were becoming increasingly conscious of the danger from the air; and they much preferred to work in the 800-mile mid-ocean gap which aircraft from Iceland and Newfoundland could not yet reach.

While the battle of the convoy routes was thus being renewed with rising intensity, there took place in the Atlantic a series of surface ship actions which, for drama and excitement, as well as for the importance of the issues which hung in the balance, have few parallels in all the long annals of naval warfare.

On 18th May Admiral Lütjens, whom we last encountered in command of the *Scharnhorst* and *Gneisenau* during their recent ocean foray,[1] sailed from Gdynia for the Atlantic in the brand-new battleship *Bismarck*, with the heavy cruiser *Prinz Eugen* in company. The *Bismarck*, which was armed with eight 15-inch and twelve 5.9-inch guns, displaced 42,500 tons and had a maximum speed of 28 knots, was without doubt the most formidable fighting ship then

[1] See pp. 122–4.

afloat. There was no single British capital ship which could both catch and sink her, and the days when carrier-borne aircraft would convincingly demonstrate the vulnerability of even the most modern battleships still lay hidden in the future. The Germans had originally intended that the *Scharnhorst* and *Gneisenau* should make a simultaneous sortie from Brest into the Atlantic; but that part of their plan was frustrated when the Royal Air Force severely damaged the *Gneisenau*.[1]

On 21st May the Admiralty received warning of the northward movement of Lütjens's squadron, and Admiral Tovey at once strengthened his watch on the northern passages to the Atlantic. That evening a reconnaissance aircraft sighted the German ships in a fiord south of Bergen, and the Commander-in-Chief at once sent his two fastest heavy ships, the battle cruiser *Hood* and the battleship *Prince of Wales*, from Scapa to Iceland to support his patrolling cruisers; but the *Prince of Wales* was a new ship, and had not yet worked up to full fighting efficiency, while the *Hood* was more than twenty years old and had never been properly modernised. At Scapa Admiral Tovey kept his fleet flagship, the *King George V*, a squadron of five cruisers and half a dozen destroyers at short notice for sea; while the Admiralty cancelled the departure of the fleet carrier *Victorious* and the battle-cruiser *Repulse* with a Middle East troop convoy, and placed them at Admiral Tovey's disposal. But the *Victorious*, like the *Prince of Wales*, was new and not yet fully worked up, and the *Repulse* was even older and more lightly protected than the *Hood*. It will thus be seen that, although on paper the Home Fleet possessed greatly superior strength to the enemy, it was far from being a homogeneous force; and the advanced age of some of its ships was as much a source of weakness as the inadequate training undergone by the newest ones.

On the 22nd visibility was very bad in the North Sea, but late in the evening a naval aircraft flying from the Orkneys penetrated into the fiord where the enemy had been sighted the previous day, and carried out such a skilful and thorough reconnaissance that she was able confidently to report to Admiral Tovey that the German squadron had put to sea again. At 10.45 p.m. the Commander-in-Chief accordingly left Scapa with his main body, and set course to the west. Meanwhile the Denmark Strait was being patrolled by the

[1] See p. 124.

An Atlantic convoy

U.243 attacked and sunk by a Sunderland of 10th Squadron R.A.A.F., 8th July, 1944

The *Bismarck* engaging
H.M.S. *Hood*, 24th May,
1941

The end of H.M.S.
Ark Royal, 13th
November, 1941

heavy cruisers *Norfolk* and *Suffolk* under Rear-Admiral W. F. Wake-Walker, and the Iceland-Faeroes passage by three smaller cruisers.[1]

After leaving their anchorage near Bergen on the evening of 21st May the *Bismarck* and *Prinz Eugen* actually passed well to the north of Iceland, and then turned south towards the Denmark Strait; but visibility was so bad that we received no news of their movements from our air patrols. At 7.22 p.m. on 23rd May, however, the *Suffolk* suddenly sighted the German squadron at the northern entrance to the Denmark Strait, steering a south-westerly course. A short time later the *Norfolk* also made contact, and the two ships now carried out the traditional cruiser duty of shadowing a superior enemy and reporting his movements, with the object of bringing our heavy forces to the scene. At the moment when Lütjens's ships were sighted Vice-Admiral L. E. Holland, with the *Hood* and *Prince of Wales* and four destroyers was about 220 miles away, off the south-west corner of Iceland. The Admiral at once turned to an intercepting course, increased to full speed, and prepared for action;[2] for in those latitudes in mid-summer twilight lasts all night, and if the enemy held to the course first reported by the shadowing cruisers contact could be expected in the very early hours of 24th. Unfortunately just after midnight Wake-Walker's cruisers temporarily lost touch, and Admiral Holland therefore altered course to the north and reduced speed to 25 knots while waiting for the situation to clarify. This movement had the unfavourable effect of causing the battle cruiser force to "lose bearing" on the enemy, who actually had held to his south-westerly course while all our ships were temporarily out of touch with him. At 2 a.m. Holland swung his heavy ships round to the south again, on to a course nearly parallel to the enemy's; but his four destroyers still carried on to the north. It is probable that the Admiral detached them for reconnaissance purposes; but the result was that the destroyers never regained touch with the battle cruisers. At 2.47 a.m. the period of uncertainty was ended by the *Suffolk* resighting the enemy, and it was now plain that Lütjens had not altered course. Because of the British squadron's turn to the north between midnight and 2 a.m.

[1] See Map p. 130.
[2] As Admiral Holland's title at the time was Admiral, Battle Cruisers, and the *Prince of Wales* was serving in the same capacity as the *Hood*, the squadron is referred to here as the battle cruiser force.

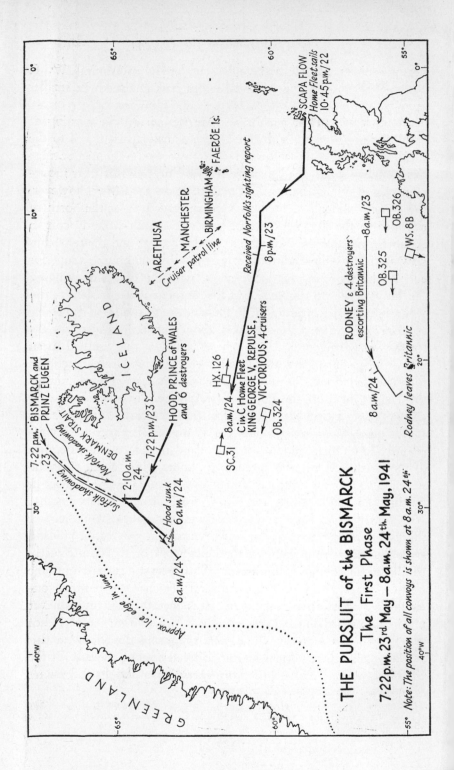

THE PURSUIT of the BISMARCK
The First Phase
7·22 p.m. 23rd May — 8 a.m. 24th May, 1941

Note: The position of all convoys is shown at 8 a.m. 24th

he had, however, gained considerably on his adversary, who was now in a far less favourable tactical situation.

At 3.40 a.m. Admiral Holland, who must have been receiving a steady flow of enemy reports from the cruisers for the previous hour, turned towards his quarry and increased to 28 knots. Visibility was now improving, and by 4.30 was about 12 miles. For some unexplained reason, but possibly because the Admiral was anxious not to reveal his presence, the *Prince of Wales* was not allowed to fly off her reconnaissance aircraft, nor did the battle cruisers use their search radar sets during the approach. Though the achievement of surprise might have brought a substantial advantage, the main-tenance of wireless and radar silence did prevent our forces co-ordinating their movements; for our own cruisers were as much in the dark as Lütjens with regard to the position and intentions of the battle cruiser force. The *Hood*, which was leading the *Prince of Wales*, sighted the enemy at 5.35 a.m. fine on the starboard bow—on a bearing which prevented the British ships' after turrets coming into action; but to the German squadron Holland's ships were only slightly before the beam, and Lütjens thus gained an important tactical advantage. The British squadron actually went into action with only four 15-inch and five 14-inch guns (one of the *Prince of Wales's* having developed a defect) against their adversaries' eight 15-inch and eight 8-inch. Moreover, Holland took his two ships into action in close order, allowing no freedom of manœuvre to individual captains—such as might have enabled more guns to be brought to bear.

All four ships opened fire between 5.52 and 5.53 at a range of about 25,000 yards; but the *Hood* almost certainly did not realise that the *Prinz Eugen* was now leading the *Bismarck*, and so directed her fire at the cruiser. The *Prince of Wales* on the other hand realised that the German ships, whose silhouettes were very similar, had changed stations; and she certainly engaged the battleship. But the error in identification further weighted the scales in the German favour, since the *Bismarck* did not receive half the weight of fire that Holland had plainly intended to direct on her. The loss of the British squadron's most important advantage—namely, its heavier broadsides was aggravated by the fact that, whereas neither the *Hood's* nor the *Prince of Wales's* initial salvos told against the enemy, the *Bismarck's* were very accurate. She hit the *Hood* heavily with her second or third salvo, and at 6 a.m., just as Holland was executing a turn which would have brought his ships' main armaments fully into action, the battle cruiser blew up with a tremendous explosion. Only three of her crew of 1,419 officers and men survived, and the probability is that one or more of her main magazines was penetrated by plunging shells, against which her armour protection was quite inadequate. The *Prince of Wales* had to alter course sharply to avoid the wreckage, and soon came under heavy fire herself. Within a few moments she received four 15-inch and three 8-inch hits, and at 6.13 her Captain turned away under cover of smoke. The odds had plainly become too heavy for his partially defective ship to take on; but we now know that she had in fact obtained two 14-inch hits on her formidable adversary; and one of them, which damaged some of the *Bismarck's* fuel tanks, was to have very important consequences. At 8 a.m. Lütjens signalled that, as his flagship's endurance had been considerably reduced, he intended to abandon the Atlantic foray and make for western France.

Even when every allowance has been made for the very real difficulties which faced Admiral Holland—caused by his squadron's lack of homogeneity, the great age of one of his ships, and the fact that the other was not properly worked up—it is difficult to justify the tactics employed during the final approach. Had he used the *Prince of Wales's* aircraft, or even his squadron's search radar sets, he would surely have realised in time that he was coming in from a very unfavourable bearing; by breaking wireless silence he could have gained the co-operation of Admiral Wake-Walker and the support of the *Norfolk's* and *Suffolk's* sixteen 8-inch guns, and perhaps have brought the destroyers back into touch with himself; and the rigid control exercised over his ships certainly proved an additional self-imposed handicap. The method of handling his squadron may, however, have owed a good deal to the fact that the 1939 issue of the Admiralty's " Fighting Instructions " which were then in force, not only laid down the tactics to be employed by heavy ships in very rigid terms, but in terms which were redolent of an earlier age —the age of great battle fleets—such as fought at Jutland.[1]

[1] The following extract from the 1939 Fighting Instructions may well have been in Admiral Holland's mind: " Prior to deployment the Admiral will control the movements

After the disaster to the *Hood* Admiral Wake-Walker took command of the damaged *Prince of Wales* as well as his own two cruisers; but the British force was now far too weak to re-engage the enemy, and could only continue to shadow him, hoping to bring Admiral Tovey's heavy ships into contact. They, however, were still some 330 miles away to the south-east, and could not expect to join action until early on 25th—unless the enemy's speed could be reduced, or he altered course to the east.[1] During the afternoon of 24th the cruisers, which were now maintaining touch by radar in poor visibility, reported that Lütjens had reduced to 24 knots and turned to a southerly course, and hopes rose correspondingly in the British fleet flagship.

We must now take temporary leave of the pursuers and pursued, and glance at the Admiralty's operational maps. There the need to draw a net around the German squadron was all too plain. To the north and north-east the seas were reasonably well covered by British ships; but there were huge gaps to the south through which it could easily slip. As a first step towards closing these gaps the Admiralty called Admiral Somerville's Force H north from Gibraltar in the very early hours of 24th, and also released the battleships *Rodney* and *Ramillies* from convoy escort duty. Other pieces on the vast Atlantic chessboard were also moved towards the critical area, some from as far away as Halifax; but it would take time for any of these ships to reach a favourable position—the more so because we still had no firm indication of Lütjens's intentions. Thus the need to reduce his ships' speed was still paramount.

At 2.40 p.m. on 24th Admiral Tovey accordingly sent the *Victorious*, accompanied by four light cruisers, ahead to reach a position from which the carrier's torpedo-bombers could get in an attack. Unfortunately the *Victorious*, which had been on the point of sailing for Gibraltar with a cargo of fighters for Malta, only had nine Swordfish and half a dozen Fulmar (fighter-reconnaissance planes) on board; but at 10 p.m. the striking force and shadowers

---

of the Battle Fleet as a whole. He will dispose the guides of divisions on a line of bearing at right angles to the bearing of the enemy battle fleet. . . ." The rigid wording of those instructions may usefully be compared with Nelson's Trafalgar Memorandum which, as Sir Julian Corbett has remarked, contained "a clear note of discrimination against the long-established fallacy of the old order of battle in single line." (See *Fighting Instructions*, 1530-1816, Navy Records Society, 1905.)

[1] See Map p. 135.

were flown off to find and attack the enemy, then about 120 miles away. In spite of abominable weather the Swordfish got in their attacks just after midnight, and obtained one torpedo hit; but it struck the battleship's main armour belt and did her little damage.

On the evening of 24th Lütjens detached the *Prinz Eugen* to operate alone in the Atlantic and then make for Brest; and at about 3 a.m. next morning, some three hours after the attack by the *Victorious's* torpedo-bombers, he himself altered to the south-east to make for western France. This movement achieved what Lütjens had been trying for ever since he had first been sighted by the *Suffolk* thirty hours earlier; for the cruisers, which had been shadowing at extreme radar range, lost touch. So far events had worked out very favourably for the German Admiral. He had sunk the *Hood*, and had damaged the *Prince of Wales* so badly that she no longer counted as a fighting unit; he had escaped serious injury in the gun action and in the carrier air attack; he had shaken off the pursuit by freeing himself from the cruisers which had been so stubbornly clinging to his tail; and he knew that his colleague, Admiral Dönitz, had called off all U-boat operations against our convoys, and had moved a group of seven boats to positions off southern Greenland where they might well trap important units of the Home Fleet. As the sun rose on 25th May he may well have felt satisfied; nor did that day bring any drastic change of fortune.

When the cruisers lost touch Admiral Tovey was only about 100 miles away to the south-east, and was closing the enemy rapidly. At about 4 a.m. on 25th his flagship must actually have crossed the enemy's track some 110 miles ahead of her; but the Commander-in-Chief was wholly unaware of how close he was to his quarry. The Admiralty now transmitted some bearings which the British direction-finding stations had taken of the *Bismarck's* wireless transmissions; but the manner in which they were signalled, combined with plotting errors made in the fleet flagship, produced the impression that she was moving to the *north-east*.[1] At 10.47 a.m. Admiral Tovey accepted the indications shown on his plot, and turned in the same direction; but he was now pursuing a false scent, and the distance between him and his principal adversary was

[1] Admiral Tovey, in his report, explained that the D/F bearings were plotted on a normal " Mercator's Projection " chart, instead of on the special " Polar Co-ordinate " chart supplied for the purpose.

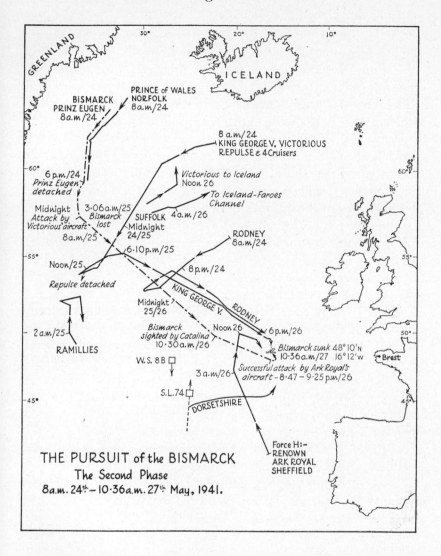

THE PURSUIT of the BISMARCK
The Second Phase
8a.m. 24ᵗʰ – 10·36a.m. 27ᵗʰ May, 1941.

actually widening as each hour passed. At 11 a.m., however, the Admiralty told Somerville to place his Force H (the *Ark Royal*, *Renown* and the cruiser *Sheffield*) athwart the course which Lütjens would take if he was heading for Brest; and in the evening they told firstly the *Rodney* and then all our forces to assume that port to be the enemy's destination. This message reached the fleet flagship just after Admiral Tovey had come to a similar conclusion, and had therefore turned again to the south-east; but he was now some 150 miles behind the *Bismarck*, and unless she could be slowed up the prospects of catching her were not at all good.

During the night of 25th-26th the Admiralty's net was drawn gradually tighter, but no one yet knew whether the *Bismarck* was within the vast ocean area which it was enclosing. The critical problem now to be decided was the placing of Coastal Command's shore-based air patrols at daylight next morning. Air Chief Marshal Bowhill, the Commander-in-Chief, who had served many years at sea as a young man, insisted that Lütjens would not set course direct for Brest, but would steer to make a landfall at Cape Finisterre. He therefore proposed to establish one air patrol well to the south of the direct course towards Brest, his suggestion was accepted by the Admiralty, and at 10.30 a.m. on 26th the crisis suddenly came when the long-range Catalina flying-boat ordered to fly that patrol sighted the enemy in a position some 690 miles west of Brest.[1] If the knowledge that the *Bismarck* was inside the Admiralty's widely cast net brought profound relief in London and the fleet flagship, everyone realised that the problem of catching her was not by any means yet solved. For she was only some 30 hours' steaming from safety, and as our own ships were getting very short of fuel time was plainly running out. Force H was, however, ideally placed to attack; at 6 p.m. the *Rodney* joined the Commander-in-Chief, and five fine destroyers under Captain P. Vian, which the Admiralty had ordered to leave a south-bound troop convoy, were also hastening to the scene to replace the big ships' original destroyer screen, all of whom had been forced to seek harbour to replenish their tanks.

Soon after the Catalina sighted the *Bismarck* the *Ark Royal's* reconnaissance aircraft also gained touch; and Somerville detached his only cruiser, the *Sheffield*, to shadow the enemy as well. In spite of the visibility being very bad, and the rough sea making aircraft handling extremely difficult, at 2.50 p.m. the carrier flew off a striking force of 14 Swordfish armed with torpedoes. An hour later they gained radar contact with a ship, and came down through very low cloud to attack. Too late did they realise that they had aimed their torpedoes—not at the *Bismarck*, but at the *Sheffield*! She, however, successfully avoided the torpedoes; but many precious minutes had been lost, and the enemy was still undamaged. The first

[1] See Map p. 135.

striking force returned to the carrier, and at 7.10 p.m. a second one, consisting of 15 Swordfish, took off. This time they made no mistake in target identification; but the fading light, stormy seas and heavy enemy A-A. fire made their task very difficult. Though co-ordination of attacks was, not surprisingly, far from perfect, two torpedoes found their marks. One struck the battleship's armour belt and, like the earlier hit by the *Victorious*'s aircraft, did little damage; but the other struck the enemy right aft, damaged her propellers, and jammed her rudder. That hit sealed the *Bismarck's* fate; for her speed dropped drastically and her course became erratic.

During the night Captain Vian's destroyers gained touch, and pressed in to close range to make a series of torpedo attacks. But all the German battleship's armaments were still intact, her crew defended their ship stoutly, and the destroyers were lucky to escape damage. It is possible, though by no means certain, that they obtained two more torpedo hits. These successes allowed Admiral Tovey, with the *King George V* and *Rodney*, to come up with the enemy; but the Commander-in-Chief decided against fighting a night action with an adversary who was so plainly delivered into his hands, and therefore held off to await daylight. Soon after dawn on 27th May he closed in from the north-west, and at about 8.45 a.m. his two battleships opened fire at 16,000 yards, gradually closing in to what amounted to point-blank range. By 10.20 the *Bismarck* had been reduced to a flaming shambles, and all her guns were silent. But our heavy shells had not penetrated to her vitals, probably because at the comparatively short ranges at which the action was fought the trajectories were too flat; and it needed several more torpedoes to send her to the bottom. She sank at 10.36 a.m. in 48° 10' North 16° 12' West, with her colours still flying. Only 110 survivors were rescued from her crew of over 2,000 men. Though a German account published long after the war states that the battleship did not finally sink until her engineers fired scuttling charges in the sea water circulation inlets, it is impossible to accept such a statement.[1] Nor would it seem greatly to matter; for no

[1] See Berthold, *The Sinking of the Bismarck* (Eng. Trans. Longmans, 1958) pp. 160–167 and 186–190. This "popular" account includes, however, so much plainly apocryphal dialogue, and is so inaccurate on verifiable matters of fact, that the scuttling story must be viewed with grave suspicion. It is based entirely on statements by Lieut-Commander (Engineer) Jumack, who was the senior surviving officer. He alleges that he concealed the matter from our interrogators in order not to reveal that our torpedoes failed to sink the ship. But his post-war recollections did not come to our notice until as late as 1956; and if they are

one has ever suggested that Lütjens and his men did not fight their ship most valiantly, and finally against overwhelming odds.[1] On the British side the news of the sinking of the giant battleship was heard with heartfelt relief; for everyone realised what a terrible danger she could have been loose in the Atlantic. Moreover, the success was as timely as it was encouraging; for 1941 had so far brought little relief to ease the enormous strain borne by the British Commonwealth. But the most important result did not at once become apparent; for we could not have realised at the time that the frustration of the ambitious German plan to raid our Atlantic shipping with all their most powerful warships marked the conclusion of a phase. Never again did the Germans throw down such a challenge, and henceforth—except in the Arctic—it was the U-boats, and not the surface warships, on which they chiefly relied to prosecute their intensive *guerre de course*.

The loss of their newest and finest battleship did not, however, lead to the Germans at once abandoning attacks on our shipping with surface warships; for on 10th June the Admiralty became aware that an important unit—possibly the *Tirpitz*—was on her way out from the Baltic, and issued a warning to the Home Fleet. It was not, in fact the *Tirpitz*, but the pocket-battleship *Lützow* (formerly the *Deutschland*), which was bound for Trondheim as a preliminary move to breaking out into the Atlantic. Late on the evening of 12th June two squadrons of Coastal Command torpedo-bombers took off from bases in Scotland, and in the small hours of the following morning they obtained one torpedo hit which damaged the pocket-battleship severely. Only with considerable difficulty was she safely escorted back to Kiel; and she had to go into dock for six months to effect

---

correct it seems odd that neither Dönitz nor Raeder mentions the scuttling story in their accounts of the sinking of the *Bismarck*—which were also compiled long after the war. See Karl Dönitz, *Ten Years and Twenty Days* (Weidenfeld and Nicolson, 1959) and Erich Raeder, *The Struggle for the Sea* (Kimber, 1959).

[1] It is a curious feature of post-war German naval apologists' writings that they claim with monotonous regularity that nearly all their losses occurred through scuttling their own ships. If it comes to the preservation of service "honour" one might think that to be sunk in action was more creditable; yet, for example, the *Marine Rundschau* has published a comprehensive list of U-boat losses, the vast majority of which are shown as "selbst versenkt." The implicit suggestion that the enemy had nothing to do with the losses is surely somewhat casuistic!

repairs. Thus was another of the German Navy's dwindling number of major warships put out of action. In the following month the heavy cruiser *Prinz Eugen*, which had achieved no successes at all during her brief Atlantic foray after parting company with the *Bismarck* on 24th May,[1] was hit by a bomb while lying in the French base; and when the battle cruiser *Scharnhorst* moved from Brest to La Pallice on 24th July Royal Air Force bombers obtained no less than five hits on her, and damaged her severely. With the *Gneisenau* still out of action from damage received in earlier air attacks[2] the Germans were thus left with very few major warships fit for sea; and by July the threat of attacks on our Atlantic shipping by powerful surface raiders, which had loomed so large on the British horizon earlier in the year, had declined very substantially.

The sinking of the *Bismarck* had an important sequel affecting the struggle for control of the more remote oceans as well as the North Atlantic; for the Admiralty guessed that a carefully planned operation such as her sortie must have included the despatch of supply ships to secret rendezvous at sea, and had been patiently collecting evidence of their movements. By June we had built up a clear picture of the enemy's plans, and were ready to strike. The Admiralty quietly ordered warships to leave their bases and search the most likely areas, and in a matter of twenty days no less than nine large supply ships, six of them tankers, were sunk or captured in widely separated spots in the north and south Atlantic oceans. These successes were the more important because some of the intercepted ships had been sent out to supply U-boats and disguised raiders, as well as the *Bismarck* and *Prinz Eugen*. Thus their loss greatly shortened the time that these other raiders could remain at sea, and seriously dislocated all the enemy's plans for the prosecution of the *guerre de course* against our merchant shipping.

We must now return to the U-boat campaign against our North Atlantic shipping, which we left at the time when all our efforts were concentrated against the *Bismarck*. In May, although our convoys were routed farther north in order to gain the maximum protection from the newly-established sea and air bases in Iceland, losses had reached the uncomfortably high figure of 58 ships (325,000 tons); and in the following month there was only a slight

[1] See p. 134.   [2] See p. 124.

decline. Towards the end of June there took place what may justly be regarded as the first of the big convoy battles between a large number of U-boats and a fairly powerful escort force; and as this fight set the pattern for the entire Atlantic battle for the next two years it should be recorded in some detail. On 23rd June the enemy located convoy HX 133 to the south of Greenland, and ten U-boats closed in to attack. This concentration did not, however, pass unnoticed in the Admiralty's submarine tracking room, and the escorts of two outward-bound convoys were diverted to strengthen the defenders of the threatened one. With thirteen escort vessels thus assembled the contestants were fairly evenly matched, and a ding-dong struggle, which lasted for five days and nights, developed around the convoy. We lost five merchantmen in the process, but as U.556 and U.651 were both sunk by the surface escorts the result may be said to have been a drawn fight. In the strategy of reinforcing the escort of a threatened convoy, as was done on this occasion, we may see the genesis of the Atlantic "support groups" which were to render such decisive service later on, at the crisis of the struggle.[1]

On 22nd June, just as the battle of HX 133 was developing, Hitler launched his attack on Russia. Many of the German bombers, which had caused us serious trouble earlier in the year, were now diverted to the eastern front, and the German Navy was required to support the advance along the southern shore of the Baltic. Taken together these factors eased the severity of the pressure against Britain. Shipping losses fell sharply in July and August, and when Dönitz tried to improve the U-boats' performance by moving them from the mid-Atlantic to the waters between Ireland and Iceland, he suffered a sharp reverse. On 27th August U.570 surfaced directly below Squadron Leader J. H. Thompson's Hudson, which attacked so quickly and accurately that the U-boat surrendered. British warships soon arrived on the scene, and in spite of very bad weather managed to tow the prize to Iceland. Though the crew had destroyed most of their secret material, the capture and recovery of an intact U-boat was an important accomplishment, and U.570 rendered good service to her captors as H.M.S. *Graph*.

In the summer of 1941 the German U-boat fleet was increasing its strength rapidly, and by 1st September nearly 200 had been commissioned. As we had sunk only 47 since the outbreak of

[1] See pp. 273-7.

hostilities it was plain that a renewal of the onslaught, in greater strength than ever before, was to be expected. Yet the comparative lull which prevailed in July and August led to pressure on the Admiralty to release Coastal Command aircraft in order to reinforce the bomber raids on Germany. The Admiralty, however, resisted such proposals on the grounds that as soon as the nights started to lengthen, the enemy's effort was bound to increase again; and the events of September, when two slow North Atlantic convoys and two others homeward bound from Sierra Leone suffered heavily, soon proved that prognosis accurate. Sinkings by the U-boats rose to 53 ships of over 200,000 tons during the month. Dönitz's plan to send a number of his larger boats to distant waters, including those off the Cape of Good Hope—where our traffic was very heavy —was however frustrated when our patrolling cruisers intercepted and sank the supply ships *Kota Pinang* and *Python* on 3rd October and 1st December respectively. Once again, as in the previous June,[1] it was shown how vulnerable was an enemy who totally lacked overseas bases and had therefore to depend on supply ships to sustain his commerce raiders; and the Admiralty's policy of seeking and striking at those vessels was again amply justified. Furthermore, the scouring of the outer oceans for the German supply ships led to the destruction of another disguised raider; for on 22nd November the cruiser *Devonshire* caught and sank the *Atlantis* in the southern waters of the ocean after which she had been named. Her cruise had lasted for no less than 20 months; but her victims numbered only 22 merchant ships (146,000 tons).

In addition to the *Pinguin* and *Atlantis* one other disguised raider was eliminated during 1941; but the price that she exacted in her last fight was heavy. On 19th November the *Kormoran* encountered the R.A.N. light cruiser *Sydney* off the coast of Western Australia. While trying to establish whether she was, the Dutch ship she claimed to be, the *Sydney* incautiously steamed parallel to the raider, and as close as 2,000 yards from her. Choosing her moment with skill the *Kormoran* suddenly cast off her disguise, discharged her torpedoes, and opened fire with every weapon she possessed. The *Sydney's* crew was at "action stations," but that was not enough to prevent the raider inflicting grave damage before she could retaliate effectively. The cruiser finally disappeared over the southern horizon

[1] See p. 139.

a mass of flames. As not one man of her company survived it seems likely that she blew up some hours after the two ships had drawn apart. The *Kormoran* herself received serious enough damage to make it impossible to continue her cruise, and she finally scuttled herself; but most of her crew reached the Australian coast in safety. The Admiralty had already issued several warnings regarding the danger of making a close approach to suspicious ships while trying to establish their identity; but we shall never know why the *Sydney* disregarded them. The clever use of disguise by the German raiders and supply ships was finally frustrated by a system under which a warship in contact with a suspect communicated at once with her base, where a plot of all our own shipping was maintained. If the plot revealed that the identity claimed by the suspicious ship was false, the base sent the answer "Checkmate," whereupon the warship was entitled to sink her without further ado; but before the system was perfected not a few enemies succeeded in bluffing our cruiser patrols—though none achieved a success comparable to that of the *Kormoran*.

Though the German attack on Russia in June, 1941, brought us an easement in the Atlantic battle, it also produced a whole crop of new problems for the Home Fleet; for an entirely new theatre of maritime war was at once opened up in the Arctic. The first requirement was to attack the enemy's supply ships, which carried men and stores from ports in Norway to the new front in northern Finland. As the Germans hoped to capture Murmansk, which was Russia's only ice-free northern port, and we were planning to use that same port as an entry for the supplies and equipment of which the Russians stood in great need, the campaign in the far north at once became critically important. In the summer a number of British submarines were sent to work from Kola Inlet, at the head of which stands Murmansk, and they contributed a good deal to bringing the German seaborne traffic to a standstill. But it was in the organisation of convoys to north Russia that we had to overcome greater difficulties; and we soon found ourselves involved in operations of a more exacting and arduous nature than in any other theatre of the war. In the first place whereas we had no advanced base anywhere in the new theatre, and the Russian harbours were very undeveloped, the enemy possessed many excellent sea and air bases in Norway right on the southern flank of a route from which little deviation was possible. Thus the convoys were exposed to heavy attacks by surface ships, bombers and U-boats throughout the greater part of their 2,000-mile journeys.[1] Secondly, the escorts had to carry along with them the fuel and supplies they would need for the return journey; and to extricate damaged ships was bound to be very difficult. Thirdly, the waters of the far north are some of the most stormy in the world, with temperatures far below freezing point throughout the long winter months; and as none of our ships were properly equipped for working in such conditions, the operations were bound to place an immense strain on the officers and men of the merchantmen and warships. It was true that in winter the perpetual darkness would afford some shield against air attack; but the storms then blew their fiercest, and journeys were certain to be prolonged by the terrible weather commonly encountered. In summer, on the other hand, the perpetual daylight would wholly favour the enemy, and we would be forced to keep as far as possible from his bases, hugging the edge of the Arctic ice and traversing the most dangerous stretch of the route in the high latitude of some 75° North. This would increase the average duration of the convoys' ordeal from perhaps ten days in winter to twelve or thirteen days in summer, when unloading would be possible in the more distant White Sea port of Archangel instead of at Murmansk, which lay uncomfortably close to the front in Finland and to the German air bases in north Norway. In terms of strategy the scales were thus heavily weighted in the enemy's favour; but some months were actually to elapse before the Germans took full advantage of this fact—probably because they were slow to realise the scale on which we were sending supplies to our Russian allies by the Arctic route.

The traffic to north Russia actually began in August, 1941, when the old carrier *Argus*, with two dozen Hurricanes on board, and seven merchantmen filled with munitions and crated aircraft were sent from Britain. Next, on 29th September, the first of the famous series of PQ convoys left Iceland for Archangel under the charge of escorts from the Home Fleet. Before the end of the year we had dispatched 55 merchantmen in eight separate convoys, and had also organised homeward (QP) convoys to bring back the empty ships. After QP 4 had been caught in the White Sea ice

[1] See Map p. 144.

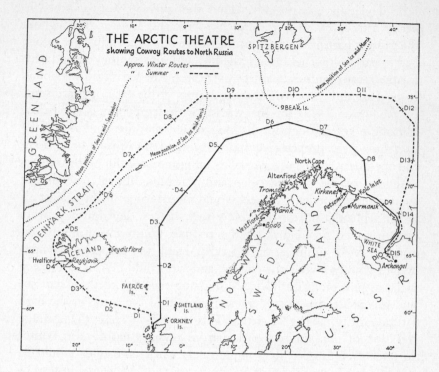

in November, however, the convoys were directed to Murmansk instead of Archangel. No losses at all were suffered on the Arctic route in 1941, and valuable experience of conditions in those distant waters was gained by the Home Fleet. In retrospect it seems to have been very unwise of the Germans to allow us to start these difficult movements with practically no interference. It thus came about that in the closing months of 1941 the focus of the Home Fleet's main activities shifted from the guardianship of the north Atlantic to the waters between Iceland and Archangel. The value of the bases gained in Iceland now became even greater than before, and Admiral Tovey's ships saw as much of them as of their main base at Scapa. But to the British sailors the treachery of the Icelandic climate made this a change for the worse, arousing all their well-known capacity for sardonic humour regarding the discomforts of their own circumstances.

Meanwhile, the meeting between Mr. Churchill and President Roosevelt off Argentia on 10th August had produced important results concerning the U.S. Navy's participation in the Atlantic Battle; and on 16th September convoy HX 150 sailed with an American escort, which was to take it as far as the Mid-Ocean Meeting Point south of Iceland. At the same time our organisation for the escorts to relieve each other in mid-ocean was adjusted to achieve greater economy of force, and this enabled three escort groups to be transferred from the north Atlantic to the Sierra Leone and Gibraltar routes, where our convoys had so far never had adequate protection throughout their long, outflanked passages past the enemy's Bay of Biscay bases.

It was inevitable that the American Navy's active participation in Atlantic convoy work should lead to incidents with the U-boats. On 4th September the destroyer *Greer* replied to an attack by U.652 with depth charges, on 17th October the destroyer *Kearney* was torpedoed, and on the last day of that month the *Reuben James* was sunk while escorting the British convoy HX 156. These were the first casualties to be suffered by the American Navy.

The practice now was for the Canadian Navy to escort east-bound convoys to the Western Ocean Meeting Point south of Newfoundland. There American escorts took over the fast HX convoys, while Canadian groups, generally reinforced by some British ships, looked after the slower SC convoys. At the Mid-Ocean Meeting Point in about 22° West British groups from Iceland would take over both fast and slow convoys, and escort them as far as the rendezvous with the local escorts of the Western Approaches Command, which had generally come out from Londonderry or the Clyde. At the same time U.S. Navy or Army long-range aircraft began to work with the R.C.A.F. from bases in Newfoundland, while others came to the Coastal Command bases in Iceland. The extension of the zone over which air escort could be provided to our convoys was very soon to bring substantial benefits; for the "air gap" in mid-Atlantic in which the U-boats sought to avoid the prying eyes and searching radars of the aircraft, was appreciably narrowed. Furthermore, in November the Americans sent two battleships and two cruisers to Iceland to take a share in the burden of watching the northern exits to the Atlantic. This development was the more welcome because powerful detachments had recently been sent from Admiral Tovey's fleet to replace losses suffered in the Mediterranean, to fight our convoys through to Malta, and to increase the pressure on the Axis supply traffic from Italy to North Africa; and the increasingly threatening attitude of Japan had made it plain that steps had also to be taken to rebuild our maritime power in the Far East. The full impact of those developments, which combined to place a heavier strain on the Royal Navy than ever before, will, however, be discussed more fully in succeeding chapters.

In the autumn of 1941 our slowly rising escort strength, the increasing American participation in the Atlantic battle, and the redefinition of Coastal Command's duties placing first priority on reconnaissance for enemy surface ships and submarines, began to take effect. Furthermore, it was at this time that, on Hitler's orders, Dönitz was forced to divert a considerable portion of his U-boat strength to the Mediterranean in the endeavour to avert the collapse of Italy and the loss of the Axis armies in Africa, and also to station other U-boats to the west of the Straits of Gibraltar. The combined result of all these various influences was that the onslaught by the U-boats on our Atlantic shipping declined, and in October their sinkings amounted to no more than 32 ships totalling 157,000 tons —about half the achievements of the previous May and June. The despatch of U-boats to the Mediterranean and the concentration off Gibraltar did, however, force us to strengthen the sea and air forces stationed at that base, in order to deny the passage of the Straits to the enemy and ensure the safety of the convoys sailing between Britain and Gibraltar. In December the Admiralty held back the homeward-bound convoy HG 76 until its escort had been reinforced to a total of thirteen ships, including our first escort carrier the *Audacity*.[1] With Commander F. J. Walker in command these ships fought the convoy through the U-boat pack, and also frustrated the reinforcements which Dönitz sent to join in the attack. Though the *Audacity* herself was sunk, her aircraft helped substantially in scoring a notable success; for no less than five U-boats were destroyed during the convoy's passage home, and only two of its merchantmen were lost.

It thus fell to the *Audacity*, first of a distinguished line of British and American escort carriers, to close the "air gap" on the Gibraltar route; and her achievements stressed the urgent need to build many more ships of her class. Everyone now realised that only the escort

---

[1] This ship was actually an ex-German prize, the *Hanover*, which had been converted to escort carrier in Britain.

carrier could fulfil the need for a convoy to carry its own fighter and anti-submarine protection along with it; and a large programme of construction was accordingly put in hand, especially in the United States, where such ships were built under " Lend-Lease " for Britain as well as for the U.S. Navy. We shall meet many ships of this class later in our story.

The lull in the North Atlantic, which first became noticeable in October, 1941, and whose causes have already been discussed, became even more marked during the last two months of the year. In November the U-boats only sank 13 ships of rather more than 60,000 tons, and in December our losses of merchant ships *from all causes* in the theatre amounted to no more than 10 ships; but any optimistic feelings which that favourable trend may have aroused in London were utterly dispelled on 7th December; and one result of the sudden and treacherous Japanese attack was to cause us enormous shipping losses in the Far East. It thus came to pass that, just when we seemed to have gained a degree of mastery over the German surface warships and U-boats, the onslaught of a powerful new enemy deprived us of all the relief and benefit of that improvement.

CHAPTER VIII

THE MEDITERRANEAN FLEET IN TRIUMPH AND ADVERSITY

January–December, 1941

"It takes the Navy three years to build a ship. It would take three hundred to rebuild a tradition."

> Admiral Sir Andrew Cunningham, to his
> staff at Alexandria, May, 1941.

WE SAW earlier how, when Italy's prospects were plainly moving to a crisis at the end of 1940, Hitler transferred a powerful force of 150 bombers to Sicily with orders that it was "to attack the British Navy, particularly in Alexandria . . . and in the straits between Sicily and North Africa." There were at the time precisely 15 Hurricanes in Malta to oppose this dangerous concentration of enemy air power, and although another 18 were flown to the island in January, 1941, the odds in the air remained very heavily in the Axis favour throughout the first six months of the year. While ominous portents were thus beginning to appear in the sky the Army of the Nile, whose offensive had begun on 9th December, 1940, was still driving victoriously westward. Tobruk and Derna were captured in January, and on 6th February General Wavell's men triumphantly entered Benghazi;[1] but the British government's decision to send troops to reinforce the Greeks in their hour of trial then brought the land offensive to a halt—just when there seemed to be nothing to prevent it reaching Tripoli. Though we will return later to the military consequences of that decision we may here note that it was the basic cause of all the tribulations which beset the Mediterranean Fleet in 1941.

Throughout the Army's sweeping advance across Libya it was

---

[1] See Map pp. 112-13.

supported and supplied by the little ships of Cunningham's Inshore Squadron which carried stores, petrol, water and ammunition right up to the front line, bombarded targets which were giving trouble to the soldiers, evacuated wounded and prisoners, and carried out a multitude of other tasks. Though the squadron was composed of a remarkably heterogeneous collection of ships, from flat-bottomed China river gunboats to heavy-gunned monitors, its work once again emphasised the immense benefits which accrue to an Army whose flank rests on waters controlled by its own side's Navy.

Meanwhile, the Chiefs of Staff in London had decided to send another fast convoy through the Mediterranean to carry urgently needed stores to Malta and Greece.[1] On 6th January the four merchantmen left Gibraltar, and next day Admiral Somerville followed with Force H. Plans to take full advantage of the opportunity had also been prepared at Alexandria; for Admiral Cunningham would not lose the chance to run reinforcements and supplies into Malta, and bring out from the island the empty ships which had remained there since delivering their cargoes in earlier convoy operations. He therefore took almost his entire strength to sea to cover the double movement, and early on the 10th he met the cruiser and destroyer force which was escorting the east-bound convoy in a position about 100 miles west of Malta. So far all had gone exceedingly well; and Somerville reversed course for Gibraltar with his share of the task successfully completed. But the main Mediterranean Fleet had been continuously shadowed from the air ever since leaving Alexandria, and on the afternoon of the 10th, when some 60 miles west of Malta, it was subjected to very heavy and skilful attacks by about 40 Ju.87 and Ju.88 dive-bombers from Sicily, assisted by Italian high-level and torpedo-bombers. It was only the Germans who were effective, and they concentrated against the fleet carrier *Illustrious*. Within a few minutes she was hit by six heavy bombs, and also sustained damage from three near misses. Though her armoured flight deck saved her from destruction she was put completely out of action, and only reached Malta with difficulty after dark. Over 200 of her crew were killed or wounded. Nor was that the end of the story, for next day the cruisers *Southampton* and *Gloucester*, which Cunningham had detached from his main force to support the convoy from Malta, were also attacked

[1] No through convoy had been run since November 1940. See p. 114.

by the German bombers from Sicily. The *Southampton* was heavily hit, caught fire, and had finally to be sunk by our own forces. Though the dual object of the operation—namely, the passage of the through-Mediterranean convoy and the release of the empty store ships from Malta—was successfully carried out, and none of the fourteen merchantmen involved suffered any damage, the 10th and 11th January, 1941, marked the end of the first period of dominance by the Mediterranean Fleet. Even had another modern aircraft carrier been immediately available to replace the *Illustrious* it would have been difficult, and probably costly, to challenge the Luftwaffe in the central basin: without a carrier it was obviously impossible. Though the *Illustrious* slipped out of Malta on 23rd and reached Alexandria safely two days later, she had to be sent to America for repairs. To replace her the Admiralty at once ordered her sister-ship the *Formidable* to proceed to Alexandria by the Cape of Good Hope; but many weeks would pass before she could arrive.

The Germans fully realised that, if their reinforcements were to reach North Africa in time to save the situation, they must neutralise Malta; for it was from that island base that our surface ships, submarines and aircraft had been taking a rising toll of the Italian troopships and supply vessels on which the land forces in Libya entirely depended. Thus to send Rommel's Afrika Korps overseas without ensuring a reasonable control over the waters across which all his supplies had to be carried, would be to offer a substantial hostage to fortune. Malta was the key to control over the disputed waters, and both sides saw clearly enough that the issue on land would depend on the outcome of the siege which opened on the day that the damaged *Illustrious* berthed there. Throughout February and March the air onslaught continued with scarcely a break, and by the middle of March the state of the island was becoming critical; for no supplies had reached it since the January convoy. Aided by bad weather Cunningham managed, on 23rd March, to slip in a small convoy; but as two of its ships were damaged by bombs while unloading the relief obtained was slight. Nor was Malta the only anxiety at this time, for the Germans had begun to drop magnetic mines in the Suez Canal; and the delays thus caused to the ships on which our land and air forces in the Middle East depended for their supplies and reinforcements were very ominous —the more so because the transport of troops and equipment from

Egypt to Greece, in accordance with the War Cabinet's decision mentioned earlier, began early in March.

The change in the strategic situation in the Mediterranean, brought about by the arrival of the Luftwaffe in Sicily, emphasised the acute shortages from which all three British services were suffering. Against the Italians it had been possible to achieve remarkable successes whilst working on the proverbial shoe string; but against the Germans even the most ingenious improvisations could not act as substitutes for the weapons and equipment we did not possess. More fighter aircraft was an obvious and urgent need, and it was in January that the first cargo of crated Hurricanes was carried by the *Furious* to Takoradi on the Gold Coast, where they were assembled and then flown across Africa to Egypt. But the need for more anti-aircraft guns, for modern minesweepers to keep the Gulf of Suez and the Canal open, and for specialised troops and equipment for combined operations was little less urgent. The Prime Minister had for some time been pressing for the seizure of the small island of Pantelleria, in the Sicilian "narrows" about 120 miles north-west of Malta;[1] but neither the Chiefs of Staff at home nor the Middle East commanders felt any enthusiasm for the idea. To the latter it seemed clear that, with the Luftwaffe reaching out to Greece and the Ægean, the islands of the Dodecanese were far more important; and they hoped to attack and seize some of the smaller ones as a preliminary to assaulting the key position of Rhodes. All such plans depended, however, on acquiring the necessary specialist troops and assault shipping; and we still possessed very few of either. In January, however, the Chiefs of Staff decided to send out by the Cape of Good Hope three converted Glen Line ships, prototypes of the Landing Ships Infantry (L.S.I.s) which were to play such an important part in later combined operations, with their Special Service troops; and the Admiralty's Mobile Naval Base Defence Organisation (M.N.B.D.O.), with its 5,000 Royal Marines, was to follow soon afterwards. In fact, however, they all arrived too late to play the offensive role which the Middle East commanders had foreseen for them.

While the first three months of 1941 was thus a period of acute difficulty, and of yet more ominous portents, the naval forces in the eastern and western basins of the Mediterranean and also those

---

[1] See Map pp. 112-13.

supporting the land operations against the Italian East African possessions were far from remaining idle. Thus on 6th February Admiral Somerville took Force H to sea from Gibraltar, and in the early hours of 9th he penetrated right into the Gulf of Genoa. While the *Ark Royal's* aircraft laid mines off Spezia and bombed the oil refinery at Leghorn, the *Renown*, *Malaya* and *Sheffield* bombarded the harbour works, docks and factories of Genoa. Though the main Italian fleet put to sea from Naples it failed to intercept Somerville on his return passage, and all the British ships reached Gibraltar completely unscathed. The chief result of this bold penetration into Italian waters probably was to impress on the enemy how vulnerable his ports were to attacks from the sea, and to emphasise that we had no intention of allowing the arrival of the Luftwaffe, nor the check suffered on 10th January off Malta, to force us back on the defensive. Events in East Africa drove home the same lessons almost simultaneously. With Vice-Admiral R. Leatham's East Indies squadron in firm control of the Indian Ocean, supplies and reinforcements reached the land forces which were attacking Italy's East African possessions almost unhindered; and wherever the fighting front came down to the sea there were the grey warships waiting to support the soldiers with their guns and aircraft, and to land their supplies. In February both Kismayu and Mogadishu in Italian Somaliland were captured, and of the 16 Axis merchantmen sheltering in the former port only one escaped.[1] Much the same occurred when our land forces advanced into Eritrea early in April and captured Massawa, the principal Italian naval base in East Africa. That event marked the final elimination of Italian naval opposition in the Red Sea; for nearly all their warships had been sunk or captured.[2] By the end of that month our control of the vital route to Suez was virtually undisputed; and an important consequence of that accomplishment was that President Roosevelt decided to allow American merchant ships to sail to Suez—since in his view the Red Sea was no longer a "combat zone."

The heartening successes achieved in East Africa were, however, soon overshadowed by the storm clouds gathering over Greece. Towards the end of February a mission consisting of the Foreign

[1] See Map p. 153.

[2] Four Italian submarines escaped from Massawa, and all reached Bordeaux safely by way of the Cape of Good Hope. The accomplishment of one of them, the *Perla*, which was of the small coastal type, was particularly remarkable.

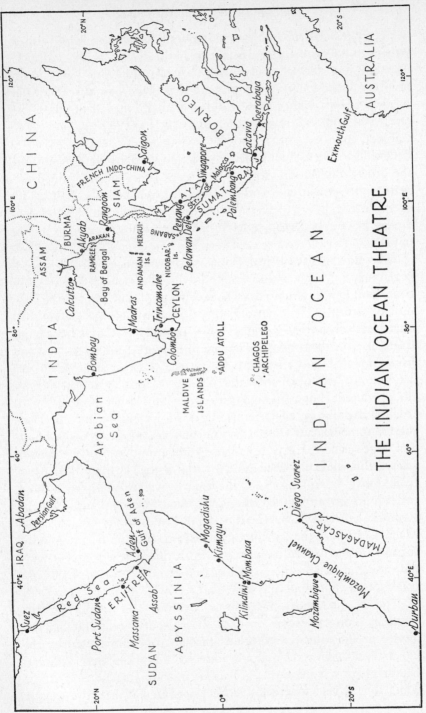

THE INDIAN OCEAN THEATRE

Secretary (Mr. Eden) and representatives of all three services visited Athens to discuss British participation in the defence of that country. The mission, though fully aware of the difficulties and perils involved, unhesitatingly recommended that we should send all the help we could—rather than abandon a small but gallant ally to its fate; and, after anxious debate, the Chiefs of Staff and the War Cabinet endorsed the proposal. "Therefore," telegraphed Mr. Churchill to Eden, "while being under no illusions we all send you the order 'Full Steam Ahead.'" A week later Bulgaria joined the Axis, and German land and air forces moved into the Balkans in strength. Such were the consequences of Mussolini's attack on Greece in October, 1940—which had been as unsuccessful as it was unprovoked.

The movement of British troops to Greece (operation "Lustre") began on 5th March, and for the following three weeks convoys ran continuously every three days between Egypt and Piræus, the seaport of Athens. The chief difficulty arose through the inability of our weak air forces, working from partially developed bases in Crete, to give the convoys adequate fighter protection; nor did we have enough bomber strength to put the German airfields out of action. Twenty-five merchantmen (115,000 tons) were lost during the operation; but as the majority were sunk either after they had reached harbour or while returning to Egypt empty, the effect on the reinforcement of Greece was not serious. Over 58,000 soldiers and large quantities of vehicles, stores and ammunition were landed safely. But while this large movement of British fighting men away from Libya was in progress, the enemy was making the utmost endeavours to strengthen the same front by shipping General Rommel's Afrika Korps in the opposite direction; and because Malta was under the lash of the Luftwaffe and the fleet was fully engaged in the eastern basin, we failed to interfere effectively with the movements. By the end of March Rommel, aware that only weak forces were opposing him, was ready to strike.

The Mediterranean Fleet was covering and supporting the "Lustre" convoys when, on 25th March, our wireless intelligence service produced clear indications that a strong movement by the Italian fleet against those same convoys was imminent. Admiral Cunningham was anxious to give every encouragement to a purpose which might lead to a decisive fleet action. He therefore quietly moved our shipping away from the disputed waters, and set about giving an impression of unpreparedness; but he ordered his second-in-command, Vice-Admiral H. D. Pridham-Wippell, to concentrate the light forces (four cruisers and nine destroyers) to the south of Crete by daylight on 28th March, and other sea and air forces in Greece, Crete and Egypt were put on the alert. At noon on 27th an R.A.F. flying-boat reported three Italian cruisers some 320 miles to the west of Crete, steering south-east. Cunningham waited a few hours longer, and, as dark closed down on Alexandria harbour, his three battleships (the *Warspite*, *Barham* and *Valiant*), the carrier *Formidable* (which had recently arrived from home by way of the Cape of Good Hope), and nine destroyers quietly slipped out to sea. All that night they steered to the north-west, while the Light Forces, whom Cunningham had called to meet him, moved towards a rendezvous south of Crete.

At dawn on 28th the *Formidable* flew off her reconnaissance aircraft, which soon reported an enemy force of cruisers and destroyers south of Crete, in the waters where our own light forces were operating.[1] A short while later Pridham-Wippell himself reported sighting the same ships, and Cunningham turned to close the position. The next air reports suggested that there was another enemy force, possibly of battleships, to the north of the cruisers; but the situation was far from clear. Then, at 11 a.m., Pridham-Wippell reported two enemy battleships sixteen miles away to the north. His position was indeed uncomfortable; for the Italian cruisers were on his starboard quarter and the battleships to port. He therefore turned to the south-east under cover of smoke, while Cunningham ordered the *Formidable* to send her striking force against the battleships. Just before 11.30 six torpedo-bombers attacked the *Vittorio Veneto*, the only battleship actually present, but failed to hit her. Their intervention did, however, relieve the pressure on our light forces; for Admiral Iachino, the Italian Commander-in-Chief, broke off the pursuit and turned to the north-west. Meanwhile our reconnaissance aircraft had reported a third Italian force farther to the north as consisting of two *Cavour* class battleships and three heavy cruisers. Though it actually comprised five heavy cruisers accompanied by four destroyers, it was now plain that most of the Italian fleet was at sea and that

---

[1] See Map p. 156.

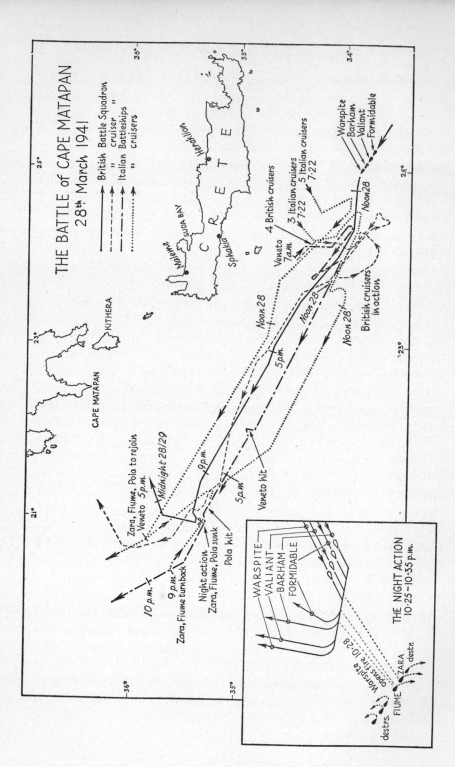

THE BATTLE of CAPE MATAPAN
28th March 1941

British Battle Squadron
" cruiser "
Italian Battleships
" cruisers

KITHERA

CAPE MATAPAN

CRETE

Malème
SUDA BAY
Sphakia
Heraklion

Zara, Fiume, Pola to rejoin
Veneto 5 p.m.

Midnight 28/29

9 p.m.

5 p.m.

Veneto hit

10 p.m.
9 p.m.
Zara, Fiume turnback

Night action
Zara, Fiume, Pola sunk
Pola hit

5 p.m.

Veneto
7 a.m.

4 British cruisers
3 Italian cruisers   7.22
5 Italian cruisers   7.22

British cruisers
in action

Noon 28

Noon 28

Noon 28

Noon 28

Warspite
Barham
Valiant
Formidable

THE NIGHT ACTION
10·25–10·35 p.m.

WARSPITE
VALIANT
BARHAM
FORMIDABLE

Warspite
opens fire 10·28

FIUME
ZARA
destr.

destrs.

destrs.

Cunningham's forces were heavily outnumbered. That knowledge, however, made no difference to the Commander-in-Chief's determination to bring the enemy to action as soon as possible.

At 12.30 p.m. Admiral Pridham-Wippell joined the Commander-in-Chief with all his ships unscathed—in spite of their having been the target of the *Veneto's* 15-inch guns for about half an hour. Cunningham now pressed on in pursuit of the Italian flagship, and ordered the *Formidable* to strike at her again; for it was urgently necessary to reduce her speed. Between 3.10 and 3.25 p.m. five Swordfish accordingly attacked the battleship, and obtained one hit. This slowed her down quite drastically, and hopes of catching her rose correspondingly in the British battle squadron; but she soon recovered sufficiently to increase speed to 19 knots. Nor did attacks by R.A.F. Blenheim bombers, and by a few naval aircraft from Cretan bases, succeed in inflicting more damage on the Italian fleet. By 4 p.m. it was clear to Cunningham that his chances of overtaking the *Veneto* before dark were receding. He therefore sent the light forces ahead to regain contact, and told the *Formidable* to make a third attempt at the battleship with her torpedo-bombers.

The *Warspite* herself next sent off one of her catapult aircraft to report the enemy's formation, and by 7.30 p.m. her experienced observer had sent an admirably accurate series of signals. Cunningham now knew that his principal quarry was steaming north-west in the centre of a massed array of cruisers and destroyers—no easy target for a small force of torpedo-bombers to attack. As the sun was setting ten Swordfish pressed in through so dense a concentration of gunfire that it was difficult to identify the targets. The *Veneto* escaped further damage; but one torpedo hit the heavy cruiser *Pola*, and brought her to a standstill. At 8.30 p.m. Admiral Iachino, who was all this time quite unaware that the British battle squadron was at sea, let alone hotly pursuing him, ordered the heavy cruisers *Zara* and *Fiume* and four destroyers back to assist the *Pola*; and that order was to have important results.[1] At about the time when Iachino sent back the *Zara* and *Fiume* Cunningham decided to accept the risks of night action with his heavy ships, and ordered his destroyers to press ahead and attack the enemy; but as so often in war, things did not work out as intended.

At 9.11 p.m. the Commander-in-Chief learnt from his light

---

[1] See Map p. 156.

forces that an unknown ship, actually the *Pola*, was lying stopped to the southward of his course, and decided to investigate. About an hour later the *Valiant's* radar picked up a contact six miles away on the port bow, and Cunningham turned his battleships to close the position. Hopes ran high that the stopped ship was the *Vittorio Veneto*. Suddenly, at 10.25, on quite a different bearing, two large ships with a smaller one ahead of them loomed up through the night fine on the battle squadron's starboard bow. Cunningham instantly swung the battleships to starboard together, thus bringing them back into line ahead and placing the enemy—which was the *Zara* and *Fiume* with one destroyer ahead and three astern of them —on his port bow.[1] The *Formidable* was told, for her own safety, to haul out of the line; and the heavy ships' turrets swung round and steadied on these new targets. For a few seconds the silence was breathless, with only the swish of the big ships' bow waves and the low hum of their machinery disturbing the night. Then the silence was shattered by the *Warspite's* first 15-inch broadside, which she fired at the *Fiume* almost simultaneously with a destroyer illuminating her by searchlight. Salvo after salvo of 15-inch shells now poured into the unlucky Italian cruisers, which had been caught quite unprepared for action. In a few minutes they were burning like torches from end to end, and Cunningham told his destroyers to finish them off. They also sank two of the four large destroyers which had been with the *Zara* and *Fiume*, and before daylight the immobilised *Pola* was located and sunk as well. The Italians thus lost five valuable warships and over 2,400 officers and men—against the British loss of precisely one Swordfish aircraft. The only unsatisfactory feature of the night's work was that the injured *Vittorio Veneto* was never found by our searching forces. An increase of speed and an alteration to the north at 9 p.m. had prevented the destroyer striking force reaching a favourable position to attack from ahead; and a signal sent by Admiral Cunningham soon after the night action, ordering all forces "not engaged with the enemy" to retire to the north-east, was wrongly taken as applying to the striking force. None the less the Battle of Cape Matapan was a substantial victory; and it provided complete justification for the emphasis placed on efficiency in night fighting by the Royal Navy. Moreover, it came at a time when it was essential that our control

[1] See Map p. 156 (*Inset*).

of the eastern basin, on which the fate of the army in Greece depended, should be fully asserted. Indeed, Sir John Jervis's remark before the Battle of Cape St. Vincent (14th February, 1797) that "a victory is very necessary to England at this time" could aptly have been repeated on the Admiral's bridge of the *Warspite* on 28th March, 1941.

Next morning Cunningham took his fleet back through the scene of the night action, and rescued many survivors from the sunken Italian ships—a work of mercy which could have been completed had not German bombers intervened. On 30th March the main fleet re-entered Alexandria, to be greeted by rousing cheers from the ships in the harbour; but there could be no resting on the laurels gained off Cape Matapan, for many pressing and difficult problems were raising their ugly heads.

Early in April we lost Benghazi, and within the next few days Rommel had driven our outnumbered land forces out of the whole of Cyrenaica except for a perimeter around Tobruk. Simultaneously with this drastic reversal of fortune in Africa the Germans attacked Greece and Yugoslavia in overwhelming strength, and the soldiers we had so recently carried to Greece soon stood in grave peril.

The most urgent need was to stop Rommel's eastward advance, and that could best be done by attacking his supply convoys while they were at sea; for a ship sunk at sea is a permanent loss, while one damaged in harbour may yet discharge her cargo, and even be repaired for the homeward voyage. With that object in mind, Cunningham detached four destroyers to Malta, and on 16th April they destroyed an entire Italian convoy (about 14,000 tons of shipping) off Sfax; but Mr. Churchill's eyes were resolutely fixed on blocking the port of Tripoli, and very heavy pressure was applied on Admiral Cunningham to carry out that purpose. The War Cabinet and Admiralty were even prepared to sacrifice the battleship *Barham* as a blockship—a proposal which did not at all appeal to the Commander-in-Chief. This was undoubtedly a case where the authorities in London would have been better advised to state their strategic purpose, and leave the manner of execution to the man responsible for carrying it out. In a somewhat heated exchange of signals with London Cunningham refused to sacrifice the *Barham*, and gave his reasons for rejecting the blocking proposal. As an alternative he took his whole fleet to sea on 18th April, seized the chance to run a supply ship into Malta, and in the early hours of 21st he subjected the town and harbour works of Tripoli to a heavy bombardment. Although he achieved complete surprise, and the fleet suffered no loss or damage during its incursion into the enemy's waters, the results of the bombardment were—apart from moral effect—disappointing; for only one ship was sunk, and unloading was little delayed. The lesson was plain—that only by catching and sinking the supply ships at sea could we decisively curtail the flow of men and equipment to the Afrika Korps; and henceforth the struggle for control of the short sea routes from Italy to Africa was chiefly waged by the surface ships, submarines and aircraft based on Malta. But that strategic island was itself still in considerable peril, and the need to reinforce its fighter defences had again become urgent. On 2nd April the *Ark Royal* of Force H accordingly flew off twelve Hurricanes, which had been ferried out from England; and on 27th a bigger reinforcement, of 23 Hurricanes, successfully reached the island in the same manner. At the same time substantial reinforcements of warships, including the light cruiser *Dido* and six modern destroyers arrived at Malta from the west, with the object of increasing the pressure against the enemy's supply traffic to Tripoli. But the mounting damage caused by bombing, the frequent obstruction of the harbours by mines, and the need to concentrate as much strength as possible in the eastern basin to cope with the crisis which was all too plainly approaching in Greece, combined to frustrate our purpose; and all surface ships soon had to be withdrawn from Malta. The opposition which the island's defenders could as yet put up against the Luftwaffe was far too weak to allow the Navy to make full use of the base for offensive purposes; but after the withdrawal of the surface warships the few submarines and strike aircraft based on the island continued to work against the enemy's supply traffic; and it is certain that it was their efforts that prevented Rommel from fully exploiting the very favourable position which, by the middle of April, he had won in Cyrenaica. To mention only two of the submarines' successes the *Upright* sank the Italian cruiser *Armando Diaz* on 24th February, and the *Upholder* accounted for the 18,000-ton liner *Conte Rosso* on 24th May in a brilliant attack which gained for her Captain (Lieut-Commander M. D. Wanklyn) the Victoria Cross.

The German attack on Greece opened on 6th April, and that

night an ammunition ship caught fire during an air raid on Piræus, and blew up with such violence that ten other ships were destroyed and the port was put almost completely out of action. It would have been hard to devise a worse beginning to a campaign in which the scales were already heavily weighted in the enemy's favour. By the 16th it was plain that the troops so recently carried to Greece were in a hopeless position, and five days later the War Cabinet approved their withdrawal. As the port of Piraeus was still out of action the Navy could only use small harbours; and with the Luftwaffe in virtually undisputed control of the skies the ships had to embark the soldiers during the short hours of darkness and get clear of the coast before dawn. Admiral Cunningham threw in virtually the whole of his light forces, except those recently detached to Malta; and evacuation from eight different harbours started on the night of 24th-25th. Except at Kalamata, from which the ships sailed prematurely in the belief that German troops were in control of the town, so leaving large numbers of our men behind, the evacuations were remarkably successful. Nearly 51,000 men (about 80 per cent of those carried to Greece) were brought away safely; but the cost was heavy—especially among the lightly-armed transports, of which four were sunk by bombs. By 4th May the fleet had reassembled in Alexandria. But the portents for the future could hardly have been more ominous; for the enemy was now in full control of Greece and the Ægean islands, and the peril in which Crete and its weak garrison stood was all too plain.

The next task which fell to Admirals Somerville and Cunningham was, however, to pass straight through the Mediterranean a convoy of five fast merchantmen loaded with tanks and fighter aircraft, of which the Army of the Nile stood in urgent need. At the same time the battleship *Queen Elizabeth* and two light cruisers from home were to join Cunningham's fleet. The convoy passed Gibraltar on 6th May, and thereafter the operation followed the usual pattern, with Force H taking the merchantmen to a point south of Malta, where they were met by a strong force sent from Alexandria. One of the merchantmen struck a mine and blew up; but the other four got through safely with their precious cargo of 238 tanks and 43 Hurricanes. As soon as Somerville's ships got back to Gibraltar they were required to reinforce the fighter defences of Malta yet again, and on 21st May the *Ark Royal* and *Furious* flew another four dozen Hurricanes to the island. Though the defences were now in much better shape than six months previously, the casualty rate among the fighters was extremely high, and it was plain that more would have to be sent to the island before long. In May, however, the Germans transferred a large proportion of their bombers from Sicily to the east to prepare for the attack on Russia; and that brought welcome relief to Malta's hard-pressed garrison. The transfer of the Luftwaffe and the decision not to attempt the invasion of Malta underline the inability of Hitler and his advisers to hold to one objective up to the point of decision; for it seems true to say that in the early summer of 1941 the complete neutralisation of the island as an air and naval base, if not its actual capture, was within the enemy's grasp. Just as it was the gallant work of our fighter pilots and the steady pressure of our maritime power which thwarted Germany's invasion plans against England in the summer of 1940, so did the defenders of Malta and the many resolute actions fought by Cunningham's and Somerville's ships frustrate the enemy's purpose in the central Mediterranean a year later; but in the latter case the margin of success was probably even more narrow than in the former.

For Force H the improvement in the central basin brought no period of rest. We saw earlier how the *Bismarck* broke out into the Atlantic by the Denmark Strait on 23rd May, and late that same evening the Admiralty called Somerville's ships north from Gibraltar to cover the approaches to the French Biscay ports.[1] Rarely can the flexibility of maritime power have been more convincingly demonstrated than by the *Ark Royal's* accomplishment in flying Hurricanes to Malta from a position well inside the Mediterranean on 21st May and crippling the *Bismarck* with her torpedo-bombers 500 miles to the west of Brest six days later.

While the Home Fleet was harrying the great German battleship to her doom far out in the Atlantic storm clouds were again gathering over the eastern basin of the Mediterranean, where Admiral Cunningham had made all possible preparations to counter the expected invasion of Crete. Cruisers and destroyers were constantly on patrol to the north of the threatened island, while the heavy ships were at sea ready to give them their support. But the greatest handicap under which the fleet laboured was that, because the

[1] See p. 133.

enemy held virtually undisputed control of the air, it could not make much use of the fine harbour of Suda Bay on the north coast of Crete, but had instead to work from Alexandria, some 400 miles away. Moreover, while the warships were at sea they had only their own guns to rely on for defence against air attacks; and if a ship was damaged so far from any properly equipped base it was bound to be difficult to extricate her.

The German attack on Crete opened on 20th May with very heavy bombing, followed by the landing of airborne forces; and it was not long before the ill-equipped defenders were hard pressed. However, on the night of 21st-22nd Rear-Admiral I. G. Glennie, who had with him three cruisers and four destroyers, encountered a convoy of some 25 small craft crowded with German troops off the north coast of Crete. Many of the convoy were sunk, and none of the 2,300 German troops embarked in it reached their intended destination; but the losses suffered by the fleet next day largely off-set this encouraging start to the battle for Crete.

Early on 22nd May four cruisers and three destroyers under Rear-Admiral E. L. S. King, which were pursuing another enemy convoy to the north of Crete, were heavily attacked from the air, and withdrew to join Rear-Admiral H. B. Rawlings's heavy support squadron to the west of the island. During the withdrawal the cruisers *Naiad* and *Carlisle* were both hit by bombs and, just as King's ships met the support force, Rawlings's flagship the *Warspite* was also seriously damaged. Worse was soon to follow. Early in the afternoon the destroyer *Greyhound* was caught by the bombers unsupported and sunk off the north-west corner of Crete. Admiral King detached two of his destroyers to rescue her survivors, and then ordered the cruisers *Gloucester* and *Fiji* to support them. All these ships were heavily attacked during the rescue work; and while the cruisers were withdrawing towards Rawlings's squadron the *Gloucester* was hit and brought to a standstill badly on fire. The *Fiji* carried on, only to be sunk by a single bomber late in the evening—after she had survived about a score of concerted attacks and fired off all her A.A. ammunition. The destroyers returned after dark and rescued over 500 of the *Fiji*'s men; but of the *Gloucester*'s company the few who survived all fell into German hands.

Meanwhile the five destroyers which had recently arrived at Malta under Captain Lord Louis Mountbatten had been called east by Cunningham to take part in the struggle for Crete, and on the night of 22nd-23rd it was their turn to patrol the dangerous waters to the north of the island. Unfortunately a signalling error gave the Commander-in-Chief the impression that the heavy ships were running out of ammunition, and he therefore ordered them back to Alexandria. This deprived Mountbatten's destroyers of support during their withdrawal at dawn on 23rd, and the *Kelly* and *Kashmir* were quickly sunk by German bombers. Happily the flotilla commander and nearly 300 of the two ships' companies were picked up by the *Kipling*—although she herself was being heavily attacked at the time.

Meanwhile on land the garrison was faring badly, Suda Bay was being so heavily bombed that not even light craft could use it in safety, and it had become virtually impossible to run in further supplies and reinforcements. Plainly the hour of crisis could not be far off. Yet on the 24th the Chiefs of Staff, almost certainly acting as the mouthpiece of the Prime Minister, urged on Cunningham the need for a greater effort to prevent seaborne landings, and signalled that the risks of operating to the north of Crete "must be accepted." The message ended by stating that "only experience would show how long the situation could be maintained." To Admiral Cunningham, whose fleet had been striving to the utmost to carry out the War Cabinet's intentions with regards to Crete, and who had in the preceding three days lost two cruisers and four destroyers, and had many other ships damaged, this message seemed "singularly unhelpful." For the truth was plain—that his ships could not work off the north coast of Crete while entirely lacking air cover, and that he could not therefore guarantee to prevent seaborne landings; furthermore to continue the attempt might lead to his fleet suffering such losses as would cripple it—without securing any commensurate advantage.

By the afternoon of 27th May the situation on land had so far deteriorated that the War Cabinet decided to evacuate the island; and that meant that the already overstrained warship crews must carry on, regardless of the cost, in an attempt to rescue the garrison of some 32,000 soldiers. Very early on 29th Admiral Rawlings, who had taken three cruisers and six destroyers to Heraklion on the north-east coast of the island, left with about 4,000 men embarked. Unlucky delays, however, prevented his ships getting well clear of the coast before daylight, and the result was that two of the destroyers were sunk and two cruisers badly damaged. Casualties among the troops crowded on board were heavy, and the surviving ships struggled into Alexandria that evening almost out of both fuel and ammunition. Happily the ships sent to the tiny port of Sphakia on the south coast on three successive nights fared better, and large numbers of men were brought away safely. In all, some 18,000 soldiers were rescued from Crete; but about 12,000 had to be left behind, and the cost of the evacuation to the Navy had been very heavy. Two battleships, one aircraft carrier, six cruisers and seven destroyers suffered more or less severe damage; and three cruisers and six destroyers were sunk. In his despatch Admiral Cunningham wrote that his men "had started the evacuation already overtired . . . and it is perhaps even now not realised how nearly the breaking point was reached. But that these men struggled through is the measure of their achievement." British history is studded with disasters in which the bitterness of defeat is mitigated only by the endurance and self-sacrifice of the fighting men involved. Though there may be little of logic in the pride with which we look back on such episodes, they have undoubtedly helped to create some of our finest traditions; and the tradition that the Royal Navy will never abandon British soldiers to captivity, so long as any hope of rescue remains, is one of them. Off Greece and Crete in April and May, 1941, that tradition was worthily upheld.

Hardly had the battered survivors of the Mediterranean Fleet returned to Alexandria from Crete when yet another new commitment arose in the Middle East. To understand the background to events in Iraq, Iran and Syria at this critical period it is necessary to return briefly to the early days of April, when a *coup d'état*, in the planning of which Axis intrigue played a big part, was staged in Baghdad against the Regent and his government. Warships of Vice-Admiral G. S. Arbuthnot's East Indies squadron were hurried to Basra, to which port troops were also carried in two convoys from India. Hostilities against the forces of the usurper Rashid Ali started on 2nd May, and on 1st June the Regent re-entered his capital. Our control of the seas had enabled us to forestall a potentially dangerous threat to our oil supplies. But events in Iraq raised anxieties in London regarding the possibility of German infiltration into the French-mandated territory of Syria, which had

adhered to the Vichy régime, and through which ran the best overland route to the oilfields of Iraq. Though we now know that, after
the failure of Rashid Ali's revolt, the Germans decided that it would
be futile to continue with their plans to gain control of Syria, the
War Cabinet decision that the risk to our oil supplies had to be
eliminated was certainly reasonable. In the middle of May they
therefore ordered the Middle East Commanders to go into action
against the Vichy French forces in Syria. The land campaign, which
was mounted from Palestine and Trans-Jordan, opened on 8th
June; and light naval forces (three cruisers and eight destroyers)
were sent to support the Army's flank where it came down to the
sea, and to prevent interference by the French warships stationed
in Beirut. The clash with the Vichy-French was marked by
singularly bitter fighting on land and sea, and the intervention of
German bombers from Crete added to the difficulties of dealing
with the large and fast French destroyers. Several of our ships were
damaged in sea and air actions; but on 15th June the French flotilla
leader *Chevalier Paul* was sunk by naval torpedo-bombers from
Cyprus, and thereafter the campaign moved steadily in our favour.
On 11th July the Vichy-French High Commissioner accepted our
terms, and the potential danger to Iraq was thus dissipated. With
the elimination of the last vestiges of the Italian threat to our Red
Sea shipping routes by a surprise assault from the sea against Assab
in Eritrea on 11th June, the northern and southern bulwarks of our
Middle East position were thus strengthened almost simultaneously;
and the strategic gains of the Axis powers in Greece and Crete were
to some extent offset.

Hardly, however, had the warships of the East Indies command
completed their tasks of supporting our army in East Africa and
securing the Red Sea shipping routes when a new threat to the
sources of Britain's vital oil supplies arose, this time in Iran (Persia).
In midsummer our intelligence service had reported that German
"tourists" were arriving in the country in considerable numbers, and
apprehensions that a pro-Axis *coup d'état*, similar to that attempted
in Iraq in the previous April, were aroused in London. The War
Cabinet decided that it was essential to forestall such an attempt, and
ordered the Commander-in-Chief, East Indies, to seize the naval
base at Korramshar and the port of Bandur-Shahpur, where a
number of Axis merchantmen were sheltering, and also to secure

the great oil refinery at Abadan. Meanwhile, British land forces from Iraq would occupy the oilfield in northern Iran. A mixed force of British, Australian and Indian warships was quickly assembled, troops were again embarked in India, and on 25th August all the named objectives at the head of the Persian Gulf were seized. The Iranian Government resigned two days later, and a potentially dangerous extension of Axis influence was thus totally frustrated. Nor were many months to elapse before the value to Russia of our temporary occupation of Iran became apparent; for not only was her southern flank made more secure, but an alternative to the ice-bound Arctic ports was soon developed for the delivery of urgently needed war supplies. The events of mid-1941 in Syria, Iraq, East Africa, the Red Sea and Iran provide a striking example of the way in which a maritime power can, by the swift and judicious use of its forces, decisively influence events on land territories of vast extent. Indeed, Francis Bacon's famous aphorism, written early in the 17th century—" he that commands the sea is at great liberty, and may take as much or as little of the war as he will "[1]—receives renewed and powerful confirmation from those events of the mid-20th century.

Although the actions just described did much to improve our position in the Middle East, which in April–May, 1941, had appeared to be precarious, the commanders of all three British services in the theatre were still beset by many difficult and daunting problems; and high on the list of commitments which had to be met without delay was the further reinforcement of Malta's defences. On 15th June the carriers *Victorious* and *Ark Royal*, covered and escorted by Admiral Somerville's Force H, accordingly flew off to the island 47 Hurricanes, which had been ferried to Gibraltar from Britain by the much older *Furious*. All but four of the fighters arrived safely, and ten days later another 64 had reached Gibraltar from home. They too were flown to their destination at the end of June; and although some of the 142 fighters which thus reached Malta were later sent on to Egypt, the island's defences had been greatly strengthened. Meanwhile, our submarines, and especially the large minelayers, were carrying in cargoes of aviation fuel, ammunition and other urgently needed stores. The crisis which had loomed so

[1] Essay No. 29 "Of the true greatness of Kingdoms and estates 1612-1625 " (London, 1819 Ed. Vol, II, p. 329).

large in the early spring thus became less acute; but the danger to Malta had not by any means yet been permanently removed.

Second only to Malta as a source of anxiety was the besieged garrison of Tobruk, which had been left isolated by the Army of the Nile's retreat from Libya in the previous April, and was entirely dependent on supplies run in by sea. Though a wide variety of ships was employed, it was the destroyers which carried the main brunt of this hazardous work, and two of them generally ran the gauntlet of the German bombers on every suitable night. The siege of Tobruk lasted for 242 days (12th April–8th December, 1941), and during that long ordeal the Navy carried in 72 tanks, 92 guns, 34,000 tons of stores and 34,113 fresh troops. The garrison was thus successfully maintained in fighting trim, and was able to play its full part when the new land offensive (operation "Crusader") opened on 18th November; but the cost to the Navy was heavy, and no less than 25 warships and five merchantmen were sunk on the notoriously dangerous "Tobruk run."

As the heavy commitments of the naval forces in the eastern basin in June and July made it impossible to run another convoy to Malta from that direction, the Admiralty decided to send six supply ships and one troop transport, covered and escorted by Force H, which would be temporarily strengthened by ships detached from the Home Fleet, from the west. The convoy left the Clyde on 11th July and reached Gibraltar safely; but when the eastward movement (appropriately called operation "Substance") started on 21st the troopship ran aground and had to be left behind. As the R.A.F. maintenance crews for Malta were on board her this was a serious blow. By dawn on 23rd Admiral Somerville had concentrated all his forces to protect the convoy while it passed to the south of Sardinia, where the Italians had numerous air bases. The expected air attacks soon began, the cruiser *Manchester* was hit by a torpedo and had to be sent back to Gibraltar, and a destroyer was so badly crippled that our own ships had to sink her. The merchantmen, however, thanks largely to the work of the *Ark Royal's* fighter pilots, were unscathed. That evening, on reaching the Skerki channel off Bizerta, Somerville ordered his heavy ships to haul round to the west, and Rear-Admiral E. N. Syfret, who had three cruisers and ten destroyers under his orders, took charge of the convoy for the final stretch. Though air attacks continued, and another destroyer was disabled, the convoy reached Malta safely on 24th, and at once began discharging its precious cargoes into the island's hungry magazines and store houses. But the accident to the troop-ship had left the planned reinforcement of the defences incompletely fulfilled; and to set that right warships left Gibraltar on the last day of July with some 1,800 soldiers and airmen on board, and carried them safely to Malta. Thus were all the purposes of operation " Substance " accomplished with a success which exceeded the hopes of even the most sanguine. Moreover, during the eastward passage of the convoy seven empty merchantmen, which had been delayed in Malta since earlier supply operations, were sailed independently to the west; and they too all reached Gibraltar safely. The Italian reaction to the arrival of the " Substance " convoy was to launch attacks by aircraft, midget submarines and motor torpedo-boats against Malta's harbours on the night of 26th July; but the defenders were very alert, all attacks were frustrated and the whole of the enemy naval force was wiped out.

In September two more of the familiar air ferry operations took place, and 49 more Hurricanes flew successfully to Malta from the *Ark Royal*. At the same time steps were taken to strengthen the base's offensive capacity by flying in R.A.F. bombers and naval torpedo-bombers, which soon joined hands with the submarines of the newly-formed 10th Flotilla in a concerted onslaught on the Axis traffic to Africa. The small (630 ton) submarines of the U-class which now composed the Malta-based flotilla were far better suited for working in the shallow and restricted waters of the central basin than the large boats which had formed the earlier Mediterranean flotillas,[1] and they soon began to exact a heavy toll. An outstanding feat was the sinking of the Italian troop-carrying liners *Neptunia* and *Oceania* (both of some 19,500 tons) by Lieut.-Commander M. D. Wanklyn's famous *Upholder* on 18th September. At this time it was the sub-marines which inflicted by far the greatest proportion of the shipping losses suffered by the Axis powers in the Mediterranean; and between June and September, 1941, they accounted for 49 troop transports and supply ships totalling some 150,000 tons. These successes, which the German staff in Italy described as "catastrophic," led to strong demands that the Luftwaffe bombers should return to Sicily and renew the onslaught on Malta; but some months were

---

[1] See p. 115.

to elapse before that was done, and in the meanwhile the British authorities had good reason to be satisfied both over the rapidity with which we had recovered from the effects of the heavy losses suffered off Greece and Crete, and with the progress made towards depriving the Axis forces in Africa of the seaborne supplies which would decide the outcome of the land campaign.

In September the War Cabinet decided to reinforce Malta yet again, making full use of the experience gained in the successful July convoy operation. Strong reinforcements were therefore again sent out to Admiral Somerville from the Home Fleet, which always acted as our central strategic reserve of maritime strength; and on 24th he sailed from Gibraltar to escort and cover nine large merchantmen loaded with Malta's most urgent requirements. The operation was called " Halberd " and, as on the previous occasion, Admiral Cunningham staged a diversion in the eastern basin, and other elaborate precautions were taken to mislead the enemy regarding our intentions. None the less the convoy was heavily attacked from the air, and the main brunt of the defence again fell on the *Ark Royal's* experienced fighter pilots. On this occasion, moreover, the main Italian fleet put to sea as though intending to dispute the convoy's passage; but when Somerville sent ahead the battleships *Rodney* and *Prince of Wales* and prepared the *Ark Royal's* torpedo striking force, it had second thoughts and retired to the shelter of its harbours. On the evening of 27th, when the convoy reached the entrance to " the Narrows " between Sicily and Tunisia, Somerville returned to the west, while Rear-Admiral H. M. Burrough, with five cruisers and nine destroyers, took the convoy on to its destination. Though one transport was hit by a torpedo in a night attack, and finally had to be sunk, the other eight arrived safely. At noon on 28th September the cruisers of the escort entered the Grand Harbour with guards paraded and bands playing, as though returning from a peace-time exercise; while the islanders in their thousands lined the ancient battlements of their cities and gave the Royal Navy a tumultuous, heart-warming welcome. That evening Admiral Burrough's ships sailed again to the west, overtaking the three empty merchantmen which had already left Malta, and meeting the main body of Force H to the west of the " Narrows." Though Somerville's flagship, the *Nelson*, had been struck by an air torpedo all ships reached Gibraltar safely.

It thus came to pass that the three Malta convoys of 1941 (Operations " Excess " in January, " Substance " in July and " Halberd " in September) succeeded in passing in to or out from Malta a total of 39 large supply ships and transports; and we lost only one such ship in the process. But all three convoys had to be fought through against substantial opposition, especially from the air; and the cost to the Royal Navy was one cruiser (the *Southampton*) and one destroyer sunk, and a battleship, two cruisers and two destroyers damaged.

In the autumn, by which time the favourable trend of the fighting in the Mediterranean appeared to be gathering momentum, the Admiralty decided to increase the pressure against the Axis supply traffic to Africa by once again stationing a striking force of cruisers and destroyers in Malta. Captain W. G. Agnew was therefore ordered out from the Home Fleet with the light cruisers *Aurora* and *Penelope*, and at Gibraltar two of Somerville's destroyers joined him. The little squadron, which was known as Force K, arrived at Malta on 21st October, and in the early hours of 9th November made a brilliant night attack on a heavily-protected Italian convoy of seven merchant ships, all of which were sunk. Later in the same month Captain Agnew scored a second success by destroying two important supply ships bound for Africa with fuel. Next Force H left Gibraltar on another air ferry operation, in which the *Ark Royal* sent a squadron of naval torpedo-bombers to Malta; but the successful despatch of still more Hurricanes and Blenheim bombers in the following month by the same familiar means had a tragic sequel; for on 13th November U.81 torpedoed the *Ark Royal* amidships, and although she was only thirty miles from Gibraltar she sank before she could be towed in. The loss of this famous ship, which had endured so much and survived so many ordeals that she seemed to bear a charmed life, was a severe blow—the more so because recent damage to our few other fleet carriers made it impossible to replace her quickly.

But the setback to Force H led to no reduction of our offensive against the Axis supply traffic; and the next step was to reinforce the Malta striking force with two more cruisers and two more destroyers. On 1st December Captain Agnew's Force K scored a third success by sinking a loaded supply ship and a tanker bound for Africa; and that blow made the Germans realise that, if Rommel's army was to be saved, the Luftwaffe bombers must return from Russia to Sicily. Before, however, that measure could take effect the Italian Navy suffered yet another blow; for in the early hours of 13th December a force of three British and one Dutch destroyer under Captain G. H. Stokes encountered the light cruisers *Alberto di Giussano* and *Alberico di Barbiano* close inshore off Cape Bon, took them by surprise and sank them both. That action, however, was to mark the spring tide of British success for many months to come; for, in addition to ordering the bombers back to Sicily, the Germans had diverted a considerable proportion of their U-boat strength from the Atlantic to the Mediterranean with the object of succouring their shaky Ally and saving their army in Africa. The sinking of the *Ark Royal* by U.81 was the first fruit of that new policy; but it was not long before we were made to realise that a comparatively small number of Dönitz's boats, twenty-six of which passed successfully into the Mediterranean between September, 1941, and the end of the year, was a far more serious menace than the numerous Italian submarines with which we had so far contended very successfully.[1]

The next blow fell in the eastern Mediterranean. On 24th November Admiral Cunningham left Alexandria with his main fleet to support the Malta-based light forces, which were then searching for the Italian supply ships whose destruction by Force K has already been mentioned. Next afternoon the battleship *Barham* was struck by torpedoes fired by U.331, which had successfully penetrated through the destroyer screen, and blew up with very heavy loss of life. Then, during the night of 14th-15th December U.557 sank the cruiser *Galatea* off Alexandria; and five days later disaster of a different kind overtook the Malta-based striking force. Captain Agnew had gone to sea in the first place to meet the supply ship *Breconshire*, which Rear-Admiral P. L. Vian with a strong cruiser and destroyer force was escorting to Malta. On the evening of 17th December Vian's ships suddenly encountered a large part of the Italian fleet, including two battleships, off the Gulf of Sirte. They were actually covering a convoy of their own which was bound for Africa; but when Vian showed a bold front and moved out to attack, the Italians drew away without interfering with the

[1] Between June, 1940, and the end of 1941 38 Italian submarines had been destroyed or captured, all but ten of them in the Mediterranean or Red Sea.

British movement.[1] *The Breconshire* was successfully met and taken to Malta by Force K, which then left harbour immediately to pursue an enemy convoy which our aircraft had reported to be making for Tripoli. In the early hours of 19th December the squadron ran into a minefield which had recently been laid by Italian destroyers; the cruiser *Neptune* struck no less than four mines, and was lost with all her company except one man; Captain Agnew's *Aurora* was badly damaged but reached Malta safely, but the destroyer *Kandahar*, which was also mined had finally to be sunk by our own forces. In a few brief hours the short but brilliant career of Force K thus came to a tragic ending, and we were forced once again to rely on the submarines and strike aircraft to continue the campaign against the Axis supply traffic. The enemy at once seized the opportunity to run convoys through to ports in Tripolitania, and by the end of the year the state of his armies in Africa, which in mid-summer they had described as "precarious," had greatly improved. Thus did the loss of a comparatively small number of British warships cause a drastic swing of the pendulum in the struggle for control of the Mediterranean; and the change of fortune at sea transformed the prospects of the armies facing each other in North Africa. Nor did the misfortunes already recounted mark the end of British losses; for on the very day that Force K was crippled Italian underwater swimmers gallantly led by Prince Borghese penetrated into Alexandria while the boom defences were open to admit our own ships, and attached delay-action mines to the hulls of the battleships *Queen Elizabeth* and *Valiant*. Both were seriously damaged, and with the *Barham* sunk and his other two battleships out of action for a long time Cunningham was deprived of the battle squadron which had so long kept the far more powerful Italian fleet in a state of subdued inactivity.

In London this succession of disasters raised the most serious apprehensions; and the Admiralty again seriously considered whether we should withdraw our forces from the eastern basin, holding on only to the Suez Canal and Gibraltar.[2] The crisis was made all the more acute because, on 7th December Japan had suddenly attacked an unprepared United States and had destroyed a considerable proportion of their Pacific fleet, but fortunately not its aircraft carriers, in Pearl Harbour. But those tremendous events,

---

[1] This brief engagement is known as the First Battle of Sirte.   [2] See pp. 83-4.

if they brought to Britain the reassuring knowledge that a new ally of immense potential strength had at last joined hands with her, afforded her no immediate relief. Rather was the result to deepen the crisis which we faced; for it was plain that part of our naval strength would have to go to the East to defend the vast and rich territories for which we were responsible, and on which we depended for many important raw materials. Furthermore, our already overstrained Merchant Navy would have to carry large numbers of men and vast quantities of stores and equipment to the new theatre. Yet so heavy had been the losses suffered during 1941, especially in the Mediterranean, that there was in fact no possibility of quickly building up a balanced fleet to fight the new enemy. Never since 1796, when Bonaparte's sweeping successes on land forced the Royal Navy temporarily to evacuate the Mediterranean, had we been so hard pressed as in the closing weeks of 1941.

Looking back to-day it seems clear that 1941 was the last year when both the advantages of the moment and the prospects for the future were really favourable to the Axis powers. The reasons why the dictators were unable to exploit their advantage to the point of victory were, firstly, the stubborn British resistance on sea, land and in the air; secondly, the many defeats inflicted on Italy, which compelled the Germans either to reinforce their weaker partner or accept her collapse; and, thirdly, Hitler's blunder in attacking Russia what time he still had not subdued the resolute people of an island, supported by a Commonwealth of free nations overseas, who really understood the means and the methods whereby maritime power could withstand, and ultimately conquer, a vastly superior continental enemy.

CHAPTER IX

DISASTER IN THE EAST—AND RECOVERY

7th December, 1941–4th June, 1942

"... too late? Ah! two fatal words of this war! Too late in
moving here. Too late in arriving there. Too late in coming
to this decision. Too late in starting with enterprises. Too
late in preparing. In this war the footsteps of the Allied forces
have been dogged by the mocking spectre of 'Too late'!"

> Rt. Hon. David Lloyd George. From a
> speech in the House of Commons, 20th
> December, 1915.

BEFORE THE outbreak of war the Admiralty had made it plain
that, in the event of Japan joining forces with the European
Axis partners, it would not be possible to send a major fleet to the
East unless we left the Mediterranean entirely to the French Navy.[1]
Yet, as the storm clouds began to gather towards the end of 1941
we were required to produce a new fleet to oppose Japan—in spite
of French maritime power having been totally lost to us a year
earlier. Plans were actually prepared in August, 1941, to send six
capital ships, a modern carrier and appropriate light forces to
Singapore by the spring of 1942; but the losses and damage recently
suffered by the Home and Mediterranean fleets prevented any
substantial reinforcements being sent out until October, 1941, when
the new battleship *Prince of Wales* was designated as flagship of
Rear-Admiral (Acting-Admiral) Sir T. Phillips, lately Vice-Chief
of Naval Staff. But a clash of strategic purposes had meanwhile
arisen in London. Whereas the Admiralty wished to concentrate
all the strength they could muster in the Indian Ocean, where a fleet
would be centrally placed to cover a very important strategic area,
the Prime Minister wished to station a small force of fast and modern

[1] See p. 34.

ships at Singapore, where he considered that they would have a deterrent influence on the aggressive purposes of the Japanese. The Foreign Office supported the Prime Minister's view, and the First Sea Lord finally agreed that the *Prince of Wales* should go at once to Cape Town, and that her further destination would be reviewed after she had arrived there. But there is little doubt that both the Admiralty and Admiral Phillips expected her to go quickly on to Singapore, for on 21st October two days *before* she sailed from the Clyde, the Admiralty informed all authorities that the eastern base was her destination; and on 11th November they ordered the battle cruiser *Repulse* (an old and lightly-protected ship dating from the 1914-18 war) to meet the *Prince of Wales* in Ceylon, whence the two capital ships were to proceed in company to Singapore, where they arrived on 2nd December. Unfortunately the new carrier *Indomitable*, which was to have gone with Admiral Phillips, had been put out of action by running aground off Jamaica.

Whatever one may think, in the light of after-knowledge, of the reasoning that led to so unbalanced a force being sent to so exposed and remote a station, with no prospect of it being quickly reinforced, it was extraordinarily difficult for the War Cabinet to frame a sound strategy for the Far East in late 1941. In the first place the American, Dutch and British Commonwealth naval forces in the Pacific were scattered over a vast area, and no unified command system existed —even among those nations which were already at war. The United States were still ostensibly neutral and, for all that President Roosevelt's government had recently been giving Britain increasing assistance in the Atlantic, it would have been optimistic to assume that, if Japan attacked only the British Empire, America would declare war. Though Singapore was obviously the best and most centrally placed base for a concentration of Allied ships of all nations, the main American Pacific Fleet was at Pearl Harbour in the Hawaiian Islands, some 6,000 miles away; and there was only a comparatively weak U.S. Naval force known as the Asiatic Fleet (three cruisers, thirteen destroyers and twenty-nine submarines) based on the Philippines. The Dutch, who had rather less strength (three cruisers, seven destroyers and thirteen submarines) in the area, were mainly concerned with the defence of their own territories, and especially Java and Sumatra; while Australia and New Zealand, though both had lent a large proportion of their warships to work under British commanders in the European and African theatres, had reserved to themselves the right to decide the allocation of the ships remaining under their control. Lastly, before Admiral Phillips's arrival there were only three very old light cruisers, and a few smaller units of the Royal Navy at Hong Kong or in Malayan waters. Even if all this heterogeneous collection of ships of many nationalities could have been assembled at Singapore, and placed under unified command, much training would have been required to weld them into anything resembling an efficient fleet; and even if the American Asiatic Fleet had joined forces with the ships of the other nations the composite strength of the Allies would still have been far from adequate to fight the highly-trained and well-equipped squadrons of the Japanese Navy.

Early in December the Admiralty's anxiety over the exposed position of Admiral Phillips's force deepened, and they urged him to take the two capital ships away from Singapore. The *Repulse* accordingly sailed for Port Darwin in North Australia on 5th December; but when a Japanese convoy was reported off Indo-China next day she was recalled to Singapore to rejoin the flagship. On the 7th the Japanese suddenly struck—not only at the American Pacific Fleet in Pearl Harbour, but also at the Philippine Islands, Hong Kong, Siam and Malaya. The very situation which the Naval Staff in London had feared from the beginning thus at once arose, and the stage was set for high tragedy.

On the evening of 8th December Phillips left Singapore with the *Prince of Wales, Repulse* and four destroyers to attack the Japanese amphibious forces which had just made landings at Singora on the north-east coast of Malaya.[1] Before sailing he requested the R.A.F. to reconnoitre the seas to the north of his intended course, and to provide fighter cover over the scene of his intended attack; but early on 9th Singapore warned him that the fighter cover could not be provided, and also reported that strong Japanese bomber forces were believed to be assembling in Indo-China. This information, combined with the sighting of his force by enemy aircraft, caused Phillips to abandon his offensive purpose, and at 8.15 p.m. that same day he reversed course for Singapore. Then shortly before midnight Singapore signalled that an enemy landing had been reported at Kuantan, which lay much farther south than Singora, and was not

[1] See Map p. 178.

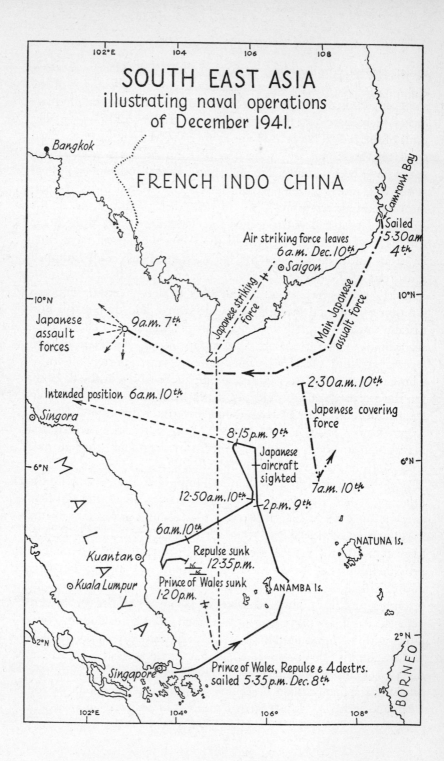

SOUTH EAST ASIA
illustrating naval operations of December 1941.

FRENCH INDO CHINA

Bangkok

Cam-ranh Bay

Sailed 5.30a.m. 4th

Air striking force leaves 6 a.m. Dec. 10th

Saigon

Japanese striking force

Main Japanese assault force

10°N

Japanese assault forces

9 a.m. 7th

2.30 a.m. 10th

Japenese covering force

Intended position 6 a.m. 10th

7 a.m. 10th

Singora

8.15 p.m. 9th

Japanese aircraft sighted

6°N

12.50 a.m. 10th

2 p.m. 9th

NATUNA Is.

6 a.m. 10th

M A L A Y A

Kuantan

Repulse sunk 12.35 p.m.

Kuala Lumpur

Prince of Wales sunk 1.20 p.m.

ANAMBA Is.

2°N

BORNEO

Singapore

Prince of Wales, Repulse & 4 destrs. sailed 5.35 p.m. Dec. 8th far off the British squadron's return course. At 1 a.m. on 10th Phillips turned to the west to close Kuantan; but he did not tell Singapore of his new intention, nor did he ask for fighters to be sent to meet him off the coast. His reluctance to break wireless silence is understandable; but it was perhaps too much to expect the authorities at the base to anticipate his reaction to the reported landing at Kuantan. In any case the report of the landing was false, and as no fighters were sent to meet him his ships were very dangerously placed to deal with a heavy air attack. In fact, the Japanese, acting on earlier sightings of Phillips's squadron by patrolling submarines, had sent 34 high-level and 51 torpedo-bombers from Saigon to attack it. They missed their quarry on the southward flight, but by ill-luck found it on the return journey. Determined and skilful attacks started soon after 11 a.m. on 10th, and the British flagship soon received two torpedo hits, which inflicted very serious damage on her propellers and steering gear, and put almost all her anti-aircraft guns out of action. At first the *Repulse*, by skilful manœuvring, avoided the torpedoes aimed at her; but before long the sheer numbers of the attackers over-whelmed her defences, she received four torpedo hits, and was plainly doomed. The *Prince of Wales* had meanwhile been hit twice more by torpedoes and was steaming slowly north with a heavy list. At 12.33 p.m. the *Repulse* rolled over and sank, and fifty minutes later the *Prince of Wales* capsized. The destroyers picked up 2,081 officers and men of the 2,921 on board the two ships; but neither Admiral Phillips nor Captain J. C. Leach of the *Prince of Wales* were among the survivors.

Thus, after only 48 hours of war, did the Japanese accomplish their purpose of crippling British and American maritime power in the western Pacific; and the virtually undisputed command of the sea which they thereby gained enabled them to strike almost at will against the vast and rich territories which were their next objectives. From the British point of view the sinking of the *Prince of Wales* and *Repulse* had immediate and disastrous effects; for the morale of the defenders of Malaya and Singapore was gravely shaken, and the fate of all our possessions in south-east Asia was plainly sealed. Rarely can a defeat at sea have had such far-reaching consequences.

In retrospect the strategy of sending out a weak and unbalanced force to an exposed position in a theatre which the enemy was threatening to command with very powerful forces is surely open to criticism; and we may regret that the Admiralty yielded to those who hoped that such a force would have a "deterrent" effect on Japan. As to the actual conduct of his last operation, Admiral Phillips's original purpose—to attack the landing force at Singora—was reasonable enough; for he could hardly stand by idle while Malaya and Singapore, whose defence provided the principal reason for his presence, were being seriously threatened. His realisation that the risks entailed in such a venture were too heavy may have been rather tardy; and it is of course impossible to say whether his squadron would have escaped had he not accepted the report of the Kuantan landing. The failure to keep his base informed of his change of intentions on the night of 9th-10th December is harder to explain; but even had he done so it is unlikely that the hard-pressed R.A.F. would have been able to protect his ships adequately. The Admiralty plainly foresaw the danger in which the British force stood early in December, when they urged Phillips to take his ships away from Singapore; and one may regret that they did not send an order to him rather than advice. It may be that the defence of the Singapore base, and the large quantities of fuel, stores and ammunition which we had assembled in it, exerted excessive influence in London. But the truth was that the base, on which so much time and money had been expended, was useless while we had no proper fleet to work from it.

After the loss of the *Prince of Wales* and *Repulse* Admiral Sir Geoffrey Layton resumed command of the Eastern Fleet, which post he had recently handed over to Admiral Phillips; but in fact there was nothing resembling a fleet for him to command, and the reinforcements for which he at once called simply did not exist. Only light naval forces remained in Malaya and Hong Kong, and although a new command, called ABDA was hastily set up early in January, 1942, with headquarters in Java, to co-ordinate American, British, Dutch and Australian resistance, the naval commander of the theatre (Admiral T. C. Hart, U.S.N.) had only a motley collection of cruisers, destroyers and submarines with which to meet vast responsibilities and oppose what was temporarily the most powerful navy in the world.

The first duty placed on the ABDA command was the reinforcement of Malaya and the Dutch East Indies, and that duty fell mainly on the surviving units of the Royal Navy and their Dutch comrades. Between 1st January and 8th February, 1942, 44 troop and supply ships in seven convoys were escorted to Singapore, and only in the last one, when a large liner was bombed and set on fire, was any ship lost. Some 45,000 fighting men were carried to Malaya during those five weeks; and in addition large numbers of fighter aircraft were brought out from the Middle East. Thus late in January the carrier *Indomitable* flew off fifty Hurricanes to airfields in Java. All these efforts were, however, of little avail; for the situation in Malaya deteriorated steadily, and one reason for the difficulties which beset the land forces was that, whereas the Japanese made excellent use of their sea power by making repeated small landings on the flanks and in the rear of the defenders, we possessed hardly any light warships with which to contest control of the coastal waters of the peninsula. The few remaining ships, most of which were ill-armed converted auxiliaries, did their best, and often accomplished feats of outstanding gallantry; but the scales were weighted far too heavily for them to be able to influence the outcome of the land campaign.

By the end of January Singapore was being so heavily bombed that the naval base could no longer function. Preparations were made to destroy the store and fuel depots; but much was actually left intact. On 9th February the Japanese gained a foothold on Singapore island, and the inward flow of British reinforcements was stopped. Three days later every possible vessel was sent away from the beleaguered base; but by that time Japanese warships had closed the escape route to the south, and many of the lightly armed craft were sunk or captured by them. Disintegration followed rapidly on the successive defeats suffered at sea and on land, and on 15th February Singapore surrendered. Of all the factors which contributed to that shattering disaster the complete collapse of our maritime power was undoubtedly the greatest. The consequence was not only the loss of vast and immensely rich territories, but a cataclysmic decline in the status of the European races throughout the whole of Asia; for the removal of some 130,000 British Empire fighting men and many thousands of white civilians into the most brutal form of captivity created an ineradicable impression of the decline of western power and prestige.

Long before the issue was decided in Malaya Japanese amphibious forces had begun to move south against the British and Dutch islands of the eastern archipelago; and, although Dutch submarines sank a few ships, little could be done to impede their progress. The most westerly arm of the three-pronged offensive mounted by the Japanese was aimed at the eastern end of Sumatra, while the centre and eastern arms were to strike at the key island of Java, with the object of seizing the great port of Batavia and the naval base of Soerabaya.[1] Between 9th and 11th February the expeditionary force destined for Sumatra sailed from Indo-China and, as soon as the purpose of this movement was recognised, the ABDA command organised a naval striking force of five cruisers (one British, one Australian and three Dutch), and ten destroyers (four Dutch and six American). This force concentrated off Batavia on 14th February, and then steered north to intercept the enemy invasion convoy; but on being heavily attacked from the air the Dutch Admiral Doorman, who was in command, withdrew. Two days later the Japanese landed on the eastern tip of Sumatra, thus isolating Java from the west. The focus of activity now moved to eastern Java, where the next threat was all too plainly developing. A number of inconclusive naval engagements were fought, and several of Doorman's ships were damaged; but Japanese plans and progress were impeded little, if at all. On 18th February they landed on the island of Bali, so cutting off Java from the east. Meanwhile, their main naval striking force, consisting of four fleet carriers, two battleships and many smaller warships had swept into the Timor Sea, and on 19th February some 150 bombers and torpedo-bombers made a heavy attack on shipping in Port Darwin—the only base in North Australia from which Java could be supplied and reinforced. The defences, which were in any case very weak, were caught by surprise; eleven transports and supply ships were sunk, and a great deal of damage was done to store dumps on shore. This devastating blow made it virtually certain that Java could not hold out for long; but a naval striking force was again assembled under Admiral Doorman, this time with the object of contesting the control of the approaches to the eastern end of the island. As had so often happened before in this theatre the naval forces (consisting of five British, American, Australian and Dutch cruisers, and ten destroyers of equally mixed nationalities) were ill-suited to meet their powerful

[1] See Map p. 178.

and well-trained adversaries; for they had done practically no tactical training together, and air co-operation and cover was almost completely lacking.

On 26th February, the very day that Admiral Doorman's squadron assembled, a large enemy invasion force was reported some 200 miles to the north-east of Soerabaya. Doorman at once went to sea, but when no enemies had been sighted by the following afternoon he returned to refuel his destroyers. Just as he was entering harbour two Japanese convoys were reported only 80 miles away, and he therefore reversed course. At 4 p.m. on 27th the Battle of the Java Sea began; but the first phase of the gun action with the four Japanese cruisers and 14 destroyers which were escorting their invasion force took place at such long range that only the 8-inch cruisers *Exeter* (R.N.) and *Houston* (U.S.N.) could engage, while the smaller cruisers were no more than spectators. Then an 8-inch shell struck the *Exeter*, and reduced her speed so drastically that the Allied line fell into confusion; and at that moment a Japanese torpedo struck and sank one of the Dutch destroyers. Doorman next ordered the three British destroyers to counter-attack, while the damaged *Exeter* steered for Soerabaya; but so weak a striking force could do little against such heavy odds, and the attempt ended in the *Electra* (R.N.) being sunk. Night having now fallen Doorman took his surviving ships south towards the Java coast, while his four American destroyers, which had expended all their torpedoes, returned to Soerabaya to refuel. Shortly afterwards he suffered another blow, for the destroyer *Jupiter* (R.N.) suddenly blew up—probably on a Dutch mine. None the less, the Admiral, now left only with the American cruiser *Houston*, which had been damaged in the first engagement, his two Dutch light cruisers (*De Ruyter* and *Java*), the *Perth* (R.A.N.) and one British destroyer (the *Encounter*), returned northwards; and at about 10 p.m. the action was renewed. Twenty minutes later the *Java* and *de Ruyter* were both hit by torpedoes and blew up. The *Houston* and *Perth* then made for Batavia, to try and escape out of the trap which had closed on them in the Java Sea by way of the Sunda Strait.[1] There, late on the evening of 28th February, they encountered vastly superior Japanese forces and were overwhelmed after a most gallant fight. Four of the five American destroyers had meanwhile sailed from

[1] See Map p. 178.

Soerabaya and made their way out of the Java Sea by way of the Bali Strait; but the damaged *Exeter* could not follow by the same shallow water route. She, the *Encounter* and the American destroyer *Pope* therefore left harbour at dusk on 28th to try and reach the Sunda Strait. Next morning they were caught by powerful enemy forces, and all three ships were sunk. The Battle of the Java Sea thus ended in the virtual annihilation of the Allied striking force, and the Japanese were able to proceed with their invasion plans unhindered. They next swept the waters south of Java to catch the ships which were trying to make their way south towards Australia. By the beginning of March, 1942, there remained nothing of Allied maritime power in south-east Asia except the memory of the way in which the *Exeter, Perth, Houston* and their smaller consorts had fought to the finish against hopeless odds.

Meanwhile, far away to the south, the surviving warships of the Australian and New Zealand Navies had been formed into an Anzac Squadron; but they were mainly employed in reinforcing the key islands of Fiji, the New Hebrides and New Caledonia, which lay athwart the route by which American troops and supplies were being sent to Australia.[1] Otherwise the White Ensign had disappeared from the entire South Pacific.

There now followed a short lull at sea while the Japanese consolidated their vast conquests and shaped their plans for further aggrandisement; but the invasion of Burma had meanwhile begun, and on 8th March the great port of Rangoon fell into their hands. One day later Java surrendered, and the disintegration of the ABDA command was complete. Such were the bitter consequences of the succession of defeats suffered at sea between 10th December, 1941, and 27th February, 1942; and if ever students of the future should seek an example of the costliness of failure by a maritime power to provide the instruments needed to safeguard the territories overseas for which she was responsible, and to protect the shipping on which their safety and prosperity depended, they cannot find a better example than the events here briefly described.

By the beginning of March, 1942, we realised that it was in the Indian Ocean that our maritime power would have to be reconstructed, with Ceylon as the main base—the policy which the Admiralty had originally wished to adopt;[2] and, secondly, that

[1] See Map p. 185.   [2] See pp. 175-6.

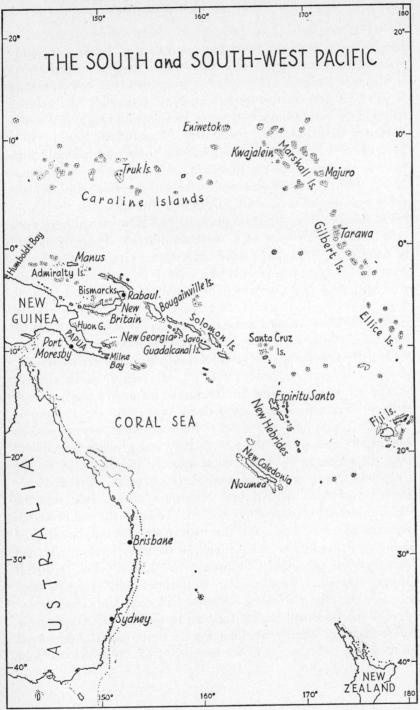

THE SOUTH and SOUTH-WEST PACIFIC

Eniwetok

Kwajalein

Marshall Is.

Majuro

Truk Is.

Caroline Islands

Tarawa

Gilbert Is.

Humboldt Bay

Manus

Admiralty Is.

NEW
GUINEA

Bismarcks

Rabaul

*New
Britain*

Bougainville Is.

Huon G.

Solomon Is.

Ellice Is.

PAPUA

New Georgia

Savo

Guadalcanal Is.

*Santa Cruz
Is.*

*Port
Moresby*

*Milne
Bay*

CORAL SEA

Espiritu Santo

New Hebrides

Fiji Is.

A U S T R A L I A

New Caledonia

Noumea

Brisbane

Sydney

NEW
ZEALAND

Australia would have to provide the rearward bases needed to prepare for a counter-blow in the South Pacific. But it was plainly essential to secure temporary bases much farther forward than Brisbane or Sydney, and it was for this reason that strenuous steps were taken to prepare Nouméa in New Caledonia and Espirito Santo in the New Hebrides—quite undeveloped though they were.[1] Not until we could base a reconstituted fleet (which would plainly have to be almost entirely American) on those islands would it be possible to oppose a new southward movement by the Japanese Navy; and the same fleet would safeguard the vital reinforcement route from the west coast of America to Australia.

But before those strategic purposes had been carried very far a new crisis suddenly blew up in the Indian Ocean. There by the end of March the Admiralty had managed to scrape together a new Eastern Fleet consisting of two large aircraft carriers and a small one, five battleships (four of which belonged to the old and slow R Class), seven cruisers, sixteen destroyers, and seven submarines. Its commander was Admiral Sir James Somerville, who had made his reputation while in command of Force H working from Gibraltar. Although on paper the strength allocated to him appeared substantial, in reality he was very unenviably placed. Firstly, his air element was far too weak to enable him to oppose the main Japanese carrier striking force. Secondly, many of his ships were old and not in first-class condition; and thirdly, his bases were ill-equipped to supply his needs. Thus there were very real grounds for anxiety over the outcome of an incursion into the Indian Ocean by the splendidly trained and so far consistently successful Japanese carrier force commanded by Admiral Nagumo; and Ceylon was the obvious place for him to strike at next. Towards the end of March we received strong indications that such an attack was to be expected in the very near future, and Admiral Sir Geoffrey Layton, who had recently been appointed Commander-in-Chief, Ceylon, with full powers over all civil and military authorities, took energetic steps to meet the expected blow. Because Colombo and Trincomalee were ill defended and too far forward to provide security, Somerville's fleet was actually working from a secret base at Addu Atoll in the Maldive Islands.[2] On the last day of March he moved from

[1] See Map p. 185.   [2] See Map p. 153.

there to concentrate his forces to the south of Ceylon, while reconnaissance aircraft searched the waters to the east through which the
enemy was almost certain to approach. By 2nd April, however,
no sign of Japanese movements had reached Somerville; and he
therefore decided to allow normal shipping movements to be
resumed, and himself returned to Addu Atoll to refuel. Just when
he was approaching the base the first sighting report, of strong
Japanese forces some 360 miles south-east of Ceylon, reached him.
In fact, Admiral Nagumo, with five fleet carriers (having some 300
aircraft embarked), four battleships and three cruisers had sailed
from a base in the Celebes on 26th March, passed south of Sumatra
and entered the Indian Ocean on 3rd April, what time a smaller
force under Admiral Ozawa (one light carrier and six cruisers) was
moving across the Bay of Bengal from Mergui in southern Burma,
with the object of attacking our shipping off the east coast of India.
It was Nagumo's main force which was sighted on the afternoon of
4th April, and that report caused Admiral Layton to clear every
possible ship out of the harbour of Colombo. He also sent the heavy
cruisers *Dorsetshire* and *Cornwall*, which Somerville had detached
from his main fleet on 2nd, back to rejoin the Commander-in-Chief.

At 8 a.m. on 5th April (Easter Sunday) the expected attack on
Colombo took place; but the defences were fully alert, and Admiral
Layton's timely precautions resulted in the damage to shipping and
port installations being comparatively light. The raid had nothing
like the deadly effects of that on Port Darwin in the previous
February;[1] and although Japanese aircraft losses were far fewer than
we believed at the time, they were high enough to constitute a
check to Nagumo's heretofore uniformly successful carrier aircrews.
Unfortunately the good work done by the defenders of Colombo
was partly offset that same afternoon, when the Japanese striking
forces located the *Dorsetshire* and *Cornwall* on their way south to
rejoin the fleet, and sank them both with a series of devastatingly
accurate dive-bombing attacks. Meanwhile, Somerville was steaming towards Ceylon from Addu Atoll; but his slow division was
still far behind his faster ships. The C.-in-C. next anticipated an
attack on his secret base; for Admiral Layton had signalled to him
that a powerful enemy force was believed to be between Ceylon
and the Maldives. Throughout the fifth reconnaissance aircraft from
the carriers flew wide searches; but they failed to sight Nagumo—

[1] See p. 182.

who had in fact withdrawn far to the south-east—and in the evening Somerville turned back to the north-west to safeguard his base. Meanwhile, Nagumo's aircraft were combing the waters to the south and east of Ceylon for the British Fleet, and we may be thankful that they never found it; for had they done so it is difficult to believe that Somerville's weak and motley force could have survived attack by the Japanese carrier planes. On the 8th one of our shore-based reconnaissance aircraft resighted Nagumo's ships 400 miles to the east of Ceylon, towards which they were again steering. The harbour of Trincomalee was at once cleared of shipping, and the expected attack took place early next morning. Unfortunately some of the ships sent out from Trincomalee were found by the Japanese striking forces close to the coast, after they had reversed course to re-enter the harbour. The small carrier *Hermes*, a destroyer, a corvette and two tankers were at once completely overwhelmed and sunk.

Admiral Ozawa's force had meanwhile entered the Bay of Bengal; and from the 4th to 7th April he played havoc among the unescorted and unprotected merchantmen which had been sent south from Calcutta and other ports to avoid the danger of attack while they were lying helpless in harbour. The original order to clear Calcutta of shipping was probably wise; but for some unexplained reason it was kept in force until the 6th—by which time it should have been plain that the ships would be safer where they were lying. In five days twenty-three merchantmen totalling over 112,000 tons were sunk by Ozawa's squadron off the east coast of India; and to that heavy toll Japanese submarines working off the west coast added a further five ships of 32,400 tons. British shipping movements along both coasts of the whole sub-continent were brought to a standstill; and the confidence of the men of the Merchant Navy in the protection which they had always relied on receiving from their comrades of the Royal Navy was severely shaken.

Happily the Japanese had not planned to make an extended foray in the Indian Ocean, nor to penetrate west of Ceylon. By 12th April both Nagumo and Ozawa were returning to Singapore by way of the Malacca Straits, while the Admiralty had suggested to Somerville that his slower ships should withdraw to East Africa to guard the long and vulnerable WS convoy route. Comparative calm thus descended on the Indian Ocean, and we were afforded a breathing space in which to improve the defences of our bases and the protection of our shipping; and, very gradually, reinforcements sent out from home reached Admiral Somerville. None the less, the shock sustained by the blows struck by Nagumo and Ozawa had been very severe; for the vulnerability of our maritime control over a vast and important area of ocean had been ruthlessly exposed. Looking back to-day it is plain that the disasters of April 1942, derived partly from the error we had committed in the previous autumn when, under strong pressure from the Prime Minister, the Admiralty had reluctantly agreed to Admiral Phillips's weak and unbalanced force being sent to Singapore.[1] Though it is, of course, impossible to say what proportion of the heavy losses which we suffered between December, 1941, and April, 1942, might have been averted had we adopted the Admiralty's strategic purpose of concentrating every ship that could be spared in Ceylon, it is none the less clear that the Naval Staff's views on strategy were much the sounder; for at the very least their policy would probably have resulted in Phillips's squadron surviving to play a part in the defence of the Indian Ocean. That could not, of course, have saved Malaya or the Dutch East Indies; but it might well have discouraged the Japanese from sending Nagumo and Ozawa into those waters, it might have saved Rangoon, and it would surely have reduced the time needed for us to regain the initiative at sea.

While these grievous trials were being undergone in the Indian Ocean the Allied position in the South Pacific was being slowly strengthened by the reinforcement of the Fiji group, New Caledonia and the New Hebrides, and by the preparation of new advanced bases in those islands. Then, on 20th April, a Japanese expedition sailed from the Caroline Islands with the object of seizing Port Moresby on the south coast of New Guinea, so gaining control of the northern approaches to Australia.[2] Allied Intelligence had, however, indicated what was in the wind, and the Americans sent out two powerful task forces formed around the carriers *Lexington* and *Yorktown*. Between the 7th and 9th May there took place in the Coral Sea the first of the long series of carrier air battles in which

[1] See pp. 175-6.   [2] See Map p. 185.

the contestants never sighted each other from the decks of their ships. The Japanese lost the light carrier *Shoho*, and the much larger *Shokaku* was severely damaged; but both the American carriers were hit, and the *Lexington* suffered so seriously that she had to be abandoned and sunk. Though the Battle of the Coral Sea was a drawn fight, the Japanese undoubtedly then suffered a check; for the invasion force intended for Port Moresby turned back.

Meanwhile, in London Ozawa's foray had raised grave apprehensions regarding the vulnerability of the vital troop and supply convoys sailing from the Cape of Good Hope to Egypt, on which our tenuous hold in the Middle East entirely depended; for we had only weak naval and air forces in South and East Africa, and there was no naval base between Simonstown and Kilindini (Mombasa). To strengthen the protection of the convoys against attack on their long and exposed flank the Cabinet decided to seize the key points in the French-owned island of Madagascar, where there was an excellent harbour at Diego Suarez which we had so far been unable to use because the island's government had adhered to the Vichy régime.[1] The assault force and its equipment and supplies left England in March for Durban—a distance of some 8,000 miles; while most of the supporting warships were supplied by Force H from Gibraltar. Rear-Admiral E. N. Syfret, who had taken over Force H on Admiral Somerville's transfer to the Eastern Fleet, was appointed "Combined Commander" of the expedition; for we had not forgotten the disastrous effects of a divided and indeterminate command organisation in the Dakar expedition of September, 1940.[2] Towards the end of April most of the warships allotted by the Admiralty—and some came from home waters and the Eastern Fleet as well as from Force H—had concentrated at Durban; but not until 1st May, by which time the expedition was approaching its objective, did the Cabinet give its final approval to the attack. The plan was to assault Diego Suarez by landing at its back door on the west coast of the island, thus taking the main defences in the rear; and in the very early hours of 5th May, after minesweepers had cleared the approaches and aircraft from the *Indomitable* and *Illustrious* had neutralised the French airfields and subdued the warships in the main harbour, the assault troops were successfully put ashore. The French resisted stubbornly on the narrow neck of

[1] See Map p. 153.   [2] See pp. 107-10.

land which separates Diego Suarez from the bays on the west coast where we landed; but a detachment of Marines who were carried round by destroyer penetrated into the harbour by the main entrance at night, and took the defenders by surprise. Resistance thereupon collapsed, and on the evening of 7th May, only sixty hours after the first landings, Admiral Syfret was able to lead the main body of his fleet safely into the strongly fortified harbour. The success of the expedition was the more welcome because it showed how far we had come towards achieving a satisfactory command organisation for combined operations. Careful planning, the deployment of well-trained troops, and the close co-ordination achieved between the land, sea and air forces not only contributed to the success but set a standard for the future; for by this time we fully realised that the use of our maritime power to land armies on hostile coasts must play a decisive part in the offensive campaigns which we hoped one day to open. Furthermore, the experiences of the Madagascar expedition emphasised the ability of carriers to supply the air element in combined operations; and although it was the U.S. Navy rather than the Royal Navy that was to develop that art to its final and decisive form, we ourselves exploited it later in the Mediterranean and Pacific.

At the time when the British assault forces were approaching Madagascar, far away to the east the Japanese were planning an expedition to seize Midway Island in the Hawaian group; and between 24th and 27th May their Combined Fleet and a great concourse of transports and supply vessels began to move eastwards from their home bases. Once again American Intelligence had given forewarning of the movement, and Admiral Nimitz, C.-in-C. of the Pacific Fleet, thus had plenty of time in which to prepare to meet the threat. The Japanese were, however, substantially superior in every department, and the spearhead of their offensive again consisted of Admiral Nagumo's fleet carriers, *Kaga*, *Akagi*, *Soryu* and *Hiryu*, in which some 270 aircraft were embarked. Against them Nimitz could only dispose the *Enterprise*, *Hornet* and *Yorktown*, with a total aircraft complement of 233. The first contacts took place early on 4th June, and by the end of that day the American carrier-borne dive-bombers had sunk all four of Nagumo's ships. Though the *Yorktown* was damaged by Japanese aircraft and sank on 7th after being torpedoed by a submarine, the Battle of Midway will always stand among the decisive victories of the world. From the British point of view it meant that there was no longer any fear of a repetition of the foray of the previous April into the Indian Ocean, but in terms of strategy its effects were yet more far-reaching; for the battle marked the beginning of the end of the period of Japanese maritime ascendancy. For almost exactly six months they had carried all before them; but after the dramatic encounter off Midway Island the Allies no longer needed to stand on the defensive. We could henceforth look forward to the day when, by making full use of our reviving maritime power, we could strike at the perimeter of the vast conquests which the ruthless efficiency of the Japanese had gained them at such trifling cost. Such are the great issues which can hang on a clash at sea lasting only a few hours of a midsummer's day.

CHAPTER X

THE SPRING TIDE OF AXIS SUCCESS

1st January–31st July, 1942

" By the mastery of the sea . . . by her persistent enmity to the
spirit of aggression . . . by her own sustained and unshaken
strength she [England] drove the enemy into the battlefield of
the Continental System, where his final ruin was certain."

A. T. Mahan, *The Influence of Sea Power on
the French Revolution and Empire*, Vol. II,
pp. 400-1.

WHILE Admiral Phillips's squadron and the other Allied forces in
south-east Asia were being overtaken by the succession of
disasters described in the last chapter, and Admiral Somerville's
Eastern Fleet was narrowly escaping a similar fate in the Indian
Ocean, the Royal Navy was undergoing a whole series of other
testing ordeals in the Atlantic, Arctic and Mediterranean. It might
be thought that the entry of the United States into the war brought
some immediate easement to the British maritime forces in those
theatres; yet that was far from being the case, and, in fact, there was
initially a sharp decline in American assistance in the Atlantic battle.
This arose partly because the United States Navy at once needed its
best ships in the Pacific; and partly because Dönitz quickly seized
the opportunity which American unpreparedness offered, and sent
his U-boats to work off that country's eastern seaboard, where
shipping was still sailing in peacetime fashion, and no warlike
precautions of any kind had been instituted. The number of U-boats
involved in what the Germans called operation " Roll on the drums"
was small—never more than a dozen; but because all merchantmen
were sailing independently they were able to reap a rich harvest at
very slight cost to themselves. In January and February, 1942,
the U-boats sank 44 ships in the Canadian coastal area, and in

March, when they moved farther south, 43 were sunk off the east coast of the United States and in the Caribbean; and what made those losses the more serious was that a high proportion of the sunken ships were tankers—of which we were already woefully short.

In the British Admiralty the holocaust achieved by the U-boats between January and April, 1942, the "second happy time" as the submarine captains called it,[1] aroused the gravest anxiety; for many of the sunken ships were British, but they were lost in waters where the Admiralty's writ did not run. Furthermore, we felt very strongly that such losses could be avoided—if only the Americans would institute convoy, and would employ even the slender naval and air forces available to them on escort duty instead of on patrols and hunting. Ever since a strong American mission had arrived in London in July, 1940, we had been giving the United States Navy the whole of our hardly-won war experience and the particulars of virtually all our latest technical developments; and outstanding among the former was the lesson that to convoy merchant ships, even if the escort was weak, not only gave by far the best protection but was much more likely to produce successful encounters with the U-boats than patrols or hunts. It was thus natural that the Naval Staff should have been astonished to hear about the procession of unescorted merchantmen which was proceeding up and down a well-known and narrow offshore route, still showing lights and still using their wireless freely; for they knew that such practices played straight into the enemy's hands. Pressure was brought to bear in many directions; but it was not until May that convoy was widely introduced on the American east coast routes; and two more months were to elapse before the same strategy began to be effectively applied in the Caribbean and Gulf of Mexico. The effects in each case were startling; for as soon as the U-boats encountered escorted merchantmen their successes at once dwindled, they themselves suffered losses, and they soon began to move elsewhere in search of easier targets. Thus in June and July it was only in the Caribbean and Gulf of Mexico that the U-boats, whose range had been greatly extended by the arrival of supply submarines, scored considerable

---

[1] The first "happy time" had been in the North-West Approaches to the British Isles between July and October, 1940, when easy targets were found among the considerable number of ships still sailing independently. See pp. 90-3.

successes; and after August, when the American "interlocking convoy system" became really effective, their achievements in those waters also declined sharply. At the height of the onslaught against shipping in the western hemisphere we lent two dozen anti-submarine trawlers to the Americans, we released two of our mid-ocean Atlantic groups to strengthen the escorts on the American eastern seaboard, we offered to turn over ten corvettes to the United States Navy, and we transferred an experienced squadron of Coastal Command aircraft to the west side of the Atlantic. It was difficult for us to do more, because Dönitz was far too shrewd a strategist to leave the transatlantic convoys alone at this time, and so allow us to effect a wide redisposition of our escort forces. Instead in May he sent a group to renew the "wolf-pack" attacks in the North Atlantic, and another group to work off Gibraltar; and in both cases they achieved some successes in convoy battles. In July, by which time the campaign in American waters was subsiding, the pack attacks were renewed with greater intensity, and the Atlantic battle assumed the familiar pattern once again.

The Germans had every reason to be satisfied with the results accomplished by the U-boats during the first six months of 1942; for in all waters they sank 585 merchantmen totalling over three million tons. Moreover, whereas they had commissioned over 100 new U-boats in that period, their losses had amounted to only 21; and no more than six had been sunk in the whole western Atlantic. To the Admiralty it was obvious that if such an unfavourable "exchange rate" continued we would be brought face to face with disaster within a comparatively short time.

Confronted with such a critical situation it was natural for the Admiralty to look in the one direction from which it seemed that some easement might accrue reasonably quickly, and that was by strengthening Coastal Command of the R.A.F. at the expense of bombing Germany. The Naval Staff accordingly represented that whereas the bombing offensive had so far not accomplished any very significant results—an opinion which we now know to have been well founded—we should lose the war if losses of merchant shipping continued on the scale of the early months of 1942. The best, and indeed the only way of restoring the situation was, they said, "by largely increasing the strength of our land-based air forces working over the sea"; and the Admiralty called for the Royal Air

Force to take "a permanent and increased share in the control of sea communications." To reduce the weight of the bombing offensive did not, however, hold any appeal to the Air Ministry; and the matter was referred to the Cabinet. After prolonged discussion the Prime Minister took action to achieve a slight shift of emphasis in our air effort; and the compromise arrived at provided for the gradual strengthening of Coastal Command without, so far as was possible, causing any decline in the bombing of Germany. Though the decision was no doubt a difficult one it did have the result that another year was to elapse, and further enormous losses of ships and cargoes were to be suffered, before Coastal Command's long-range aircraft began to play a decisive part in the struggle.

Perhaps the most favourable augury for the future in the Atlantic battle developed from the Anglo-American staff discussions which took place early in 1942, while the U-boat campaign in the western Atlantic was at its height. Up to this time the entire responsibility for the theatre, and for the control of all shipping moving across its waters, had rested on the Admiralty; but the entry of the United States into the war had plainly produced the need for the two maritime nations to share the burden. The outcome of the discussions was that in July the Atlantic was divided into British and American "strategic areas"—the line of demarcation following generally the meridian of 26° West; and a "Change of Operational Control" (or "Chop") Line was also established. At first it corresponded to the line dividing the two strategic areas, but in November, 1942, it was shifted to 47° West. Shipping to the east of the line was still controlled by the Admiralty, but to the west of it the U.S. Navy Department in Washington accepted responsibility for all movements. Control of each convoy or independently-routed ship was switched to and fro between the two operational centres as they crossed the Chop Line; and thus was born the full partnership in the Atlantic which was to last until the end of the war.

We must now take leave of the Atlantic and review events which took place in our home waters and the Arctic during the first six months of 1942. At the beginning of the year Admiral Sir John Tovey, the Commander-in-Chief, Home Fleet, had two main anxieties. The first concerned the German Brest squadron—the *Scharnhorst*, *Gneisenau* and *Prinz Eugen*—which we believed to have repaired the damage received in earlier air raids and to be nearly ready for sea;[1] and the second arose through the Germans moving the new and very powerful battleship *Tirpitz* to Trondheim in mid-January. While it seemed that the Brest squadron might at any time break out again to attack our Atlantic shipping, the concentration in Norway presented a serious threat to the convoys running to and from North Russia. In fact, however, the Germans were planning to bring the warships from Brest back to their home bases, and the movements to Trondheim had been ordered by Hitler because of his "intuition" that we intended to invade that country; but those plans and purposes were of course shrouded from British eyes. The Admiralty pressed for air attacks to be made on the German warships in Brest and Norway; but the bombers failed to inflict any damage, and by the beginning of February there were plentiful signs that both squadrons were likely to put to sea in the near future. None the less, the Arctic convoys ran smoothly for the first two months of the year; and in the five convoys which set out for North Russia between 1st January and the middle of February (PQ 7-11) 41 loaded merchantmen arrived safely and only one was sunk. By the latter date the nights were shortening rapidly, and the loss of the friendly shield of darkness, taken with the appearance off Kola Inlet of a number of U-boats and the activity of the warships in Trondheim, made it seem virtually certain that the lull in the Arctic was about to come to an end. It was, however, the Brest squadron and not the Trondheim ships which were the first to move. On 2nd February the Admiralty distributed to all authorities a study of the various alternatives open to those enemies, in which they concluded that the most probable was a dash up-Channel to their home bases. The main onus of dealing with such an attempt would not fall on the Home Fleet, but on the naval commands at Plymouth, Portsmouth and Dover—and especially on the last named, since interception could most easily be effected in the narrows of the Straits of Dover; but Coastal Command of the R.A.F., whose No. 19 Group was responsible for reconnaissance in the south-western approaches to the Channel, was also very intimately concerned. The Admiralty next ordered certain precautionary dispositions of destroyers, submarines, minelayers, motor torpedo-boats and torpedo-bombers. But the forces available were very slender, for we could not strip

[1]See p. 124.

the Home Fleet of its none too adequate strength in destroyers and strike aircraft, when they might at any moment be needed to deal with the Trondheim squadron; and almost all our modern submarines had already been sent to the Mediterranean. The effectiveness of our counter-measures was further reduced by the unwillingness of the Admiralty to risk sending heavy warships into the Channel, where they would be very exposed to air attacks, and by the fact that while Bomber Command's aircrews were not trained to deal with fast and fleeting naval targets, Coastal Command's striking force consisted of no more than some two dozen torpedo-bombers. Moreover, when one of its squadrons was ordered south from Scotland on 11th there was confusion and delay in bringing together the aircraft and their torpedoes. Thus the plan to meet the eventuality foreseen by the Admiralty was much vitiated by the weakness of the forces available, and by the lack of any single authority able to control the efforts of such ships and aircraft as could be provided. Early in February, however, the fast minelayers *Welshman* and *Manxman* did lay about 1,000 mines off the French coast between Ushant and Boulogne, while Bomber Command's minelaying aircraft placed 100 more between Terschelling and the mouth of the Elbe.

As soon as the precautionary orders were issued Coastal Command began to fly reconnaissance patrols off Brest and along the French coast to the east as far as Boulogne; but on the night of 11th-12th February the patrol off Brest returned to base early because of a radar failure.[1] The next aircraft to the east also had a radar failure and returned; but in this case no relief aircraft was sent out, nor was the fact that the stretch of coast was not being watched reported to the Admiralty or to Dover. This was the more unfortunate because Vice-Admiral Ciliax actually left Brest with his heavy ships, escorted by six destroyers and numerous smaller warships, at 10.45 p.m. on 11th February, and should certainly have been detected by the middle of our three air patrols—had it been on station. It thus came to pass that it was late in the following forenoon, when Spitfires making sweeps off the French coast sighted the enemy warships, before we obtained firm information that they were at sea; and even then there was delay in getting the news through to the shore authorities because, in accordance with the

[1] See Map p. 199.

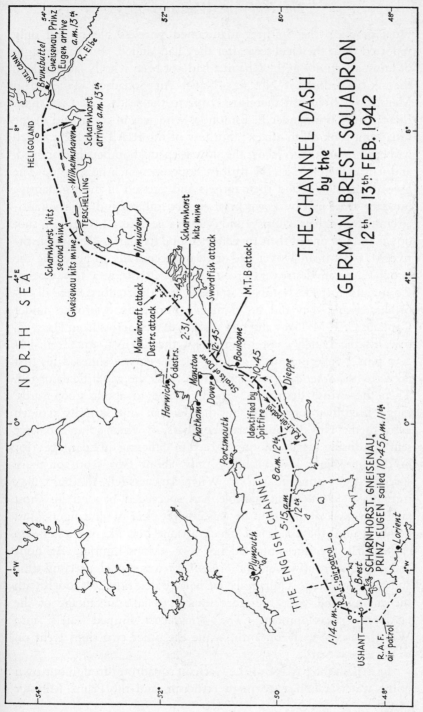

NORTH SEA

Brunsbuttel
Gneisenau, Prinz Eugen arrive a.m. 13th

R. Elbe

HELIGOLAND

Wilhelmshaven
Scharnhorst arrives a.m. 13th

TERSCHELLING

Scharnhorst hits second mine

Gneisenau hits mine

Ijmuiden

Scharnhorst hits mine

Main aircraft attack
Destrs. attack
2·31
3·45
12·45

Swordfish attack

M.T.B attack

Harwich
6 destrs.

Manston
Dover
Boulogne
Straits of Dover

Chatham
10·45
Dieppe

Portsmouth
Identified by Spitfire
R.A.F. air patrol

8 a.m. 12th

5·15 a.m. 12th

Plymouth
THE ENGLISH CHANNEL

R.A.F. air patrol

1·14 a.m.

USHANT
Brest
SCHARNHORST, GNEISENAU, PRINZ EUGEN sailed 10·45 p.m. 11th

Lorient

R.A.F. air patrol

THE CHANNEL DASH
by the
GERMAN BREST SQUADRON
12th — 13th FEB. 1942

usual practice, the Spitfires maintained wireless silence and only reported what they had seen after they had landed. But earlier signs of unusual activity in the Channel had not been wholly lacking, and the six Swordfish of No. 825 Naval Air Squadron stationed at Manston in Kent had therefore come to the ready. At 12.28 p.m. Lieutenant-Commander E. Esmonde, who was in command of the squadron, took off to attack; but few of the R.A.F. fighters which had been requested to escort the slow torpedo-bombers had arrived, and it was therefore a very forlorn hope on which he set out. The Swordfish pilots found their targets and pressed in most gallantly; but they were met by a swarm of enemy fighters and a hail of anti-aircraft fire; their clumsy and vulnerable aircraft were all shot down and not one of their torpedoes found its mark. Meanwhile the five M.T.B.s from Dover had tried unsuccessfully to penetrate the strong German destroyer screen. In the afternoon a few Coastal Command torpedo-bombers attacked, but their efforts were ill co-ordinated and they did no damage. Next, six destroyers under Captains C. T. M. Pizey and J. P. Wright dashed across from Harwich towards the Dutch coast to intercept the German squadron. At 2.30 p.m., while they were closing in, the enemy suffered his first check by the *Scharnhorst* striking a mine; but she was little damaged. Then the British destroyers, having closed to about 3,000 yards' range, fired their torpedoes; but the German ships skilfully avoided all of them. Nor did our heavy bombers, of which some 240 were sent out during the afternoon, succeed in inflicting any damage; for in the prevailing low visibility only about two score of them succeeded in getting in attacks. When darkness fell Admiral Ciliax must have felt that his gamble had succeeded beyond his most sanguine expectations; but he was not yet clear of all dangers. Just before 8 p.m. the *Gneisenau* struck a mine but, like her sister-ship earlier that day, she sustained no very serious injuries. An hour and a half later, however, the *Scharnhorst* was mined a second time and came to a stop. Unhappily we had by that time lost touch with the enemy, and were therefore unable to take advantage of the favourable development. The *Scharnhorst* limped safely into Wilhelmshaven early on 13th, while the other two ships went on to the Elbe estuary.

In Britain the passage of the German squadron through our own home waters raised a storm of criticism, and the Prime Minister

ordered a full inquiry into the matter.[1] Apart from the failure of
the air reconnaissance, on which the Board of Inquiry commented
adversely, the chief lesson appears to concern the need for a single
authority to control all the naval and air forces involved in a fast-
moving operation; for it was mainly the divided control and the
multiplicity of commands concerned which resulted in the sea and
air attacks taking place piecemeal. On the German side the "Channel
Dash" was undoubtedly well planned and executed; but, as their
own naval staff thoughtfully remarked afterwards, if the safe arrival
of the ships was a tactical success, their withdrawal from Brest was
a strategic defeat. For nearly a year they had been a constant thorn
in our flesh, and we were soon to experience the relief brought
about by their removal from a commanding position on the flank of
our main north-south convoy route.

Soon after the *Prinz Eugen* reached Germany she and the *Scheer*
were sent to join the *Tirpitz* in Trondheim; but the submarine
Trident torpedoed the cruiser off the Norwegian coast, and damaged
her severely. However, the presence of the two heavy ships and a
number of modern destroyers was enough to raise anxiety for the
safety of our Arctic convoys, and Admiral Tovey therefore asked
that in future the outward and homeward movements should take
place simultaneously, so enabling him to cover them both with his
main fleet and also strengthen their close escorts. PQ 12 and QP 8,
which left on 1st March, were the first to set out in accordance with
this plan. The *Tirpitz*, to which Admiral Ciliax had transferred his
flag, actually sailed for the very purpose that we had anticipated on
the 6th March, but was reported by a patrolling submarine. Admiral
Tovey, who had with him three capital ships and the fleet carrier
Victorious, at once steered north-east to place his fleet between the
enemy and the convoys, which passed each other to the south-west
of Bear Island at noon on the 7th.[2] That day Ciliax detached his
three destroyers to search for the convoys, and a game of blind
man's buff ensued in very low visibility, with the Home Fleet, the
two convoys and the German battleship all at one time within
about eighty miles of each other. Nevertheless, apart from the
enemy sinking one Russian straggler from QP 8, no contacts took
place, and late in the evening of the 8th Ciliax turned south again.
German signals had, however, given the Admiralty the clue to his

[1] The report was published in 1946 (Cmd. 6775). [2] See Map p. 144.

intentions, and a timely warning sent from London enabled Admiral Tovey to set course towards the Lofoten Islands with a very good chance of catching his quarry. At daylight on the 9th reconnaissance aircraft from the *Victorious* sighted the *Tirpitz* just where she was expected, and twelve torpedo-bombers at once took off to attack her. Unhappily the tactics used during the approach of the striking force gave the enemy a good chance to avoid the torpedoes, and all of them missed. Thus was a splendid opportunity to bring the German battleship to action let slip—an opportunity, moreover, which was never to recur.

After this escape the *Tirpitz* called briefly in Vestfiord, whence she steamed south in thick weather, evading all our patrolling submarines. On 13th March she was safely anchored again in Trondheim. Though it was a blessing that the two convoys had escaped all harm, the failure to catch the enemy battleship was intensely disappointing. But the Germans realised that their newest and finest ship had had a very narrow shave, and decided on a more cautious policy in the future; and that was to have far-reaching effects on later forays by their warships in the far north.

The heavy cruiser *Hipper* next joined the German squadron in Norway, and shortly after her arrival another pair of Arctic convoys (PQ 13 and QP 9) set out on their long 2,000-mile journeys. The homeward convoy had a comparatively easy passage; but the outward one was scattered by a very severe gale, and was attacked by bombers, by U-boats, and by three German destroyers sent out from Kirkenes. The encounter between the close escort and the latter on 28th March ended in one German destroyer (the Z.26) being sunk. The cruiser *Trinidad*, which was giving close cover, was however the victim of an extraordinary stroke of ill-fortune; for one of the torpedoes which she had aimed at the enemy behaved erratically (probably because of the intense cold) and returned to strike the ship from which it had been fired, damaging her severely. She got into Kola Inlet safely, but we realised that it would be impossible to repair her properly there, and difficult to extricate her.

The next two outward convoys to Russia, PQ 14 and 15, comprised 24 and 25 ships respectively; but the former ran into heavy ice, many of its ships being forced to return, and during the passage of PQ 15 and QP 11, which sailed at the end of April, the cruiser *Edinburgh* was torpedoed by a U-boat. She turned back to Murmansk, but was found by searching German destroyers on 2nd May, and in the ensuing engagement she received another torpedo hit. We finally had to sink her ourselves. The Germans lost one destroyer (the *Schoemann*) in this action; but in addition to the loss of the *Edinburgh* we had one destroyer sunk by accidental collision and two others damaged. The most encouraging feature of the operation was that only four of the 38 merchantmen involved were lost. Next we tried to get the damaged *Trinidad* home; but German aircraft quickly found her, and a bomb hit started serious fires. As with the *Edinburgh* she had finally to be sunk by our own torpedoes.

The experiences of the Arctic convoys in March and April, 1942, underlined the severe hazards involved in such operations with, as Admiral Pound put it "the dice loaded against us in every direction"; but for political reasons, and under heavy pressure from President Roosevelt, the War Cabinet decided that they must continue—notwithstanding the fact that by May continuous daylight would prevail throughout the whole of the long journey. Moreover, with the *Scheer*, *Lützow* and four destroyers in Narvik, and the *Tirpitz*, *Hipper* and six destroyers at Trondheim the enemy disposed of greater strength than ever before; and if he was prepared to risk a general engagement in the Barents Sea he might well be able to bring it off in conditions which were wholly favourable to himself.

The presence of the *Tirpitz* in Norway also aroused anxieties lest she should try to emulate the earlier exploits of the *Scharnhorst* and *Gneisenau* by breaking out into the Atlantic through one or other of the northern passages to prey on our convoys.[1] In the pursuit of the *Bismarck* we had learnt how difficult it was to prevent such a break-out, and we had no illusions regarding the damage and dislocation to our shipping which so powerful a raider could achieve in the western ocean. One way of discouraging such a sortie was to make it impossible for the battleship to dock in western France; and as there was only one dock which could take her—the huge Normandie lock at St. Nazaire—the Admiralty proposed to the Chief of Combined Operations that an attack should be made from the sea with the object of putting the lock out of action. The plan was exceedingly bold, for lightly armed assault craft would have to make their way up a five-mile-long and closely guarded estuary;

[1] See p. 122.

but by exploiting the factor of surprise to the full we had hopes that the object could be accomplished. The ex-American destroyer *Campbeltown* was accordingly filled with explosive, and she was to ram the lock gates what time some 260 Commandos landed from her and from a number of motor launches and blew up the operating machinery. The striking force, which was under Commander R. E. D. Ryder, sailed from Falmouth on 26th March, and was escorted to a position just off the Loire estuary, whence the *Campbeltown* and eighteen coastal craft began the passage up-river after dark next evening. By skilful use of deceptive ruses Commander Ryder confused the defences, and delayed the inevitable retaliation sufficiently to enable the force to reach its objective without suffering serious damage. Just after 1.30 a.m. on 28th the *Campbeltown* rammed the lock gates well and truly, and the Commandos leapt ashore from her; but the motor launches now came under a mælstrom of fire, and few of their troops could be got ashore. Commander Ryder's motor gunboat managed to rescue many of the *Campbeltown's* crew, after which he ordered the surviving craft to withdraw; but most of the soldiers who had landed had to be left behind. At about noon that same day the *Campbeltown* blew up, completely destroying the lock and inflicting heavy casualties on the Germans who had unwisely gone on board to inspect her; while the survivors of the assault force met their escort offshore, and got safely back to England. All but two of the sixteen coastal craft involved were, however, lost through one cause or another; but the casualties we suffered—under 170 killed and missing—were remarkably light, considering that the assault force had penetrated into a very well-defended enemy stronghold and had remained there for about two hours. Not only did the St. Nazaire raid eliminate the possibility of the *Tirpitz* docking in western France, but the gallantry of its execution was a tonic to the people of Britain, who were passing through a very difficult period at the time.

Meanwhile the decision to continue running the Arctic convoys throughout the summer was causing the Admiralty rising concern; for the ice edge, which is at its farthest south in about April, would force the convoys to pass close to the German bases in Norway; and the continuous daylight would make it easy for the Luftwaffe and U-boats to shadow and attack them. Admiral Tovey considered that we were gambling with fate, and foresaw heavy losses; but

naval opinion had to defer to the political influences already mentioned, and it thus came to pass that, far from suspending the convoys
during the period of greatest danger, PQ 16's thirty-five merchantmen made it the largest convoy so far sailed. The threat of the
German Narvik and Trondheim squadrons, both of which were
well able to attack the convoy while it was crossing the Barents Sea,
was regarded so seriously that Admiral Tovey allocated four of his
cruisers to reinforce the close escort and took his main fleet to sea
to cover the double movement from a position to the west of Bear
Island. On 21st May PQ 16 left Reykjavik in Iceland and QP 12,
of fifteen ships, sailed from Kola Inlet. Four days later the convoys
passed each other, and fierce air attacks were then launched against
PQ 16. For nearly five days the close escort fought an almost
continuous battle with the German torpedo- and dive-bombers; but
the convoy preserved what Commander R. Onslow, senior officer
of the escort, described as "parade ground rigidity" and on the 30th
"reduced in numbers, battered and tired, but still keeping perfect
station" it entered Kola Inlet. Only seven merchantmen were lost
in the outward convoy, and none at all from the homeward one—
a result which far exceeded our expectations. The German surface
ships did not attempt to intervene, the U-boats failed completely,
and the good discipline and fire-power of the merchantmen and
escort vessels drastically curbed the effectiveness of the Luftwaffe.
But we realised that one or two escort carriers would have added
immensely to the effectiveness of the defences, and might well have
turned a success into a decisive victory. Thus was nemesis deferred
in the Arctic—but not for long.

Because by June, 1942, the condition of Malta was again
becoming critical many Home Fleet ships were next transferred to
the south to help fight a convoy through to the beleaguered island.[1]
Not until the end of that month did the surviving ships return to
Scapa, and in consequence it was 27th June before PQ 17 and QP 13
(36 and 35 merchantmen respectively) could start out on their long
journeys. Nor were signs lacking that the German Navy was again
planning to attack the convoys in the Barents Sea with some or all
of its heavy ships—including the *Tirpitz*. Admiral Tovey discussed
this unpleasant prospect at some length with the First Sea Lord;
for the Commander-in-Chief considered that the risks had become

---

[1] This was operation " Harpoon." See p. 218

so serious as to be unacceptable. He held that if the outward convoy had to sail it should be sent in two sections, which could be more easily defended than a large mass of merchantmen; and, in the light of the experiences leading to the loss of the *Edinburgh* and *Trinidad*, he disliked sending large cruisers far into the Barents Sea. Admiral Pound however insisted that the operation should be carried out as planned; and it was during these telephone conversations that Admiral Tovey learnt, to his utter surprise and alarm, that if the dangers besetting the convoy appeared likely to become critical the First Sea Lord intended to order it to scatter. This was, as the Commander-in-Chief pointed out in no uncertain terms, contrary to all our recent experience.[1]

The general plan for PQ 17 corresponded to that which had been so successful in getting its predecessor through; but two American as well as two British cruisers were included in the escort under Rear-Admiral L. H. K. Hamilton, and the American battleship *Washington* was with Admiral Tovey's main covering force, which again included the fleet carrier *Victorious*. The influence of the latter ship was to be very important, for Hitler had told Raeder that his heavy ships were not to sail until the disposition of our carriers was known—a restriction which was likely to delay their departure so seriously that a favourable opportunity might well be missed. In fact, Raeder transferred his heavy ships northward from Trondheim and Narvik as soon as he knew that the outward convoy had sailed; but the *Lützow* and three destroyers all ran aground as they were leaving Narvik. The Admiralty quickly learned about the departure of the Narvik and Trondheim squadrons; but not until the evening of 4th July did they become aware that the *Tirpitz* had joined the *Scheer* and *Hipper* in Altenfiord. By that time PQ 17 had made excellent progress, and had passed safely to the north of Bear Island. In spite of fairly heavy air attacks only three ships had so far been lost and, in the words of Commander J. E. Broome, senior officer of the close escort, the convoy's "tails were well up." In the Admiralty, however, things looked quite differently; for it seemed that the crisis they had most reason to fear was now imminent, and that the ships in Altenfiord, which were quite capable of overwhelming the convoy escorts, would probably attack in the early

[1] Admiral Tovey told the author of this history that he informed Admiral Pound on the telephone from Scapa that if he scattered the convoy "it would be sheer bloody murder."

hours of next morning, the 5th. The First Sea Lord therefore called a staff meeting, and between 9 and 9.36 p.m. he sent three signals ordering Admiral Hamilton's cruisers to withdraw to the west at high speed and the convoy to scatter. The wording of those signals was, moreover, singularly unfortunate; for they gave the impression that a greatly superior enemy was about to appear over the southern horizon, and that the escort would shortly have to fight a desperate battle.[1] Admiral Hamilton therefore concentrated the six destroyers of the close escort with his cruisers, which was reasonable enough; and at 10.30 p.m., having told the astonished convoy Commodore to order his ships to scatter, he himself turned back to the west with his four cruisers. Unfortunately he took the six destroyers with him, thereby leaving only a few anti-aircraft ships, corvettes and trawlers to go along with the scattering merchantmen. If the Admiralty's intervention was untimely, and the wording of the signals misleading, Admiral Hamilton's removal of the destroyers was certainly an error of judgment of some magnitude. Nor was the enemy slow to seize the opportunity produced by this succession of mistakes. Between 5th and 10th July eleven merchantmen were sunk by air attacks and ten by U-boats. The remaining ships of the escort made valiant efforts to protect their charges, some of which they formed into small convoys on their own initiative; and Captain J. C. K. Dowding, R.N.R., the Convoy Commodore, after having his own ship sunk, set out again from Kola to bring in ships which had taken shelter on the unfriendly coasts of Nova Zembla. But only 13 of the 36 ships which set out on this ill-fated journey reached Murmansk.[2] "Not a successful convoy" was the concluding remark of Dowding's report—surely one of the classics of understatement.

The repercussions of the disaster were widespread—not least because American warships had witnessed its beginning, and many of the sunken merchantmen were American. Although the men who survived the ordeal could not, of course, have known the

---

[1] The three signals were as follows:

9.11 p.m. "Most Immediate. Cruiser force withdraw to westward at high speed."

9.23 p.m. "Immediate. Owing to threat of surface ships convoy is to disperse and proceed to Russian ports."

9.36 p.m. "Most Immediate. My 9.23 of the 4th. Convoy is to scatter."

[2] Of the 36 ships which set out one grounded early in the voyage and another returned to Iceland.

complex causes which lay behind the decisions taken, and the heroic efforts of the small escorts should have belied the feeling that the Royal Navy had abandoned its charges in face of danger, the disappearance of the cruisers and destroyers over the western horizon what time the dispersed merchantmen were left to plod slowly in the opposite direction created a most unhappy impression. Nor was astonishment and anger confined to the merchant seaman; for the same feelings very quickly arose among the crews of the warships. An officer in the *Norfolk* jotted down the following note at the time:

" At 26 knots the four cruisers and all the destroyers swept close past the convoy. Our last sight of the merchantmen showed them slowly opening out and separating. The effect on the ship's company was devastating. Twenty-four hours earlier there had been only one thought—that at last we were going to bring enemy surface ships to action. I had never known the men in such good heart. . . . Then in the space of a few hours we abandoned our aircraft [which had just been flown off to reconnoitre to the east] and its crew, and we abandoned the convoy. The ship was in a turmoil: everyone was boiling, and the Master at Arms told me he had never known such strong feelings before. . . . It was the blackest day we ever knew—sheer bloody murder."

The tragedy is moreover deepened by our present knowledge of how unnecessary it was; for the *Tirpitz* and her consorts actually only left Altenfiord at 11 a.m. on the 5th—more than 12 hours after the dispersal of the convoy; and that same evening they abandoned their projected attack and reversed course to regain the shelter of the anchorage. Such were the consequences of trying to control the fleet from a headquarters 2,000 miles away—the danger of which practice Admiral Tovey, like his predecessor Admiral Forbes, had repeatedly represented. Had the Admiralty done no more than send the latest intelligence to the Commander-in-Chief, together perhaps with their appreciation of the enemy's intentions, repeating their message to the senior officers of the escort, it is probable that the latter would never have withdrawn, and certain that the convoy would not have been dispersed; and in that event convoy PQ 17, with its conduct left in the hands of the men on the spot, would undoubtedly have been as successful as its predecessor.

To turn from the Arctic circle to the wide oceans, well before these tragic events had taken place three disguised German raiders had broken out into the Atlantic. In January the *Thor* escaped undetected from Bordeaux, which she had reached by passing down-Channel from Germany in the previous December; and in March and May respectively the *Michel* and *Stier* reached the Atlantic by the same route, taking advantage of darkness and bad weather to shield them from our patrols in the narrow seas. The *Thor* first went to the Antarctic in an unsuccessful endeavour to emulate the *Pinguin's* earlier success against our whaling fleets, after which she moved to the Indian Ocean, where many ships were still sailing unescorted. The *Michel* and *Stier* worked only in the South Atlantic; but all three raiders several times met supply ships at secret rendezvous in mid-ocean, and replenished themselves from them. This procedure was, however, becoming increasingly hazardous; for the Admiralty's intelligence centre kept very careful watch for signs of the supply ships' movements, and we were now able to spare more cruisers and aircraft to search for them. It thus became far more difficult for the disguised raiders to find victims, and in the first half of 1942 they accounted for no more than 17 merchantmen (107,600 tons); but we did not succeed in actually catching any of them in that period.

The Germans were now supplementing the disguised raiders' efforts by sending U-boats to distant waters, and we have already seen how, early in 1942, they achieved substantial successes against unescorted ships in the Caribbean and Gulf of Mexico.[1] In March Dönitz made a fresh probe against the focus of shipping off Freetown, where two U-boats quickly sank eleven ships; and in the same month the *Doggerbank* (originally the British *Speybank*, which had been captured in the Indian Ocean by the raider *Atlantis* a year earlier, and had since been converted to a U-boat supply ship) laid a number of mines off the Cape of Good Hope. This was always one of our most sensitive spots, because almost all the troopships and supply vessels bound for the Middle East, and many of those

[2] See p. 194.

carrying men and stores to India, had to pass that way. The *Doggerbank's* mines thus caused considerable dislocation to our traffic, as well as a few losses. An additional threat to our Middle East convoys arose in May, 1942, when five Japanese submarines appeared in the Mozambique Channel, and sank 20 ships (94,000 tons); but the occupation of Madagascar early in that month, as recounted earlier,[1] strengthened our watch on the shipping moving up and down the east coast of Africa, and after the return of the Japanese submarines to Penang in July there was a lull in those waters. None the less the threat inherent in these distant lunges by Axis submarines was very real; for we could not possibly have strong sea and air escorts everywhere, and by suddenly appearing at remote spots the U-boats were almost certain to score easy successes—until such time as our anti-submarine forces were strengthened. Then the U-boats would move elsewhere, and we could do little more than guess where they would turn up next.

The Germans and Japanese had meanwhile jointly arranged to sail fast merchantmen between Europe and the Far East to break through our blockade with especially valuable cargoes, such as edible oils and rubber in the homeward-bound ships and machinery in those outward bound. Between April, 1941, and May of the following year 16 such ships sailed from the Far East, and 12 of them arrived safely with 75,000 tons of cargo. Six ships also reached Japan safely from Europe; but those accomplishments marked the high water of success for the blockade runners, very few of which got through after 1942.

We must now turn to the Mediterranean to review the manner in which Admiral Cunningham's fleet, gravely depleted though it had been by the disasters of 1941 and by transfers to the Indian Ocean, was facing its manifold responsibilities. High on that list stood the reinforcement of Malta, the supply of the Army of the Nile through the Libyan ports, and the interception of Axis convoys running between Italy and Tripoli; but it was impossible for Cunningham to meet all three requirements simultaneously with the forces at his disposal. In January, 1942, the Italian Navy was thus able to escort two convoys safely to Africa, with substantial reinforcements and supplies for Rommel, and before the end of that month the Afrika Korps struck. Very soon we had to withdraw

[1] See pp. 190-1.

all the ships and stores which had been so laboriously carried to Benghazi, our troops were in full retreat back towards the Egyptian frontier, and the hard-worked little ships of the Inshore Squadron were once again trying to mitigate the consequences of defeat on land by supporting the Army's seaward flank, by running stores and ammunition up to the front, and by evacuating men and equipment from the ports which we were forced to abandon. To Admiral Cunningham this sudden reversal of the wheel of fortune was a bitter blow, and the abandonment of the forward airfields in the desert boded ill for his efforts to supply Malta; since the convoys would now have to run the gauntlet of enemy sea and air forces working from the ample bases they possessed on both flanks of the route. Small wonder that the naval commander, who was not given to expressing concern over the future, should have told the First Sea Lord that he was "alarmed about Malta's supplies." Actually, in January, before the situation had become critical, he had sent to the island two fast ships and also a convoy of four merchantmen, three of which arrived safely; but those were to be the last comparatively easy supply operations for a long time.

On 12th February Admiral Cunningham sailed three fast merchantmen for Malta under the guardianship of Rear-Admiral Philip Vian's 15th Cruiser Squadron and eight destroyers. Four empty ships from previous convoys were to be brought out at the same time. The west-bound ships were, however, heavily attacked from the air. One was disabled early in the passage and two were sunk; and this substantial effort thus brought no relief at all to the hard-pressed island. Nor were our submarine and strike aircraft successful against another "battleship convoy" which the Italians safely escorted to Tripoli in February. Given a battle fleet Cunningham would, of course, have challenged such movements with all his strength—as he had so often done in earlier times; but he had no heavy squadron, and the few light cruisers and destroyers left to him were no match for the enormous strength which the Italian Navy was able to deploy to command the central basin temporarily during the passage of their convoys.

Early in March Force H, now commanded by Rear-Admiral E. N. Syfret, flew off fifteen Spitfires to Malta, and the arrival of even a small number of those famous fighters was one of the few happy auguries for the future at this difficult period; for the weight of the Luftwaffe's offensive against the island was now increasing again, it was becoming more and more difficult to keep surface warships based there, and even the submarines of the 10th Flotilla were suffering damage while in harbour.

At the next attempt by the enemy to send reinforcements to Africa Cunningham and his R.A.F. colleague decided to do their utmost to interfere with the movements. On 10th March Admiral Vian accordingly left Alexandria with three light cruisers and nine destroyers; but they were heavily attacked from the air, and two days later his flagship, the *Naiad*, was torpedoed and sunk by a U-boat. Nor did the R.A.F. torpedo-bombers succeed in their attacks on the Axis convoys, which were thus able to land enough supplies and reinforcements to enable Rommel to press on towards Egypt.

As to the Axis submarines, both German and Italian boats were very active at this time—especially against the important convoys running between Egypt and the oil ports on the Levant coast; but between January and March, 1942, we sank eight of them (three Germans and five Italians), and a remarkable feature of those successes was that six of the eight enemies sunk fell to our own submarines. Between March and June we sank five more of the German Mediterranean U-boats, and by July, in spite of Dönitz having sent out reinforcements, their strength had thus declined from 21 at the beginning of the year to 16. None the less that comparatively small number continued to cause us considerable trouble and substantial losses. On the other hand, the Italian submarines, though far more numerous than their German colleagues, were never anything like as troublesome. In June and July five more of them were accounted for, and on 9th July the corvette *Hyacinth* blew one of them, the *Perla*, to the surface off Beirut, captured her intact and took her triumphantly into harbour. For all the troubles of this period the little ships and anti-submarine aircraft continued to show that they could hit hard at any enemy they detected.

To retrace our steps for a few weeks, on 20th March Admiral Vian headed west again from Alexandria with four good supply ships bound for Malta under his wing. Two days later warships sent out from Tobruk and Malta brought the escort up to four light cruisers and sixteen destroyers; but a patrolling submarine had meanwhile reported that strong Italian forces were leaving harbour.

In fact the battleship *Littorio*, two heavy and one light cruiser, and ten destroyers sailed from Taranto and Messina early on 22nd to attack Vian's convoy.[1] The submarine's report made it clear to the Admiral that an encounter with a greatly superior enemy was likely to take place in a few hours' time; but he was determined that the convoy should get through, and had already issued orders to meet the very eventuality which now seemed certain to arise. Early in the afternoon he therefore made the signal to "prepare to carry out diversionary tactics," and without further ado his ships separated into six small divisions—some to attack the enemy with torpedoes, some to lay a dense smoke screen to windward of the convoy, and others to shield the merchantmen from air attacks. Just before 2.30 p.m. the *Euryalus* appropriately (for it had been Captain Blackwood's *Euryalus* which, on 14th October, 1805, had signalled to Nelson that the combined French and Spanish fleet was preparing to leave Cadiz harbour) hoisted the ever-welcome signal " Enemy in Sight."[2] The Admiral at once gave the executive order to carry out his pre-arranged plan, and the six divisions of his ships all moved to carry out their appointed tasks. While the convoy altered to the south-west under its own escort, the smoke layers covered the sea to windward of it with a dense screen, and Vian himself in the *Cleopatra*, with the *Euryalus* in company, stood out to attack the enemy. Thus was the stage set for the " Second Battle of Sirte."[3]

The first phase of the battle took the form of a long-range gun duel between the British and Italian cruisers; but the latter soon turned right away and Vian, having accomplished his purpose of driving them off, then returned to the convoy—which was meanwhile heavily engaged with enemy aircraft. Hardly had the Admiral rejoined the merchantmen when a more serious threat developed; for the *Littorio* as well as the three cruisers hove in sight to the north-east. The British ships at once repeated their tactics of standing boldly towards the enemy, and a series of confused fights now took place, with the British cruisers and destroyers plunging at high speed through heavy seas, in and out of the smoke screen which the ships specially detailed for that purpose were still laying.

[1] See Map p. 214.

[2] It is interesting to recall that the names of the four frigates which Nelson had with him off Cadiz in October, 1805—the *Naiad, Phoebe, Sirius* and *Euryalus*—were all represented in the 15th Cruiser Squadron of 1941-42.

[3] The First Battle of Sirte was the skirmish of 17th December, 1941 (see p. 173).

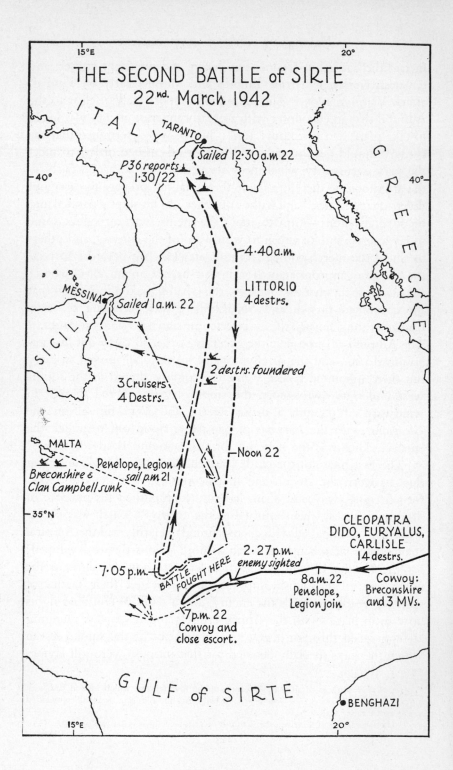

THE SECOND BATTLE of SIRTE
22nd. March 1942

I T A L Y

TARANTO

Sailed 12.30 a.m. 22

P36 reports
1.30/22

40°

GREECE

40°

4.40 a.m.

LITTORIO
4 destrs.

MESSINA

Sailed 1 a.m. 22

SICILY

2 destrs. foundered

3 Cruisers
4 Destrs.

Noon 22

MALTA

Penelope, Legion
sail p.m. 21

Breconshire &
Clan Campbell sunk

35°N

CLEOPATRA
DIDO, EURYALUS,
CARLISLE
14 destrs.

7.05 p.m.

BATTLE
FOUGHT HERE

2.27 p.m.
enemy sighted

8 a.m. 22
Penelope,
Legion join

Convoy:
Breconshire
and 3 MVs.

7 p.m. 22
Convoy and
close escort.

GULF of SIRTE

BENGHAZI

15°E

20°

Vian expected the Italians to try to work round to the east (i.e. to windward) of the smoke, but just after he had moved in that direction to head them off they suddenly appeared to the west of the smoke—and only eight miles away. Four destroyers under Captain St. J. A. Micklethwait, however, threatened them so successfully with their torpedoes that, in spite of "the unequal nature of the contest" the Italians forbore to press in towards the convoy. None the less from 5.40 to 6 p.m. the situation looked dangerous. Then the returning *Cleopatra* and *Euryalus* suddenly broke through the smoke, their little 5.25-inch guns blazing defiance at the giant *Littorio* at only 13,000 yards' range. This brought a welcome if short relief to Micklethwait's hard-pressed destroyers—one of which had been disabled by a 15-inch shell from the enemy battleship. Vian then returned briefly to the east—in case the enemy cruisers were trying to outflank him in that direction, while Captain A. L. Poland's four destroyers joined Micklethwait's depleted division, and pressed in to engage. The final phase lasted from 6.40 to nearly 7 p.m., by which time the enemy was obviously retiring for good to the north. The convoy then resumed its westerly course for Malta, the two damaged destroyers were ordered to make for the same base, while Vian and the rest of the Alexandria-based ships headed to the east—their task magnificently accomplished. Few if any sea battles have better demonstrated how, in the words of Sir Julian Corbett written half a century earlier, "a small well-handled fleet, acting on a nicely-timed offensive, may paralyse the mobilisation of an overwhelming force."[1] But for all the efforts of Vian and his men on 22nd March off the Gulf of Sirte a sad fate awaited the convoy; since its southward diversion during the battle prevented it entering Malta early next day, as intended, and that gave the German bombers their chance. Though the escorts fought, screened and towed with unflagging resolution, one ship was sunk twenty miles from her destination, the famous *Breconshire* (Captain C. A. G. Hutchinson), heroine of so many runs to Malta, was so badly damaged that she had to be beached and became a total loss, and both of the two merchantmen which struggled into the Grand Harbour were destroyed by the bombers. Only a fifth of the 26,000 tons of cargo in the convoy was delivered into the island's hungry store houses; and the Luftwaffe's attacks on the warships

[1] See *Fighting Instructions*, 1530-1816 (Navy Records Society, 1905).

lying in the dockyard and harbours of Malta now became so savage that it was obvious that all those able to steam must withdraw immediately. So opened the month of April, 1942—the period of supreme trial for Malta, when we came within an ace of losing the only position that could give us a measure of control over the central Mediterranean, and on which the fortunes of all our forces in the Middle East chiefly depended. But it was actually Admiral Cunningham's successor who had to face the final crisis; for on 1st April Cunningham hauled down his flag and came back to England to prepare for his new appointment as head of the British naval mission in America. For nearly three years (1st June, 1939–1st April, 1942) he had trained and led his fleet with unsurpassed vigour and determination, and in that period he established a clear supremacy over the Italian Navy. When the Luftwaffe and the U-boats came to the assistance of the Italians, and temporarily halted his triumphant progress, he inspired his fleet to endure the severe trials of the evacuations from Greece and Crete; and all the while he was giving every possible support to the land forces engaged in the desert campaign. His leadership was of such a quality that every man in the fleet was proud to serve under him—even though they knew full well that he would exact the uttermost effort and sacrifice from them. To the end of their days Royal Navy men will tell their children how they fought under Cunningham in the Mediterranean; and the noble words with which Joseph Conrad described the influence of Nelson—"through the fidelity of his fortune and the power of his inspiration, he stands unique amongst the leaders of fleets and sailors"[1]—may worthily be applied to the other Admiral who, a century and a half later, made his name in the same sea. On 1st April Vice-Admiral H. D. Pridham-Wippell, the second-in-command, temporarily took over the fleet; and on 20th May Admiral Sir Henry Harwood, the victor of the River Plate Battle, arrived to fill the post of Commander-in-Chief.

The heavy air raids of April, 1942, caused vast destruction in Malta dockyard and heavy losses among the warships left behind in the island's harbours; and they almost extinguished the Royal Air Force's fighter defences. The light cruiser *Penelope* finally escaped in a dramatic dash to the west; but the 10th Submarine Flotilla had to be withdrawn to Alexandria, and many warships were

[1] *The Mirror of the Sea.*

too severely damaged to get away from the island. On the 14th of this critical month, however, the American aircraft carrier *Wasp* left the Clyde with a cargo of 47 Spitfires, passed safely through the Gibraltar Straits under British escort, and on the 20th flew off the fighters to Malta. But this gallant effort ended in tragedy, for the arrangements made for the reception of the Spitfires were faulty, and nearly all of them were quickly destroyed on the island's airfields. Furthermore, our other commitments, which included fighting the Arctic convoy PQ 16 through to Murmansk,[1] were so heavy that we could not muster the forces needed to run a convoy to Malta before June; and the enemy was meanwhile able to send his supply ships from Italy to Africa with little hindrance except from our submarines. But a gleam of hope came at the end of April, when the Germans—believing that Malta was completely neutralised—transferred most of their bombers from Sicily to other fronts; and the island to which the King had recently awarded the George Cross quickly showed its remarkable powers of recovery. Then on 9th May the U.S.S. *Wasp* and the *Eagle* together flew off 64 more Spitfires to Malta. All but three arrived safely, and the arrangements for their reception were so much improved that when the enemy bombers came in to attack the airfields they were repulsed with heavy losses. The air battles of those days marked the turning point in the long siege; but we should not forget the warships, such as the fast minelayer *Welshman*, which repeatedly rushed in ammunition and vital stores, nor the specially adapted submarines which carried in small but precious quantities of fuel during the crisis; for without their efforts the fighters would have been grounded and the gun defences would have fallen silent for lack of ammunition. In the middle of May the old *Eagle* sent a further 17 Spitfires to the island, and in June she made two more ferrying trips which together added 55 more to the defences. By the end of June the situation on Malta's airfields had been transformed; but we were still a long way from restoring our sea and air offensive against the Axis convoys to Africa, and on 11th May an ill-co-ordinated attempt to strike at one of them led to the sinking by German bombers of three valuable destroyers. This was a tragic experience, and moreover one that should surely have been avoided so late in the war; for we had long since learnt, at bitter cost, that surface warships could not work

[1] See p. 205.

without adequate fighter cover in waters where the enemy held command of the air.

Early in June reinforcements from the Eastern Fleet began to assemble at Alexandria to escort a convoy of eleven supply ships to Malta simultaneously with the passage of another convoy, of six ships, from Gibraltar under the guardianship of Force H, which had been substantially strengthened from the Home Fleet. The double operation was an excellent example of the capacity of a maritime power rapidly to switch its forces from one theatre to another; for many of the warships had very recently been involved in other operations from the Arctic to Madagascar. The convoy from the west (called "Harpoon") passed into the Mediterranean on the night of 11th-12th June, and by the time it reached the Narrows between Sicily and Africa only one merchantman had been lost. On the morning of the 15th, however, after the main escort had turned back to the west, an Italian squadron of two cruisers and five destroyers sent out from Palermo endeavoured to molest the convoy to the south of Pantelleria. The five escorting fleet destroyers at once stood out to attack in traditional manner; but heavy air attacks developed almost simultaneously—while the convoy had little protection. Another merchantman was lost, and two others were so gravely damaged that the senior officer of the escort reluctantly decided to sink them. Then the survivors ran into a minefield just outside Malta, and suffered further losses. Only two of the six merchantmen entered harbour safely—a result which was hardly commensurate with the effort made; but the convoy from the east (called "Vigorous") was meanwhile faring even worse.

Admiral Vian was once again in command, and on 13th June he left Alexandria with 7 cruisers and 17 destroyers to meet the merchantmen, which had sailed from Haifa and Port Said in two sections, off Tobruk. But enemy aircraft found the convoy very early in its passage, and at once attacked in force. By the 14th two merchantmen had been sunk and two others damaged; and that evening Vian learnt that the main Italian fleet, consisting of the 15-inch battleships *Littorio* and *Vittorio Veneto*, four cruisers and a dozen destroyers, had sailed south from Taranto. Knowing that he had little hope of holding off such enemy strength throughout a long summer's day, as he had done off Sirte in the previous March, Vian asked the Commander-in-Chief if he was to retire; for the persistence of the air attacks and the likelihood of a surface action in very unpropitious circumstances made the prospects of the convoy appear slender—if it steamed farther to the west. Admiral Harwood, however, told him to hold on towards Malta until 2 a.m. on 15th, when Vian accordingly carried out the difficult manœuvre of reversing the course of some fifty ships. Five hours later Harwood ordered the convoy to steer for Malta again; but when the Italian fleet was reported only 150 miles away he ordered a second withdrawal. Next he signalled to Vian that the situation was so obscure that he must leave it to the cruiser Admiral to decide whether to go on or not— a principle which it might have been better to adopt from the beginning of the operation. None the less in the afternoon Harwood sent another message urging Vian to renew the attempt to get through to Malta; but by that time the escorts, which had been cruising to and fro in the waters known to the British sailors as "bomb alley" for nearly twenty-four hours, were running short of ammunition. Moreover, to Vian, who had been subjected to almost continuous attacks by every weapon in the enemy's armoury ever since leaving Alexandria, and whose charges were also plainly threatened by the overwhelmingly superior Italian fleet, the outlook appeared hopeless. He therefore continued his retirement to the east, and late in the evening the Commander-in-Chief accepted the inevitable by ordering all forces to return to Alexandria. Operation "Vigorous" thus not only ended in total failure but involved us in the loss of a cruiser and three destroyers which we could ill spare. Several important lessons derived from this unhappy experience. In the first place the remote control of the fleet exercised by the C.-in-C. from ashore not only broke down at the crisis of the operation, but actually added to the difficulties of the senior officer afloat. In Admiral Cunningham's time no attempt was ever made to direct the movements of forces at sea in that manner, and although it was the understandable desire to achieve close co-ordination of the sea and air aspects of the operation which caused his successor to adopt the practice, experience proved beyond doubt that its disadvantages far outweighed its anticipated advantages. Secondly, the accuracy of the attacks on the Italian fleet by our shore-based aircraft left much to be desired, and the exaggerated claims made by the R.A.F. aircrews misled the shore authorities regarding the prospects of fighting the convoy through. In fact all they achieved was one bomb and one torpedo hit on the battleship *Littorio*, which did her no serious injury, and one torpedo hit on the cruiser *Trento*, which slowed her down sufficiently for the submarine *Umbra* to catch and sink her. There was no doubt at all that aircraft for aircraft the German attacks had been far more deadly than our own. Lastly, we realised that as long as we lacked anything resembling a balanced battle fleet, and while the enemy remained in possession of the airfields in western Libya, it was impossible to run a convoy to Malta from the east. The island's salvation must therefore lie in supplying it from the other direction, and in our next effort we would therefore stake everything on a bigger and better version of operation "Harpoon." Meanwhile we would continue to seize every possible chance to run in essential stores by fast supply vessels and submarines.

On 21st June, only a week after the failure of the " Vigorous " convoy, Tobruk, which we had struggled so long to keep supplied during the protracted seige of 1940-41,[1] fell to Rommel's forces, and the threat to the fleet's main base at Alexandria became too plain to be ignored. Steps were therefore taken to transfer some warships to Haifa and Port Said, to send others south of the Suez Canal, and to move at any rate some of the vast quantities of valuable stores which we had so laboriously accumulated in Egypt to safer places. Fortunately it proved unnecessary to carry the evacuation of Alexandria very far; for early in July the Eighth Army stopped Rommel's advance at a hitherto obscure spot in the desert about sixty miles west of Alexandria called El Alamein. Meanwhile Malta's defenders had again been reinforced, air attacks on the island had declined, and the 10th Submarine Flotilla had therefore been able to return to its proper base. These favourable developments enabled us to intensify the three-pronged offensive by surface ships, strike aircraft, and submarines against the Axis armies' seaborne supplies; and that was bound to affect the prospects of Montgomery's next blow against the Afrika Korps. Though we still had a long way to travel before we had gained a firm measure of control over the central basin of the Mediterranean, the crisis which had arisen in April had plainly passed.

In retrospect it now seems clear that the month of July, 1942, marked the spring tide of Axis success. For Rommel then reached

[1]See p. 168.

El Alamein, in Russia the Germans had captured Rostov on the Don, in the Pacific the Japanese had gained a foothold in the Solomons and the Aleutians, in the Indian Ocean our maritime control was precarious, we had recently lost the whole of Burma, in the Arctic we had just suffered a serious disaster to convoy PQ 17, and in the Atlantic our shipping losses had recently been very heavy. Though no one would have dared to foretell it at the time, in the latter half of 1942 the pendulum, which had swung so severely against us since the false dawn of mid-1941, gradually lost its unfavourable momentum; and before the end of that year it was to show the first signs of returning to a central position.

CHAPTER XI

THE HOLD AT SEA RESTORED

1st August–31st October, 1942

"The English never yield, and though driven back and thrown into confusion, they always return to the fight, thirsting for vengeance as long as they have a breath of life."

Giovanni Mocenigo, Venetian Ambassador in France, to the Doge, 8th April, 1588 (State Papers Venetian, Public Record Office).

THE REVERBERATIONS of Dönitz's "Roll on the drums" operation in the western Atlantic, which had started in January, 1942, were still being felt in the following August; but the U-boats had shifted from the east coast of America to the Caribbean and Gulf of Mexico, where unescorted ships could still be found in some numbers. A particularly sensitive spot was the focus of shipping, including many tankers plying to and from the Venezuelan oil ports, off Trinidad; and in September it was there that the U-boats reaped their richest harvest (29 ships totalling 143,000 tons). Next they moved still farther south, to the waters off the mouth of the Orinoco, and there too they found many ships sailing independently. Not until October was the American "Interlocking Convoy System" extended southwards to include ships sailing between Trinidad and Pernambuco; and then, as always happened, the U-boats' successes declined and Dönitz transferred them elsewhere. But well before that time the decrease in tonnage sunk in the western ocean had caused the Admiralty to expect a renewal of pack attacks on the main North Atlantic route; for Dönitz could deploy his forces far more economically there than against shipping in more remote waters. Nor was it long before those expectations proved correct. Early in August convoy SC 94, of 33 merchantmen protected by seven escorts, was heavily attacked when south of Greenland. The battle lasted five days, during which both sides sent reinforcements to the scene. Fog at first handicapped our long-range aircraft; but four more surface escorts joined the convoy in mid-ocean. None the less our forces were never strong enough to deal decisively with the 18 U-boats involved. Two enemies were destroyed and four others severely damaged; but eleven ships of the convoy (53,000 tons) were sunk. Though the battle of SC 94 could perhaps be classed as a drawn fight, on the next occasion the U-boats definitely gained the upper hand; for in September convoy ON 127 lost seven ships and one of its escorts when a "wolf-pack" attacked it in mid-ocean; and no enemies were destroyed in return. In that month, however, progress was made with two measures which were ultimately to have a profound effect on the Atlantic battle. Admiral Noble, the Commander-in-Chief, Western Approaches, had long ago realised the need to form special " Support Groups" of highly trained escort vessels, which could be sent to reinforce threatened convoys; but until September, 1942, when the first group entered the fray, we had never been able to spare the ships for such purposes. At about the same time the first escort carriers to commission since we had lost the *Audacity* in December, 1941, were ready for service;[1] but the many compelling demands for special escorts for troop convoys which arose in the autumn of 1942 actually prevented either the Support Groups or the escort carriers making their weight felt on the main Atlantic convoy route for another six months. If the ships which we had so long planned to throw into the struggle could not yet be spared, certain technical developments had greatly strengthened the armoury of our escort vessels and aircraft. Supreme among them stands the short-wave (10 centimetre) radar developed by British scientists; for it enabled our escort vessels to detect a surfaced U-boat at several miles' range, and so remedied the inability of their Asdic sets to locate such enemies. Secondly, heavier depth charges, the new shallow-set (25 feet) detonating pistol, and the ahead-throwing weapons being fitted in escort vessels helped greatly to increase the deadliness of our actual attacks. Unfortunately the production of the short-wave radars for Coastal Command clashed with fitting the heavy bombers with a similar set, which was urgently needed to improve the effectiveness of their raids into

[1] See p. 146.

Germany; and, as so often happened when the needs of the maritime war conflicted with those of the strategic bombers, it was the latter that were given priority. Our maritime aircrews thus had to continue to make do with the old 1½-metre radars, whose transmissions the U-boats were able to detect; and that reduced almost to zero the effectiveness of the patrols over the U-boat transit routes in the Bay of Biscay and round the north of Scotland. Later experience was to prove how extremely effective the short-wave radars were when used in conjunction with the " Leigh Light " fitted in our aircraft; for the searchlight could be switched on suddenly when the radar had brought the aircraft within a few hundred yards of the enemy, and so the attack could be made before he could seek safety in the depths; but it was not until March, 1943, that supply of the new radar sets enabled our aircraft fully to exploit such tactics. None the less it is certain that of all the many factors which combined to cause Dönitz increasing uneasiness in the summer of 1942 the far-ranging escort and patrol aircraft, able to reach some 800 miles out to sea, were among the greatest; and both in the North Atlantic and on the Sierra Leone route he began increasingly to deploy his boats in the ever-narrowing "air gaps" which we could not yet cover from our shore bases in Northern Ireland, Iceland, Newfoundland, Gibraltar and elsewhere.

In September, 1942, a group of U-boats and a "milch cow" (as the Germans called their supply submarines) arrived south of the equator, and there on the 12th U.156 sank the homeward-bound troopship *Laconia*, which had 1,800 Italian prisoners on board. On learning from survivors what he had done Hartenstein, the U-boat's captain, sent a series of messages *en clair* calling for help in the rescue work and promising immunity to ships sent to the scene, provided that he himself was not attacked. Though Hartenstein's messages certainly reached the Admiralty, the *Laconia's* SOS, which was probably sent on a low-power emergency set, was not picked up by any British ship or shore station. A Vichy French sloop in the Gulf of Guinea did, however, hear her call for help; and she informed Dakar, whence the cruiser *Gloire* sailed on the 15th to join in the rescue work. On the same day the headquarters of the Flag Officer, West Africa, at Freetown ordered two ships to proceed to the scene. All went well until the next afternoon when an American Army aircraft from the newly established base on Ascension Island arrived, flew around the surfaced U-boats for about an hour, and then attacked U.156 with bombs. It is as impossible to justify that act as it is difficult to explain why it was committed. The aircraft unquestionably reported by wireless that it was over a U-boat, and an order to attack was sent to it either from the American air base at Ascension or from the British naval base at Freetown, which were not in direct wireless touch with each other. The Flag Officer, West Africa (Rear-Admiral F. H. Pegram), was away from Freetown at the time, and he did not return there until 16th September; the station records make no mention of the dispatch of an order to attack, and the balance of probabilities suggests that it was an American authority which signalled the order. The consequence of the bombing of U.156 was that on the 17th Dönitz issued an order that "all attempts to rescue the crews of sunken ships will cease forthwith"; and at his trial before the International Military Tribunal at Nürnberg after the war the prosecution sought, unsuccessfully, to prove that this was an order to murder survivors. Such were the lengthy repercussions of the sinking of the *Laconia*. To-day two things seem clear. The first is that throughout the days following the torpedoing of the troopship, Hartenstein and the other U-boat captains involved behaved with marked humanity towards the survivors, doing their utmost to rescue friends and foes alike; and the second is that, on the Allied side, whoever sent the order to the aircraft to bomb the U-boat committed a serious blunder.

In October the pressure of the wolf-packs in the North Atlantic increased. As in the preceding month neither side gained a distinct advantage; but if our losses continued at a high rate we could draw some comfort from the fact that the sea and air escorts were exacting a slowly rising toll from the attackers. Thus in the middle of the month the slow convoy SC 104 lost eight ships; but the escorts sank three U-boats. The enemy always found it easier to concentrate against the slow SC convoys than against the faster ones from Halifax (HX); and it was around the former that many of the most protracted and bitter battles were fought. Thus at the end of October a lucky wireless interception enabled Dönitz to deploy a large force against SC 107, which lost no fewer than 15 ships (88,000 tons); but again we destroyed three U-boats. At the same time convoy SL 125, homeward bound from Sierra Leone, was beset by ten enemies and lost 13 ships in a seven-day battle; but, as we shall see later, the ordeal undergone by that particular convoy actually had very fortunate repercussions for the Allies.[1]

To sum up the progress of the struggle against the U-boats between July and October, 1942, the losses they inflicted on our merchant shipping had continued at a very high level (396 ships totalling more than two million tons during the four months); but a large proportion of those losses was incurred around the "soft spots" which Dönitz's probes into the western hemisphere had located. On the main Atlantic routes the results were far more favourable to the Allies; for British and Canadian escorts had given a good account of themselves in those convoy battles in which they had met their adversaries on something like equal terms. With the steady strengthening of our sea and air escorts, the improved training of the groups, and the new equipment now entering service there was ground for cautious optimism; but the uncomfortable facts were that the enemy's strength was still steadily rising, and that whereas 61 new U-boats had commissioned during the period, bringing the total to 365, all our efforts had only succeeded in destroying 32. Plainly we had to do much better than that to tilt the balance firmly in our favour.

In the outer oceans the German disguised raiders fared ill during the latter part of 1942. Three of them were at large in the middle of the year,[2] but the *Stier* met her end on 27th September in the South Atlantic in a duel to the death with a gallant American " Liberty ship" the *Stephen Hopkins*. The *Komet* tried to break out down-Channel early in October, but was intercepted and sunk by British destroyers and M.T.B.s off Cape de la Hague on the 14th; and the *Thor*, which had made her way from the Indian Ocean to Japan, was destroyed in Yokohama harbour on 30th November by an internal explosion. Thus at the end of 1942 only one of the nine disguised raiders which the Germans had fitted out so ingeniously was still at sea; and she, the *Michel*, was finding it so difficult to keep herself supplied that she was no longer capable of doing us serious harm. But the Japanese had meanwhile taken a leaf out of their Axis partner's book, and had sent two very powerful disguised raiders, the *Hokoku Maru* and *Aikoku Maru*, which were 10,400-ton ships armed with six 6-inch guns, into the Indian Ocean. On 11th November the Royal Indian Navy's little minesweeper *Bengal* (733

[1] See p. 244.   [2] See p. 209.

tons and armed with one twelve-pounder gun), which was escorting
the Dutch tanker *Ondina* (armed with one 4-inch gun), encountered
both those enemies some 1,300 miles to the north-west of Perth.
The *Bengal* and *Ondina* fought their ancient weapons to such good
effect that, incredible though it may seem, they sank the *Hokoku
Maru* and drove off her sister ship, while they themselves escaped
serious injury. Rarely can so one-sided an encounter have ended so
satisfactorily for the inferior party.

It will thus be seen that as 1942 drew to a close the days of the
disguised raider were plainly numbered. By putting most of our
shipping into convoy we had deprived them of easy targets, and by
catching their supply ships we had severely limited their sea-keeping
capacity. But the Germans were very far from abandoning the
guerre de course in the distant oceans; they had already arranged
with their Japanese allies to share in the underwater onslaught on
our traffic in the Indian Ocean, and early in October five U-boats
arrived in the focal area off Capetown. The Admiralty's Submarine
Tracking Room had, however, anticipated the move, and reinforcements had already been sent out; but they were not enough to
prevent our suffering some unpleasant losses—including three of the
large liners employed as troopships on the WS convoy route to and
from the Middle East. By the end of October the five U-boats had
sunk no less than 24 ships (161,000 tons); and when we strengthened
our patrols and escorts off the Cape of Good Hope they moved
north to the Mozambique Channel. There too they found a large
number of easy targets, for the Eastern Fleet did not possess anything
like the number of flotilla vessels needed to convoy all shipping in
the vast theatre for which it was responsible. Another successful
long-distance probe by Dönitz was the despatch of a group of nine
U-boats to the Brazilian coast in December, 1942; and there too
they did unpleasantly well for a time. And so it continued, and was
to continue for many months more. We could not convoy all
shipping everywhere and all the time, and the enemy constantly sent
the U-boats, sometimes thousands of miles, to find "soft spots" in
our defences. Having found one such spot they would do very
well for a few weeks. Then we strengthened our sea and air escorts
and patrols, the U-boats suffered losses, and the survivors moved
elsewhere to repeat the process.

We must now return from the distant oceans to our home waters

to review events in the Arctic since the shock we had suffered in
the disaster to PQ 17 in July, 1942.[1] By August Admiral Tovey's
strength in heavy ships was more satisfactory; for the new battleships *Howe* and *Duke of York* had joined his fleet, and their
sister ship the *Anson* was working up efficiency. In consequence the
U.S. Navy's contribution, known as Task Force 99, which we had
welcomed to Scapa in the previous April, was no longer essential,
and the battleship *Washington* and the heavy cruisers *Wichita* and
Tuscaloosa returned to their own country. On the German side the
light cruiser *Köln* had joined the *Tirpitz*, *Scheer* and *Hipper* in
Narvik; while the *Lützow* successfully slipped through our patrolling
submarines and aircraft, and reached Germany to repair the damage
she had sustained in grounding on 3rd July.[2] Admiral Tovey was
not, however, allowed for long to enjoy any appreciable increase
of strength; for in August many of his best ships were detached to
fight a critically important convoy through to Malta,[3] and that
prevented any ships being sent to North Russia before September.
Apart from a foray by the *Scheer* into the White Sea, during which
she only found one victim, the enemy heavy ships in the far north
remained idle during this period; but the highly efficient German
cryptographic service had revealed the position where our next
homeward and outward Arctic convoys were to pass each other,
and they therefore set about infesting the shallow waters on the
Barents Sea route and off Nova Zembla with mines.

Admiral Tovey used the breathing space gained by the postponement of the August convoy to Russia to recast the plans for those
difficult operations, and earlier experiences were put to good effect
in the orders for the conduct of PQ 18 and QP 14. The former
was to be a large convoy of 43 ships (including 4 tankers and a
rescue ship), and it was given an anti-submarine and anti-aircraft
close escort of 17 vessels of various types. What was new in the
plans was, firstly, that an escort carrier, the *Avenger*, was available;
and, secondly, that a " Fighting Destroyer Escort," consisting of the
light cruiser *Scylla* and no less than 16 fleet destroyers, would
reinforce the close escort during the critical part of the outward and
homeward journeys. Cover for the convoy was to be provided as
usual by three heavy cruisers; while the *Anson* and the remainder

[1] See pp. 206-8   [2] See p. 206.
[3] This was operation " Pedestal." See pp. 233-7.

228

of the Home Fleet, which did not amount to much, would cruise to the north-east of Iceland. Lastly, a special force would carry reinforcements and stores to Spitzbergen during the passage of the outward convoy. The 15 homeward-bound ships comprising QP 14 were not to sail until the loaded merchantmen had nearly reached their destination, thus ensuring that both convoys received the maximum protection for the longest possible period; but this arrangement did, of course, add greatly to the strain on the crews of the escorts, who would have to keep the seas under very exacting conditions for about three weeks with only the briefest of breaks for refuelling.

PQ 18 sailed for Archangel from Loch Ewe on 2nd September, and by the 9th Rear-Admiral R. L. Burnett, flying his flag in the *Scylla*, had joined it with part of the Fighting Destroyer Escort, and had taken command of the whole operation. The rest of the special escort had gone ahead to refuel in Spitzbergen. Meanwhile the enemy was doing his utmost to repeat the success he had achieved against PQ 17. On the 10th the *Scheer*, *Hipper*, *Köln* and some destroyers moved from Narvik to Altenfiord in the very north of Norway;[1] but when Hitler insisted that risks should not be taken with the heavy ships Raeder cancelled their intended foray, and they all remained in harbour throughout the convoys' passages. The Luftwaffe, however, personally urged on by Göring, threw in great strength; and a dozen U-boats were stationed in three patrol lines across the outward convoy's route. The first air attacks took place on the afternoon of the 13th, when some 40 torpedo planes, coming in " like a huge flight of nightmare locusts," almost obliterated the two starboard wing columns of the convoy at a moment when the carrier-borne fighters were engaged with enemy high-level bombers. This was a heavy blow; but when the enemy tried to repeat his success next day the *Avenger's* Hurricanes were ready at the critical moment, only one more ship was sunk, and a heavy toll was exacted from the attackers. Though the battle continued with scarcely a break until PQ 18 reached the entrance to the White Sea, the escorts kept the upper hand, and losses were never again as severe as in the first attack. In all PQ 18 lost 13 merchantmen—ten to air attacks, and three to U-boats' torpedoes; but the fighters and the anti-aircraft gunners destroyed no less than 41 enemy aircraft, and the

[1] See Map p. 144.

surface escorts sank three U-boats. The safe arrival of 27 loaded merchantmen, taken with the heavy losses inflicted on the enemy was, from our point of view, a substantial success; and it did much to offset the unhappy fate of PQ 17. The homeward convoy, QP 14, though protected by Admiral Burnett's special escort and by the *Avenger* for the greater part of its passage, had a very difficult time. Stormy weather handicapped flying, and the exhaustion of the warship crews may have helped to give the U-boats their chance. They sank two warships of the escort and three merchantmen. An outstanding feature of the double operation was, however, the effectiveness of the *Avenger's* work; and she should be remembered for having first closed the "air gap" on the Arctic route just as the *Audacity* had accomplished the same purpose on the Gibraltar route nearly a year earlier.[1]

The very heavy commitments which fell on the Royal Navy in the autumn of 1942, mainly in connection with the invasion of North Africa, made it impossible to run another outward convoy to Russia before the end of the year. A number of British and American ships were, however, sailed independently in both directions during the interval; and five of the thirteen loaded ships which set out alone on the long journey arrived safely. In November we also managed, aided by the shield of continuous darkness, to bring home a convoy of empty merchantmen (QP 15) with a comparatively light escort, and only two of the 29 ships in it were lost. It is now plain that the passages of PQ 18 and QP 14 marked the turning point in the Arctic; for although some later convoys underwent severe ordeals, events in Africa and on the Russian front prevented the Luftwaffe ever again throwing in such substantial strength; and our sea and air escorts had taken the measure of the U-boats in the far north, as they had done in the Atlantic. The only feature of the operations which remained constant, and caused very bitter feelings among the crews of the warships and merchantmen who risked so much to bring aid to our Ally, was the extraordinarily unco-operative attitude of the Russians at the receiving end. Not only did their naval and air forces, such as they were, rarely exert themselves to drive the U-boats from their own back door or sweep the mines which the enemy regularly laid there, but for a long time they put every obstacle in the way of our establishing the necessary shore

[1] See p. 146.

organisation to look after and administer the large numbers of Allied ships arriving at Murmansk and Archangel; and they even refused permission for us to land the medical staff necessary to look after our sick and wounded. Yet every time a convoy was postponed— and no matter what the reason—Stalin telegraphed protests and accusations couched in such intemperate terms that even Mr. Churchill's monumental patience finally became exhausted. One may doubt whether the rulers of Russia ever came near to under- standing the exertions which the Royal and Merchant Navies of Britain made on their behalf.

While these events were in progress in the far north the British and American leaders had for their part been earnestly considering ways and means whereby the weight of the German land offensive against Russia might be reduced, and in particular whether we could mount a cross-Channel assault in 1942 with any prospect of success. But the conclusion of the planners was that lack of trained men and of specialised equipment made it quite impracticable. There remained, however, the possibility of carrying out a large-scale raid on the French coast, and in the previous April Combined Operations Headquarters had therefore begun to plan an assault on Dieppe, the only place where we considered worthwhile objectives existed. The War Cabinet desired, moreover, to make active use of some of the large numbers of Canadian troops, who had assembled in Britain but had so far seen no fighting. Early in July unfavourable weather and the possibility that the enemy had gained foreknowledge of our intention caused us to cancel the operation; but towards the end of the same month the Prime Minister, in consultation with Admiral Mountbatten, the Chief of Combined Operations, decided to revive it in a modified form. The naval forces, which were under Captain J. Hughes-Hallett, consisted of 237 vessels, and were to carry across some 5,000 Canadian soldiers and 1,000 British Commandos. Some of the troops were to make landings on each side of Dieppe harbour with the object of capturing the enemy gun positions which commanded the direct approach to the port; while the main body was to make a frontal assault on the town itself. In the wisdom of after-knowledge it is plain that the plan suffered from several serious defects. The first was that, for a variety of reasons but chiefly to help gain surprise, no preliminary air bombardment was arranged; and the second was that the naval forces included no ships larger than destroyers, and there was little possibility of their light guns putting the enemy coast defences out of action before the landings. Success thus depended entirely on achieving surprise, and on whether the flank assaults accomplished their objects; for if they failed the main landing was bound to have to face an alert enemy established behind well-designed and intact gun positions.

The assault forces sailed from Portsmouth, Newhaven and Shoreham on the evening of 8th August, sweepers cleared a way for them through the German minefield in mid-Channel, and by the early hours of 19th the various groups had formed up for the approach. All seemed well set to achieve surprise when, just before 4 a.m., one group of landing craft ran into a German coastal convoy. It is not clear whether the engagement that followed gave the enemy warning of the approach of our forces; but it certainly delayed the landing craft carrying the troops for the eastern flank assault, and caused them to fall into some confusion. The result was that the assault on that flank was a complete failure. On the western flank a measure of success was achieved; but the Germans were not dislodged from the batteries and strong points commanding the beaches where the main landing was to take place. None the less the force commanders went ahead with the frontal attack, and at 5.20 a.m. the landing craft touched down in front of the town—almost exactly on time. But the enemy then opened up a murderous enfilading fire, the troops were pinned to the beaches, and the tanks—on which much depended—failed to force their way into the town. The destroyers and smaller vessels did their best to silence the German batteries; and although the weight of their fire was nothing like heavy enough the Royal Marine Commandos were sent in to reinforce the Canadians—an action which one of its officers described as "a sea parallel to the charge of the Light Brigade." The frontal assault was thus a complete and costly failure, redeemed only by the gallantry of the men involved. At 11 a.m. landing craft moved inshore again, to try and rescue at any rate some of the unfortunate soldiers; but the weight of the enemy's fire made this a desperate undertaking, many craft were lost, and only about 1,000 soldiers were brought away. By 12.30 p.m. it was obvious that no more could be done, and the naval forces began to withdraw—under heavy air attacks. Casualties among the Canadians were very heavy (68 per cent of those engaged), and the Royal Navy lost one

The second battle of Sirte, 22nd March, 1942. H.M.S. *Cleopatra* laying
a smokescreen seen from the bridge of H.M.S. *Euryalus*

The German Brest squadron in their up-Channel dash, 12th February, 1942

"Pedestal" convoy entering the Mediterranean with escort of battleships, aircraft-carriers, cruisers and destroyers, August, 1942

H.M.S. *Victorious* leading H.M.S. *Indomitable* and *Eagle* on "Pedestal" convoy to Malta, August, 1942

destroyer and 33 landing craft. Undoubtedly the lack of preliminary bombing and of heavy naval bombardment contributed a good deal to this unhappy failure; but we also learnt that permanent naval assault forces were essential to success in combined operations. After Dieppe it became our practice to keep such forces together once they had been formed, and to arrange that they trained with the troops whom they were to carry overseas and put ashore in hostile territory. The naval assault forces which were a constant feature in all later combined operations thus had their genesis in the failure off Dieppe on 19th August, 1942; and never again did we pit our troops against prepared enemy positions without giving them the strongest possible naval supporting gunfire.

We have already seen how in 1942 the fate of Malta fundamentally affected all our maritime plans and purposes, from the Arctic to the Indian Ocean; and how our inability to run a convoy to the beleaguered island in July had made it essential to fight one through in August. The principal change in the plan for operation " Pedestal," as it was called, was that this time fighter protection was to be provided by no less than three fleet carriers—the *Victorious*, *Indomitable* and *Eagle*; while the old *Furious* was also included in order to fly off yet another batch of Spitfires to reinforce the island's defenders. Vice-Admiral E. N. Syfret, commander of Force H, came home to meet the fourteen merchantmen forming the convoy and the Home Fleet reinforcements off the Clyde on 3rd August, and a week later the entire force, which included two battleships, the four carriers already mentioned, seven cruisers and two dozen destroyers, passed safely through the Gibraltar Straits in thick fog. This was by far the biggest convoy we had ever despatched to Malta, and the escort was the most powerful ever provided; for the War Cabinet and Admiralty fully realised that the fate of the island hung upon the safe arrival of a reasonable proportion of the merchantmen —and especially of the precious tanker *Ohio*, which was an American-built ship chartered by the Ministry of War Transport and manned by a British crew.

On the day that the Pedestal convoy passed Gibraltar the Mediterranean fleet staged a diversion in the eastern basin, to give the impression that, as on the previous occasion,[1] we intended to send convoys from both directions; but it seems unlikely that this

_____
[1] Operations " Vigorous " and " Harpoon " in June, 1942. See pp. 218-20.

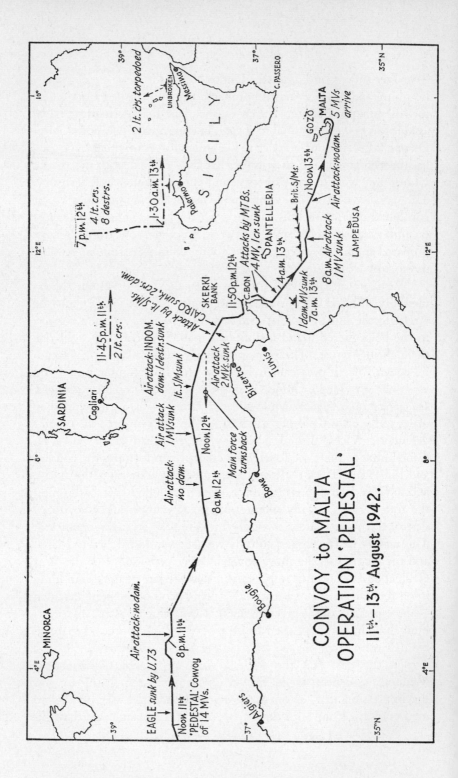

CONVOY to MALTA
OPERATION 'PEDESTAL'
11th–13th August 1942.

deceptive ruse influenced the enemy to any appreciable extent, since his aircraft gained touch with Syfret's large body of ships soon after they entered the Mediterranean. On the 11th the *Furious* successfully flew off her Spitfires in a position 550 miles from Malta; but early that afternoon U.73 struck a hard blow when she torpedoed and sank the faithful old carrier *Eagle*, which had performed such splendid service in those same waters since the earliest days.[1] Happily most of her crew were rescued by the ever-alert destroyers. At dusk that evening, and again in the early hours of the 12th, the fighters and A-A. gunners successfully beat off air attacks; but it was when the convoy came within range of the Sardinian airfields that the enemy's real effort began. Some 80 torpedo- and dive-bombers attacked on the afternoon of the 12th, hit the *Victorious* but did not damage her seriously, and caused the first casualty among the merchantmen. At about the same time the convoy passed safely through the enemy's main U-boat concentration, sinking an Italian submarine in the process; but towards evening the air attacks were renewed in dangerous strength, and this time the *Indomitable* was so badly hit that her flight deck was put out of action. Only the *Victorious* now remained to give the convoy fighter cover.

Meanwhile Italian cruisers and destroyers had put to sea from bases in Sicily and Sardinia, as well as from Naples, with the object of attacking the convoy; but we had stationed submarines to the north of Sicily and in "the Narrows" to the south of that island in anticipation of such a move, and on the 13th one of the former, the *Unbroken*, torpedoed the cruisers *Bolzano* and *Attendolo*. This time no major units of the Italian fleet ventured to come south of Sicily.

Shortly after the *Indomitable* was hit the convoy reached the position off Bizerta where Admiral Syfret and the heavy ships were to return to the west, leaving Rear-Admiral H. M. Burrough to carry on to Malta with four cruisers and twelve destroyers—a sufficient force to prevent interference by the Italian Navy, such as had produced unhappy consequences for the June convoy.[2] So far the warship and Merchant Navy crews had good reason to be

---

[1] The *Eagle* was designed in 1913 as a battleship for Chile, but was taken over by the Royal Navy and converted to aircraft carrier during the 1914-18 war. Her aircrews took part in the attack on Taranto on 11th November, 1940, and in many other operations in the Mediterranean. In 1942 she made nine aircraft ferry trips for Malta, sending 183 Spitfires to the island.

[2] See p. 218.

satisfied with the progress of the operation; but the next few hours were to produce a drastic change of fortune. Hardly had Admiral Burrough taken charge when his flagship the *Nigeria* and the A.A. cruiser *Cairo* were both torpedoed by the Italian submarine *Axum*, and the *Cairo* had to be sunk by our own ships. The Admiral transferred his flag to a destroyer and sent the *Nigeria* limping back to Gibraltar. Next enemy aircraft attacked—just when the convoy was changing its formation to a narrow front to pass through the Skerki Channel—and two merchantmen were sunk. A short while later the cruiser *Kenya* was torpedoed by a submarine, but managed to stay with the convoy. Admiral Syfret, hearing of these troubles, ordered back a light cruiser and two of his destroyers to replace Burrough's lost and damaged ships; but the reinforcements had not joined when, at midnight on 12th-13th, the convoy rounded Cape Bon and turned south, hugging the Tunisian coast.[1] It was now in shallow, easily mined waters, and close off bases where Axis light naval forces were known to be stationed. The minesweeping destroyers were ahead of the merchantmen, successfully clearing the passage; but the escort soon realised that enemy E-boats were about, and they were extremely difficult targets to see on a dark night. In the small hours of the 13th the cruiser *Manchester* was torpedoed by one of them, and came to a dead stop. Having failed to get his ship under way again by 5 a.m. her captain gave the order to scuttle her. This was not, however, the worst blow suffered during the night; for no less than five merchantmen were hit by E-boats' torpedoes, and four of them sank. Still the depleted convoy fought its way on towards its destination.

Soon after daylight on 13th the German bombers renewed their onslaught, destroying one more merchantman, and severely damaging three others, among them the precious *Ohio*. Destroyers came back to look after the cripples, while the survivors of the convoy—now reduced to three ships—struggled on to the east. Malta-based fighters were now patrolling overhead, minesweepers and light escorts had come out to meet them, and in the afternoon they entered the Grand Harbour safely. Meanwhile a tremendous effort was being made to save at any rate some of the crippled ships. At dusk one of them was sunk in yet another air attack, and the *Ohio* was hit for the third time; but the destroyers, the minesweepers

[1]See Map p. 234.

and her own crew were all determined to get her in. From noon on the 13th until the morning of the 15th they towed, escorted, swept the mines and fought off air attacks; and their efforts were finally crowned by success. Totally disabled, her decks almost awash, but her cargo practically intact, Captain D. W. Mason's indomitable *Ohio* finally reached safety, as did one other of the damaged merchant ships. So ended operation "Pedestal." Only five out of the 14 ships in the convoy reached Malta, and the losses suffered by the naval escort had also been heavy. But the 32,000 tons of general cargo and 15,000 tons of oil delivered into Malta's nearly empty store houses and fuel tanks were enough to enable the island not only to continue to defend itself but to intensify the offensive against the Axis supply traffic to Africa; and there is no doubt that, if we paid a heavy price for that accomplishment, its influence on the land campaigns was decisive. The First Sea Lord put the matter in a nutshell in a letter to Admiral Cunningham in which he said, "personally I think we got out of it lightly considering the risks we had to run, and the tremendous concentration of everything which we had to face." But the partial success achieved by the Pedestal operation was not by itself enough to restore the striking power of Malta for an indefinite period. On 17th August the *Furious* therefore flew yet another batch of Spitfires to the island, and for the next three months submarines continued to run in specially valuable cargoes such as aviation spirit. Between January, 1941, which marked the beginning of the siege of Malta, and the arrival of the "Pedestal" convoy in August of the following year 82 merchantmen had set out for the island from the east or west, and our submarines had made 31 supply trips; but only 49 of the merchantmen had arrived safely, and in recent months the number sunk on passage had risen very sharply. Though the "Pedestal" ships had brought essential relief to the hard-pressed islanders, it was plain that we were still far from raising the siege.

While the August convoy was on passage to Malta a plan had been prepared at the urgent request of General Auchinleck to take some of the weight off his Eighth Army; and when General Montgomery relieved Auchinleck on 13th August the decision to make an assault from the sea on Tobruk, combined with a sudden lunge by raiding forces from the desert, was not amended. On 13th September the destroyers *Sikh* and *Zulu*, in which 350 Royal

Marines had embarked, sailed from Alexandria to meet other forces, including about a score of M.T.B.s and M.L.s with 150 soldiers on board. The intention was to land the marines on the north side of the harbour and the soldiers on the south side to seize the enemy gun positions; after which the destroyers were to enter the harbour, destroy the shipping present, and finally re-embark the assault forces. But the weather on the night of 13th-14th was far from suitable for that most hazardous of enterprises—an assault in darkness on a hostile coast; and from the beginning the plan went awry. Very few of the marines or troops ever got ashore, and when the *Sikh* closed the coast to find out what had happened she was quickly disabled by the German batteries. The *Zulu* tried unavailingly to tow her clear, and she finally sank close inshore. During the withdrawal the survivors were heavily attacked by German bombers, and the A-A. cruiser *Coventry* and the *Zulu* were both sunk. In retrospect it is plain that to attempt an attack on an enemy stronghold with such very slender forces was bold to the point of rashness. The outcome certainly caused serious heart burnings in London, and Admiral Harwood himself described it as a "desperate gamble" which was justified only by the Eighth Army's call for help. General Montgomery also was critical of the undertaking, and it is likely that his lack of confidence in his naval colleague, which was to culminate in the latter being relieved of his command six months later, originated in the failure off Tobruk in September, 1942.

Meanwhile with Malta revivified the pressure against the Axis supply traffic to North Africa was rising steadily. In September only about one-fifth of the tonnage which sailed from Italy was sunk; but in the following month Axis losses increased sharply, and little more than half the ships which set out on the short but dangerous passage to Africa arrived safely.[1] It was the 10th Flotilla's submarines and the strike aircraft of the Navy and R.A.F. based on Malta which inflicted by far the greatest proportion of those losses; and their combined efforts produced a critical situation for Rommel's Afrika Korps which, only a few months earlier had seemed likely to overwhelm our entire position in the Middle East. With supplies for our own Army pouring in through the Red Sea ports, the Levant convoys

---

[1] Bragadin, *The Italian Navy in World War II*, p. 216 gives the following figures:
    August, 1942   25% of supplies and 41% of fuel sent to Africa lost.
    September, 1942 20% of total tonnage sent lost.
    October, 1942   44% of total tonnage sent lost.

steadily bringing in cargoes of precious fuel, and our escorts taking a heavy toll of the German and Italian submarines which tried to interfere with them, our control of the eastern Mediterrean had been reasserted; and the strategic situation throughout the Middle East theatre had in consequence undergone an astonishing transformation. By the beginning of October it was plain that it would be Montgomery's men, and not Rommel's, who would strike the next blow; and on 23rd the hearts of the free world lifted to the news that the Eighth Army had resumed the offensive at El Alamein. The Inshore Squadron had meanwhile made itself ready once again to support the Army's flank where it came down to the sea, and to carry its supplies right forward to the front; while the submarines and Malta-based striking forces redoubled their efforts to prevent fuel, stores and reinforcements reaching the enemy. Other submarines and the fast minelayer *Welshman* again ran urgently needed supplies to Malta, and late in October the *Furious* sent the island yet another consignment of Spitfires. Thus did all arms and all services strive towards one objective—to give the Eighth Army the striking power it needed to gain a decisive victory. Their reward came on the night of 4th-5th November when they heard that, after twelve days of gruelling battle, General Montgomery had made a complete break in the Axis defences, and that Rommel was in full retreat.

CHAPTER XII

NORTH AFRICA HOLDS THE BALANCE

1st November–31st December, 1942

" Like other amphibious animals we must come occasionally
on shore: but the water is more properly our element, and in
it . . . as we find our greatest security, so we exert our greatest
force."

Bolingbroke, *Idea of a Patriot King* (1749).

EVER SINCE our expulsion from Europe in the summer of 1940
it had been the intention of the British war leaders that, when
the day came that we were able to assume the strategic offensive, they
would exploit our maritime power to strike at the perimeter of the
enemy's defences. Not only was such a strategy backed by centuries
of experiences of war against far more powerful continental enemies,
but we were fully aware that, even after the greater part of Germany's
military might had been committed in the titanic campaigns against
Russia, we had little hope of winning important victories on land
unless we could surprise the enemy by landing troops in a theatre of
our own choice, where his own defences were weak and ill-prepared.
Furthermore, the Prime Minister himself was deeply conscious of
the fact that in the 1914-18 war we had not employed our maritime
power to the best advantage; and that the seaborne expeditions to
the Baltic and the Dardanelles, for which he had so strenuously
pleaded, might well have gained us great benefits, and saved our
armies from the "carnage incomparable and human squander" of
the long-drawn campaigns in France and Flanders. With Mr.
Churchill now in supreme control of the British war machine it was
certain that our previous error would not be repeated, and that our
grand strategy would be based on striking a succession of blows at

key points far overseas, with the object of gradually improving our position until the time came when we would be able to launch a decisive expedition aimed at the heart of the enemy's territory. For over two years, however, all such aspirations had seemed more than a little unreal; for our control of the seas, on which the fate of Britain—let alone the prospect of assuming the offensive—entirely depended, had been continuously and seriously threatened; and we had been forced to devote our utmost energies to countering that threat. Not until the middle of 1942 had the adverse movement of the balance at sea been sufficiently checked to enable us to review future purposes with some sense of reality. Secondly, even after an unprepared America had suddenly found itself at war, our combined resources of merchant ships, of landing craft and of trained men long remained totally inadequate to such purposes; and our Ally had moreover to devote a considerable proportion of what was available on his side of the Atlantic to containing Japanese ambitions in the Pacific. Thus it was plain that the first offensive blow in the west would have to be mounted on a fairly modest scale, and aimed at a point where stubborn resistance was unlikely to be encountered. It was those considerations which ruled out the possibility—long-favoured by the Americans—of striking across the Channel at the coast of France in 1942, and led to the Allied leaders accepting, on 25th July of that year, the alternative all along favoured by the British—namely, the despatch of an expedition to the French North African territories, so timed as to assist a westward offensive by the Eighth Army from Egypt. We saw that by establishing a new army in Rommel's rear at the same time as his old adversaries hammered at his front there was a good hope of clearing the Axis forces right out of Africa; and by exploiting the fact that French sentiments towards the United States were very much friendlier than towards Britain, we hoped that their troops in Algeria and Morocco would, if faced with overwhelming strength, offer no more resistance to Allied landings than was consistent with maintaining their jealously guarded honour.

Though it was not until October that the British and American Chiefs of Staff gave their final approval to the plan, the Admiralty did not wait upon them to assemble the shipping and escorts, and to organise the convoys. From the British point of view by far the greatest difficulty was the provision of the necessary troopships, landing craft, escort vessels and supporting warships; but in mid-summer the Admiralty had far-sightedly instituted very extensive changes in our world-wide shipping control organisation in order to release the large mercantile tonnage and the scores of warships needed. Convoys to North Russia were temporarily stopped, as were those running between the British Isles and Gibraltar or Sierra Leone; reinforcements for some overseas theatres, and in particular South-East Asia, were held back; our own coastal convoys were stripped almost bare of escorts, and the Home Fleet was called on to provide many ships, thus acting, as so often in its history as the strategic reserve of our maritime power. The diversion of merchant shipping involved in these measures was, of course, bound to slow down the arrival of essential imports in Britain; for, to give only one example, homeward-bound vessels from the Cape of Good Hope were re-routed via Trinidad, or even by the Straits of Magellan and then eastwards through the Panama Canal to New York or Halifax. But such handicaps, as well as the risks involved in reducing the mercantile convoys' escorts, were accepted in the interests of our first major overseas expedition. The Admiralty's chief anxiety was that large numbers of U-boats might concentrate against the troop and supply convoys; for at the end of October more than one hundred of these enemies were at sea and, if the Germans gained foreknowledge of our intentions, a high proportion of them could be redisposed in time to catch the special convoys. We will discuss later how and why the threat never reached anything like its anticipated scale.

In mid-August Admiral Sir Andrew Cunningham was appointed "Allied Naval Commander Expeditionary Force" for operation "Torch," and on 1st November he hoisted his flag at Gibraltar to take command, under General Eisenhower, of the maritime side of the whole complex undertaking, and of all naval forces in the western Mediterranean. His return to the station where he had made his name famous during his first period of command was a good augury for the success of the new enterprise.

The plan for operation "Torch" involved making two assaults inside the Mediterranean, at Algiers and Oran, and one on the Moroccan coast near Casablanca. The forces for both the landings in Algeria were to set out from Britain, while those destined for Morocco were to be carried there direct from the United States, and would be wholly American. But the assault forces for Algeria included many American troops, who had previously been carried across the Atlantic, generally in the British "giant liners" such as the *Queen Mary* and *Queen Elizabeth*, whose high speed and great carrying capacity, increased by June, 1942, to 15,000 men, made them remarkably well suited to such purposes.[1] The naval forces for escorting, covering and supporting the Algerian assaults were British, and were commanded respectively by Vice-Admiral Sir Harold Burrough (Algiers) and Commodore T. H. Troubridge (Oran). Force H from Gibraltar, under Vice-Admiral Sir Neville Syfret, was to be specially reinforced from the Home Fleet, and was to cover the Algerian landings against interference by the Italian fleet. The date originally fixed for all three assaults was 30th October; but, chiefly because the U.S. Army could not be ready in time, in mid-September it was postponed until 4th November. A week after that decision had been taken an aircraft which was carrying an officer with papers in his possession giving the actual date of the landings crashed off the Spanish coast, and the fear that our plans had been compromised caused a further postponement to 8th November. In fact it is now plain that the Germans gained no hint of our intentions from this accident. In order to improve the chances of achieving surprise all the assaults were to take place in darkness, " H-Hour " being 1 a.m. at Algiers and Oran and 4 a.m. on the Moroccan coast. From the naval point of view this was far from ideal, since confusion was much less likely to arise during the hoisting out and forming up of the landing-craft flotillas, and they would find it much easier to arrive at the right beaches, if the landings took place in daylight; but military needs were held to outweigh those considerations, and not until much later in the war did we accept that the advantages of night assaults had been over-estimated.

Long before the expeditions set sail the Admiralty had been creating the necessary organisation at Gibraltar to handle, supply and administer the hundreds of warships and merchantmen which would pass through the Straits; and it is no exaggeration to say that the base formed the hub around which the wheel of the whole great

---

[1] The other giant liners were the *Aquitania* and *Mauretania* (British), the *Ile de France* (French) and the *Nieuw Amsterdam* (Dutch). They made the greater part of their passages, which were known as "operational convoys," unescorted; and special measures for their safety were always instituted by the Admiralty.

enterprise revolved. On the British side the 160 warships detailed to take part were recalled well in advance from many different stations and duties, in order to refit and replenish with stores; while the 240 merchantmen gradually assembled in many different ports, but chiefly in the Clyde and Loch Ewe, to embark military stores, vehicles, ammunition and all the multifarious equipment needed by the overseas expedition. Early in October a series of "Advance Convoys," mostly comprising store ships of various types, began to sail outward-bound to Gibraltar. Then, between 22nd October and 1st November, four large "Assault Convoys" carrying the troops for the landings at Oran and Algiers followed. The main naval forces from Britain also began to move from Scapa towards Gibraltar at the end of October; and during the first week of November a vast concourse of merchantmen and warships was thus steaming south from the British Isles, most of them passing to the west of Ireland and keeping well out into the Atlantic before heading east towards Gibraltar. As was inevitable several U-boats sighted and reported the presence of our convoys and warships; but even so the enemy remained totally unaware of what was in train. We had, of course, taken elaborate precautions both to conceal our intentions and to mislead the enemy regarding them; but the immunity of the expedition from U-boat and air attacks while on passage none the less remains an astonishing feature. In fact, the most dangerously placed U-boat group was busily engaged in attacking the slow homeward-bound convoy SL 125 at the time when the assault ships slipped through Dönitz's net. Though 13 merchantmen were sent to the bottom in the seven-day battle that followed, their unintended sacrifice proved so beneficial that the Convoy Commodore sardonically remarked to the author of this history that it was the only time he had been congratulated for losing ships. Even taking account of the fact that the element of luck, which must always play some part in operations of war, seems on this occasion to have favoured the Allied cause, the safe passage of the entire expedition, including the section which started out from America, and the complete surprise achieved, surpassed the hopes of the most sanguine.

As darkness was falling on 5th November the expeditionary force rounded Cape St. Vincent and passed Cape Trafalgar. Then the grey loom of the Rock of Gibraltar hove in sight in the still evening air. These were waters with which the Royal Navy had been intimately connected for more than two hundred years; and memories of Rooke, Howe, John Jervis, and of Nelson himself, must have flooded into the minds of those taking part in the latest of the Service's many ventures through them. Quite recently Somerville's few ships had fought for and held control of the Gibraltar approaches, making it possible to keep Malta supplied and to send Cunningham's reinforcements off on their hazardous passages through the narrow seas. Now some of those same ships, and others bearing names made famous in earlier Mediterranean sea fights, were ploughing their way steadily eastwards, with the troop convoys sheltering under the safety of their wings, bound on an expedition which their crews knew full well would mark a turning point in the war. And high on the Rock which had seen so much British history, had so often listened to the booming of her Navy's guns out to sea, and watched the torn and shattered ships struggle into the shelter of its harbour, stood the Naval Commander himself— that same Cunningham whose leadership in triumph and adversity had made possible the events now come to pass. To him the safe passage of the " Torch " convoys must indeed have seemed a prominent milestone on the long road towards victory; and that night in his headquarters inside the Rock and in the quiet rooms deep down beneath the Admiralty everyone waited, with natural anxiety, for the first reports on the expedition's fortunes.

Once inside the Mediterranean the expeditionary force from Britain divided into two main bodies consisting of the ships destined for Algiers and Oran respectively; and on arriving off their destinations each assault force divided again, into the components allocated to the different beaches. Next the troop transports anchored in the " lowering positions " about seven miles offshore, where the assault craft were manned, hoisted out, formed up into their various flotillas, and then set off towards their distant objectives. Accuracy of timing and of pilotage were among the most important requirements in such an undertaking—especially when, as on the present occasion, the approach and landings were to take place in darkness. Submarines were therefore stationed offshore in each sector to act as navigational beacons, and specially trained pilotage craft were attached to the assault flotillas. None the less there remained plenty of room for human error and unforeseen difficulties, and matters did not go exactly according to plan either at Algiers or

Oran. In the former case, however, resistance was slight, and by daylight on 8th November the assault troops were ashore and the two local airfields had been captured. Meanwhile, the destroyers *Broke* and *Malcolm* (both of them veterans of the 1914-18 war) had made a frontal attack on the powerfully defended harbour, with the object of landing troops to prevent the French destroying their ships and port installations. During the approach the *Malcolm* was badly damaged; but the *Broke* successfully charged the boom and got inside the harbour. She disembarked her troops but was then forced by heavy fire to withdraw, and sank the next day. By the afternoon of the 9th the bombarding ships had silenced the coast defences, and at 7 p.m. that evening French resistance ceased. Algiers had been won remarkably quickly, and at relatively small cost.

The assault on Oran was on a larger scale than that against Algiers; and, as we had expected, resistance was much stiffer. As happened off Algiers—and indeed is likely in any operation as complex as an amphibious assault—some unforeseen troubles arose. Thus a fortuitous encounter with a French convoy caused confusion in the western assault force, and sandbars close offshore damaged many landing craft in the centre sector. A frontal assault on the harbour by two ex-American British-manned coastguard cutters was frustrated by the defenders, and both ships were sunk; but the French destroyers which came out to attack the invasion shipping were severely handled by our covering forces. By daylight on the 8th the situation in all three assault sectors was reasonably satisfactory, and troops and tanks were pouring ashore; but the French continued to resist stubbornly until noon on the 10th, when our armoured vehicles penetrated into the city and the authorities thereupon capitulated. Thus passed into Allied hands a splendid naval base, which had been a source of anxiety to Britain ever since June, 1940, on account of the powerful French warships present in it. But of all the assault forces in operation " Torch " those landed at Oran had much the hardest fight.

Meanwhile off the Moroccan coast Rear-Admiral H. K. Hewitt, U.S.N., was carrying out three landings—two to the north and one to the south of Casablanca. They should all have taken place three hours later than the assaults at Algiers and Oran (that is to say, at 4 a.m. on 8th November); but various difficulties, the chief of which was the heavy surf breaking on the beaches, caused delays. Moreover, when the landing craft reached the shore many of them broached to in the surf and were lost. The covering American warships fought several sharp and successful actions with French ships which came out from Casablanca harbour, and the bombarding squadron put the battleship *Jean Bart* out of action. The powerful French squadron in Dakar, whose intervention might have proved awkward, did not however put to sea. On 10th November, by which time the assault forces were poised to attack Casablanca itself, Admiral Darlan broadcast an order from Algiers to all French troops to cease resistance, and that afternoon the Americans occupied all their principal objectives.

Thus within three days of the first soldiers stepping ashore, did the Allies, by the skilful application of maritime power, gain possession of positions which vastly improved their strategic situation both in the western basin of the Mediterranean and in the central Atlantic; for we were now able to make use of excellent naval and air bases close on the southern flank of the route to Malta, and also give our north-south Atlantic convoys far better protection than had been possible while we had to depend entirely on Gibraltar and Freetown, which are about 2,100 miles apart.[1] Rarely can so much have been gained at such small cost as in operation " Torch " in November, 1942.

The German reaction to the landings was, to say the least of it, slow; but by the middle of November nine U-boats had arrived off the Moroccan coast, a dozen were concentrated in the western approaches to Gibraltar, and seven had penetrated inside the Straits with the object of attacking the follow-up convoys running to Algiers and Oran. We had always expected that, in waters through which such heavy traffic was flowing, the U-boats and the enemy bombers would cause us some losses; but they never came anywhere near to endangering the expedition, and the U-boats themselves soon began to suffer at the hands of our anti-submarine forces. Thus in November we sank two in the approaches to Gibraltar and one off the Moroccan coast, as well as five Germans and two Italians in the western Mediterranean.

The object of operation " Torch " was, however, far wider than merely to gain control of Algeria and Morocco—important though

[1] See Map p. 91.

those territories were in terms of strategy. We aimed to demolish for good the Axis barrier across the narrows of the central basin between Sicily and Tunisia; and the key to that barrier was held by the ports of Bizerta and Tunis.[1] This latter fact was as obvious to the enemy as to ourselves; and it was therefore natural that, as soon as our troops were well established in Algeria, the race for Tunisia should begin. Land communications in North Africa were, however, far too primitive to enable a large army to advance rapidly eastwards, while keeping itself adequately supplied; and in order to gain more advanced bases through which to nourish our land forces, on 11th and 12th November we assaulted Bougie and Bone from the sea. The Navy again carried the assault forces safely to their destinations, and both ports were seized without undue difficulty; but the shipping in those harbours was much more vulnerable to air attacks from the enemy's Sardinian and Sicilian bases, and our land-based fighters were slow to get established on the adjacent French airfields. It thus came to pass that we lost a number of valuable ships, and the build-up of the Army's supplies did not take place as fast as we had hoped. By the end of November the First Army was still held up some forty miles west of Bizerta, and as the enemy had meanwhile been able to reinforce Tunisia it was obvious that we had lost the race. In retrospect it does seem that, hazardous though a lunge by sea direct to Bizerta undoubtedly would have been, the value of the prize would have justified accepting the risks; and had we got sufficient forces ashore in Tunisia to stiffen the timid and vacillating French authorities we would undoubtedly have cleared North Africa of Axis forces in the autumn of 1942. As it was, another six months were to elapse, and a great deal of hard fighting was to be undergone, before we achieved that purpose. If in that respect the results of operation "Torch" fell short of what they might have been—and Admiral Cunningham was at the time firmly convinced that a landing at Bizerta would have succeeded—in many other respects the gains it brought were substantial; and the greatest of them were that Malta could now be permanently relieved and our Atlantic shipping rendered far more secure.

On 11th November the fast minelayer *Manxman* and six destroyers dashed to Malta from Alexandria with urgently needed

[1] See Map pp. 112-13.

The damaged tanker *Ohio* entering Grand Harbour, Malta, 15th August, 1942

Ships of the main assault convoy *en route* for North Africa, November, 1942

The Invasion of North Africa, November, 1942. The main assault convoy on passage

The Invasion of North Africa, November, 1942. The heavy ships of the covering force. H.M.S. *Duke of York*, *Nelson*, *Renown* and *Formidable* seen from H.M.S. *Victorious*

stores—just as the *Welshman* had done a few days earlier from the west. If our fast minelayers had accomplished nothing else during the entire war their contribution towards keeping Malta supplied would alone have justified their design. In fact, if one had to single out a few from all the ships of many classes and types which helped to save the island, the choice would probably fall on the U.S. Navy's *Wasp*, the Royal Navy's supply ship *Breconshire* and fast minelayer *Welshman*, and the Merchant Navy's tanker *Ohio*. But such distinctions are in fact invidious, since the salvation of Malta was accomplished by all arms of all three British services—and, perhaps above all, by the steadfastness of the islanders themselves.

While the "Torch" assault forces were gaining control of Algeria and Morocco, in the eastern basin of the Mediterranean Admiral Harwood's Inshore Squadron was, as so often before, supporting the Eighth Army in its rapid advance across Cyrenaica, and on 13th we regained the much-contested harbour of Tobruk. A week later Benghazi was recaptured, and we were once again in possession of the advanced desert airfields which meant so much in the struggle to keep Malta supplied. These successes on land transformed the prospects of getting a convoy through to Malta from the east, and on 17th November four merchantmen set out from Alexandria under a powerful cruiser and destroyer escort. In spite of bad weather and heavy air attacks they all arrived safely, and that operation (called "Stoneage") marked the final and effective relief of the island whose ordeal had lasted only a few weeks short of two years.[1] And, as a sign that the Axis supply lines to Africa were very seriously imperilled, ships of the famous 15th Cruiser Squadron, now commanded by Rear-Admiral A. J. Power, and many destroyers soon berthed alongside Malta's battered wharves, another squadron of naval torpedo-bombers moved to the island's airfields, and the submarines of the 10th Flotilla, which had borne the main burden of the offensive against Axis shipping throughout the worst months of the siege, received welcome reinforcements. To make the attempts by enemy supply ships to reach the ports of Tunisia and Tripolitania yet more precarious the Commander-in-Chief next established a new cruiser and destroyer striking force based on Bone. Thenceforth either the Malta or the

[1] The siege of Malta may be said to have started with the German air attacks which followed the arrival there of the damaged *Illustrious* on 10th January, 1941 (see pp. 149-50).

Bone striking force was out on every suitable night, and Axis losses rose sharply to more than forty ships a months in November and December. The year thus closed with our hold over " the ancient waterway" through the Mediterranean greatly strengthened; but until the enemy had been driven from Tunisia we could not sweep the many mines laid in "the Narrows" south of Sicily, and so were unable to send our convoys straight through the Mediterranean to the Suez Canal. The success of the North African enterprise had, however, enabled the Admiralty to reorganise our convoys sailing on the north-south Atlantic route, and a special series of fast and slow convoys (called KMF/MKF and KMS/MKS respectively) had started to run between Britain and the North African ports. Though the U-boats and bombers repeatedly attacked those convoys as they moved slowly along the African coast, and on occasions we lost some valuable ships, the Royal Navy and Royal Air Force gradually and jointly developed an extremely effective offensive-defensive system of protecting the merchantmen and counter-attacking their assailants. Supplies and reinforcements for the First Army in the west, as for the Eighth Army in the east, continued to pour ashore; and during the two months following the landings in North Africa the " Torch " command area received no less than 437,200 fighting men, 42,420 vehicles, and many thousands of tons of stores. Thus was our maritime power first exploited on a large scale to launch an overseas offensive; and by the turn of the year it was plain that the situation in the whole Middle East theatre had been completely transformed. The balance had not only come central, but was now swinging unmistakably in favour of the Allies.

CHAPTER XIII

THE JAPANESE FORCED BACK ON THE DEFENSIVE

1st August, 1942–31st May, 1943

" Command of the sea is the indispensable basis of security, but whether the instrument that commands swims, floats, or flies is a mere matter of detail."

Admiral Sir Herbert Richmond, *Statesmen and Sea Power* (O.U.P., 1946), p. 136.

W E SAW earlier how the drawn battle in the Coral Sea on 8th May, 1942, checked the Japanese lunge at Port Moresby in New Guinea, where they had hoped to establish forward bases from which they could threaten Australia; and how the decisive battle of Midway on the following 4th June totally frustrated their plans to seize some of the Hawaiian Islands, and so extend their control of the central Pacific towards America.[1] But neither of those battles, and not even the loss of Admiral Nagumo's entire carrier striking force in the second of them, immediately curbed Japanese ambitions. Nor was this at first sight unreasonable; for they still possessed great strength in their Combined Fleet, the skill and efficiency of their amphibious forces had been proved in many assaults from the sea, and the morale of their Navy was still very high. Moreover, the losses suffered at Midway, though serious, cannot have seemed irreparable; for they still had five fleet or light fleet carriers in commission and six more were building or being converted. What they did not appreciate was that America's power of recovery was far greater than they had supposed; that her vast industrial capacity was bound to produce ships, aircraft, combined operations vessels, and all the other instruments of modern warfare far more

[1] See pp. 189-90 and 191-2.

quickly than they themselves could construct them; that Japanese aggression had united the people of the United States as never before, and that the American people's lately aroused resolution made them absolutely determined to see the matter through to victory. There was, furthermore, a serious weakness in the Japanese position of which her war leaders were as yet totally unaware: namely that the merchant shipping available to them, which in mid-1942 had amounted to no more than some six million tons, was nothing like sufficient to support and exploit the territories they had already gained—let alone extend their conquests still farther from their sources of supply. They had, moreover, taken no adequate steps to safeguard the mercantile tonnage they did possess, and to employ it economically; and American submarines had already begun to exact a heavy toll from ships which they encountered sailing independently. Not until the autumn of 1943, by which time they had lost about half their original tonnage, did the Japanese attempt to put their shipping into convoy and give it proper protection; and it seems certain that their long and costly disregard of that ancient principle derived from the belief that such a strategy was purely "defensive," and therefore both inimical to their pride and inferior to so-called "offensive" measures. In passing we may remark that the same fallacious reasoning has often been heard in British circles, even in recent times; but the strength of our maritime traditions has so far saved us from its worst consequences.

It thus came to pass that in the middle of 1942, the Japanese, quite undeterred by recent set-backs, planned to renew the attempt to gain Port Moresby, and also sent forces to the southern islands of the Solomons chain, with the object of reaching out thence to the New Hebrides, Fiji and New Caledonia, so cutting the supply line from America to Australia and New Zealand.[1] This latter threat was a serious one, and the Americans realised that it had to be countered quickly. Though the White Ensign ships in the Pacific were now few—consisting only of the half-dozen cruisers and smaller vessels of the Australian and New Zealand navies which, after the creation of the South and South-West Pacific commands in April 1942 generally served under American flag officers—it is none the less desirable to follow briefly the progress of the campaigns in those theatres; for not only did they profoundly affect

[1] See Map p. 185.

the conduct of the war in other and far distant waters, but they themselves are replete with lessons on maritime strategy and the waging of sea warfare in modern conditions.

As soon as the Americans heard of the Japanese landing in the southern Solomons they prepared a counter-offensive, and towards the end of July an amphibious expedition sailed from New Zealand to assault the island of Guadalcanal, where the Japanese were building an airfield. The landings took place on 7th August, while Admiral Somerville's Eastern Fleet carried out diversionary movements in the Bay of Bengal, and were completely successful; but two nights later disaster very nearly overtook the entire expedition. The Japanese sent down from the north, a strong cruiser force with the object of attacking the American transports, and in the early hours of 9th August, they caught the covering Allied warships, which were under Rear-Admiral V. A. C. Crutchley— a Royal Navy officer then commanding the Australian cruiser squadron—completely by surprise. Within a few minutes the heavy cruiser *Canberra* (R.A.N.) and three American cruisers were sunk, and the way was wide open for the Japanese to launch themselves at the almost defenceless transports. Happily they returned instead by the way they had come; but the " Battle of Savo Island " was the sharpest defeat suffered by the Allies since the disastrous clash in the Java Sea in the previous February.[1]

There now followed a period of great anxiety for the Allies, whose expedition to the Solomons was left in a very exposed condition, and of extremely stubborn fighting on land and sea and in the air. For both sides realised that the balance in the South Pacific depended on the outcome of the struggle for Guadalcanal; and both tried to run in reinforcements and to prevent their adversaries doing the same. On 24th August, there took place another carrier air battle to the east of the Solomons, in which the Japanese *Ryujo* was sunk and the American *Enterprise* damaged. But that drawn fight was soon followed by events which came very near to restoring the initiative to the Japanese. On the last day of August a Japanese submarine torpedoed and damaged the big American carrier *Saratoga*, and a fortnight later another submarine sank the *Wasp*—the ship which had recently earned the admiration and affection of the Royal Navy for her two reinforce-

[1] See pp. 183-4.

ments of Malta.[1] There was now only one American carrier—the *Hornet*—in the theatre; but the *Enterprise* repaired the damage received in the battle of 24th August remarkably quickly, and early in October she rejoined the South Pacific fleet. On the night of 11th-12th October there was another sharp, close-range encounter between cruisers and destroyers in the narrow waters to the north of Guadalcanal colloquially known as " the Slot," and this time it was the Japanese who were caught by surprise and lost several ships. The " Battle of Cape Esperance ", as it was called, did something to avenge the Allied defeat off Savo Island two months earlier. Then, on 26th October, the two sides' aircraft carriers met in yet another tense encounter off the Solomons. The Japanese *Zuiho* and *Shokaku* were damaged, as were the American *Enterprise* and *Hornet*; and the latter caught fire so badly that she had to be abandoned and sank next day. The " Battle of Santa Cruz " thus left the Allies with only the much-battered *Enterprise* to support their land expedition, and it was now the U.S. Navy's turn to appeal to the Admiralty for help. But to send a big ship half-way round the world to undertake active operations in a theatre where there was no British shore organisation to support and supply her, nor any spare aircraft, ammunition or accessories, was not as simple a matter as sending the *Wasp* across the Atlantic to ferry Spitfires to Malta—though some Americans seem to have regarded it so. To the Admiralty it was plain that a British carrier would have to be re-equipped with American aircraft if she was to undertake extensive service in the new theatre, and when they asked for particulars of how and when this was to be done, the exchanges generated a certain amount of heat in Washington. Admiral E. J. King, the American Chief of Naval Operations, was never an easy man to work with; and on the present occasion he seems to have regarded the Admiralty's questions as indicative of a reluctance to help the U.S. Navy tide over a very real crisis. In the end, however, the *Victorious* was ordered to the Pacific early in December; but, as the Admiralty had foreseen, she had to spend some months at Pearl Harbour re-equipping with American aircraft and re-training her aircrews; and by the time she was ready for active operations the worst of the crisis had in fact passed.

Meanwhile the struggle for Guadalcanal was continuing with

[1] See p. 217.

unabated fury, and on 13th November, there took place off Savo Island one of the very few close-range night actions between battleships. It ended with the sinking of the Japanese *Kirishima*, and in the total defeat of their plans to bombard the airfield and reinforce their troops on Guadalcanal. Thereafter the Japanese confined themselves to sending down cruisers and destroyers to contest control of the narrow waters; and in the next phase there were many fierce night encounters between them and similarly composed Allied forces. It was, however, some time before the Americans—for all their advantage in having by far the more efficient radar sets—developed really effective night fighting tactics. Again and again did the Japanese use their very efficient long-range torpedoes to good effect; and it was mainly the superiority of their tactics and torpedo fire which enabled them to inflict a sharp defeat on a superior American force on the last day of November in the " Battle of Tassafaronga," when one American heavy cruiser was sunk and three others were damaged. As 1942 drew to a close, it was none the less plain that the Americans were slowly gaining the upper hand on Guadalcanal, and were establishing a sufficiently firm control over the adjacent waters to enable the counter-offensive to be extended northwards.

Meanwhile in New Guinea, the renewed Japanese attempt to win Port Moresby had been decisively checked, after very stubborn fighting in the jungle-clad Owen Stanley mountains; and early in September, General MacArthur, commander of the South-West Pacific forces, seized Milne Bay on the south-east tip of Papua. This greatly improved the Allies' strategic position; for the bases which the Americans now developed in Papua lay on the western flank of the main Japanese bastion in New Britain.[1] MacArthur's chief difficulty lay at this time in his lack of a properly organised and trained amphibious force. The Australian Navy's light craft did their best to act as substitutes, and that service and its Dutch and American colleagues showed great ingenuity in extemporising what they did not possess; but in this as in every other theatre of the war, shortage of landing craft and other combined operation vessels long remained the most intractable of the many problems which the commanders had to face.

While the tense struggles for Guadalcanal and eastern New

[1] See Map p. 185.

Guinea were in progress, Somerville's Eastern Fleet had remained very weak. Though the American victory at Midway had eliminated the possibility of another Japanese foray into the Indian Ocean in strength, such as Nagumo had made in April, 1942,[1] we were still very far from building up our strength to a point at which Somerville could assume the offensive. True the Admiralty had sent out some reinforcements; but by the end of August, the Commander-in-Chief had only the carrier *Illustrious*, the battleships *Warspite* and *Valiant* and a few cruisers in his fast squadron; his destroyer strength was far from adequate to screen the big ships and deal with the U-boats which had appeared at various points off the coast of East Africa, from the Mozambique Channel to the Gulf of Aden; and he had not even got the nucleus of landing ships and craft whereon he could build an amphibious striking force. Moreover, whenever specially urgent requirements arose in the eastern Mediterranean, such as fighting a convoy through to Malta,[2] he was called on to reinforce that theatre from his own slender strength. The Prime Minister, however, was impatient over the apparent inactivity of the Eastern Fleet, and in October he asked the First Sea Lord whether Somerville's ships could not be better employed in the Mediterranean. Admiral Pound, however, firmly opposed the proposal, pointing out that to strip the Indian Ocean bare would expose our shipping to the depredations of quite modest enemy forces; and Mr. Churchill, even though he continued to regard what he called " idle ships " as a " reproach," finally accepted his views. In war it is inevitable that, once a nation's leaders have decided on the form which their offensive strategy should take, all other interests should defer to that purpose. In the autumn of 1942, our primary object was the invasion of North Africa, and it was impossible for us to take the offensive in the Indian Ocean until the success of the Mediterranean strategy was assured. In the meanwhile the Eastern Fleet had to stand on the defensive, and deploy such forces as could be spared for it on safeguarding the very important traffic from the Cape of Good Hope to the Middle East and across the Indian Ocean to India and Ceylon.

To return to the Solomons campaign, after the very heavy fighting which had marked the first phase, it was natural that a

[1] See pp. 186-8.   [2] See pp. 218-20 regarding the June, 1942, convoy to Malta.

lull should follow, and early in 1943 both sides were recouping their strength and preparing for a renewal of the contest. The Japanese actually took the decision to evacuate Guadalcanal on 4th January; but another month elapsed before they were ready to make the effort to save their garrison. Between 1st and 7th February, their destroyers successfully removed some 12,000 men, in spite of local sea and air superiority resting with the Allies; and so ended one of the most stubborn and prolonged contests for control of a strategic island in the whole history of war. But the Japanese had no intention of abandoning the whole Solomons chain, and in the next phase the fighting therefore moved to the central islands of the group, around which a new series of sharp night actions between the two sides' cruiser and destroyer forces now took place. Though the Japanese fought well, and still continued to use their torpedoes effectively, the advantage generally rested with the Americans, whose numerical and technical superiority was becoming ever more marked.

The Allied strategy, which was endorsed by the Casablanca conference in January, 1943, was to mount twin offensives from the Solomons and New Guinea with the object of breaking through the Bismarck barrier into the open seas leading towards the Philippine Islands;[1] and in March the Americans therefore reorganised their naval forces into the Third and Seventh Fleets, under Admiral Halsey and General MacArthur respectively, to support the two offensives. The surviving Australian and New Zealand warships now joined the various task forces comprising those fleets, serving with distinction in both theatres. On 29th January, the New Zealand Navy's little minesweepers *Kiwi* and *Moa* scored a creditable success by driving ashore and destroying the 2,000-ton Japanese submarine I1; but later in the year the same service's cruisers *Achilles* and *Leander* were both severely damaged in action in the Solomons, and had to withdraw for repairs. In May, 1943, the *Victorious*, now equipped with American aircraft, arrived to join Halsey's fleet, and from then until the beginning of August she and the *Saratoga* provided the whole of the carrier air power in the South Pacific theatre. To the disappointment of the British aircrews, however, the Japanese did not provoke another carrier battle in that period; and as Halsey himself was still too

[1] See Map p. 185.

weak deliberately to seek such an encounter, the *Victorious* finally returned to the Home Fleet without ever getting the chance of showing her mettle against the Japanese carriers.

The chief difficulty which the naval forces in the Pacific always had to contend with was that of distance; for the Solomon Islands are 3,000 and 1,500 miles from Pearl Harbour and Sydney respectively, and more than 5,000 miles from the western seaboard of the United States, from which most of the supplies and reinforcements for the theatres of active operations had to start out. Furthermore, at the beginning of the campaign there were absolutely no base installations in the advanced areas, where jungle-clad islands and coral atolls, on which there existed nothing except a few coconut palms, had to be equipped with fuel tanks, ammunition depots, workshops and store houses to meet all the multifarious needs of the fleets. It was in this work that American energy and ingenuity in improvisation showed to great advantage. Within a remarkably short time they had put afloat a great part of the necessary base facilities, while their specially trained Construction Battalions, for which no counterpart existed in the British services, had developed a positive genius for rapidly clearing and levelling the ground needed for airstrips, for building roads, and for erecting temporary buildings. But the problems of distance, the lack of shore installations, and the scale on which operations were being planned did produce very heavy demands for mercantile tonnage; and to Britain, whose Merchant Navy had already suffered enormous losses, whose import programme had been cut to the bone, and to whom every tramp and tanker counted a very great deal, the knowledge that large numbers of ships were being held in Pacific bases for very long periods made it seem that American methods were unjustifiably extravagant, and that the combined resources of the two maritime Allies were not being pooled to the best advantage —as their respective governments had agreed. To-day it seems that there was some justification for the feeling that our Ally had not studied closely enough the complex problems involved in the economical use of merchant shipping; and that shortages in other theatres—which undoubtedly did cramp our offensive strategy— could have been mitigated had the needs of the Pacific campaigns been scrutinised as carefully as was our own habit. But it must none the less be admitted that, even if American methods were unduly lavish, the efficiency of the mobile and temporary bases was quite remarkable; and that without them the active fleets could never have kept themselves efficient so far from any permanent bases.

In March and April, 1943, there took place two events which were to have important consequences on the plan to breach the Bismarck barrier, already referred to. The first was the total destruction by shore-based aircraft on 2nd-3rd March of a Japanese expedition sent to reinforce their garrisons in New Guinea; and the second was the complete failure of Japanese attempts to strike at the main Allied bases in the Solomons and at Milne Bay with naval aircraft which Admiral Yamamoto, commander of their Combined Fleet, had disembarked from the fleet's carriers to work from shore airfields. The very heavy losses suffered by them in attacks on Allied bases deprived the Japanese fleet of the striking power which might still have been capable of regaining the initiative at sea; for, as we have seen, Allied carrier strength was still at a very low ebb. Nor was the chance ever to occur again since, after the middle of 1943, new American carriers began to appear in such numbers, and were equipped with such greatly improved aircraft, that the Japanese were thereafter totally outclassed in that vital element of maritime power. The wastage of her irreplaceable aircrews was one of the Japanese Navy's costlier errors.

Meanwhile Somerville's Eastern Fleet was being run down to a level even lower than the modest strength possessed at the end of 1942; for plans to invade the mainland of Italy in the autumn of 1943 were now far advanced, and the Admiralty was also preparing for a great cross-Channel operation against Hitler's European fortress in the following year. In consequence his last fleet carrier (the *Illustrious*) was brought home, his only two modern battleships (the *Warspite* and *Valiant*) were transferred to the Mediterranean, and a redistribution of our forces not very different from that which Mr. Churchill had urged in October 1942,[1] thus took place some six months later. What was left in the Indian Ocean was little more than an anti-submarine escort force; and there were not even enough flotilla vessels to give all convoys adequate protection against the U-boats which Dönitz was now sending to probe

[1] See p. 256.

for " soft spots " in remote waters. Thus when a new group of six U-boats arrived off South Africa in May, 1943, they were able to sink a disproportionately high tonnage—nearly all of it consisting of ships sailing independently. Losses continued until August, when the U-boats started to withdraw towards the Japanese base at Penang. Meanwhile the last German disguised raider, the *Michel*, was working off western Australia; but her successes were extremely small. In the middle of the year she moved right across the Pacific to try her luck off the west coast of South America; but there too, she accomplished very little. In September she set course for Japan, only to be sunk by an American submarine patrolling off that country's coasts on 17th October. So ended the German attempt to wage the *guerre de course* in that traditional and perfectly lawful manner. In all the disguised raiders sank 133 ships, totalling nearly 830,000 tons—which was almost insignificant when compared with the losses inflicted by the U-boats, by mines and by enemy aircraft;[1] but for a time they had caused us considerable trouble, and forced us to expend a large effort on trying to bring them to book.

To sum up the progress of the war against Japan, by the middle of 1943, Allied prospects had been totally transformed. The victory of Midway had started the turn of the tide, and the gruelling campaign in the Solomons had slowly confirmed our superiority at sea. In the vital element of mercantile tonnage too, the advantage now lay with the Allies; for the Japanese Merchant Navy, which had never been really adequate to support the grandiose plans of conquest conceived by her war leaders, was now disappearing at an alarming rate—chiefly at the hands of the far-ranging American submarines. In the field of maritime strategy, the Americans had shown remarkable understanding of the traditional principles governing the use of amphibious expeditions, and had developed the capacity to exploit their sea-power for such purposes with astonishing speed. The Solomons campaign had moreover, taught them that it was unnecessary to reduce each island garrison in turn, and that so long as they held command at sea, they could safely by-pass such positions as were not essential to them, attacking

---

[1] The total losses they inflicted were:

    U-boats—2,828 ships totalling 14,687,231 tons.
    Aircraft— 820 ships totalling 2,889,883 tons.
    Mines— 534 ships totalling 1,406,037 tons.

only those on which they desired to establish new advanced bases. With the balance in the Pacific now brought firmly central, and the offensive phase about to open, it was possible to employ the " leap-frog " strategy to the fullest possible extent; and the economy of time and of resources thereby achieved became one of the most outstanding features of the entire war.

CHAPTER XIV

THE VICTORY OF THE ESCORTS

1st November, 1942–31st May, 1943

" The defeat of the U-boat . . . is the prelude to all effective aggressive operations."

Mr. Churchill, at a conference of Ministers of the Crown, 11th February, 1943.

SINCE THE reader's attention was last concentrated on the Atlantic battle he has been conducted far overseas. He has shared in the trials of Malta while the Axis sea and air forces were doing their utmost to prevent the relieving ships getting through; he has watched the Arctic convoys battling their way slowly through ice floes, snow storms and the worst that the enemy could do to them to reach Murmansk or Archangel with their precious cargoes of tanks, aeroplanes and every type of war material; he has seen the " Torch " convoys set out from Britain and America, and the snowy Atlas mountains look placidly down on the landing craft as they groped their way towards the beaches of Oran and Algiers, or were hurled helpless on to the rocks of the Moroccan coast by the breaking surf of the Atlantic rollers; and he has viewed from afar the deadly struggles in the fetid, exhausting heat of the Solomon Islands and New Guinea. Yet it is no exaggeration to say that Allied fortunes in all those theatres depended ultimately on the issue which was all the time being fought out in the wastes of the North Atlantic. For if Britain had ever lost her grip there, she would in a very short time have been brought face to face with final disaster; and if she had gone down in defeat the repercussions would without doubt, have been tremendous. Would the Russians then have been able to hold off the Axis onslaught, with no American and British supply ships reaching them, and their enemies able to concentrate their entire resources on the eastern front? And if the whole of Europe and Africa, as well as most of Asia, had fallen under the control of the dictatorships would the United States, with no maritime Ally, and themselves as yet far from fully geared to war, have been able alone to cope with an encircling attack on all the oceans? Whatever answer the reader may give to those imponderable questions, there can be no doubt on two points. The first is that an Axis victory in the Atlantic would have vastly improved their chances of achieving their objective of world power; and the second is that throughout the whole course of the long struggle, it was mainly the overdriven, battle-scarred escort flotillas of Britain, and their colleagues of the Royal Air Force's Coastal Command, which held the enemy at bay, and finally turned the tables on him. As long as those unresting flotillas, few in number but indomitable in spirit, went out from Liverpool and the Clyde, Londonderry and Iceland, Newfoundland and Halifax to meet the convoys, and brought them safely to harbour under the guardianship of their storm-torn White Ensigns, Britain could fight on; and, turn where they would, victory would elude the grasp of the dictators.

As 1942 drew to a close, the real issues involved in the Battle of the Atlantic seem to have been understood by the Axis leaders more clearly than ever before, and they prepared to put their utmost effort into the struggle. The German underwater fleet was now approaching the 400 mark, about half of which were fully operational; and Hitler was at last heeding Raeder's requests for the highest priority to be given to U-boat construction. On the British side as well, greater strength was now available, and at the beginning of the fourth year of the war we had some 450 escort vessels of all types working from bases stretching from Iceland to the Cape of Good Hope, and from Newfoundland to Murmansk.[1] But the Admiralty knew full well that our resources were still far from adequate to the needs, for it was inevitable that many of our ships should always be out of action for refitting, or to repair storm and battle damage; and their crews had to be given short periods of rest if the limits of human endurance were not to be overstepped.

In mid-November, 1942, Admiral Sir Max Horton took over

[1] This figure includes the Royal Canadian Navy's escort vessels stationed in the western Atlantic.

the Western Approaches command from Sir Percy Noble. He was a submarine officer of long experience, possessed of ruthless determination; while his shrewd, clear brain and profound knowledge of submarine tactics provided exactly the equipment needed to outwit Dönitz. But he would have been the first to admit the debt that he owed to his predecessor; for it was Noble who had organised and trained the Western Approaches flotillas to a high pitch of efficiency, and had established the remarkably intimate understanding with the Coastal Command squadrons which co-operated with them in every single convoy operation; and it was he who had created the smoothly working headquarters in Derby House, Liverpool, whence our Atlantic dispositions and movements were controlled. If it was Horton who was to wield the weapon at the crisis of the battle, the forging of it had mainly been Noble's work. Nor should we forget that it was the labours of our scientists and technicians in designing new instruments and weapons, such as the short-wave radar mentioned earlier and the ahead-throwing anti-submarine mortar projector, which were making our sea and air anti-submarine tactics far more deadly; while the scientific study given to such problems as the optimum size of convoys and strength of escorts by the Admiralty's Operational Research department kept our methods one step ahead of the enemy.

In the last two months of 1942, for all that Dönitz had been able to strengthen his wolf-packs, they achieved no substantial successes until, almost at the end of the year, the outward convoy ONS 154 lost 13 ships. But the Admiralty could draw little comfort from the safe passages made by several convoys; for they knew that during the whole of 1942 we had lost the enormous total of 1,664 merchantmen totalling nearly 8 million tons, that new construction had not by any means replaced those losses, that our imports had fallen to one third less than the 1939 figure, and that we had sunk far fewer enemy submarines than had entered service.[1] Most serious of all was the fact that stocks of commercial oil fuel in Britain had fallen so low that little more than two months' consumption was on hand. To the naval staff the graphs kept by the statisticians revealed all too plainly that " our shipping situation

[1] In 1942 we actually destroyed 87 German and 22 Italian submarines, and new deliveries of the former amounted to 238. Thus the net increase in Dönitz's fleet was 151 boats.

The beach at Dieppe after the raid, 19th August, 1942

Convoy PQ 18 to North Russia, September, 1942. H.M.S. *Eskimo* in foreground

Convoy **PQ** 18 to North Russia, September, 1942. A merchantman blows up

Convoy JW 53 to North Russia, February, 1943

has never been tighter," and that the crisis of the battle could not be long deferred. But our promise to the Russians that we would send them another big convoy as soon as the ships diverted to operation "Torch" had returned home, prevented us at once concentrating our efforts in the North Atlantic. In accordance with Admiral Tovey's wishes, the convoy actually sailed in two parts, and the first section (called JW 51A[1]) was never sighted by the enemy. Its 15 ships arrived safely on Christmas Day as a timely present for Stalin; but the passage of the second section (JW 51B of 14 ships) told a very different story. The Germans now had the *Tirpitz, Lützow, Hipper, Nürnberg, Köln* and about a dozen big destroyers in Norwegian waters, and had also strengthened the U-boat flotilla based on Narvik. To the Admiralty, who could not know that it was chiefly Hitler's obsession about an Allied invasion of Norway that had brought about those dispositions, nor that he had imposed severe restrictions on the offensive use of the big warships, it seemed certain that another attempt to attack an Arctic convoy was imminent.

Convoy JW 51B sailed from Loch Ewe on 22nd December, escorted by six destroyers and five smaller vessels under Captain R. St. V. Sherbrooke in the *Onslow*. Rear-Admiral R. L. Burnett's two cruisers, the *Sheffield* and *Jamaica*, which had gone right through to Murmansk with the first section, were to return to cover the second section while it was in the Barents Sea. On 30th December, a U-boat reported the convoy's position, and Vice-Admiral Kummetz at once put to sea from Altenfiord with the *Hipper* (flagship), *Lützow*, and six destroyers.[2] Admiral Burnett expected the enemy to approach from astern of the convoy, and had therefore taken station to the north of its route; but he was very uncertain of its actual position. In fact heavy weather had delayed and scattered the merchantmen, some of whom had not yet rejoined the main body; and early on 31st the convoy itself was some 150 miles to the west of the position which Admiral Tovey,

---

[1] For security reasons the Arctic convoys were given new code letters and numbers at this time. PQ 18 and QP 15 were the last of the old series, and for the new series the letters were changed to JW. (outward) and RA. (homeward), with numbers for both starting at 51.

[2] The German destroyers displaced 2,260–2,690 tons and were armed with five guns (5-inch to 5.9-inch) and 8 torpedo tubes. The destroyers of the *Onslow* class displaced 1,540 tons, and their armament consisted only of four guns (4-inch to 4.7-inch) and 8 torpedo tubes. Moreover, the five ships of that class originally with Captain Sherbrooke were reduced to four before the battle, for the *Oribi* lost touch when a gale struck the convoy off Bear Island.

whose main fleet was giving distant cover, signalled to the cruiser Admiral as his best estimate. It thus happened that as the total darkness of the Arctic night gave way to the faint glimmer of dawn on New Year's Eve, 1942, none of the British forces in the Barents Sea was aware of the exact whereabouts of the others.

Captain Sherbrooke, however, had always felt that an attack by enemy warships was likely, and before setting out he had described to his subordinates and the Convoy Commodore how he would meet such an eventuality. His plan, which bore a strong resemblance to that which Admiral Vian had used so effectively in the Second Battle of Sirte,[1] was to concentrate the destroyers of his own flotilla on the threatened flank of the convoy, and stand out boldly to attack the enemy, while the merchantmen would turn away under cover of a smoke screen laid by the other escorts. Thanks to Sherbrooke's foresight the captains of all ships present were thus absolutely clear regarding the parts they were to play, and if an emergency arose, no signalling would be necessary beyond telling them to "act in execution of previous orders." On the German side, Admiral Kummetz planned to approach from astern of the convoy, just as Burnett had anticipated, but he meant to divide his forces and attack simultaneously from both flanks; and that plan, if it worked out as intended, was bound to produce serious difficulties for Sherbrooke's few ships.

The first contact took place astern of the convoy at 8.30 a.m. on 31st December; but for about an hour our ships were doubtful whether the dim shapes seen in the half-light against a background of snow-laden clouds were friends or foes—for a reinforcement of Russian destroyers, which actually never turned up, was expected at that time. At 9.30, however, the uncertainty was dispelled by the enemy, which was in fact the three destroyers of the *Hipper's* group, opening fire on the *Obdurate*, which Sherbrooke had detached to investigate. The escort commander at once sent an enemy report, and that message gave Admiral Burnett the position of our destroyers as well as telling him that they were in contact with the enemy. Sherbrooke's pre-arranged plan was now put into effect, the convoy turned to the south, and the small escorts laid their smoke screen. A short while later the *Onslow* and *Orwell*

[1] See pp. 212-16.

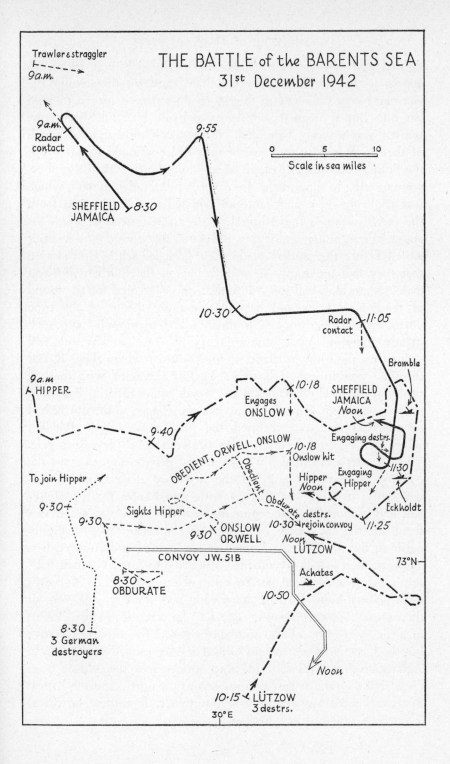

THE BATTLE of the BARENTS SEA
31st December 1942

Trawler & straggler
9 a.m.

9 a.m.
Radar
contact

9.55

0   5   10
Scale in sea miles

SHEFFIELD
JAMAICA   8.30

10.30

Radar   11.05
contact

Bromble

9 a.m.
HIPPER

Engages
ONSLOW   10.18

SHEFFIELD
JAMAICA
Noon

9.40

Engaging destrs.

OBEDIENT, ORWELL, ONSLOW   10.18
Onslow hit

Obedient

Engaging
Hipper   11.30

To join Hipper

Hipper
Noon

Eckholdt

9.30

Sights Hipper

9.30

Obdurate

Obdurate destrs.

11.25

ONSLOW
ORWELL   9.30

10.30   rejoin convoy

CONVOY JW. 51B   Noon   LÜTZOW   73°N

8.30
OBDURATE   Achates

10.50

8.30
3 German
destroyers   Noon

10.15   LÜTZOW
3 destrs.

30°E

sighted and engaged the *Hipper* herself, which was trying to approach the convoy from the north; and by threatening the German heavy cruiser with their torpedoes they managed to hold her off. But at 10.20 the *Onslow* was badly hit, and Sherbrooke himself was severely wounded. Lieutenant-Commander Kinloch of the *Obedient* now took command, and continued to carry out the flotilla commander's plan. Meanwhile the two British cruisers were moving to support the destroyers; but a radar contact, which was probably on a merchantman which had got separated from the convoy, caused the Admiral to steer east instead of south for about half an hour; and it thus happened that about another hour passed before the cruisers made their presence felt.[1] Considering that they had previously sighted flashes on the southern horizon it does seem that, had the Admiral at once " steered for the sound of the guns " he would have considerably shortened the time during which Sherbrooke's four ships had to grapple with such greatly superior forces; for at 10.45 the *Lützow* was suddenly sighted on the southern flank of the convoy—where there was at the time very little to protect it. Luckily she acted with marked timidity, and held off while (in the words of her captain) " waiting for the weather to clear." Meanwhile the *Hipper*, to the north, had encountered and overwhelmed the little minesweeper *Bramble*, which had become detached from the convoy in the earlier gale. Then at 11.15 she suddenly re-appeared dangerously near to the convoy, and quickly crippled the destroyer *Achates*, which was devotedly shielding her charges with smoke. So far the *Hipper* had had matters altogether too much her own way; and it was fortunate that at 11.30, just when the situation looked highly perilous, the *Sheffield* and *Jamaica* at last sighted and engaged her. They at once scored several hits which reduced the German flag-ship's speed, and forced her to retire westwards. Then Burnett's ships sighted two German destroyers, and quickly sank one of them—the *Friedrich Eckholdt*. The *Lützow* was meanwhile closing in again, and at 11.45 she suddenly opened fire on the convoy; but the *Obdurate*, *Obedient* and *Orwell* at once moved out to attack, and again they held her off. No sooner had that threat been countered than the *Hipper* re-appeared to the north, and the British destroyers had to switch their attention to her. Kummetz, however,

---

[1] See Map p. 267.

did not press his advantage, but ordered all his forces to withdraw westwards; and when no more enemies could be seen, the three effective British destroyers therefore steered to overtake the convoy, on which the damaged *Onslow* had already taken station. The *Sheffield* and *Jamaica* were meanwhile pursuing the retiring *Hipper*; but by 2 p.m. they had lost contact, and Burnett then took up a covering position to the south of the convoy. So ended the " Battle of the Barents Sea." On the British side there was every reason to be satisfied with the outcome, for although we lost the *Achates* and *Bramble*, the sinking of the *Eckholdt* and the damage inflicted on the *Hipper* balanced the material account fairly evenly; and, most remarkably, not one ship of the convoy suffered more than superficial damage. Even though the German ships, and particularly the *Lützow*, had shown a marked reluctance to seize the opportunities which came to them, let alone force a decision on their much weaker adversaries, the accomplishment of Sherbrooke and his men was an outstanding example of what determined leadership, supported by complete mutual understanding between individual captains, can accomplish—even in the face of a greatly superior enemy. The German Naval Staff admitted that the action had been " obviously unsatisfactory," but in the enemy's camp the battle had astonishing repercussions; for when Hitler learnt how five British destroyers supported by two 6-inch cruisers had held off a pocket-battleship, an 8-inch cruiser and six far more powerful destroyers for four hours, and had finally forced them to withdraw, he flew into an ungovernable rage, and so insulted Raeder and his service that the Grand Admiral tendered his resignation. On 30th January, 1943, Dönitz thus became Commander-in-Chief of the German Navy; and the man who had all along been the chief advocate of the U-boat arm was at last given the power to direct his country's entire naval effort—just when the events in the Atlantic were plainly moving towards a climax. We may, however, note that the new C.-in-C. very soon had to get Hitler to rescind the order to pay off all the big German warships, which had been one of the chief causes of the breach between him and Raeder.

While this seismic disturbance was taking place in the Nazi hierarchy, the Allied leaders were quietly considering their future strategy at the Casablanca conference, which opened a fortnight after the battle just described had been fought in the Arctic twilight. Among other matters it was then decided that, since none of our offensive purposes could prosper until the U-boats had been decisively defeated, that objective had to be made a first charge on Allied resources. One consequence of this decision was that Bomber Command was required to devote a big effort to the German U-boat bases and building yards; for we believed that, even where concrete shelters had been completed, heavy air attacks would reduce the efforts of the U-boats and put some of them out of action. Between January and May, 1943, British and American bombers accordingly aimed 11,000 tons of high explosive and nearly 8,000 tons of incendiary bombs at those targets; but we now know that not one U-boat was put out of action, nor was the German building programme appreciably delayed. In fact, it was not until 24th July, 1943, that the first enemy U-boat was destroyed in a bombing raid. In no other respect does Allied reasoning and planning appear to have fallen so wide of the mark as in this matter of the effect of bombing raids on the Battle of the Atlantic, and it is difficult not to feel that we would have done better to equip and train more of our best long-range bombers for duty as air escorts with the convoys; for in February, 1943, there was precisely one squadron of " Very Long-Range " aircraft—the type most needed —to cover the whole Atlantic; and Britain and America between them had only some 300 aircraft of lower performance allocated to such work. Observing that at the stage now reached in our story, it was very rare for a merchantman to be sunk from a convoy which had both sea and air escorts, it is hard to convince oneself that the relative priorities given to the bomber offensive against German cities and the Atlantic Battle were correct; since every merchant ship and cargo lost at sea was bound to delay the build-up for the strategic offensive by all arms which was the acknowledged aim of the Allied governments.[1] Moreover, we now know that the effects of the land bombing campaign on Germany's war potential in 1942-43 were actually very much less than we believed

[1] To illustrate the difference of emphasis placed on the bombing of Germany and the Atlantic Battle in 1942-43, when the much-publicised " thousand bomber raids " were started with the attack on Cologne on 30th-31st May, 1942, no less than 100 of Coastal Command's maritime aircraft were lent to Bomber Command; and similar loans took place on later occasions. Yet Bomber Command always put up a very stubborn resistance to the transfer of any of its aircraft to Coastal Command, to increase, even temporarily, the meagre strength allocated to the maritime war.

at the time; and not until the latter part of 1944 did they become appreciable.

In the North Atlantic, 1943 opened with a series of gales which, even for those stormy waters, were unusually severe. The little escorts and the slowly plodding merchantmen underwent the most exacting ordeals, convoys were scattered far and wide, and passages were much slower than usual. But the gales also handicapped the U-boats, and in January the only substantial success they achieved was to sink seven of the nine tankers in a convoy (TM 1) running from Trinidad to Gibraltar. By the beginning of February, Dönitz had formidable strength disposed in the north and central Atlantic. No less than 100 boats were on patrol, and 37 of them were lying in wait to the south of Greenland—in the " air gap " which we could as yet only occasionally cover from the bases in Newfoundland and Iceland. The slow convoy SC 118 was the first to feel the weight of the enemy's new offensive. It was beset by a score of U-boats, which sank 13 of its 63 ships. Then, thanks to the presence off the Azores of two supply U-boats (" milch cows ") Dönitz was able to make very heavy attacks on three successive outward convoys. ON 166 suffered particularly badly, and in a four-day battle, 14 of its ships went down. Our losses for the month of February shot up to 63 ships totalling 360,000 tons, and the apprehensions expressed by the Admiralty a few weeks earlier were thus justified unexpectedly quickly. The crisis was plainly upon us, and the Admiralty and Admiral Horton at once instituted far-reaching measures to meet it.

In January and February, Admiral Tovey had successfully sent two more convoys (JW 52 of 14 ships and JW 53 of 22 ships) to North Russia, and had also brought back safely 26 of the 30 ships comprising RA 53. But during the passage of the latter convoy, the *Tirpitz*, *Scharnhorst* and *Lützow* were all sighted in Altenfiord, and this powerful concentration, combined with the ever-lengthening hours of daylight, caused Admiral Tovey to represent that the sailing of Arctic convoys should be suspended for the time being. It was, however, the crisis in the Atlantic which actually decided the matter; for the Western Approaches command's escort strength had to be increased at once, and that could only be done at the expense of the Home Fleet. Mr. Churchill firmly declared that until we had restored the balance in the Atlantic, no more convoys could be sent to Russia, and neither the pleadings of President Roosevelt nor the recriminations of Stalin would move him from that decision.

The Arctic convoys run during the early months of 1943 were the last to be conducted by Admiral Tovey, for on 8th May, Admiral Sir Bruce Fraser succeeded him as Commander-in-Chief, Home Fleet. Admiral Tovey's long period of command will chiefly be remembered for the successful pursuit of the *Bismarck*; but throughout its duration, his ships had controlled the northern passages to the Atlantic, had fought the Arctic convoys through, and had reinforced the Mediterranean squadrons and other theatres whenever special needs, such as the running of a convoy to Malta, arose. In the offensive phase now opening, it was to continue to act as our main strategic reserve and, almost as soon as Admiral Fraser had taken over, many of his ships were sent to the Mediterranean to take part in the expeditions to Sicily and Italy. Admiral Tovey next hoisted his flag as Commander-in-Chief, The Nore— a command which was to play a vital part in the invasion of western Europe, plans for which were now being framed.

To return to March, 1943, it was in that month that representatives of the British, American and Canadian navies met in an "Atlantic Convoy Conference" in Washington. It was then agreed that the U.S. Navy would withdraw entirely from participation in the defence of North Atlantic convoys, but would take over responsibility for the tanker convoys running between Britain and the West Indies. Canada, on the other hand, would create a North-West Atlantic Command at Halifax, which would become wholly responsible for North Atlantic convoys while they were to the west of the "Chop Line" in 47° West.[1] These arrangements came into force on 1st April, 1943; and to help the Canadian Navy meet its extended responsibilities, the ships which had come across to take part in operation "Torch" were sent back to their own country, and half a dozen British destroyers were lent to the new command. From this time until the end of the war the Canadian Navy shared with the Royal Navy the entire responsibility for escort duty in the North Atlantic. The only matters which could not be resolved satisfactorily at the convoy conference were, firstly, the question of control of American naval aircraft based on

[1] See p. 196.

Morocco, where Admiral King had created an independent American command within the British sphere of strategic responsibility; and, secondly, the vexed question of the allocation of " Very Long-Range " aircraft (Liberators) to the Atlantic battle. We were well aware, that whereas in February, 1943, Coastal Command possessed no more than 18 of these invaluable aircraft, the U.S. Navy had been receiving large allocations and was, we believed, employing them on reconnaissance work of secondary importance in the Pacific. The debate on Liberator allocations was long-drawn; for to the British it seemed that the employment of such a high proportion of them in the Pacific conflicted with the policy decided by the Allied leaders at Casablanca. It appears that only when the President himself started to inquire into the uses to which the U.S. Navy was putting them did Admiral King agree to release more to the Atlantic.[1] By July Coastal Command had 37 operational Liberators, but it was the one squadron (No. 120) which it possessed at the crisis of the battle that did so much to turn the tables on the enemy in the Atlantic Battle.

It was mentioned earlier that we had long desired to form special " Support Groups " to reinforce threatened convoys in the Atlantic,[2] and it was in March, 1943, that we were at last able to put that intention into effect. Two of the first five groups were composed of destroyers lent from the Home Fleet, two consisted of experienced escort vessels from the Western Approaches Command, and the fifth was formed around the escort carrier *Biter*. Thus the escort carrier appeared on the North Atlantic convoy routes almost simultaneously with the arrival of the support groups;[3] yet the battle was to move even further against us, and we were to suffer one of the most grievous convoy disasters of the whole war, before they made their presence fully felt.

March opened badly for the Allies. The slow convoy SC 121 was heavily attacked between 7th and 11th, and lost 13 ships without any compensatory price being exacted from the U-boats; but worse was soon to follow. While SC 121 was sorely beset, the

---

[1] In March, 1943, there were 71 U.S. Navy Liberators working from the Pacific islands and the west coast of America. (From Office of Naval History, U.S. Navy Department.)

[2] See p. 223.

[3] The first escort carrier to support a North Atlantic convoy was the U.S.S. *Bogue* at the end of February, 1943. The British ships *Biter* and *Archer* entered the struggle in the following April.

next two convoys, a slow one of 60 ships (SC 122) and a faster one of 40 ships (HX 229) had sailed from New York. As the slow convoy started out only three days ahead of the faster one, and they had been sent by similar routes, they were bound ultimately to join together and form an inviting mass of shipping in mid-ocean. Nor was Dönitz slow to seize the opportunity offered him; for he concentrated 40 U-boats against the two convoys. From the 16th to the 20th very heavy attacks took place with scarcely a break between them. Though we sent out reinforcements of escort vessels and aircraft, the U-boats gained and held the upper hand, and we lost—mostly from the HX convoy—21 merchantmen totalling no less than 141,000 tons. It was a serious disaster to the Allied cause, and it provoked from Mr. Churchill—who could hardly be described as an alarmist—what was almost a cry of anguish. "Our escorts are everywhere too thin" he told President Roosevelt "and the strain upon the British Navy is becoming intolerable." Nor were the three convoys mentioned the only ones to suffer serious losses in March, 1943; for in all theatres of the war, the U-boats then sank 108 ships totalling 627,000 tons; and the proportion of those losses suffered by our North Atlantic convoys was so high, that the naval staff later recorded that the enemy then came "very near to disrupting communications between the New World and the Old." By the end of that fateful month, however, the support groups had entered the fray, and although during the succeeding weeks fierce battles continued to rage around the convoys, our losses showed a decline, and the escorts exacted a reasonable price from the enemy for the successes he did achieve. Thus in April the balance in the North Atlantic may be said to have come central again; but Dönitz then made a sudden lunge to "the old battle ground" off Freetown, where our defences were still none too strong. One U-boat sank 7 ships from a weakly escorted Takoradi-Sierra Leone convoy in a single night—a result which Mr. Churchill, who did not always remember that it was impossible for us to be strong everywhere at the same time, described as "deplorable." In the North Atlantic, however, we achieved a success by deliberately sending a well-protected Halifax convoy (HX 233) by a southerly route through waters where we knew Dönitz had disposed a powerful concentration of U-boats. Thanks to the presence of a support group only one ship was sunk. Losses for the month dropped to little more than half those suffered in March; and, better still, the last week of April produced what the Naval Staff described as "a considerable slaughter" of U-boats. Furthermore, it was on 28th April that Dönitz, misled by a report that the U-boats' search receivers, which had been fitted to give warning of the approach of our patrolling aircraft, were failing to detect the transmissions from our radar sets, and encouraged by the success of a U-boat in shooting down a Coastal Command aircraft, committed the error of ordering his captains to stay on the surface by day while crossing the Bay of Biscay and fight it out with our air patrols; and that misjudgment was to bring Coastal Command its one period of high accomplishment on the transit routes. Not until 2nd August did Dönitz take steps to mitigate the consequences of his order, and during the 94-day period that it remained fully in force (1st May-2nd August) the British aircrews seized their opportunities with both hands. Pressing home their attacks to point-blank range at very low heights, and ignoring the heavy gunfire directed at them, they achieved great results.[1]

In April, the general trend of the battle was thus encouraging, in spite of the fact that a steady stream of U-boats had, to our knowledge, been passing with little hindrance from Germany into the Atlantic round the north of Scotland. Admiral Horton and his staff now took stock of their resources, redisposed some of the increased number of escort and support groups which had become available, and prepared for what everyone at Western Approaches headquarters and in the Admiralty felt would be a decisive period. Towards the end of April, the outward convoy ONS 5 left Britain by the northern route, escorted by the experienced B7 Escort Group[2] whose leader, Commander P. W. Gretton, was in the destroyer *Duncan*. On 29th the enemy gained contact in stormy weather off Cape Farewell, the south-easterly tip of Greenland, and the 40 U-boats which Dönitz had stationed across the convoy's track in the ever-narrowing "air-gap" started to close in. But the U-boat's first sighting report had been picked up in England, and the Admiralty at once ordered the 3rd Support Group (Captain J. A. McCoy) to leave St. John's Newfoundland and reinforce the

[1] See p. 305.
[2] "B" groups were British, "C" groups Canadian and "A" groups American.

escort. A succession of gales now struck and scattered the convoy, delaying its progress so badly, that the *Duncan* and two of the 3rd Support Group's destroyers had to return to harbour to replenish their tanks; for it was far too rough to refuel at sea from a tanker in the convoy, as had been intended. To replace the departed ships, Horton now called the 1st Support Group (Commander G. N. Brewer) out from St. John's, and after dark on the evening of 4th May, by which time the storms had abated, the battle opened in earnest. Attack and counter-attack followed in quick succession and several merchantmen went down; but a corvette sank U.192. Next night the struggle was even fiercer, and attacks were almost continuous. The little ships, however, hit back hard, and between them sank U.638, U.125, U.531 and U.438. By the 6th the convoy was within range of the Newfoundland air bases, and Dönitz called off the pursuit. Though ONS 5 lost 12 of its 42 ships the total cost to the enemy was 7 U-boats—a rate of exchange which we regarded as reasonably satisfactory.

Dönitz at once reformed the survivors of the three groups of U-boats which had attacked ONS 5; but in the next two battles they accomplished little, and themselves suffered further losses; for the 5th Support Group with the escort carrier *Biter*, was skilfully switched by Horton from one convoy to another as each threat developed. Then, on 11th May, the slow convoy SC 130 left Halifax, and met Gretton's B7 Group, which was to be its mid-ocean escort, three days later. This was the type of slow convoy against which the U-boats had scored many of their earlier successes, and four groups closed in as though rubbing their hands with glee at the prospect of once more finding easy targets. But on this occasion their experience was profoundly different. The 1st Support Group arrived with timely reinforcements, No. 120 Squadron's Liberators reached south from Iceland, and in the ensuing battle, five U-boats were sunk and not a ship of the convoy was lost.[1] The sea and air escorts had unquestionably gained a resounding victory. Almost simultaneously the enemy failed as well against HX 239, which had the escort carrier *Archer* to protect it; and at the time when SC 130 and HX 239 reached Britain in safety, the

---

[1] One of the sunk U-boats was U.954, which met her end at the hands of a Liberator of the famous No. 120 Squadron from Iceland on 19th May. Dönitz's son Peter was serving in her as a watch-keeping officer. His second son, Klaus, was killed when the E-boat (S.141) in which he was serving was sunk by our destroyers in the Channel on 13th May, 1944.

Admiralty's Submarine Tracking Room noticed that wireless transmissions had ceased to be heard from the North Atlantic U-boats. In fact, Dönitz made the decision to withdraw on 22nd May, because his losses had become insupportable; and that date may therefore be taken as marking the victory of the escorts in the Atlantic battle. We now know that during May, 1943, we destroyed in all theatres no less than 41 U-boats; and the merchant ship tonnage sunk by them dropped to 50 ships of 265,000 tons. In the Admiralty and at Derby House, Liverpool, the full extent of the victory was not at once apparent. Remembering how black the prospects had appeared only a few weeks earlier, we found it hard to believe that the tables had really been turned so quickly. When it did dawn even on the most hardened sceptics that a great victory had been gained, the predominant sensation was one of profound relief; for we knew that we had shaken off what had been very nearly a stranglehold on our jugular vein. To-day it is absolutely plain that it was the escort and support groups, the few " Very Long-Range " aircraft of Coastal Command, and the tiny force of anti-submarine aircraft embarked in the escort carriers which won the victory. But at the time it was impossible to give the British and American public a full account of what they had done and how they had done it; for we felt sure that Dönitz would renew the contest as soon as he had licked his wounds and replaced his losses. For that reason, and perhaps because convoy battles are marked only by latitude and longitude, and have no names that ring in the memory like Matapan, the victory of May, 1943, is scarcely remembered. Yet it was in its own way as decisive as the Battle of Britain in the summer of 1940; for never again was the German Navy able seriously to threaten our life-line—let alone come within measurable distance of severing it.

Thus did we, in the short space of a few months, restore the balance in both the Arctic and Atlantic, so laying firm foundations for the entire offensive strategy of the Allies. But the same period also marked far-reaching changes in our coastal waters, for we then gained a mastery over all the weapons—bombers, E-boats and mines —which the enemy could deploy against our inshore shipping. Although in this chapter the reader's attention has been directed chiefly to the wide Atlantic and the ice-bound waters of the Arctic Ocean, he should never forget that the successes there gained would have availed nothing had we not simultaneously maintained our grip on the shallow, tide-swept waters which girdle these islands. Thus a share in the victories of 1943 surely belongs to the hundreds of minesweepers who, day after day and night after night, went out to seek the hidden dangers and keep the channels clear, to the small craft which shepherded the coastal convoys up and down the narrow seas, and to the fighters which kept the skies above them clear of enemies. Though their defensive activities could not be relaxed for a single day, by the middle of 1943 we were able to give our attention more and more to the prosecution of the offensive in the enemy's coastal waters. Cruisers as well as destroyers were now based once again on Plymouth, to trap enemy blockade runners and co-operate with the Biscay air patrols; M.T.B.s went out to Norway regularly from Scapa to ambush the German convoys creeping up and down the protected waters of the "Leads," off which our submarines also constantly patrolled; strike aircraft of Coastal Command were searching for and attacking enemy shipping from North Norway to the Spanish frontier; while Bomber Command's minelaying aircraft were reaching out ever farther to lay their deadly loads off enemy harbours as far away as the Baltic—which no other of our weapons could reach. The offensive against the enemy's coastal traffic was in the fullest sense a combined operation; and at the stage now reached in our story, the various arms of the Royal Navy and Air Force were between them inflicting such losses as made it increasingly hazardous for the Germans to send seaborne supplies to their armies in Norway, the Low Countries, and France; and that was bound to place a further strain on their already overtaxed land transport system. Although the coastal offensive rarely caught the limelight, and its effects have since been given scant attention, the records of our former enemies leave no room for doubt regarding the importance of its impact on their own war potential; for the Germans were compelled to allocate an ever-increasing proportion of their resources to the endeavour to keep their coastal traffic moving.

CHAPTER XV

AFRICA THE SPRINGBOARD: ITALY THE TARGET

1st January–1st October, 1943

" But the English temper, when once aroused, was marked by
a tenacity of purpose, a constancy of endurance, which strongly
supported the conservative tendencies of the race."

A. T. Mahan *The Influence of Sea Power on
the French Revolution and Empire*, Vol. II, p.
317.

WE SAW earlier (Chapter XII) how at the end of 1942 the British Eighth Army was advancing victoriously westwards from Egypt, with the little ships of the Inshore Squadron keeping pace with it. But after the capture of Benghazi on 20th November, General Montgomery's men had to cross the whole breadth of Tripolitania, on whose seaboard there were, until Tripoli itself was reached, only a few indifferent harbours.[1] Thus to maintain the momentum of the offensive it became necessary to land much of the army's fuel, water, ammunition and stores over the open beaches of the Gulf of Sirte; and the Inshore Squadron developed such skill in that task, and carried it out with such unwearying devotion, that it gained a warm commendation from General Montgomery. Both Army and Navy, however, fully realised the importance of Tripoli, which had a good harbour; and if the land forces regarded it as essential to the rapid build-up of their strength for the advance into Tunisia, the maritime services knew full well that the ability to disembark vehicles, stores and equipment directly on to its quays would greatly ease their own burden. But the enemy was also alive to the importance of Tripoli, and when on 15th

[1] See Map pp. 112-13.

January, 1943, the Eighth Army opened a new offensive, and it soon became plain to the Axis commanders that they could not hold on to the port for long, they put in hand carefully planned measures to block and obstruct it very thoroughly. Meanwhile ships and equipment for the clearance and re-opening of the harbour had been assembled at Alexandria; but the extent of the enemy's demolitions—and in particular the use of concrete-filled block ships—seems to have caught Admiral Harwood's staff by surprise. At any rate it became apparent soon after Tripoli was captured on 23rd January that the preparations had been inadequate; and although the clearance teams on the spot did very well with what they had, General Montgomery was dissatisfied over the rate of progress. It is certain that from the very beginning Admiral Harwood had not hit it off with Montgomery; and it is likely that the disastrous failure off Tobruk on 13th-14th September, 1942 had, somewhat unfairly, coloured the Eighth Army commander's views on his principal naval colleague.[1] But it is also the case that several other incidents in the eastern Mediterranean— notably the failure of the " Vigorous " convoy to Malta in June[2]— had aroused questioning doubts in London; and they now appeared to be reinforced by the Army's complaints over the re-opening of Tripoli. Furthermore Montgomery's views on Tripoli reached Cairo when the Prime Minister himself was there; and Mr. Churchill had recently been angered by Admiral Harwood's strict adherence to the agreement about the French warships immobilised in Alexandria. This had originally been negotiated on a personal basis between Admirals Godfroy and Cunningham in June, 1940,[3] and had, on the British side, come to Harwood by inheritance. But Godfroy was still vacillating about joining the Allies, and Mr. Churchill considered that the time had come when greater firmness would resolve a rather absurd situation : for many of the French ships which had been in Oran, Algiers and Dakar had already thrown in their lot with us. The result was that when the reports on Tripoli, and the views of the Minister of State in the Middle East on these matters, reached London, the First Sea Lord decided that Admiral Harwood should be relieved of his command.

Not the least curious aspect of the story of the re-opening of Tripoli, and its repercussions on the naval Commander-in-Chief,

[1] Operation " Agreement." See pp. 237-8.   [2] See pp. 218-20.   [3] See p. 85.

H.M.S. *Valiant* leads two Italian battleships and five Italian cruisers to Malta, September, 1943

Anzio: an L.S.T. approaching the assault area, while destroyers lay a smokescreen, 21st January, 1944

Landing at Reggio, September, 1943

The *Tirpitz* in her net defence at Kaafiord, 1943

is that close investigation of the progress made in restoring the port and in unloading supplies, leaves one in no doubt that the Army's requirements were in fact fully met, and that no delay was imposed on the next westward offensive. Indeed, both Mr. Churchill and General Montgomery paid tribute later to the Navy's efforts at Tripoli.[1] Thus it may be that, had all the facts been known in London, a tragic end to a war career which had opened so brilliantly off the River Plate on 13th December, 1939 might have been avoided.

On 20th February, 1943, Sir Andrew Cunningham resumed the title of Commander-in-Chief, Mediterranean, which he had made famous earlier in the war, and the area of his responsibility was extended eastwards to include the waters through which the expeditionary force bound for Sicily would sail; for the decision to launch that undertaking had just been accepted by the Allied leaders at the Casablanca conference. The eastern Mediterranean now became known as the Levant Command, and on 5th June Admiral Sir John Cunningham took over responsibility for those waters.

By the end of January the Eighth Army had crossed the Tunisian frontier, but not until two months later did Montgomery's men breach the defences known as the Mareth Line. Soon afterwards the ports of Gabes and Sfax were captured,[2] and again the Inshore Squadron moved in hard on the soldiers' heels. Meanwhile the Levant Command was sending a steady stream of supply convoys to Benghazi, Tripoli and Malta; while Sir Andrew Cunningham's cruiser and destroyer striking forces based on Malta and Bone and our shore-based aircraft were steadily tightening their hold on the Mediterranean "narrows," and the reinforced submarine flotillas were intensifying their patrols off the principal ports of departure for Axis shipping. Though the enemy continued almost to the end to try to run ships through to Tunis and Bizerta, his losses rose steeply. During the first five months of 1943 over 500 Axis merchantmen, totalling some 560,000 tons were sunk in the Mediterranean, and by the beginning of May the Afrika Korps was virtually cut off from the European mainland. At the same time our

[1] See W. S. Churchill, *The Second World War*, Vol. IV, p. 644, and Field-Marshal Montgomery, *El Alamein to the River Sangro*, p. 37.
[2] See Map pp. 112-13.

greatly strengthened convoy escorts took a heavy toll of the enemy's submarines, no less than 20 of which (9 Italian and 11 German) were sunk between January and May. As it was now very difficult for Dönitz's reinforcements to break through the Gibraltar Straits, the Mediterranean U-boats, which had caused us heavy losses when they first arrived, had become a dwindling asset.

Early in May the First and Eighth Armies struck the culminating blows in their long campaigns, and on the 7th Allied forces entered both Tunis and Bizerta. Next day Sir Andrew Cunningham signalled to all his forces " Sink, burn, destroy. Let nothing pass "; for he was determined that the Axis armies should not escape from his clutches to fight again on the European mainland. Cruisers and destroyers now vigorously scoured the waters in which less than a year earlier we had suffered heavily in our attempts to succour Malta; while M.T.B.s and other small craft searched for enemy vessels in every nook and cranny of the African coast. But they actually found few targets, for the enemy's attempts to evacuate his trapped soldiers were very half-hearted. On 13th May the last Axis soldiers in Africa laid down their arms, and the strategic purpose towards which Britain had striven for nearly three years, and which we had always regarded as the essential preliminary to re-entering the European continent, was triumphantly fulfilled. Although in the last phase the issue in North Africa was decided by the land battles, it was our command of the sea which had enabled our armies to recover from their earlier defeats, and then to build up their strength for the final offensives; and had the enemy ever succeeded in gaining firm maritime control in the Mediterranean it is certain that the land campaigns would have gone the other way.

Well before the surrender in Tunisia the Navy had been preparing to sweep the dense minefields in the " Narrows," and on 15th May Cunningham signalled to the Admiralty that " the passage through the Mediterranean was clear." A week later the first through convoy since May, 1941, reached Tripoli safely, and thereafter we ran a regular service between Gibraltar and Alexandria. The WS convoys, sailing by the long Cape of Good Hope route, which had been the life-line of the Middle East forces ever since June 1940, were now stopped; and ships sailing to India and Australia could again use the Suez Canal. To Britain this meant an enormous saving in mercantile tonnage, which offset a proportion of the heavy losses suffered during the preceding three and a half years. With the " ancient waterway " through the Mediterranean reopened and firmly controlled by the White Ensign ships or their comrades flying the Stars and Stripes, and the shortage of merchant shipping which had so long been the chief source of our anxiety mitigated, we were able to turn to the planning of the next offensive with renewed vigour and firm faith in its success.

The next step after reopening the Mediterranean was to re-organise our mercantile traffic so as to make the fullest possible use of the Tunisian ports. Tobruk and Benghazi in the east had now declined in importance, as had Bone and Bougie in the west. Bizerta and Tunis on the other hand stood in an excellent strategic position right in the middle of the route from Gibraltar to Alexandria, and thus became the central hub around which the protection of the through convoys revolved.[1] Furthermore, the Tunisian ports (Bizerta, Tunis, Sousse and Sfax) became, with Tripoli, the main assembly points for the landing craft required for the next combined operation. The outward Mediterranean convoys from Britain (KM) and those from the U.S.A. (UG) now joined together at Gibraltar, and became a British responsibility during their eastward passages. Ships joined them from various ports as they progressed through the Mediterranean, and some of the combined convoys became very large indeed. To give one example, UGS 8A, which sailed from Gibraltar early in June, consisted of 129 merchantmen, and was protected by 19 escort vessels. These large, slow-moving convoys, which could not deviate from the 2,000-mile route along the North African coast, were inviting targets for the U-boats and for the German bombers working from their well-placed bases in Sardinia, Sicily and Crete; but losses never approached those which some of our Atlantic convoys had suffered early in 1943. The still numerous Italian submarines did us little harm, and during the whole of the latter half of 1943, the Mediterranean U-boats sank only 31 ships (136,000 tons), while the bombers accounted for 41 more totalling 225,000 tons. Furthermore a substantial proportion of those losses was incurred during the great combined operations against Sicily and southern Italy, shortly to be described, when the Allied shipping massed close offshore presented the enemy with

[1] See Map pp. 112-13.

exceptionally favourable targets. On the through-Mediterranean route, our shipping suffered only light losses at the hands of the U-boats and bombers—for all that the latter had been reinforced to a total of about 1,000 on the airfields around the central basin. The chief reason for the comparative immunity of these important convoys was that the Royal Air Force and its comrades of the U.S.A.A.F., now possessed many excellently placed bases close off the southern flank of the route; and they and the surface escorts were working together in increasingly intimate harmony. In the anti-submarine field the new technique, developed jointly by the naval and air commanders and colloquially known as " Swamp," proved extremely effective. Shore-based aircraft would patrol continuously over the waters where a U-boat had been sighted, so keeping the enemy submerged, what time flotilla vessels rushed to the scene to hunt the enemy to destruction. The result of these measures was that, although Dönitz continued to send reinforcements to try and break through the Gibraltar Straits, few succeeded in doing so; and those that did penetrate into the Mediterranean were very roughly handled by the sea and air escorts and patrols. During the six months June-December, 1943, twenty more Axis submarines (9 German and 11 Italian) were destroyed in the Mediterranean, and at the end of the year the U-boats' numbers had declined from a peak of 25 in November, 1942, to no more than 13. It may therefore be said that the defeat of the Mediterranean U-boats took place about four months after the Allied escorts had achieved their great victory of May, 1943, in the Atlantic.[1]

On 11th and 12th June, after very heavy preliminary sea and air bombardments, we seized the small islands of Pantelleria and Lampedusa in the Mediterranean narrows,[2] thus strengthening our hold over the waters through which the assault shipping bound for Sicily would sail, and also improving the security of the convoys running between Gibraltar and Alexandria. Meanwhile we had set up combined operation training centres at the head of the Red Sea, and had shipped out large numbers of landing craft from Britain and America. After a period of intensive training for the naval crews and the military units which they were to embark, in June the assault forces began to move to the assembly ports from which they would sail to Sicily; and it is therefore time that we

[1] See pp. 275-8.   [2] See Map pp. 112-13.

looked at the plan for operation " Husky "—the first attack on the European mainland.

The Americans came to the Casablanca conference in January, 1943, determined to press for the invasion of Europe to be launched across the English Channel in the following summer, and it was only after long discussion that they accepted the British view that the shortage of shipping and landing craft, and of men specially trained in assaults from the sea, ruled out such a purpose for another year—unless they were prepared to risk a disaster on a scale which would have made the failure at Dieppe seem like a minor setback.[1] The British representatives first proposed to attack Sardinia, because such an undertaking could be launched soonest, but deferred to the American view that Sicily should be the next objective— even though the larger forces needed would mean postponing the new offensive until July or possibly August. This strategy was approved by the Combined Chiefs of Staff on 7th April; but the original intention to land in the west of the island, in order to capture the fine harbour of Palermo quickly,[2] as well as on the east coast, was finally dropped in favour of concentrating the assaults at the south-east corner. Here we may note that this change of plan, which was pressed by General Montgomery, undoubtedly reduced the risks of failure—as did his insistence on strengthening the assault force with an extra division; but the late date on which the decisions were taken, produced serious and, one may feel, avoidable difficulties for the naval commanders and their staffs, who had to revise the entire intricate convoy and escort programme. On 13th May, however, the new plan was approved by the Combined Chiefs of Staff. The British Eighth Army was now to be carried, mostly from Africa, to five sectors stretching from just south of Syracuse to a point west of Cape Passero; while the American Seventh Army would land in three sectors on the south coast of Sicily with a gap of about 30 miles between it and the most westerly British assault. The initial objectives were the ports of Augusta and Syracuse, which were essential to the rapid unloading of stores and reinforcements, and the group of airfields in south-east Sicily, which were needed to enable the Allied Air Forces to establish themselves close to the scene of operations; while the final purpose was the expulsion of the Axis armies from the whole

[1] See pp. 231-3.   [2] See Map p. 286.

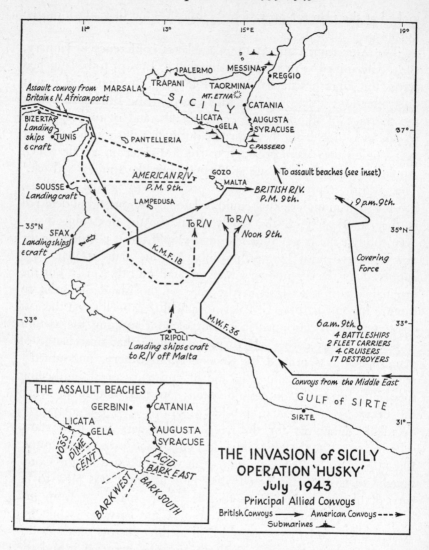

island. Under the Commander-in-Chief, Sir Andrew Cunningham, the naval forces for the British (or eastern) assaults were to be commanded by Admiral Sir Bertram Ramsay, of Dunkirk fame; while Vice-Admiral H. K. Hewitt, U.S.N., was made responsible for the American (or western) assaults.

The expedition to Sicily consisted of five assault forces drawn from the British Empire, and three provided by the United States.

In the British expeditionary force the troops allocated to the three northern sectors (called " Acid North," " Acid South " and " Bark East ") were to embark in and sail from the ports of the Middle East: the " Bark South " assault force was to come from North Africa and Malta, while the 1st Canadian Division and Royal Marine Commandos were to be sent out from Britain to carry out the assault in the " Bark West " sector.[1] Of the three American assault forces two would start out from North African ports and one from the east coast of the United States. In all some 115,000 British Empire and 66,000 American soldiers were involved in the undertaking; and we may here note that it was undoubtedly the fact that the British contribution in all elements greatly outnumbered that of our Ally which brought about the acceptance of the strategy which we favoured; for the country which pays the piper by supplying the majority of the men and weapons will always, in the ultimate issue, be entitled to call the strategic tune—as we were to learn to our sorrow during the following year.

One interesting feature of operation " Husky " was that, whereas in operation " Torch " all the assault forces had been carried to the scene in large transports, from which they transferred to the landing craft which were to carry them in to the beaches (called " ship to shore " assaults), on the present occasion a new technique (called " shore to shore " assaults) was introduced. The main force for the British " Bark South " sector, and certain elements of those destined for the other sectors, thus embarked in North African ports or in Malta in the landing ships and craft from which they would actually step ashore in enemy territory. Though this technique could not be applied in cases where a long sea passage had to be made, where the distances between the embarkation ports and the assault area were comparatively short it possessed considerable advantages; for the difficult and sometimes lengthy task of transferring the troops from the transports to the landing craft was eliminated. On the other hand if the sea was in unkindly mood, a " shore to shore " assault might subject the soldiers to so unpleasant an ordeal that their efficiency would be impaired; for seasickness, though it can be mitigated by modern drugs, can scarcely fail to damp the ardour and determination which are so essential to success in assaults from the sea. Another new feature in operation " Husky " was the

[1] See Map p. 286.

introduction of a " Senior Naval Officer, Landings " for each sector. Aided by specially trained parties of Naval Beach Commandos his functions were to control boat traffic, to maintain communications with the offshore shipping, and to produce order out of the confusion which is almost inevitable during the first hours after the " touch-down."

In the final plan " D-Day " was named as 10th July and " H-Hour " as 2.45 a.m.—which was about three hours before dawn. It was the British Army which favoured an assault in darkness—holding that the possibility of achieving surprise was thereby increased. From the naval point of view a landing soon after daylight would have been greatly preferred, because darkness was bound to make navigation and pilotage more difficult, and increased the likelihood of confusion and error among the landing craft flotillas. Later experience—especially that of the Americans in the Pacific—was to prove that the arguments put forward in favour of the night assault were not altogether well founded. More serious perhaps, was the Army's insistence that preliminary bombing and bombardment of the defences should be sacrificed in the interests of surprise. Again the Navy deferred to military opinion; for it is an ancient tradition of the service that in combined operations the Army's needs should take priority over all other considerations. But we were soon to find out that the benefits to be gained from preliminary bombardments far outweighed the arguments against them.

On 20th May, only about seven weeks before D-Day, Admiral Cunningham issued his naval plan to his subordinate British and American commanders, and to the shore authorities. In all 2,590 warships and landing craft (1,614 British, 945 American and 31 from other nations) were involved in the transport of the assault forces from the embarkation ports to the beaches, in covering them and supporting them after they had landed, and in seeing that reinforcements and supplies thereafter flowed in unimpeded. Rear-Admiral T. Troubridge was in command of the forces coming from the Middle East, which were to land in the Acid North, Acid South and Bark East sectors, Rear-Admiral R. R. McGrigor led the contingents from North Africa and Malta destined for Bark East, Bark South and Bark West, while the convoys from Britain were commanded by Rear-Admiral Sir Philip Vian.[1]

[1] See Map p. 286.

In addition to the escort vessels, bombarding ships, minesweepers and other warships allocated to the assault force commanders, a very strong covering force (4 battleships, with 2 more in reserve, 2 fleet carriers, 6 cruisers and 18 destroyers) was provided to Vice-Admiral A. U. Willis, commander of Force H, to defeat any attempt at intervention by the main Italian fleet; while Rear-Admiral C. H. J. Harcourt had a cruiser and destroyer force to work close inshore in support of the Army. Lastly, submarines were to act as navigation beacons for the assault forces, to land small raiding parties in the enemy's rear, and to lie in wait off Italian ports in case their still powerful fleet came out. All these White Ensign ships, as well as the American Navy's contribution to the western assault, remained under the C.-in-C. until they reached the invasion area, when the assault force commanders would assume full authority in their several sectors.

The outward movements actually began at the end of May, with the departure of the convoys from America; then the Canadian Division sailed in 4 convoys from British ports between 20th June and 1st July, shortly followed by the assault forces from the Middle East. Last to leave were the landing craft and L.S.T. convoys from Tunisian ports earmarked for the " shore to shore " assaults already described. Meanwhile all the " follow-up " convoys had started to move from Britain, America and North Africa; and to a celestial observer the island of Sicily might have appeared to resemble a magnetic spot on the earth's surface towards which hundreds upon hundreds of ships were being drawn by some invisible but irresistible force. What such an observer could not have realised was that the control of all those far-flung movements was in fact being exercised firstly from the quiet rooms beneath the Admiralty, then from Admiral Cunningham's headquarters at Algiers, and finally from the Headquarters Ships in which the assault force commanders flew their flags.

Losses while the convoys were on passage were insignificant—only four ships being sunk by U-boats; but we had, as in " Torch," made elaborate preparations to deceive the enemy regarding our intentions. In the present case, feints were made to suggest an invasion of Crete and Greece in the east, and of Sardinia and Corsica in the west; and we even adopted the macabre ruse of depositing an officer's dead body off the Spanish coast in a position where the false papers which it carried were almost certain to fall into the hands of German agents. We discovered after the war that this had been entirely successful; and there is no doubt that the enemy, though he knew that a new overseas expedition was being prepared, remained completely in the dark about where and when the blow would fall.

Early in July Admiral Ramsay transferred to Malta, and on the 4th of that month the Commander-in-Chief gave the executive order to " carry out operation Husky," thus setting in motion the whole intricate machinery of the carefully worked out plan. The 9th July was a critical day—for the landing craft convoys were then moving north from Tunisia. Dawn broke on a clear sky, but the north-west wind then freshened sufficiently to produce a nasty lop, which taxed the seamanship of the landing craft crews severely, and caused the unfortunate soldiers embarked in them considerable internal discomfort. But it was then too late even to consider postponing the operation, and naval headquarters could only let matters take their course. Daylight on 9th July saw the main covering force manœuvring as though on a peace-time exercise right in the middle of the waters which Mussolini had once rashly claimed as " *mare nostrum*"; while the great troop convoys coming from the east and west steamed steadily towards each other along the North African coast, turning towards Malta when they reached a point off Tripoli. In the evening the British convoys passed in succession through a datum point which had been established to the south of that island, and Admiral Ramsay came out to watch the junction of the hundreds of ships which had started out from so many different points of the compass. The small craft were labouring badly; but they battled manfully to the north and, after passing through the datum point, all convoys set course for their final destinations. Shortly before midnight the wind mercifully started to ease, and first light on D-Day revealed to the anxious watchers at headquarters that the swell was decreasing, and the weather seemed to be set fair. In fact it now seems that the unfavourable conditions encountered but overcome by the landing craft crews on the night before the assault, contributed to the achievement of surprise—for the defenders of the beaches relaxed their precautions in the belief that, as Admiral Cunningham put it, " to-night at any rate, they can't come." But they were wrong:

for, in spite of all that the sea and wind could do " they came."

The first bombardments took place soon after dawn on D-Day, the 10th, when warships struck at Catania and Taormina on the east coast of Sicily and at Trapani and Marsala in the west with the object of diverting the enemy's attention from the actual scene of the landings.[1] Meanwhile in the three northern sectors of the British assault area the troop convoys from the Middle East had arrived at their " lowering positions " about seven miles off shore as intended at 12.30 a.m.; but the swell and sea caused difficulties in getting the troops embarked in the landing craft, and in forming up the flotillas for the passage inshore. Most of the craft touched down on time, but some soldiers were landed on the wrong beaches and a certain amount of confusion resulted. Luckily resistance was slight, and by the time that full daylight had come, the assault troops were well established everywhere. As soon as the big troop transports had unloaded they were sent away under convoy, thus escaping the first air attacks—which took place early in the afternoon. The landing craft for the " shore to shore " assault in the Bark South sector near Cape Passero were late in arriving, on account of the severe buffeting they had received the previous day; and when they moved inshore they encountered " false beaches " on which some of them grounded well to seaward of the proper disembarkation points. It was now that the American-designed amphibious vehicles known as DUKWS proved their remarkable versatility, by unloading grounded craft and carrying their men and stores right up on to the proper beaches. The Bark West force had the most difficult experience of all, for its beaches were more exposed to the swell, and again offshore reefs and sandbanks caused trouble. None the less, by daylight the Canadians were in firm possession of their beaches; but here too it was fortunate that the enemy's initial resistance was slight. By dusk on D-Day, in spite of the troubles encountered, the Eighth Army's assault elements were firmly established in Sicily, the first reinforcement convoys were arriving, and losses had been almost insignificant. Best of all was the news that Syracuse had fallen to our troops on D-Day; and the minesweepers cleared the approaches to the port so quickly that on 13th the first convoy was sent in to unload there. As its facilities were practically undamaged the Army was now much less

[1] See Map p. 286.

dependent on what could be unloaded over the beaches. That same day, the 13th, Augusta was captured, and again the naval forces moved in quickly with the object of getting the port working. These two successes enabled us to close down the original beach organisation considerably earlier than we had anticipated.

Meanwhile to the west of Cape Passero, Admiral Hewitt's three assault forces had met rather more difficult conditions than the British crews; for their beaches were more exposed to the wind and sea than those on the east coast. Delays resulted, and when the landing craft moved inshore " false beaches " again caused trouble. Moreover enemy air attacks were at first more frequent and severe than those experienced by Ramsay's ships; and when the Germans launched a heavy counter attack on the 11th, the close air support proved inadequate. Luckily the bombardment ships stepped into the breach, and broke up what at one time appeared a dangerous thrust against the newly landed troops. Once these difficulties had been overcome, and the Seventh Army had consolidated its beach-heads, General Patton's men swept right across central Sicily to capture Palermo on the 22nd. They then turned east, driving the enemy before them towards Messina.

Meanwhile in the British sector the naval forces were kept very busy answering the Army's calls for bombardments, opening up the captured ports, beating off air attacks and dealing with the submarines which endeavoured to attack the shipping crowded in the offshore anchorages. After the first few days the enemy bombers concentrated their efforts against the British rather than the American task force, and it was they who caused the majority of the losses suffered. Yet none of the British flag officers represented in their reports that the fighter cover provided by the Air Forces was inadequate—as did the American Admiral Hewitt. In fact the Commander-in-Chief himself found it " almost magical that great fleets of ships could remain anchored on the enemy's coast . . . with only such slight losses." The difference in outlook probably arose from the fact that whereas we had been in constant action with the Luftwaffe for more than three years, and knew exactly how deadly its bombers could be against warships and convoys which lacked fighter protection, the Americans had undergone no similar experiences, and therefore expected to enjoy too high a degree of immunity from air attacks. In the British fleet, because less was expected, there was better understanding of the problems involved in giving air cover, and a sensible appreciation of what the Air Forces actually accomplished. As to the Axis submarines which tried to intervene, they inflicted fewer losses than the bombers,[1] and were themselves very roughly handled. In the three weeks following the invasion of Sicily we sank three German and eight Italian submarines; and another Italian, the *Bronzo*, was blown to the surface and captured intact off Syracuse on 12th July, to be towed triumphantly into harbour by British minesweepers.

After the capture of Augusta and Syracuse, and of the adjacent airfields, the Eighth Army's next objective was Catania; but while still some miles from the town our troops encountered stiff resistance, and their advance was halted. Early on 17th July, Admiral Cunningham sent the battleship *Warspite*, his former flagship, up from Malta at full speed to bombard the defences; but neither her 15-inch shells, nor a paratroop operation, nor a frontal attack by the infantry succeeded in breaking the enemy's grip. General Montgomery now switched his main effort from the direct advance towards Messina up the east coast of Sicily to an encircling movement around the massif of Mount Etna.[2] This decision surprised the naval commanders, who had expected to exploit our overwhelming sea-power by lifting a proportion of the Army and landing it farther up the coast, behind the main enemy defences on the Catania plain. Though it is true that the conformation of the coast between Catania and Messina, and the strong shore defences, would have inhibited a large scale landing, it does seem that comparatively small forces could have cut the line of retreat up the very vulnerable coastal road and railway. Twice in July the Navy prepared to carry out such a purpose, but each time the Army cancelled it; and the only landing actually made (on the night of 16th-17th August) was too late to interfere with the enemy's retreat. On the north coast the Americans did form a special force, and endeavoured on three occasions to cut the coastal communications by landings from the sea. Unfortunately the assault forces were too

---

[1] Between D-Day and the end of July we lost six merchantmen or auxiliaries (41,509 tons) and three small craft to air attacks, and had a number of other ships damaged. The American task force lost only one merchantman, two L.S.T.s, a destroyer and a minesweeper. Enemy submarines only accomplished the sinking of four British merchantmen and two American L.S.T.s in the same period.

[2] See Map p. 286.

weak to accomplish much, and they arrived after the main body of
the enemy had already passed the points at which they disembarked.
The efforts made were, however, on the right lines; and one can
only regret that greater strength was not allocated to such purposes.
It thus happened that the British and American armies both drove
the defenders of Sicily back towards Messina—the point from which
they were bound in any case to evacuate the island; and our
sea-power was hardly exploited at all in order to close the trap on
them. To-day one may feel, as indeed Admiral Cunningham felt
at the time, that more could have been done by way of landings
from the sea; and the correctness of the strategy actually adopted
appears even more questionable, because we now know how greatly
inferior to our own strength were the Axis forces deployed before
Catania.[1] Thus it seems that holding attacks against the main
defences, combined with landings in the enemy's rear might have
disorganised his retreat and led to the capture of a substantial
proportion of his forces.

From the middle of July until the end of the campaign, naval
light forces, and sometimes heavy bombardment ships, worked
constantly in the southern approaches to the Messina Straits; but
the gun batteries on both coasts were extremely numerous and
powerful, and we never succeeded in gaining anything like a firm
hold over the waters—only $2\frac{1}{2}$ miles wide at their narrowest point
—which the enemy had to cross if his troops were to escape from
Sicily. On 3rd August indications of a large scale evacuation became
strong, and the Naval and Air Commanders considered what could
be done to stop it. No co-ordinated plan was, however, issued;
the main strength of the Strategic Air Force continued to be deployed
against targets in Italy, and another ten days elapsed before the
Tactical Air Force was told to concentrate its effort against the
heavy traffic across the straits. On the enemy's side very thorough
preparations had been made by Rear-Admiral P. Barone of the
Italian Navy and his German colleague, Captain von Liebenstein;
and the chief credit for the success achieved must go to those two

---

[1] We had landed four infantry divisions and two armoured brigades, plus ancillary
forces, in the original assault, and a fifth division was carried in late in July. The defenders
of Catania appear to have consisted of one "gruppe" (Schmalz) of the Hermann Goering
Division, elements of the 1st Parachute Division, and a miscellaneous collection of Italian
units of doubtful military value. Though the contemporary records do not enable us to
assess the strength of the German units in late July, 1943, with any accuracy, there is no doubt
that they had recently suffered heavy losses, and were far below establishment.

officers. We may, however, note that von Liebenstein was astonished that the Allied air effort against the terminal ports and the ships and barges which he had assembled was so light and sporadic. The outcome was that between 3rd and 16th August, 62,000 Italian soldiers, nearly 40,000 Germans, and great quantities of vehicles, guns and equipment were removed—mostly by day—to temporary safety in Italy; and when Allied forces entered Messina on 17th August they found that their quarry had escaped. To-day it seems plain that, on the Allied side, it was the lack of any co-ordinated plan which made this achievement possible. Our naval and air forces, though present in overwhelming strength, went into action piecemeal, and the bombers were constantly switched from one duty to another. The correct policy undoubtedly was for the strategic bombers to attack the terminal ports until they had made embarkation impossible, and for the tactical bombers to neutralise the coastal batteries sufficiently to enable our warships to seize control of the narrows; and had a joint plan been made to accomplish those objects, it is difficult not to believe that we could have stopped the evacuation. Such a purpose was, after all, similar to that of launching a great offensive combined operation, though in an inverted sense; and we were well aware of the care in planning which was essential to success in such undertakings. Yet in July and August, 1943, we made no parallel preparations to deal with the enemy withdrawal from Sicily by sea. This may be attributed in part to the physical separation of the three Service commanders between Sicily, Malta and North Africa, and in part to the fact that their staffs were at the time greatly occupied with planning the next assault from the sea; but the main cause of the enemy's success seems to have been that the full value of the prize to be gained from blocking the Messina Straits simply was not appreciated at the time.

After the clearance of Sicily in the middle of August, 1943, there was a pause of about a fortnight—chiefly because, although the Allied commanders in the Mediterranean had long since been preparing for the next offensive, and the loading of ships had actually begun—their governments had not yet decided where to strike. All that the Commanders-in-Chief had to work on was the agreement of the Combined Chiefs of Staff, reached on 21st July, that the mainland of Italy should be invaded; and the Americans had complicated the execution of that purpose by insisting that the combined operations vessels earmarked for the South-East Asia Command should not be held back, and by refusing to allocate any more long-range fighters to the Mediterranean theatre, on the grounds that they were all required to escort the strategic bombers on their raids into Germany. Those decisions, though not un-expected, caused a good deal of concern in London, and steps to mitigate their effects were at once considered. Adequate fighter support over the scene of the landings was, of course, essential; and when we realised that the shore-based Air Forces were not going to be able to provide more than a part of the necessary aircraft, the Admiralty promptly sent out the fleet carrier *Illustrious* and a specially organised escort carrier force equipped with naval fighters under Rear-Admiral Sir Philip Vian. To relieve the shortage of shipping they also ordered back to the Mediterranean ten large troopships, which had returned home after the assault on Sicily.

Hardly had we re-organised our forces to meet the Mediterranean theatre's needs when, on 25th July, the fall of Mussolini introduced totally new factors; since for several weeks we were uncertain whether the new Italian government would continue to fight alongside the Germans or not. The first peace feelers, put out in great secrecy, were actually received almost simultaneously with the opening of the Quebec conference on 13th August; but the possibility that Italy would sue for peace did not eliminate the need to proceed with the invasion, since we were aware that the Germans were tightening their grip on that unhappy country. After considering all possible alternative landing places, on the south as well as the south-west coast of Italy, the Allied leaders finally accepted General Eisenhower's recommendation that the new assault should be made in the Gulf of Salerno, to the south of Naples;[1] and by the end of August the Mediterranean planning staffs had, by working at great pressure, managed to complete the operation orders.

The plan provided for General Montgomery's Eighth Army to be carried across the Straits of Messina (operation " Baytown "), and for the Fifth Army under the American General Mark Clark

[1] See Map pp. 112-13.

to make the assault at Salerno (operation " Avalanche "). This Army consisted of VI Corps, composed of American troops, and the British of X Corps; and the latter was considerably the stronger of the two. A " Western Naval Task Force " commanded by Vice-Admiral H. K. Hewitt, U.S.N., was organised to carry the troops to the scene of the assault, and to support them after they had landed. It consisted of a Northern Attack Force under Commodore G. N. Oliver, which was responsible for landing X Corps, and a Southern Attack Force under Rear-Admiral J. L. Hall, U.S.N., which was to embark the American Army's VI Corps. The maritime forces comprised some 700 warships, merchantmen and landing craft; and each Attack Force commander was given a number of heavy ships for bombardment purposes, minesweepers to clear the inshore waters, and other vessels of all the numerous types needed for a combined operation. The convoys carrying the troops for the northern (British) assault assembled at and sailed from Bizerta and Tripoli, while those carrying the American troops for the southern assault used Algiers and Oran. All convoys were to pass to the west of Sicily, thus keeping out of range of the enemy's main air bases as long as possible, and also aiding our deception plan— which was designed to give the impression that we were moving against Sardinia or Corsica. The landings at Salerno were to be made by a combination of " ship to shore " and " shore to shore " assaults;[1] and the employment of the latter method necessitated the landing craft convoys calling at ports on the north coast of Sicily in order to refuel. Follow-up convoys were organised in the usual manner, and once the assault forces were established on shore, L.S.T.s and L.C.I.s were to run shuttle services between the Gulf of Salerno and the loading ports.

By the beginning of September all preparations had been completed; but the Admiralty was still anxious about whether Admiral Cunningham had enough ships, and of the right types, to build up the assault forces with the necessary speed. They realised that, by landing at so great a distance from our established sea and air bases, we might place the Fifth Army in a very dangerous position; for there was little doubt that, in the early stages, the enemy would be able to reinforce the defenders quicker than we could strengthen the assault forces. There was, however, little more

[1] See p. 287.

that could be done at this late hour, and on 1st September, Admiral Cunningham accordingly named the 9th as D-Day, with H-Hour at 3.30 a.m. (one hour before sunrise). It will thus be seen that, as in the invasion of Sicily, the Army's preference for an assault in darkness was given priority over the naval preference for a landing in daylight; and once again preliminary air and naval bombardments were sacrificed in the interests of achieving surprise. On 3rd September, the day that the first of the " Avalanche " convoys sailed, the Eighth Army was carried across the Messina Straits in some 300 landing ships and craft, and stepped ashore in Italy unopposed; for the Axis forces which had escaped from Sicily were in the main regrouping around Naples. General Montgomery's men now advanced north along the coastal road; but the slow pace of their progress soon made it plain that they were unlikely to link up with the Fifth Army as soon after the assault from the sea at Salerno as had been intended.

On 7th September the main naval covering force (four battleships and two fleet carriers, with a powerful destroyer escort) left Malta under Vice-Admiral Willis, and passed west-about Sicily into the Tyrrhenian Sea. Though heavily attacked by German torpedo-bombers on the night of 8th-9th (an attack which the enemy probably intended for the invasion convoys) it escaped damage, and by D-Day Willis's ships were in position to fulfil their main task of providing air and naval cover for the assault forces. Admiral Vian's escort carrier force sailed from Malta on the 8th, about 24 hours after the main fleet, and steamed up the Messina Straits into the Tyrrhenian Sea, where it took up its station off Salerno Bay and prepared to fly off the covering fighters. Meanwhile the Italian government had accepted the Allied terms for an armistice, and on the evening of 8th, when the assault convoys were approaching the assault area, they were publicly announced. The naval clauses provided for the Italian fleet to be immediately transferred to " such points as may be designated by the Allied Commander-in-Chief"; and Admiral Cunningham accordingly ordered their main body to come south from Spezia by a special route. The battleships *Roma*, *Vittorio Veneto* and *Italia* (formerly *Littorio*), six cruisers and a number of destroyers accordingly sailed in the early hours of the 9th; but some curious vacillations by the Italian Commander-in-Chief, Admiral Bergamini, gave the Germans their chance, and that afternoon they attacked their former allies with their new wireless-controlled bombs. The *Roma* was hit and blew up with heavy loss of life. Meanwhile Cunningham had ordered a detachment from the Salerno covering force to meet the Italian fleet, and early on the 10th the famous *Warspite* and her sister ship the *Valiant* conducted them to Malta. The other principal Italian warships were at Taranto; and they too—including the battleships *Andrea Doria*, *Caio Duilio* and *Giulio Cesare*, and several more cruisers—were met at sea and taken to the British base. Thus did the main part of the Italian fleet pass into Allied control without a shot being fired. To the British sailors who watched its submission, it was an unforgettable occasion; since for over three years those warships had been their principal adversaries. On 11th September, Cunningham signalled to the Admiralty in traditional language " Be pleased to inform Their Lordships that the Italian battle fleet now lies under the guns of the fortress of Malta."[1]

As soon as the armistice terms were announced Cunningham rushed a powerful naval force, with troops embarked, to Taranto; and on 9th September we took possession of that important base— the scene of the Fleet Air Arm's brilliantly successful attack on 11th November, 1940.[2] Within a few days, with the willing co-operation of the local Italian authorities, we had extended our hold to Brindisi, Bari and other harbours, which were soon to prove very valuable entries for the supplies and reinforcements needed by the Allied armies in Italy. Furthermore, the possession of all the naval and air bases in the south of that country enormously strengthened our hold over the sea routes through the Mediterranean. Thus, within the space of a few days, were maritime prospects in the whole theatre transformed.

To return to the Salerno invasion convoys, early on 9th September, they reached their lowering positions, and the landing craft moved inshore; but for the first time since Dieppe we now encountered an alert enemy installed in strongly defended positions which had not been subdued, let alone neutralised, by preliminary bombardments. During the approach the landing craft were heavily fired on by German guns, and as soon as the troops stepped

[1] This is the form of address used by a Commander-in-Chief in a letter to the Permanent Secretary of the Admiralty, whose function it is to lay correspondence before the Lords of the Admiralty.

[2] See pp. 110-14.

ashore they found themselves involved in a bitter contest for possession of the beaches. The destroyers and support landing craft moved close inshore to support the soldiers, while the heavier bombarding ships (cruisers and monitors) fired on the more distant enemy batteries, and the fighters from Admiral Vian's carrier force (which flew 265 sorties on D-Day) kept watch overhead. In spite of all difficulties, by nightfall on D-Day the British beach-head was firmly held; but penetration inland was nowhere more than three miles, and the local airfield, which was urgently needed for use by our defending fighters, had not been captured. Moreover, there was a gap of about five miles between the British and the American assault forces, which latter had encountered even more stubborn opposition than X Corps. This was a situation which a skilled and determined enemy was bound to exploit, and on 13th the Germans launched a powerful attack aimed to reach the shore at the junction between the British and American sectors, so cutting the invasion army into two. By the 14th the situation looked precarious; for German penetration had been deep, and the American beaches were being shelled. Admiral Hewitt now stopped all unloading, ordered the assault shipping to keep steam at short notice, and signalled urgently to Admiral Cunningham for reinforcements. The response was immediate. While cruisers steamed at full speed to Tripoli to embark more troops, the *Warspite* and *Valiant* rushed up from Malta to support the embattled armies with their heavy guns; and Allied bombers and fighters struck at the German salient and their lines of communication with all their might. Though the situation on 14th was certainly anxious it never became anything like desperate; and the naval authorities were therefore astonished to receive a request from General Clark to prepare plans to re-embark either VI Corps or X Corps, and then put the withdrawn troops ashore again in the other sector. To them it seemed that re-embarkation from a rather shallow beach-head in the face of stiff opposition would certainly prove suicidal; and they took immediate steps to ensure that the attempt should not be made.

On 15th and 16th the offshore warships—battleships, monitors, cruisers and destroyers—were almost continuously in action against enemy gun batteries and concentrations of troops and vehicles; and by the latter day it was plain that the German thrust had been

defeated. The bombarding ships did, however, attract the attention
of the German wireless-controlled bombers. Two American and
one British cruiser were hit quite early on, and on 16th the *Warspite*
was so badly damaged that she lost all power, and had to be towed
to Malta. The enemy's records make it plain, however, that the
naval gunfire was probably the greatest factor in the defeat of their
attempt to divide the Allied army and then drive it back into the
sea.

While this bitter fighting was proceeding around the Salerno
beach-heads Admiral Vian's fighters continued to provide cover
for the offshore shipping; but the experiment of using carrier-
borne aircraft for such purposes was not an unqualified success—
chiefly because the naval Seafires were too slow to catch the German
bombers, and too fragile for the heavy wear and tear of deck
landings. But their efforts proved that the principle of giving fighter
cover from carriers during the early stages of a combined operation
was entirely sound; and on future occasions, when better aircraft
were available, the results were much more satisfactory.

After the defeat of the German thrust towards the coast in
Salerno Bay the build-up of the Allied armies proceeded rapidly.
On 16th September, the advance forces of the Eighth Army gained
touch with General Clark's troops—an event which many people
considered could have taken place a good deal earlier—and thereafter there was never any likelihood of the enemy regaining the
initiative. Towards the end of the month, however, a severe gale
struck the assault area, and did a good deal of damage to the smaller
ships and landing craft. One can only feel thankful that it did not
occur a fortnight earlier, at the crisis of the struggle for the beaches;
for had it done so, complete disaster might well have overtaken the
assault forces.

On 1st October, Allied troops entered Naples—21 days after
they had stepped ashore at Salerno; and the naval authorities at
once set about clearing the harbour and restoring the great port to
use. Five days later the Western Naval Task Force was dissolved,
and the ships engaged in operation " Avalanche " turned to other
duties—the chief of which was to support and supply the Fifth and
Eighth Armies during their advance up Italy.

The events at Salerno in September, 1943, provided a very
valuable example of the difficulties and dangers inherent in any

large scale combined operation; and the experiences were closely studied in London and Washington with a view to applying them on future occasions. Chief among them was the lesson that— as the invasions of North Africa and Sicily had already suggested— the somewhat abstract advantages of tactical surprise had been overrated; and that the inescapable troubles involved in assaulting by night were not compensated for by any very material gain to the soldiers. Even clearer was the lesson that the sacrifice of pre-liminary naval and air bombardments in the interests of surprise was wholly mistaken—as indeed the Americans had been insisting for some time. Operation " Avalanche " thus confirmed the view of the Royal Navy that it was preferable to land shortly after day-light, having previously done our utmost to subdue the defenders by the heaviest possible sea and air bombardments; and that view was accepted in the plans for the great assaults on Hitler's " Fortress Europe " whose preparation was now at hand.

CHAPTER XVI

ATLANTIC AND ARCTIC COMMAND ASSURED

1st June–31st December, 1943

> "The decisive point in warfare against England lies in attacking her merchant shipping in the Atlantic."
>
> Dönitz to Raeder, Memorandum dated 1st September, 1939.[1]

W E LEFT the Atlantic battle at the time when the sea and air convoy escorts had just gained their great victories of May 1943, and Dönitz had withdrawn the surviving U-boats from the theatre to lick their wounds and await the arrival of the new equipment with which he confidently expected to regain the initiative. First among the improvements stood an efficient search receiver capable of giving warning of the approach of our radar-fitted ships and aircraft, but Dönitz was also providing his boats with much more powerful anti-aircraft armaments; and he set great store by the new acoustic torpedo, which he intended to use against our escort vessels rather than the merchantmen under their charge. As to longer term measures, the output of the building yards was to be increased to 40 boats per month, and Hitler had approved that the development of new types (called Types XXI and XXIII) with much higher under-water speeds (17 knots for short periods) should be given the highest priority. None of the improved boats could, however, be ready before the spring or summer of 1944; but in the meanwhile the fitting of breathing tubes, colloquially called " Schnorkels," would give the older U-boats the ability to

---

[1] Parts of this memorandum are quoted in *Brassey's Naval Annual* for 1948 under the heading *Führer Conferences on Naval Affairs*. Fuller extracts are given in Admiral Dönitz's *Memoirs*, pp. 43-4 (Eng. trans. Weidenfeld & Nicolson, 1959).

recharge their batteries while submerged, so making them much harder to locate by radar. On the Allied side, however, the escort and support groups, and the long-range air squadrons with whom they co-operated daily, were gaining constantly in strength and efficiency: and the development of centimetric radar had provided them with a location device which was far superior to the early metric sets. But perhaps the greatest gain to the Allies lay in the fact that, whereas the Admiralty's intelligence organisation was now working with great speed and assurance, the change in our ciphers which had been introduced in May 1943, had at last defeated the highly skilled German cryptographers. Thus while we were able to keep our forces well informed regarding enemy dispositions and intentions, the Germans had been deprived of what had for a very long time been their most fruitful source of intelligence.

In June 1943, not one North Atlantic convoy was attacked, and the group of 16 U-boats which Dönitz sent to the waters north of the Azores suffered losses at the hands of the American escort carriers which had recently begun to patrol the New York–Gibraltar convoy route. Meanwhile boats from the Bay of Biscay bases were sailing outward-bound in groups, in order to afford each other mutual protection; and Dönitz's order that they should stay on the surface by day and fight back against our patrolling aircraft was still in force. On our side, however, the new tactics had not passed unobserved, and Coastal Command at once strengthened its Biscay air patrols; but for a time successful attacks on U-boats were few and far between, and the low-flying bombers quickly found that their adversaries could hit back hard with their greatly strengthened gun armaments. It was plain that surface ships were needed to co-operate with the aircraft; and as comparative quiet reigned in the North Atlantic, the Admiralty was able to order Captain F. J. Walker's redoubtable 2nd Escort Group into the Bay of Biscay. Towards the end of June his sloops there sank two U-boats in quick succession; but the results of the Bay offensive in that month were none the less not very satisfactory, with only four enemies destroyed.[1] The Admiralty and Coastal Command therefore took prompt steps to improve the ratio between aircraft

---

[1] In all waters 17 U-boats were destroyed in June, 1943. It was the small proportion of successes achieved in the Bay of Biscay which was disappointing.

sightings of U-boats and successful attacks—which had so far been disappointingly low. Shore-based aircraft from Gibraltar were brought into the patrol scheme, the co-operation of U.S. Navy planes based on French Morocco was sought, and Air-Marshal Slessor introduced new tactics for his Coastal Command aircrews. These laid down that a sighting aircraft would at all costs keep in touch with the enemy, and would call his nearest colleagues and also the surface patrol groups to the scene. The aircraft would then make a succession of attacks, pressing them right home at very low height; while, if the enemy dived deep, the warships would hunt him to destruction. These measures soon reaped a rich reward. The greatest success came at the end of July, when an entire group of three U-boats including two of Dönitz's precious U-tankers or " milch cows " (of which only ten were ever completed) was destroyed by the air patrols and the 2nd Escort Group. Such disastrous experiences compelled Dönitz reluctantly to accept that his policy of crossing the Bay on the surface was mistaken, and he substituted an order that inward-bound boats should creep home submerged along the Spanish coast, while those outward-bound were to abandon the attempt to fight back against our bombers. During the 94 days that the order had been fully in force (1st May to 2nd August) Coastal Command aircrews sank 28 U-boats, and damaged 22 others;[1] but the loss of 57 aircraft was a heavy, if not unreasonable price to pay for those successes.

Early in August the sudden decline in U-boat sightings made it plain that the enemy had changed his tactics; and we soon realised that Dönitz had in fact found a measure of safety on his most important transit route. Though the air patrols continued to fly from Britain, Gibraltar and Morocco, and surface escort groups— now given cruiser support against the powerful German destroyers based in western France—were always on hand, the successes of the previous month were not repeated. We can, moreover, now see that the short period just described marked the climax of Coastal Command's entire Bay of Biscay offensive; since once Dönitz had rescinded his fatal order the results achieved by our patrolling aircraft returned to the comparatively low level at which they had stood before it was introduced. Furthermore we may here notice how, taking the war as a whole, the air patrols were far less effective

---

[1] This figure includes those sunk off the coast of Portugal.

than the convoy air escorts as U-boat killers. None the less we should remember that the constant harrying to which the U-boats were subjected on the transit routes undoubtedly increased the strain on their crews and, by slowing their passages, also reduced the time they could spend in their operational areas.

We saw earlier how Dönitz's strategy always was to probe constantly in distant waters, seeking " soft spots " in our defences, and hoping thereby to force us to divert part of our strength from the defence of our vital Atlantic shipping; and we have also remarked how impossible it was for the Allies to be equally strong everywhere. Thus the sudden arrival of even a small number of U-boats in a remote theatre might enable them to achieve some quick successes. After the recall of the Atlantic U-boats following on their heavy defeats in May 1943, Dönitz continued his distant probes; but in June the boats sent to the west coast of America, West Africa and the Cape of Good Hope achieved nothing very substantial. The Indian Ocean, however, seemed to the enemy still to offer good prospects of easy targets; for the theatre was too vast and Admiral Sir James Somerville's Eastern Fleet was too weak to enable us to sail all shipping in convoy. In June the seven U-boats present sank 10 ships, mostly off the south-east coast of Africa; and they all replenished successfully from the supply tanker *Charlotte Schliemann*. In the following month the Indian Ocean U-boats did even better, sinking 17 merchantmen, some of which were valuable ships loaded with supplies for India or the Middle East; and a new group, originally of nine boats, which Dönitz had ordered out was on the way to join them. Also in July, U-boats turned up off Brazil, in the West Indies, and on the shipping routes off the west coast of Africa; and for a short time they too did quite well. But as soon as attacks were reported we strengthened the air patrols and convoy escorts in the threatened area, whereupon sinkings of merchantmen quickly declined and the U-boats themselves suffered losses. Furthermore the fortunes of Dönitz's distant lunges depended very largely on " milch cows " being able to replenish the operational boats, since by this time it was only in the Indian Ocean that surface supply ships enjoyed a reasonable chance of survival. Nor was the enemy left for long in any doubt regarding whether his supply submarines would be allowed to fulfil their function. During the last days of July and the first days of August, British ships and aircraft sank four of them, while the American escort carrier groups which were constantly sweeping the enemy's favourite fuelling area some 400 miles north-west of the Azores also achieved remarkable successes. Between the beginning of June and the end of August 1943, the groups centred on the U.S.S.s *Bogue*, *Core*, *Santee* and *Card* destroyed one " milch cow," two reserve tankers (i.e., ordinary boats acting as additional supply vessels), and eleven operational submarines; and by the end of August it was plain that, except in the Indian Ocean, Dönitz's distant lunges had failed.

To complete the picture of the period June–August, 1943, which saw the second major defeat suffered by the U-boats, we may remark that in all waters excluding the Mediterranean they sank no more than 58 Allied merchantmen; and for those very moderate successes they paid the heavy price of 74 of their own number sunk —the great majority (58½) by shore-based or carrier borne aircraft in the Bay of Biscay, the North Atlantic and the waters remote from Europe. Many factors, such as the improved training and tactics of the aircrews, closer co-operation between them and the surface ships, and the arrival of rocket projectiles contributed to this highly satisfactory result; but the greatest benefit of all was probably derived from our 10-centimetre radars, of whose existence the German Navy still remained sceptical—in spite of a similar set having recently been captured from a crashed British bomber.[1] From the Allied point of view the only theatre where there was still serious grounds for concern was the Indian Ocean; for the five survivors of the group ordered out by Dönitz in June reached the Cape of Good Hope at the end of August, fuelled from the supply tanker *Brake* off Madagascar, and then joined forces with the eight Japanese submarines already working in those waters. Losses of merchantmen continued in September and October, by which time some U-boats had reached up as far as the Persian Gulf and the approaches to the Red Sea—where our traffic was extremely

[1] Enemy records make it clear that the scientists who inspected that set realised that it worked on the centimetric wave-band, and that their report was passed to the German Navy. The latter, however, preferred to accept a statement made (perhaps with intent to deceive) by an R.A.F. prisoner-of-war, to the effect that our aircraft "homed" on to the radiations emitted by the U-boats' search receivers. Not until early in 1944, when the subject was brought up again almost by chance, did the truth dawn upon the German Navy; and Dönitz then at once pressed for a search receiver which would react to the short-wave radars. The long delay in arriving at the truth emphasises the failure of the Germans to integrate the work of their scientists with that of their service staffs.

valuable. Before the end of 1943, however, the situation had improved; for reinforcements of escort vessels had reached the Eastern Fleet (which had been drastically stripped to meet the needs of the combined operations against Sicily and southern Italy), air co-operation had greatly improved, convoys were sailing on more routes; and, lastly, the German boats had begun to withdraw towards Penang to refit and replenish. None the less, during the seven months June–December, 1943, a small number of enemy submarines (never more than seven German and eight Japanese) inflicted on us the substantial loss of 57 merchantmen, totalling some 337,000 tons; which demonstrates how hard it is for Britain to protect her commerce in a theatre far remote from her home bases.

In the autumn of 1943 the Germans attempted to renew the blockade-running campaign between Japanese and French ports, which had achieved considerable success earlier in the war.[1] But by this time our counter measures had been greatly strengthened, and only one of the five homeward-bound ships (the Italian *Osorno*) reached her destination. We were aware that blockade-runners were approaching Europe, and had sent the cruisers *Glasgow* and *Enterprise* from Plymouth to intercept them; but the Germans had sailed ten destroyers or " fleet torpedo-boats " from western France to escort them in, and early on 28th December an air sighting report enabled the cruisers to chase and engage these enemies. While severe fighting went on overhead—for both sides sent out aircraft to protect their own ships and attack the enemy's—a high speed gun action, lasting from 1.30 until 4 p.m., took place in the rough seas of the Bay of Biscay. It ended in the sinking of the large German destroyer Z.27 and two fleet torpedo-boats.[2] By the evening of 29th the two British cruisers, unscathed in spite of being attacked by a variety of aircraft, including glider bombs, were back in Plymouth. They had convincingly demonstrated that the enemy could no longer hope to exert even temporary control in the Bay of Biscay.

The heavy losses suffered by the homeward-bound blockade-runners convinced the Germans that it was futile to send to Japan the eight ships which had been waiting loaded in western France,

---

[1] See p. 210.

[2] The Z.27 (2,688 tons) belonged to a class sometimes erroneously referred to in British circles as " Narvik class." The torpedo-boats were the T.25 and T.26 (1,318 tons).

and early in 1944 Hitler agreed to the cancellation of their departure. So ended the German blockade-running campaign. In all 16 ships carrying 111,500 tons of cargo, reached Europe, while 15 ships delivered 57,000 tons at Japanese-controlled ports; but that comparatively small accomplishment cost the enemy 20 merchantmen sunk or captured.

To return to the Atlantic theatre, in mid-summer Dönitz was planning to resume the assault on our convoys as soon as his boats were equipped with acoustic torpedoes; and he intended again to employ his favourite " group tactics," or " wolf-pack " attacks as we called them. His hope was that, by sinking or damaging a sufficient number of a convoy's screen, some U-boats would be able to get in among the merchantmen—as they had often done in 1940-42, when our escorts were still lamentably weak; but, unfortunately for him, the acoustic torpedo, unlike the magnetic mine in the early months of the war, did not catch us by surprise.[1] Not only were we making similar weapons ourselves, but the Admiralty had prepared the necessary antidote—a noise-making device (colloquially called " Foxer ") which was towed astern of a ship and attracted the " Gnats " to itself instead of to the ship's propellors.

In the middle of September the three months of quiet in the North Atlantic was broken by 28 U-boats—some from Germany or Norway and some from the Biscay bases—taking up a patrol line designed to catch our outward-bound convoys in mid-ocean. Thanks to the re-adoption of submerged passages through the transit areas, this considerable concentration was effected without serious difficulty; and with improved search receivers, strengthened A-A armaments, and acoustic torpedoes for use against the escort vessels there were reasonable grounds for Dönitz's belief that he might regain the initiative. The ever-watchful Submarine Tracking Room in the Admiralty had, however, gained wind of his intention; the escort groups which had been co-operating with our Biscay air patrols were promptly recalled, and Coastal Command switched a proportion of its aircraft back to Northern Ireland and Iceland in readiness for the renewal of the struggle around the Atlantic convoys.

The slow convoy ONS 18 of 28 ships left Milford Haven on

[1] See pp. 47-8.

12th September, 1943, and ON 202 of 40 ships sailed from Liverpool three days later. As the Liverpool convoy was the faster of the two, and they had been given similar routes, it would overtake the Milford Haven ships in mid-ocean; but the Western Approaches command welcomed the possibility of the combined escorts fighting a battle with the new wolf-pack: strong air escorts had been arranged for both convoys during the critical period of their passages, and a Support Group was kept in the offing ready to reinforce whichever of them might be threatened. On 20th September, by which time the fast convoy was only 30 miles behind the slower one, Dönitz unleashed all his wolves, and in the very early hours they sank two merchantmen and severely damaged one of the escorts with an acoustic torpedo; but as a Liberator sank U.338 soon afterwards, the lost ships did not long go unavenged. By noon of that same day the two convoys had joined together, and Commander M. J. Evans, whose group (B3) had originally been responsible only for the slow convoy, took charge of the whole escort—now reinforced to a total of 18 destroyers, frigates and corvettes. During the next night the U-boats made frequent attempts to pierce the powerful screen, all of which were frustrated; but astern of the convoy a fierce battle developed, with rapid attacks and counter-attacks; and the acoustic torpedoes brought the enemy more successes by sinking a Canadian destroyer and a British corvette. On the 21st dense fog shrouded the convoys, and there was a lull until after dark, when the previous night's pattern was repeated. This time however no merchantmen were sunk, and Evans's own *Keppel* rammed and sank U.229. Dawn on 22nd, by which time honours were about even, again found the convoys protected by fog, and when it cleared in the afternoon the warship crews found " the air filled with Liberators." Once again attacks were held off, while the merchantmen plodded slowly but steadily to the west. Soon after dark on 22nd another prolonged battle started; and this time the U-boats gained the advantage. They first sank the frigate *Itchen* which, by ill-chance, had on board all the survivors from the two escort vessels which had been sunk earlier. Only three men from the three ships' companies were picked up. Then, very early on the 23rd, the U-boats at last penetrated the screen, and sank four merchantmen. After daylight still stronger air escorts joined; but by that time Dönitz had called off the attackers—for the convoys were well within range of the air bases in Newfoundland and Canada. Three of the 19 U-boats engaged in the five-day battle were sunk; but we lost the same number of escort vessels, as well as six merchantmen. Though Dönitz had some reason to be satisfied at the outcome, he was misled by exaggerated claims into believing that his success was much greater than was actually the case. The truth was that his new weapons and equipment had not by any means turned the tables on our sea and air escorts—as was to be very convincingly demonstrated during the succeeding weeks.

In October, Commander P. W. Gretton's B7 escort group, whom we last encountered stoutly defending convoy ONS 5 at the crisis of the struggle in the previous May,[1] and Commander R. A. Currie's B 6 group fought a double convoy (ON 206 and ONS 20) through a wolf-pack. During the five-day battle only one merchantman was lost; and the sea and air escorts destroyed no less than six of their adversaries. There next followed a whole series of convoy battles which made it abundantly plain that the initiative still rested with the little ships and the long-range aircraft. Very few merchantmen were lost, and the U-boats suffered heavily. Towards the end of October Dönitz switched one of his groups to the Gibraltar route, where he hoped to benefit from the co-operation of Luftwaffe planes; but in an attack on the combined convoys SL 138 and MKS 28[2] they found conditions no easier than in the North Atlantic. Moreover it was in that month that, after very prolonged negotiations, we at last gained from the Portuguese government the right to establish air and naval bases in the Azores; and that development greatly strengthened our hold on the central Atlantic and on the route between Britain and Gibraltar. It thus came to pass that the return of the U-boats to the Atlantic in September-October, 1943 and the re-introduction of wolf-pack tactics only brought the enemy further discomfiture. In those two months 2,468 merchantmen crossed the ocean in 64 convoys; and no more than nine were sunk. On the other hand the enemy suffered heavily at the hands of our escort vessels and aircraft, and off the Azores the American carrier groups again proved their

[1] See pp. 275-6.
[2] The SL convoy came from Sierra Leone and the MKS one from North African ports. They joined together to the west of Gibraltar.

deadliness. In October the U.S.S.s *Card, Core* and *Block Island* sank six U-boats, including another " milch cow " and an emergency tanker; and the latter successes imperilled the whole enemy refuelling programme. In all Dönitz lost 25 boats in mid-Atlantic in September and October 1943; and the return obtained for those substantial losses was almost insignificant. Moreover the reinforcements which he sent at this time to the Mediterranean, the Indian Ocean and to other remote waters fared badly while on passage; for the Gibraltar Straits were now very strongly patrolled, and long-range aircraft had begun to work from bases in Brazil, along the West African coast, and on Ascension Island. Thus the distant U-boats had poor prospects of making their long journeys undetected.

The autumn months of 1943 must have been a very disheartening time for the U-boat command; for, as one of Dönitz's staff despondently noted " the enemy holds all the trump cards . . . his aircraft have curtailed the mobility of the U-boats . . . the enemy knows all our secrets, and we know none of theirs." None the less they were still very far from throwing up the sponge, and November found several small groups of two or three boats widely dispersed in the North Atlantic. We, however, were determined to press our advantage right home, and were keeping several escort carriers and support groups constantly at sea, ready to pounce on any enemy who was bold enough to show himself. To give one example of our strategy and tactics at this time, Captain Walker's 2nd Escort Group had been joined by the escort carrier *Tracker*, and her aircraft did invaluable work in bringing the hard-hitting sloops into contact with the enemy. Moreover Walker had developed simple but deadly tactics against U-boats which tried to find safety by going very deep. His method was to station a " directing ship " astern of the enemy to hold Asdic contact, while two others, not using their Asdics, crept up on either side, to release a barrage of depth charges by signal from the directing ship at the critical moment. The U-boat thus never knew when the depth charges were released, and could not take avoiding action while they were descending. It was by these tactics that in November Walker's famous sloops—the *Starling, Kite, Woodcock* and *Wild Goose* (the *Wren* being absent on this occasion)—sank two of the U-boats which Dönitz had stationed to the east of Newfoundland.

In that same month (November) another prolonged sea and air battle took place on the Gibraltar route between the escorts of the combined convoys SL 140 and MKS 30 and more than 30 U-boats. As so often before, timely reinforcements were sent to the convoys as soon as the threat was seen to be developing; and large numbers of Coastal Command aircraft, firstly from Gibraltar, then from the Azores, and finally from British bases, patrolled and searched around the merchantmen by night as well as by day; while long-range R.A.F. fighters flew as far as the Spanish coast, and engaged the German shadowing aircraft. The defence of this convoy was indeed a splendid example of integrated action by the Royal Navy and Royal Air Force; and the results were, from the Allied point of view, highly satisfactory. The only merchantman lost was a straggler against which the Germans concentrated attacks by some two dozen of their wireless-controlled glider-bombs; and three U-boats were sunk by the sea and air escorts. Nor did Dönitz's next attempts against the large outward- as well as homeward-bound convoys on this route fare any better. By the end of the year he was forced to admit that his favourite group tactics had failed him; that his new weapons and equipment had not come up to expectations; and that throughout the whole wide Atlantic his prospects of challenging Allied maritime control were slight. Though he still entertained high hopes from the improved performance of the new types of boat, delays and difficulties over completing them were increasing; and it was becoming plain that their entry into service would be far slower than he had originally hoped. In the meanwhile he intended to fit every possible boat with the " Schnorkel " breathing tube, and would continue the development of a search receiver which would respond to our 10-centimetre radar sets; for it was at this time that the Germans at last realised that the instruments fitted in our ships and aircraft worked on a very short wave-length.

We must now leave the unceasing struggle against the U-boats to review events in the far north during the latter half of 1943. At the beginning of that period the Home Fleet, now commanded by Admiral Sir Bruce Fraser, had been so much weakened by detachments sent to the Mediterranean for the invasion of Sicily that it was unable to guarantee the security of the northern passages to the Atlantic; and as the *Tirpitz, Scharnhorst* and *Lützow* were still lying poised in an excellent strategic position in north Norway another attempt to break out on to our main convoy routes seemed quite likely. An appeal to Washington, however, met with a quick response, and the balance was restored by two American battleships coming temporarily to Scapa to join Admiral Fraser's command. In August they were replaced by two heavy cruisers, but the arrival of the U.S. Navy's *Ranger* did something to mitigate the Home Fleet's lack of carrier air power; for the *Victorious* had not yet returned from the Pacific,[1] and the *Illustrious* was shortly to leave for the Mediterranean to support the Salerno landings.[2] To cover the Atlantic convoys, and to guard the Denmark Strait and the Iceland-Faeroes passage against a break-out by the German heavy ships, Admiral Fraser kept either the American squadron or a similarly composed force of his own ships stationed at Hvalfiord in Iceland; but during the summer months he was too weak, especially in carrier air power, to undertake any large offensive operations. The successful reinforcement in June of Spitzbergen, whose importance lay in the fact that it lay close off the northern flank of our Arctic convoy route,[3] and a diversionary movement against southern Norway in July, designed to deceive the Germans into the belief that we intended to invade that country, and so distract their attention from Sicily, marked the limit of the Home Fleet's capacity at this time. Moreover the turn to the offensive, and the immense demands for ships and men which the new combined operations were producing, had made it essential to save man-power wherever possible; and the Admiralty had therefore decided to release all ships employed on purely defensive purposes. Thus the 1st Minelaying Squadron, which had been engaged since 1940 on laying the vast minefield between the Shetlands and Iceland was disbanded; all minelaying in the east coast barrier was stopped; and almost all the liners which had been requisitioned to serve as Armed Merchant Cruisers in the early days were released and reconverted to troopships. In retrospect it seems that some of these measures might well have been put in hand considerably earlier. For example, the northern barrage, in which 110,500 mines were laid, must be classed as a singularly unprofitable undertaking, and

[1] See pp. 257-8. [2] See p. 296. [3] See Map. p. 144.

was indeed more of a menace to our own ships than to the enemy—who only lost one U-boat in it. As to the A.M.C.s, we had learnt in 1940-41 that they were too weakly armed to stand up even to a German disguised raider,[1] and they were always extremely vulnerable to U-boat attack. After America had entered the war there was little useful service that they could perform on the convoy routes.

The problems which beset the Naval Staff in the summer of 1943 were made more acute by the First Sea Lord, Admiral of the Fleet Sir Dudley Pound, suffering a stroke while in Canada for the second Quebec conference in August, and having to lay down the immense burden which he had borne since the beginning of the war. The choice of a successor did not prove easy; for Mr. Churchill, who probably remembered his conflict with Lord Fisher in 1915 which led to his replacement as First Lord, was reluctant to accept the man who was the unquestionable choice of the whole Royal Navy—namely Sir Andrew Cunningham.[2] He therefore first offered the appointment to Admiral Fraser, who tactfully stated his wish to stand aside; and in the end, though still reluctantly, the Prime Minister agreed to Cunningham's appointment. But it was 15th October before the new First Sea Lord took over, and a week later, on Trafalgar Day, Sir Dudley Pound died. Perhaps he had served the Navy best by the affection and confidence which he won from Mr. Churchill; and by the steadiness of his hands on the reins controlling our maritime power throughout the crisis of 1940-41. During that difficult period he succeeded in holding steadfastly to the essentials in the maritime war; and that repeatedly

[1] See pp. 96 and 125.

[2] Mr. Churchill had good reason for his determination to avoid a repetition of the conflict between "the frocks and the brass" of the 1914-18 war; and some of Cunningham's answers to his "prodding signals" (e.g. at the time of the Battle of Crete in 1941) probably made him feel that the Admiral's personality was too strong to ensure smooth working in the Chiefs of Staff Committee, of which Churchill, as Minister of Defence, was chairman. Moreover, the long opposition of the Admiralty to the introduction of convoy in 1917, until Lloyd George overruled professional opinion, probably left him with a strong impression of the fallibility of expert advisers. See Robert Blake, *The Unknown Prime Minister* (Eyre & Spottiswoode, 1955), Marder, *Fear God and Dread Nought, the Letters of Lord Fisher of Kilverstone*, Vol. III (Cape, 1959), and Lord Beaverbrook *Men and Power* (Hutchinson, 1956) regarding Fisher's quarrel with Churchill, whose own *World Crisis*, Vol. IV, Chapter XV (Thornton Butterworth, 1927) sets out his views on naval policy in 1917. Lord Cunningham's autobiography, *A Sailor's Odyssey* (Hutchinson, 1951) gives many examples of the type of message which the Admiral, while C.-in-C., Mediterranean, considered unnecessary and provocative.

involved deflecting the Prime Minister from his less sound strategic purposes.[1]

The reader will remember that no convoys had been sent to North Russia since February 1943.[2] The initial reason for stopping them had been that the risks were regarded as unacceptable as long as powerful German naval and air forces were stationed close off the exposed southern flank of their long route—especially during the period of continuous daylight. Then the crisis in the Atlantic of March forced the Admiralty to switch a powerful proportion of the Home Fleet's flotilla strength to the Western Approaches command, in order to reinforce the escort groups;[3] and after the May victory over the U-boats many Home Fleet ships were sent to the Mediterranean to take part in the combined operation against Sicily. In the summer, however, the possibility of restarting the Arctic convoys was reviewed: for the period of continuous darkness was approaching, and political pressure to send more cargoes to Russia was heavy—especially from President Roosevelt. The Admiralty and Admiral Fraser considered that the essential preliminary step was to immobilise the *Tirpitz* and, if possible, the *Scharnhorst*; and ways and means of doing so were therefore considered. Altenfiord, their normal advanced base, was too far from Britain to enable the R.A.F.'s heavy bombers to reach it by direct flight, and conditions on the airfields in North Russia were so primitive that it was difficult to organise a heavy bomber attack from the other direction; while the Home Fleet, which only had the old *Furious*, was far too weak in carrier air strength to enable it to strike a telling blow from the sea. The best hope lay in carrying out an " attack at source " with submersible craft; for they stood a reasonable chance of penetrating into the anchorage. Such tactics had been exploited by the Royal Navy on innumerable occasions in the past; and the raid on St. Nazaire in March 1942, had confirmed that, given very careful planning and great resolution in execution, there was, even under modern conditions, a good chance of achieving surprise and of inflicting great damage on specially important targets.[4] The Admiralty had accordingly designed a midget submarine of about 35 tons, whose four-man

---

[1] Such as the proposal to seize Pantelleria and then the Dodecanese Islands (operation "Workshop") in 1941. See p. 151.

[2] See pp. 271-2.   [3] See p. 273.   [4] See pp. 203-4.

crews could, if carried to a point near enough to their objective, force their way through or under the most up-to-date defences to place heavy charges of explosive, which would be detonated by time fuses, on the seabed beneath the target. They were known as X-craft, and may be regarded as the descendants of the fireships which Drake had used to such deadly effect off Gravelines in 1588. The planning of the operation and the training of the crews were carried out in darkest secrecy, and at the end of August six submarines specially fitted for towing arrived at the Scottish loch where the X-craft had assembled. While the final preparations for the attack were in progress the German squadron itself suddenly showed unusual activity; for on 6th September the *Tirpitz*, *Scharnhorst* and 10 destroyers sailed from Altenfiord. Two days later we heard that they had bombarded Spitzbergen. The Home Fleet at once put to sea; but there was in fact little chance of catching the enemy before he regained the shelter of Altenfiord. It is an interesting fact that this was the only occasion during her entire life that the *Tirpitz's* big guns fired at what may be called an enemy target. Yet her influence on our maritime strategy and dispositions was profound; nor had the end of her story by any means yet been reached.

On 11th-12th September the six submarines allocated to operation " Source "—the attack on Altenfiord—sailed from their Scottish base to the north-east, each with an X-craft in tow; but one of the midgets was lost with all hands during the long passage, and a second one suffered so many harrowing vicissitudes that she finally had to be abandoned. The other four little submersibles, with 16 men between them, set off on the 20th to penetrate into one of the most strongly defended harbours of all time. Three of them (X5, X6 and X7) were to attack the primary target, the *Tirpitz*, while the fourth (X10) was allocated to the *Scharnhorst*; and the parent submarines would wait at the offshore rendezvous in the hope of recovering the crews, if not their craft, after the attack had been completed. From the release position the attackers had to cross a German minefield, and then make their way 50 miles up the fiord to the enemy anchorage. X5 lost touch sometime during the following night, and was never seen again; but by the early hours of the 22nd, X6 and X7, commanded by Lieutenant D. Cameron, R.N.R. and Lieutenant B. G. C. Place, R.N., were ready for the final approach to the *Tirpitz*. Though Cameron's craft developed serious defects to its periscope at this critical moment, and Place became entangled in the defensive nets, soon after 7 a.m. they both reached their objective. But the enemy had been alerted by X6 accidentally breaking surface, and the *Tirpitz's* captain thereupon shifted his ship on her cables as far as possible from the spot where the midget submarine had submerged again. Cameron, however, groped his way beneath the target, released both his two-ton charges, surfaced again and scuttled his craft. He and his crew were picked up and taken on board their giant adversary. Lieutenant Place had meanwhile surfaced involuntarily almost alongside the target; but he managed to submerge again, and to release his charges. He then tried most determinedly to force his way out through the nets, but was still entangled when at 8.12 a.m. the explosion of the charges severely damaged his craft, which became quite uncontrollable. Place and one of his crew managed to escape, but the other two were lost when X7 sank. On board the *Tirpitz* the explosion of the charges caused the huge ship " to heave several feet out of the water," and apparently produced widespread confusion. But the most serious damage, probably caused by the charge which X7 had released in an almost ideal position, was to the main turbines, all three sets of which were put out of action. X10 had meanwhile met with a series of misfortunes on her way up the fiord, and finally found herself without compass or periscope. In those circumstances her captain reluctantly decided to abandon the attack on the *Scharnhorst*, and made his way out to sea again. We now know that he would not in any case have found his target, as the battle cruiser had left her usual berth on 21st to carry out exercises in the more open waters at the entrance to Altenfiord. X10 successfully met her parent submarine off the coast, but was lost in heavy weather during the long tow home. Though the results of the operation thus fell short of complete success, the primary purpose—namely the immobilisation of the *Tirpitz*—was accomplished; and the strategic results were far-reaching. Plans to restart the Arctic convoys were now pressed ahead, and in November the American squadron which had come to reinforce the Home Fleet at the time of its lowest strength, returned to its own country.

The next endeavour to catch one of the major German warships in north Norway had a less happy outcome. Towards the end of

September the Admiralty began to suspect that some important movement was being planned; for we had noticed unusual sea and air activity. The *Lützow* actually left Altenfiord on 23rd September for Narvik, whence she sailed south again on the 26th, bound for the Baltic. An agent reported her departure, but we realised that she would not be within range of the home-based Coastal Command aircraft until next day, and that the U.S.S. *Ranger* which had an efficient dive-bomber squadron on board, could not reach a flying-off position in time to catch the pocket-battleship. By chance a squadron of Tarpon torpedo bombers had just disembarked from the *Victorious*, and was available in the Orkneys;[1] but there now ensued one of those sequences of orders and counter-orders, and of plans made and plans cancelled, which was always one of the dangers inherent in the British system of divided control of maritime aircraft. The officer commanding No. 18 Group of Coastal Command had been made responsible for all the air operations against the *Lützow*—even though the squadrons in the *Ranger* and the one landed from the *Victorious* belonged to the Home Fleet; and his group actually had very few strike aircraft available at short notice. Nor was Coastal Command willing to send them out without a fighter escort, for which purpose only a handful of Beaufighters could be collected quickly. Early on the 27th a reconnaissance aircraft sighted the *Lützow*, and Admiral Fraser thereupon pressed Coastal Command to send out whatever was ready by way of a striking force—if necessary without a fighter escort. But there was little or no cloud cover over the target, and the Commander-in-Chief, Coastal Command, supported the group commander's view that the risks were therefore too great. A short while later the ban was withdrawn, and early in the afternoon the Fleet Air Arm torpedo-bombers, lately belonging to the *Victorious*, took off with three R.A.F. Beaufighters as escort. The striking force made its landfall correctly, and then searched to the north; but their target was actually about 40 miles to the south at the time, and they therefore missed it. That evening the *Lützow* was met by a fighter escort, and next day she entered the Baltic in safety. The escape of so important a warship led to an

[1] These were American aircraft, with which the *Victorious* had been equipped while serving in the Pacific (see pp. 257-8). They were known as Avengers in the U.S. Navy, and were excellent aircraft—far superior for carrier work to the British Barracudas.

investigation by the Admiralty and Air Ministry; but the joint committee's report made no recommendations on the matter of achieving unified control—the lack of which, as in the escape up-Channel of the German Brest squadron in February, 1942,[1] was surely the chief cause of the failure. Though one may feel that Coastal Command, having accepted responsibility for the conduct of the operations, can hardly escape criticism for the failure, we may none the less regret that Admiral Fraser did not send out the Tarpon squadron earlier on his own responsibility—perhaps with an escort of the *Ranger's* Wildcat fighters.

By the autumn arrangements to send 40 ships a month to Russia had been completed, and in accordance with Admiral Fraser's recommendations the new convoys were to be run in two sections. The chief opposition was likely to come from the two U-boat flotillas in north Norway; for we knew that the Luftwaffe's strength in the theatre had been reduced by diversions elsewhere. As, however, the *Scharnhorst* was known to be fit for sea, and might at any time be ordered out, a powerful cruiser escort and heavy covering force were still essential. In November and December the first two pairs of outward and homeward convoys (JW 54A and B and RA 54A and B) made safe passages; but the Admiralty expected the enemy soon to attempt retaliation, perhaps using the *Scharnhorst*; and in mid-December, during the passage of the next outward convoy (JW 55A) Admiral Fraser therefore went right through to Kola Inlet in the *Duke of York*—the first time that a British battleship had appeared in those waters. We now know that Dönitz had in fact just obtained Hitler's agreement to committing the *Scharnhorst*, though the German Naval Staff seems to have had serious misgivings over the decision. In November, Admiral Kummetz, who commanded the northern task force was, rather surprisingly, allowed to go on prolonged leave; and command devolved on Rear-Admiral Bey, who had been in charge of the destroyer flotilla. He seems to have favoured using the battle cruiser at the next opportunity, and on 19th December Dönitz told Hitler that she would attack our next east-bound convoy. The Admiralty's forecast thus proved extraordinarily accurate, and

[1] See pp. 196-201.

H.M.S. *Starling* carrying out a depth-charge attack in February, 1944

H.M.S. *Emperor* ferrying Hellcats across the Atlantic, February, 1944

" Milch-cow " U-boat returning to base, Spring, 1943

Admiral Fraser's preparations had not been put in hand a moment too soon.

On 20th December convoy JW 55B, of 19 ships, sailed eastbound, and two days later the corresponding homeward convoy (of 22 ships) left Kola Inlet. Each had a close escort of about a dozen destroyers or smaller vessels, while Vice-Admiral R. L. Burnett, with the cruisers *Belfast*, *Sheffield* and *Norfolk* was to cover the double movement. Admiral Fraser himself, with the *Duke of York* and the cruiser *Jamaica* sailed from Iceland on 23rd—the same day that Burnett's ships left Kola. The outward convoy was reported by enemy aircraft early in its passage, and on Christmas Eve the continuous presence of shadowers convinced Fraser that attack by the *Scharnhorst* was imminent. He therefore hastened his progress towards the critical waters of the Barents Sea. By Christmas Day the homeward convoy had passed the danger point south of Bear Island, and the C.-in-C. therefore switched four of its destroyers to the outward convoy, which he diverted farther to the north. JW 55B now had 14 destroyers in company, and Admiral Burnett's cruisers were closing towards it from the south-east.[1]

Admiral Bey, with five destroyers to escort the battle cruiser, actually left Altenfiord on the evening of Christmas Day, and in the early hours of the next morning the Admiralty signalled to Fraser that they considered the *Scharnhorst* was at sea. The weather was stormy, and enemy reconnaissance planes had been grounded; but one of the eight U-boats stationed on a patrol line west of Bear Island had reported the convoy's position and the composition of its escort fairly correctly at 9 a.m. But in spite of Fraser having several times broken wireless silence to co-ordinate the movements of his various forces, the Germans were quite unaware that the Home Fleet flagship was in the offing. On 26th December, as the Arctic night gave way to the faint glimmer which was all the daylight that would come in those latitudes at that time of year, the convoy was actually about 50 miles south of Bear Island, Admiral Fraser was some 200 miles to the south-west of it, while Admiral Burnett's cruisers were steering to intercept the German squadron as it came north. A heavy sea was running, and the smaller ships on both sides were having a difficult time. At 7.30 a.m. Admiral Bey detached his destroyers to search for the convoy to the south-

[1] See Map p. 322.

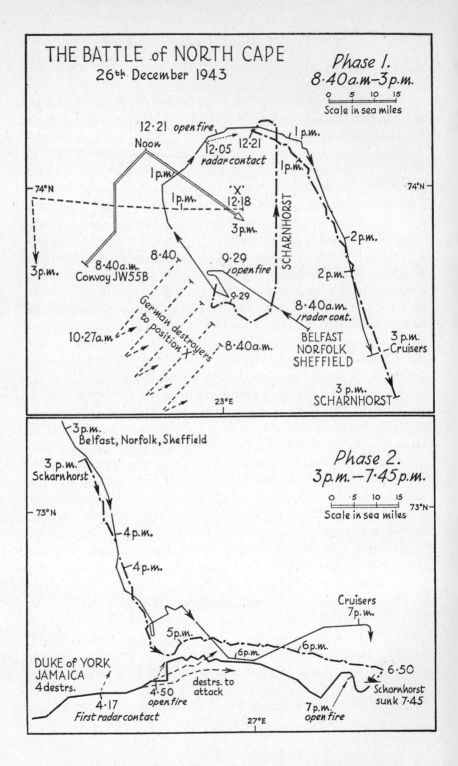

THE BATTLE of NORTH CAPE
26th December 1943

Phase 1.
8·40 a.m.–3 p.m.

0   5   10   15
Scale in sea miles

12·21 open fire
Noon

12·05   12·21
radar contact

1 p.m.

1 p.m.

1 p.m.

74°N

'X'
12·18

3 p.m.

SCHARNHORST

2 p.m.

2 p.m.

74°N

8·40 a.m.
Convoy JW55B

8·40

9·29
open fire

9·29

German destroyers
to position X

10·27 a.m.

8·40 a.m.

8·40 a.m.
radar cont.

BELFAST
NORFOLK
SHEFFIELD

3 p.m.
Cruisers

3 p.m.
SCHARNHORST

3 p.m.

23°E

3 p.m.
Belfast, Norfolk, Sheffield

3 p.m.
Scharnhorst

Phase 2.
3 p.m. — 7·45 p.m.

0   5   10   15
Scale in sea miles

73°N

73°N

4 p.m.

4 p.m.

Cruisers
7 p.m.

5 p.m.

6 p.m.

6 p.m.

6·50

DUKE of YORK
JAMAICA
4 destrs.

destrs. to
attack

4·50
open fire

Scharnhorst
sunk 7·45

4·17
First radar contact

7 p.m.
open fire

27°E

west, and they must actually have passed within a few miles of it later in the forenoon; but they sighted nothing, and lost touch with their flagship. At 2 p.m. Bey ordered them to return to harbour, and they reached Altenfiord with nothing accomplished.

Shortly before 9 a.m., the *Belfast* obtained a radar contact on the *Scharnhorst*, which was actually (though she did not know it) within 30 miles of the convoy at the time. The range closed rapidly, and the *Norfolk* briefly engaged and probably hit the battle cruiser soon afterwards. Bey did not reply, but turned to the south, and his superior speed enabled him quickly to draw away. Shortly after this first action four destroyers, diverted from the convoy by the C.-in-C., joined Burnett, who now took a bold decision. Rather than pursue a faster enemy in the endeavour to shadow her —the traditional function of a cruiser force in contact with a superior enemy—he turned to the north-west to close and protect the convoy; but the loss of contact caused the Commander-in-Chief grave anxiety. However Burnett's guess—that Bey would come round again towards the convoy—proved correct; and soon after noon the *Belfast* again reported a radar contact. A second gun action, this time with all three British cruisers engaged, followed. It lasted for about 20 minutes, and hits on the *Scharnhorst* were again observed; but the *Norfolk* was hit by two 11-inch shells, which did her a good deal of damage, and the four destroyers with the cruisers were unable to get in a torpedo attack—because the Admiral had concentrated them on his own port bow and the enemy turned away in the other direction.

The *Scharnhorst* next steered south again, with Burnett's cruisers shadowing by radar. Their enemy reports had relieved the Commander-in-Chief's main anxiety; for not only was he now well informed regarding his adversary's position and course, but he knew that he was excellently placed to intercept her. Moreover his plot made it plain that the two main British forces had almost closed the trap on the unsuspecting Bey, and it thus came as no surprise that at 4.17 p.m., the *Duke of York* herself gained radar contact at about 22 miles. The range closed rapidly, and Admiral Fraser ordered his four destroyers to take up position to attack with torpedoes; but, rather surprisingly, he told them not to attack until told to do so—an order which resulted in the postponement of a favourable opportunity.

At 4.50 the *Belfast's* star shell illuminated the *Scharnhorst*, which was obviously caught unawares, and had her turrets trained fore and aft. She turned north, with the *Duke of York* and *Jamaica* engaging from one side and Burnett's cruisers from the other. Meanwhile both divisions of British destroyers were battling through the heavy sea in the endeavour to reach a position of torpedo advantage. Soon the *Scharnhorst* was taking heavy punishment from the *Duke of York's* 14-inch shells, and at 5.24 Bey signalled desperately to Germany " am surrounded by heavy units." Though she fought on gallantly, after an hour's gun duel with her far more powerful adversary her main armament was silenced and her speed had been reduced. The British destroyers, like foxhounds on a breast-high scent, now closed in for the kill. In a series of attacks from both flanks they and the cruisers fired 55 torpedoes, of which 11 probably hit. By 7.30 p.m. only a faint glow could be seen from the once proud battle cruiser, and a quarter of an hour later she had sunk. The British ships searched for survivors, but only 36 of her crew of nearly 2,000 could be rescued from the icy waters of the Barents Sea. Thus did a ship which had caused us immense trouble since the very beginning of the war meet her end; and the strategic situation in the far north was altered still further in the Allied favour.

CHAPTER XVII

NO QUICK VICTORY IN THE MEDITERRANEAN

1st October, 1943–4th June, 1944

"Whereas the success of this expedition will very much depend upon an entire good understanding between our land and sea officers, we do hereby strictly enjoin and require you . . . to maintain and cultivate such a good understanding and agreement. . . . As the commander-in-chief of our squadron is instructed, on his part to entertain the same good understanding and agreement."

William Pitt's Secret Instruction to General Wolfe for the expedition against Quebec, 1759 (Public Record Office. C.O. 5/214).

IN SOME Allied circles the fall of Mussolini, the Italian request for an armistice, and the landings on the European mainland which quickly followed on those events produced hopes that the entire Axis position in the Mediterranean theatre was about to collapse. But the wave of optimism was in fact ill-founded; for it took little account of the resilience and determination of the German military leaders, nor of the fighting qualities of the men whom they commanded. The enemy realised full well that Sardinia and Corsica, which had been very valuable as long as control of the through-Mediterranean sea route was in dispute, had now lost most of their importance; but they took strong steps to quell revolts in Corfu and Cephalonia, which commanded the southern approaches to the Adriatic, and on 11th September they overpowered the Italian garrison and seized the island of Rhodes, which was the key to control of the Ægean.[1] In the same month Sardinia fell to the Allies without a shot being fired, and French troops were then

[1] See Map pp. 112-13.

carried from North Africa to Corsica; but the Germans succeeded in evacuating to Italy the garrison of some 25,000 men, as well as much equipment—chiefly because we were fully occupied with the struggle for the Salerno beach-head at the time. Though they lost some 17,000 tons of shipping to Allied submarines and air attacks during the evacuation, the cost was not unreasonable in relation to the accomplishment. By the end of September the Germans had so far restored their position in the central basin that they could turn their attention to the Ægean, and especially to the Dodecanese islands close off the coast of Asia Minor. Not only did those islands command the approaches to the Dardanelles, with the Danube estuary and Black Sea ports beyond them, but possession of them was bound to exert a powerful influence on the military situation in Greece and on the political outlook in neutral Turkey.

In London, however, the imminent collapse of Mussolini's government, and the possibility that Italy might join hands with the Allies, had caused the Prime Minister's eyes to turn in the same direction; for his long experience of war and sense of history made him deeply conscious of the richness of the prize to be gained from possession of the oft-contested Ægean islands; and the narrow channels between Europe and Asia Minor to the north of them were probably a reminder to him of the opportunities which were lost at Gallipoli in 1915—and of the influence of that failure on his own career. The Middle East Commanders-in-Chief, whose head-quarters were still in Cairo, answered the Prime Minister's urgings with proposals to seize Cos, Leros and certain other islands; to which Mr. Churchill replied on 9th September " Good. This is the time to play high. Improvise and dare." The need to improvise must already have been clear to the men on the spot; for diversions to the Italian theatre and to the South-East Asia Command had left them very weak in all three elements—but especially in the air; and there was no properly organised and trained amphibious force in Egypt. There were moreover grave risks in sending troops to the Dodecanese what time the island of Rhodes remained in enemy hands. The outlook for an Ægean venture was thus far from wholly favourable: and the problems which were certain to arise were made more difficult by the fact that the Middle East authorities would have to depend for reinforcements and support on the inter-Allied commanders in the central theatre, who were under General

Eisenhower; and they already had on their hands the conduct of the main campaign in Italy, where prospects of a long and costly struggle were becoming very plain. But the risks of the undertaking, and the grave disadvantage of dependence on a different command, were accepted by the British Chiefs of Staff in the belief that the speed and daring which Mr. Churchill had urged would offset the unfavourable factors. In mid-September the warships of the Levant command accordingly carried small bodies of lightly armed troops to Cos, Leros and certain other of the Dodecanese islands, where they installed themselves without difficulty.

The Germans had, however, already strengthened their air forces in Greece and Crete, and were also reinforcing their garrisons in Rhodes and other islands held by them; and we may here note that the enemy's air bases were very much closer to the scene of operations than were the bases from which the Royal Air Force had to work in Cyprus—let alone in Egypt or Libya.[1] Thus it was hardly surprising that the British forces engaged in the Ægean soon encountered serious difficulties; for we had in fact sent military expeditions overseas far from any well-found naval or air bases, and we could not command the adjacent waters sufficiently firmly to ensure their support. The burden of supplying and reinforcing the British garrisons mainly fell, as was inevitable, on the Royal Navy; and the sinking by enemy bombers of two destroyers in Leros harbour on 26th September quickly showed that it would be no easy task. Though more warships were sent from the central Mediterranean to the Levant command, no amount of pressure from London would persuade General Eisenhower or his Air Force commander, Air Chief Marshal Tedder, to release aircraft from the main theatre. True the strategic bombers did plaster some of the German airfields in Greece; but it was direct tactical support for the troops ashore and for the ships working in the Ægean or on passage to and from Egypt that was needed—and that essential purpose could not be fulfilled by the few aircraft available in the Levant. Early in October the Germans sailed a convoy from Greece towards Cos and, although it was sighted from the air, it was missed by the warships on patrol. Shortly after daylight on 3rd October,

[1] See Map pp. 112-13. Whereas Rhodes and Crete were only some 70 and 150 miles respectively from Cos, Cyprus was 350 miles away; and aircraft working from Egypt and Libya had to fly at least double that distance.

seaborne and airborne troops attacked the island under cover of heavy bombing, and by the following evening the survivors of the ill-equipped garrison of some 900 British troops surrendered. Mr. Churchill was reproachful about this setback; but to the Middle East authorities it was plain that the seizure of Cos was only a preliminary step towards the larger and more important island of Leros. They therefore renewed their appeals for more air support—and especially long-range fighters. On 6th October two groups of U.S.A.F. Lightnings lent from the Mediterranean Air Command began to work in support of the Ægean forces from a Libyan air-field; and those splendid aircraft at once showed what quite modest numbers of modern fighters could do. On the night of 6th-7th the warships on patrol destroyed an entire German landing craft convoy bound for Cos, and it seemed that things might be about to take a turn for the better. Unfortunately the relief gained by the hard-pressed warships was very brief; for after only four days Air Marshal Tedder recalled the Lightnings to the central theatre—in order that they should escort the strategic bombers on their raids against distant targets in north Italy and the Balkans.

It was now plain that if we were not to suffer further reverses in the Ægean something had to be done immediately about organis-ing proper air support; and a conference, to which all the com-manders concerned were called, therefore took place in Tunis on 9th October—the day before the Lightnings were recalled. Fully supported by his service Commanders-in-Chief, General Eisen-hower then decided that the situation in Italy was such that forces could not be diverted for a combined operation against Rhodes—a purpose which the Middle East authorities had long wished to carry out, but for which the forces at their own disposal were wholly inadequate. The logical corollary to this decision was that Leros and the other islands still held by us should be evacuated; for with Rhodes in enemy hands the Ægean operations could not possibly prosper. But the conference accepted instead that the islands should be held, and the naval Commander-in-Chief, Levant, certainly left with the impression that the air support which was essential to that purpose would be forthcoming. Such hopes, however, proved vain. Although the Chief of the Air Staff signalled to Tedder that in his view Leros was " more important than strategic objectives in southern France or north Italy," command of the skies over the Ægean was not wrested from the Luftwaffe. In consequence losses suffered by the patrolling warships and supply vessels continued to mount, and the island garrisons were subjected to constant bombing—to which they could make no effective reply. None the less more warships, including a light cruiser squadron, were diverted from the central theatre; and small reinforcements were successfully carried to Leros. Throughout October sweeps and patrols continued in the endeavour to exercise adequate control of the waters around the threatened island; but the pattern of events remained little different from what it had been before the Tunis conference. By day our ships were constantly bombed, and the few R.A.F. Beaufighters in the Middle East could neither give them adequate protection nor strike hard enough to stop the enemy's supply traffic; and by night, when the German convoys slipped from island to island, the patrolling warships found them very difficult to locate. Furthermore among the warship crews doubts began to arise regarding the justification of the ordeal to which they were being subjected almost daily.

Early in November the Germans began to send assault forces from Greece towards the contested islands. Although we watched the convoys' progress from the air, and attacked with such aircraft as could be sent out, we did not manage to stop the movements; and, at the last stage, the destroyers which had been lying close at hand off the Turkish coast missed their quarry. Early on 12th November the Germans landed on Leros from the sea, and later in the day their paratroops cut the defenders in two. There followed four days of confused sea and air fighting around the beleaguered island, with both sides trying to send in reinforcements and prevent their adversaries doing so; but the advantage in the air always lay with the ·Germans—and that proved decisive. On the 16th the garrison of Leros surrendered.

So ended an episode whose outcome, even though the scale was too small for it to be classed as a disaster, was certainly a very unpleasant setback—the more so as it took place after we had been at war for over four years. Whether the strategic purpose which Mr. Churchill had in mind could have yielded the rewards which he visualised may be debatable; but there can surely be no doubt that in the Ægean venture the sound inter-service command organisation, the careful preliminary planning, and the thorough training of the men involved, which very recent experience had proved essential to success in combined operations, were all of them lacking. From the Royal Navy's point of view the experience was a bitter one; for its losses amounted to six destroyers and many smaller vessels; while four cruisers and six more destroyers were seriously damaged—most of them by air attacks. As we had learnt off Norway in 1940 and in the invasions of Greece and Crete in the following year, it was impossible for a military force to be sustained overseas unless command of the air was reasonably assured; and one may feel that by 1943 it should not have been necessary to relearn that lesson. Shortly after the loss of Leros we evacuated the last of the islands which we had occupied with such sanguine hopes two months earlier.

To turn to the Adriatic, the importance of those waters at this time lay in the fact that land communications in Yugoslavia and Greece were so bad that supplies for the German forces in those countries had mostly to be sent by sea from the ports on the Istrian peninsula (Trieste and Fiume) down the narrow channels threading the maze of islands off the Dalmatian coast;[1] while on the opposite shore a large proportion of the needs of the German army in Italy had also to be shipped by water to ports close up to the front. By the end of September the Germans had established themselves on most of the Dalmatian islands; but we had opened a new base for our light naval forces at Bari on the east coast of Italy, and had also gained the island of Vis as an advanced base from which we could raid the enemy's coastal communications. The destroyers and coastal forces now began to make frequent sweeps in search of German shipping, while Commandos from Vis made many descents on enemy garrisons in the islands in co-operation with the Yugoslav partisans. This was a type of irregular warfare at which the young R.N.V.R. officers in our Coastal Forces excelled, and the exploits of their motor torpedo-boats and motor gunboats were often exceedingly daring—if their actual accomplishments in ships sunk were a good deal less than we believed at the time. On the other coast of Italy, in the Tyrrhenian Sea, rather similar developments were taking place; for there too the Germans depended greatly on the coastal communications to keep their land forces supplied, and we set about disrupting them with light forces work-

[1] See Map pp. 112-13.

ing from Italian ports and from Corsica. Moreover in November there were still 13 German U-boats in the Mediterranean, and both they and the bombers from southern France caused us trouble by attacking the large supply convoys on passage from Gibraltar to Italy. The losses they inflicted were, however, rarely serious; and in the last three months of 1943 the U-boats lost three more of their dwindling number—most of them at the hands of our sea and air convoy escorts. By far the heaviest blow struck at our shipping at this time arose through an air raid on Bari on 2nd December, when an ammunition ship blew up, and fires spread so rapidly that 16 merchantmen and 38,000 tons of cargo were lost.

The closing months of 1943 thus marked a period of readjustment for the Mediterranean Fleet. Since the surrender of the Italian Navy there was no longer any need to retain big ships permanently on the station, and the battleships, aircraft carriers and many of the larger cruisers were therefore either transferred to the Eastern Fleet or came home to prepare for the invasion of Normandy. The smaller cruisers, the destroyers, the escort vessels and the coastal craft were, however, having a very busy time. In addition to the sweeps against the enemy's coastal traffic in the Adriatic and the Tyrrhenian Sea, already mentioned, and their unremitting escort-of-convoy functions, they had to support the Fifth and Eighth armies by bombardments wherever their flanks came down to the sea; and it was their traditional and primary task to ensure that the Allied land forces lacked nothing which could contribute to the success of the land campaign in Italy. At the end of the year the naval commands in the theatre were re-organised to meet the new circumstances. The Levant Command was abolished, and Admiral Sir John Cunningham, its former commander, assumed the more famous title of Commander-in-Chief, Mediterranean, in succession to Sir Andrew Cunningham who, as we have already seen, had recently taken over the office of First Sea Lord.[1] Four sub-commands were established at Gibraltar, Algiers, Malta and Alexandria, and to them the C.-in-C. delegated the responsibility for administration and operations within the zones allocated to each of them. This was very similar to the organisation that had existed in 1939; and the reversion to the earlier tradition may be

[1] See p. 315.

taken as a measure of the distance we had travelled along the road
to victory during 1943.

The success of the Salerno landing and the rapid capture of
Naples aroused hopes that Rome itself would fall to the Allies
early in 1944; and plans for the next Allied offensive, which aimed
to breach the " Gustav Line " defences along the Sangro and
Garigliano rivers, therefore included an assault from the sea near
Anzio, which lay some 30 miles to the south of Rome and 50 miles
north of the Fifth Army's front.[1] Unhappily neither the Fifth nor
the Eighth Army, who renewed their offensives in very bad weather
in late November and early December, 1943, respectively, could
make appreciable progress; and when it became plain that there
was no longer any possibility of troops landed from the sea at
Anzio linking up quickly with the Fifth Army advancing from the
south the combined operation (which was known as operation
" Shingle ") was cancelled. On Christmas Day, however, a conference over which Mr. Churchill presided took place at Tunis,
and the assault from the sea was then revived in a modified form and
with a different purpose. Whereas the original assault force had
been restricted by shortage of landing ships and craft to one division,
the conference decided that, by forgoing the much discussed
attack on Rhodes and stripping the South-East Asia command,
sufficient specialised vessels could be collected to land two divisions;
and the object of the operation became the reduction of German
pressure on the main front in order to assist the next offensive
against the Gustav Line. The decision was confirmed when the
Allied leaders met early in January, 1944 at Marrakesh, where Mr.
Churchill was recovering from a bout of pneumonia; and D-Day
was then fixed for 22nd January. Not only did this leave very
little time to complete the plans, but on the Navy's side there was a
good deal of anxiety regarding the wisdom of carrying out a big
combined operation, which was bound to entail supplying the
troops for some days over open beaches, in mid-winter. But the
prize—namely the quick capture of Rome—was held to be so
valuable that Admiral Sir John Cunningham accepted the risks
involved. His headquarters therefore moved from Algiers to Naples,

[1] See Map pp. 112-13.

where the plans were completed in the short space of two weeks. Rear-Admiral F. J. Lowry, U.S.N., was given command of the naval forces allocated to operation " Shingle," and was himself to be responsible for the southern of the two assault sectors, where the 3rd U.S. Division and three battalions of American Rangers (the equivalent to our Commandos) were to land. Rear-Admiral T. Troubridge was placed in command of the northern assault, which was to be carried out by the 1st British Division and two Commandos. By 16th January, when the orders for the operation were issued, almost all the ships and craft taking part had assembled in the Bay of Naples. In all they numbered 379, provided in about equal proportions by the Royal and United States Navies; and ships from both countries were intermingled in the two assault forces, transporting British or American troops without distinction as to the nationality of the ships. After carrying out rehearsals in the Gulf of Salerno, in which stormy weather and inexperienced handling of craft caused some losses to the American assault force, the convoys, in which some 50,000 men and 5,000 vehicles had been embarked, formed up outside the Bay of Naples on 21st January and then steered to the north. The weather was fine and calm, and sweepers went ahead to clear the anchorages and the channels leading to the beaches. This work had not, however, been completed when the first waves of assault craft moved inshore to touch down at H-Hour, which was 2 a.m. on 22nd; and unswept mines caused a good deal of trouble and some losses.

The first landing craft arrived at their beaches almost exactly on time, and it was at once clear that we had achieved complete surprise. By dusk on D-Day, in spite of the flat gradient of the beaches making things difficult for the landing craft and vehicles, all the assault troops had landed, and the empty L.S.I.s were soon on their way back to Naples under escort. Enemy gunfire and air attacks had caused insignificant damage. Meanwhile in the southern sector the U.S. Rangers had seized the small port of Anzio, where the first L.S.T.s and L.C.T.s unloaded during D-Day. By the early hours of 23rd the beach-head was securely held, and VI Corps (as the assault force was designated) was advancing slowly inland towards its main objective, which was the Alban Hills twenty miles away, whence the main enemy north-south communications could be commanded. We now know that there was, in fact, almost nothing to prevent the Army driving straight into Rome at that moment; but the American General commanding VI Corps did not seize the opportunity, and the Germans reacted with vigour. The consequence was that the highly successful landing at Anzio was not exploited in the manner which Mr. Churchill, its chief protagonist, had hoped for; and within a few days VI Corps was virtually besieged in its beach-head. To the Allied navies this meant the start of a long and trying period, during which they would have to keep the troops supplied over open beaches or through the one small port available; and the enemy soon began to use every weapon in his armoury—land artillery, dive-bombing, torpedo and glider-bomb attacks, special assault craft, human torpedoes and mines—against the shipping lying close offshore in a very exposed position. The day after the landings, when one British destroyer was sunk and another seriously damaged, brought a foretaste of what was to come; and that night the fine weather broke. Losses, especially to glider-bombs and mines, began to mount; but the cruisers and destroyers had to continue to work close inshore to support the army with their gunfire. On the 29th, while carrying out that duty, the cruiser *Spartan* was hit by a glider-bomb, and capsized with heavy loss of life. In spite of all difficulties, within a week of the first landings nearly 70,000 men, over 27,000 tons of stores and many tanks and guns had been put ashore; but German reinforcements were arriving in strength, and the initiative had plainly passed to the enemy. Admiral Cunningham, who visited the assault area at this time, forcefully expressed his chagrin at the stalemate which had developed. " It is " he wrote to the First Sea Lord, referring to the lost opportunity at Suvla Bay in August 1915, when the landing was also virtually unopposed but the highly favourable circumstances were not exploited,[1] " Suvla all over again . . . except that the Navy cannot be blamed this time for landing the wrong kind of mules." But there was very little that the Allied navies could do about it, except to continue to pour reinforcements and supplies into the beach-head, and support the troops with their guns.

On 3rd February, the Germans launched their expected counter-attack, and for about a fortnight the issue hung in the balance. At the height of the struggle four British and one American cruiser,

[1] See Moorehead, *Gallipoli*, Chapters XIII-XV (Hamish Hamilton, 1956).

and all the available destroyers of both services, came up from Naples to support the embattled land forces; and German records show that their harassing fire contributed a great deal to halting their counter-offensive. In such circumstances losses were bound to be suffered by the offshore warships; but as the mines were now being cleared as fast as the enemy laid them, and our defences against the glider-bombs had improved, they were not unduly heavy. The sinking by a U-boat of the cruiser *Penelope* on 18th February was one of the most grievous—the more so because she had done such splendid work in the Malta convoys of earlier years.

Throughout March and April the situation remained virtually static both in the Anzio beach-head and on the main front; and by the beginning of May the recall to Britain of the warships needed to take part in the invasion of Normandy could be deferred no longer. This left only very exiguous forces to support the new offensive against the Gustav Line, which opened on 11th May; but a week later the stubbornly contested key point of Monte Cassino at last fell to the Allies, and on 23rd VI Corps struck hard to break out of the Anzio perimeter. Two days later the long-awaited junction with Fifth Army troops coming up from the south took place, and on the last day of the month the Alban Hills, towards which longing eyes had been raised ever since the assault forces had stepped ashore at Anzio four months previously were at last in our hands. The Germans now disengaged all along the front, and on 4th June, Allied troops entered Rome.

The landing at Anzio will probably long remain a subject for debate, and it seems unlikely that historians will ever achieve unanimity on whether it should have been launched at all, once the break-through on the main front had failed in December, 1943. Mr. Churchill's desire to make imaginative use of our overwhelming maritime power undoubtedly played a big part in the decision to remount the operation in enlarged form. And it certainly seems true to say that if throughout the winter of 1943-44 we had made no attempt to exploit the greatest advantage we possessed, the enemy's task would have been lightened, and his defence of the lines to the south of Rome would have been even more stubborn; for the equivalent of six good German divisions were ultimately absorbed in containing the Anzio beach-head.[1] Even more difficult to decide is the question whether, had VI Corps advanced quickly to the Alban Hills, its thrust would have so disorganised the enemy that Rome would have fallen and a break-through have become possible on the main front; for many soldiers held, and still hold, that VI Corps would more probably have been overwhelmed when the enemy counter-attacked. What is beyond doubt is that the combined operation was faultlessly planned and executed, that complete surprise was achieved and that, after the chance of exploiting a favourable situation had faded, the Allied navies carried out the arduous duty of supporting, reinforcing and supplying the troops encircled in the perimeter with complete success—in spite of the enemy's utmost endeavours to disrupt their work.

While the long-drawn stalemate at Anzio was in progress we re-organised our Mediterranean convoy system to take full advantage of our possession of the great port of Naples, and of the harbours on the " heel " of Italy. This saved a great deal of transhipment in the North African ports, such as Algiers and Oran, whose importance had now declined. Though air and U-boat attacks on convoys continued in the western basin, the defensive measures organised jointly by the Allied naval and air services were by this time extremely effective. During the first five months of 1944 the U-boats and the bombers each sank only ten merchantmen, and the attackers themselves were severely handled. Twelve U-boats were destroyed in that period—most of them by air raids on their base at Toulon or by the joint Navy-R.A.F. " swamp " operations mentioned earlier.[2] By the end of May the Mediterranean U-boats' strength had fallen to eleven, and before the end of the year all of them had been accounted for. Furthermore after May, 1944, not one Allied merchant ship was sunk by a U-boat in this theatre.

While our sea and air escorts were thus establishing a final mastery over the U-boats and the bombers, our light forces were reaching ever farther up into the Adriatic, and many small combined operations were carried out by Commandos and Yugoslav partisans against German garrisons in the Dalmatian islands. The

---

[1] Field-Marshal Kesselring, commander of the Germany Army in Italy, later said, " If you had never pitted your divisions in the Mediterranean as at Anzio-Nettuno, you would not have won the victory in the west." (Quoted U.S. Naval Institute Proceedings, Vol. LXXX, p. 31.)

[2] See p. 284.

unrelenting pressure of those sweeps and raids was gradually depriving the enemy of the use of the coastal communications on which his armies in the Balkans depended; and by the middle of 1944 a complete collapse of the German position in that theatre was becoming a distinct possibility. In terms of strategy that event, if exploited energetically, opened up wide prospects; for it would make it possible for the western Allies to force their way from the head of the Adriatic into the Danube valley, and so gain command of central Europe. We now know that such a prospect caused Hitler grave alarm. In the eastern basin too we were at last able to mount a sufficiently effective sea-air offensive to imperil the German hold on Crete and the Ægean islands, and by the middle of 1944 the enemy was suffering experiences such as we had undergone during the vain endeavour to hold Cos and Leros in the previous autumn. The Germans now abandoned the attempt to use large ships to supply their garrisons, and relied instead on small craft, such as locally requisitioned caïques. But such vessels could only carry a few tons of cargo, and with our aircraft and light naval vessels making increasingly frequent sweeps off Crete and into the Ægean, the quantities unloaded in the enemy-held islands was falling rapidly. Lastly we were also extending our hold up into the Gulf of Lyon. Towards the end of 1943, soon after the Germans evacuated Corsica, we established a new Coastal Force base at Bastia on the north-east corner of that island; and at about the same time the 10th Submarine Flotilla moved from Malta to Maddalena in Sardinia, while the 1st Flotilla came from Beirut to Malta. All those measures were designed to extend our maritime control northwards, and to deprive the Germans of the use of the coastal waters off southern France and north-west Italy. In 1944 our submarines patrolled constantly in those waters and, if targets were too few for their liking, they sank several valuable ships. Meanwhile the M.T.B.s and M.G.B.s from Bastia, which were most ably organised and led by Commander R. A. Allan, R.N.V.R., searched the inshore waters for enemy convoys whenever the conditions were favourable, and struck some hard blows. Taken together these various measures restricted enemy movements by sea to an ever narrowing area of the Ligurian Sea, the Adriatic and the Ægean; and with his seaborne supplies suffering a steady attrition, the difficulties of his land forces in Italy, Yugoslavia and

Greece—let alone in the outlying islands still occupied by German garrisons—were becoming increasingly acute. On the other hand the Allied land forces in Italy were sustained and nourished by an enormous and almost unimpeded flow of men, stores, guns and vehicles—all of them brought across the seas from Britain or from far away America. By June, 1944, it seemed that, if the Fifth and Eighth Armies were given adequate priority for reinforcements, a great victory in Italy would soon be within their grasp; but a conflict of strategic views on the future of the Italian campaign had unfortunately developed between the British and American war leaders—and that was to result in the deferment of the final victory in the Mediterranean theatre for nearly another year.

CHAPTER XVIII

ADVANCE IN THE PACIFIC:
FRUSTRATION IN THE INDIAN OCEAN

1st June, 1943–31st May, 1944

" The moral effect of an omnipresent fleet is very great, but it cannot be weighed . . . against a main fleet known to be ready to strike and able to strike hard."

> Lord Fisher to Lord Stamfordham, 25th June, 1912 (Marder, *Fear God and Dread Nought*, Vol. II, p. 469. Cape, 1956).

WHEN WE last glanced briefly at the progress of the war against Japan we saw how, by the middle of 1943, the South and South-West Pacific theatre commanders (Admiral W. F. Halsey, U.S.N., and General MacArthur) were poised and ready to strike new blows aimed to breach the enemy's main defensive position known as the Bismarck Barrier. At the end of June both commanders renewed their offensives. While Halsey's amphibious forces moved up the Solomon Islands chain to seize new bases on the direct route towards the key point of Rabaul, those commanded by MacArthur attacked westward along the north coast of New Guinea in order to win the well-placed bases in the Huon Gulf, from which they could threaten the western flank of the Bismarck Barrier.[1] The invasion of New Georgia and other islands in the Solomons led to a renewal of the fierce close-range night encounters in the narrow waters of the " Slot," which had been such a marked feature of the opening months of the Solomons campaign, when the struggle for Guadalcanal was at its height;[2] but the cruiser-destroyer task forces employed at first by the Americans did not prove tactically suitable to such conditions. In July two indecisive battles were fought, and in the second of them the New Zealand cruiser *Leander*

---

[1] See Map p. 185.   [2] See pp. 253-5.

—the last major White Ensign warship under Halsey—was torpedoed and severely damaged. Early in August, however, an American destroyer squadron, working without cruiser support, did inflict a sharp defeat on a similarly composed Japanese force. That month saw the first anniversary of the start of the Solomons campaign. Though the tale of Allied losses had been heavy, they had been more than replaced by American new construction; but the Japanese Navy had undergone a process of attrition from which it never fully recovered, and its naval aircrews had been so recklessly squandered that the surviving carriers could no longer be fully manned.[1]

While Halsey's threat to Rabaul from the south was thus developing along the intended lines, MacArthur's amphibious forces, working in close co-operation with Australian troops who had been fighting their way through the difficult New Guinea mountains and jungles from the south, landed in Huon Gulf. By the early days of October all the objectives had been captured, the Allied hold on eastern New Guinea was complete, and possession of the new bases had both outflanked the Bismarck Barrier and provided a jumping off point for the next drive to the west; for MacArthur's strategy was to gain full control of the waters off northern New Guinea as the essential preliminary to a northward swing towards the Philippines.[2] The Japanese for their part recognised the threat which was developing, but still hoped to hold a vast " defensive perimeter " stretching from the Aleutian Islands in the north-east to the Andaman Islands in the Indian Ocean, and including the Gilbert and Marshall groups in the Pacific and the whole of the very rich islands of the Eastern Archipelago (Timor, Celebes, Java, Sumatra etc.). The naval defence of this enormous area was confided to their Combined Fleet, now commanded by Admiral Koga, which was based on Truk in the Caroline group; but as early as July, 1943, the Japanese had, by evacuating the last of the Aleutian islands, drawn in the far-distant northern flank of their defences. It was soon to be seen whether they could withstand a powerful punch in the centre of their perimeter; for at the first

[1] If the fighting off New Guinea and the Bismarck Archipelago be included Japanese losses between August, 1943, and August, 1944, amounted to two battleships, six cruisers, one small aircraft carrier and thirty-six destroyers.

[2] See Map p. 341.

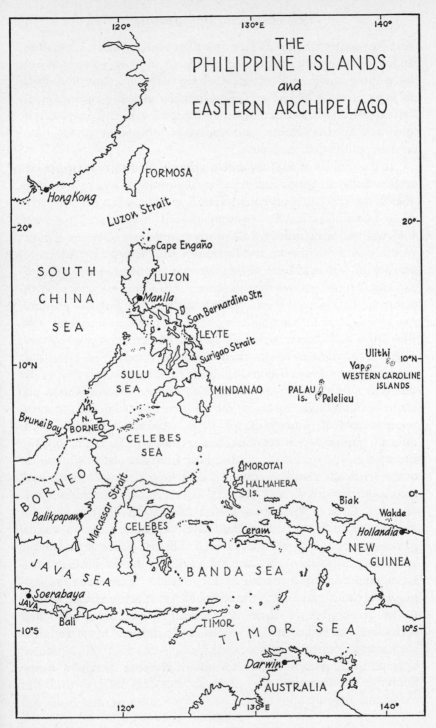

THE
PHILIPPINE ISLANDS
and
EASTERN ARCHIPELAGO

FORMOSA

Hong Kong

Luzon Strait

Cape Engaño

LUZON

Manila

San Bernardino Str.

LEYTE

Surigao Strait

SOUTH

CHINA

SEA

SULU
SEA

MINDANAO

Ulithi

Yap·
WESTERN CAROLINE
ISLANDS

PALAU
Is. ·Pelelieu

Brunei Bay

N.
BORNEO

CELEBES
SEA

MOROTAI

HALMAHERA
Is.

Biak

Wakde

BORNEO

Macassar Strait

Balikpapan·

CELEBES

Ceram

Hollandia·

NEW
GUINEA

JAVA SEA

BANDA SEA

Soerabaya·
JAVA
Bali

TIMOR

TIMOR SEA

Darwin·

AUSTRALIA

Quebec conference in August the Combined Chiefs of Staff had approved an assault on the Gilbert Islands in November, followed by a blow against the Marshall group early in 1944. The grand strategy of the Allied powers had originally included a simultaneous offensive by British forces from India against Burma and Malaya; but lack of the means, and especially of combined operation vessels, stultified that purpose.

In the middle of 1943 the situation in the British zone of strategic responsibility in South-East Asia was depressing. The Eastern Fleet, which was still based on Kilindini in East Africa, had been deprived of so many ships for the invasion of Sicily that it was impossible for Admiral Somerville to do more than provide for the security of merchant shipping in the Indian Ocean. Except for submarine patrols off Japanese bases in Malaya and the East Indies, offensive measures were out of the question. After the surrender of the Italian fleet, however, it was possible for the Admiralty to reinforce Somerville, and in September 1943, he was able to move his main base from East Africa back to Ceylon. Though this was at least a move in the right direction, the fleet's striking power—especially in carrier-borne aircraft—was still quite inadequate for any major offensive undertaking; and there was no properly organised and trained amphibious force in the theatre. In August, 1943, the appointment of Admiral Lord Louis Mountbatten as Supreme Allied Commander, South-East Asia, seemed to offer hopes of better times; but, for reasons to be discussed later, his plans to make use of our renascent maritime power by launching a combined operation across the Bay of Bengal were to be repeatedly frustrated. The directive issued to Mountbatten on 23rd October, 1943, setting out his responsibilities produced, moreover, difficulties both with the naval commander in the theatre and with the Admiralty; for the Admiralty insisted that, because Somerville's responsibilities as naval Commander-in-Chief extended far outside Mountbatten's geographical theatre, and it was the invariable practice for naval C.s-in-C. to be responsible to them for maritime control within their commands, he could only be regarded as being under the Supreme Commander when it came to employing the fleet on combined operations. This decision was, for obvious reasons, distasteful to the Supreme Commander—the more so as he wished to base his command organisation on the same principles as the American

South-West Pacific theatre, rather than on General Eisenhower's Mediterranean model; and the naval forces of the American Seventh Fleet were at all times directly under General MacArthur's control. The ideal solution undoubtedly was for Mountbatten to be given a Flag Officer and a fleet which would act solely in furtherance of his strategic aims; but to the Admiralty the Eastern Fleet was the guardian not only of the vital sea communications off the East African coast, but of the Persian Gulf and Red Sea—which were not in the South-East Asia Command's area of responsibility. Thus, in spite of a great deal of discussion, no solution acceptable to all parties could be found, and Somerville continued to serve two masters separately and simultaneously, according to the purpose on which his ships were employed. Happily the Japanese were so fully occupied by the Solomons and New Guinea campaigns, and in preparing to meet Nimitz's threat in the Central Pacific, that they were unable to devote any serious attention to the Indian Ocean during the time that the British fleet was very weak. Apart from sending a few submarines to join with Dönitz's U-boats in the *guerre de course* against our shipping, as already told,[1] there was little enemy activity in the theatre during the latter half of 1943.

On 1st November Halsey struck still higher up the Solomons chain, making a series of "leap-frogs" over islands garrisoned by the enemy but not essential to his own strategy, to assault the northernmost island of Bougainville. The Japanese, though initially taken by surprise, reacted strongly; for with the Americans firmly established on Bougainville the threat to Rabaul was too plain to be ignored. When, however, they sent a cruiser and destroyer force to attack the invasion shipping on 1st November, the covering American warships successfully frustrated their purpose. But Admiral Koga had also detached seven of his heavy cruisers to Rabaul, and as Halsey possessed no comparable ships he could not afford to disregard their arrival so close to the scene of the new combined operation. He therefore switched his main carrier striking power on to those targets, and in two heavy attacks on 5th and 11th November he inflicted such losses that all danger to the Bougainville expedition was eliminated. Furthermore, the successful defence of his fleet against attack by shore-based aircraft while working close off the enemy's bases in New Britain showed that

[1] See p. 210.

the days when it had been considered too risky to expose the precious carriers to such forms of attack had passed; and that realisation was to have important repercussions on the conduct of future operations.

While Halsey's assault forces were establishing themselves in the northern Solomons a gigantic pincer movement aimed at the Gilbert Islands and directed by Admiral Nimitz was also in progress; for assault forces had sailed from Pearl Harbour and the New Hebrides on 10th and 12th November, and the whole available strength of the Central Pacific command had gone to sea in support of them. The two forces met on the 19th, and next day, after very heavy preliminary bombing and bombardments, the American marines landed in the Gilberts. As always the Japanese garrison fought to the last man, but by the 23rd the key islands had been captured. Admiral Koga's Combined Fleet which, for reasons already explained, was desperately short of carrier air strength, did not attempt to intervene; and their defensive perimeter, if not yet pierced, was thus severely dented right in the centre. With the Gilberts firmly secured Vice-Admiral R. A. Spruance swept to the west with his Fast Carrier Task Force, and treated the enemy bases in the Marshall Islands to the first of many demonstrations of his redoubtable strength and hitting power.

In London and Washington discussions were meanwhile in progress regarding the employment of the naval forces which the Admiralty was able to release from the European theatres, now that the situation in the Mediterranean had been transformed by the elimination of the Italian fleet, and the German threat in the far north had been reduced by the immobilisation of the *Tirpitz*. The big question which had to be resolved was whether we were to build up our strength in the Indian Ocean, in order to strike across the Bay of Bengal against Malaya and Sumatra, or whether we should send out all we could to join the Americans in the great offensives in the Pacific now pending. At the Cairo conference in November, 1943, it became plain that the proponents of the Pacific strategy would win the day, and we therefore offered immediately to send out by the Panama Canal a " British Pacific Ocean Force " consisting of three battleships, one or two fleet carriers, and a number of cruisers and destroyers. The proposal was not actually carried out, because the recall of the American ships which had been working with our

Home Fleet and the decision to restart the Arctic convoys forced us to retain more strength at home than had at one time seemed necessary.[1] Furthermore, the Eastern Fleet had to be reinforced if the plan to strike against the Andaman Islands and Sumatra early in 1944, then under discussion, was to be carried out. But one may see in the offer to send out the Pacific Ocean Force in November, 1943, the genesis of the British Pacific Fleet, which was to join with its American comrades in the final phase of the war against Japan.

Towards the end of 1943 the Japanese modified their plans by accepting a considerably shrunken defensive perimeter, including only the Marianas and Carolines (which were the essential bulwarks of their position in the Philippine group), the parts of northern New Guinea which were still held by them, and the islands of the Eastern Archipelago.[2] But in truth their strategy was based on a fundamental fallacy: since unless they could defeat the main Allied fleets, and so regain a measure of the maritime control which was plainly slipping from their grasp, they could not hope to defend the rich territories within their perimeter. Nor was the extent of the illusion under which they laboured to remain unexposed much longer; for on 1st February, 1944, the Central Pacific forces struck right at the heart of the Marshalls, and within a few days they gained possession of Kwajalein, which possessed a very extensive harbour capable of serving as an advanced base for hundreds of ships. While other islands in the Marshalls were being secured or neutralised Vice-Admiral Spruance then swept still farther to the west with most of the powerful Fifth Fleet; and on 17th February he attacked Truk, the principal Japanese base in the Carolines. Though most of Admiral Koga's Combined Fleet had already retreated to the Palau Islands, the American carrier aircrews wiped out the defending Japanese aircraft, and then did heavy execution among the merchant-men and the warships which had stayed behind. Next one part of the Fast Carrier Task Force drove on westwards to the Marianas; for the American strategists had decided to " leap-frog " over Truk and the rest of the Carolines, and to strike at that important bastion of the Philippines. Thus was a great gap torn in the very centre of the Japanese defensive perimeter in the early months of 1944.

After the seizure of the key islands in the Marshalls there was a

[1] See pp. 314 and 320-2.   [2] See Maps pp. 185 and 341.

pause in the Central Pacific while the amphibious forces prepared for the next combined operation. The Fifth Fleet was therefore switched temporarily to support MacArthur's New Guinea campaign, since the naval forces in that theatre, known as the Seventh Fleet were, by comparison with the Fifth Fleet, very weak. Its commander, Vice-Admiral T. C. Kinkaid, U.S.N., possessed no carriers at all, and his principal strength consisted of the Australian heavy cruisers *Australia* and *Shropshire*, under Rear-Admiral V. A. C. Crutchley of the Royal Navy, and three American cruisers. By the beginning of 1944 MacArthur was planning to exploit the new " leap frog " strategy to the fullest possible extent; and he had therefore decided to by-pass the strongly defended Japanese bastion at Rabaul, merely keeping the garrison neutralised by air attacks. But that decision made it essential for him to find another harbour which could be developed to serve as an advanced base for his naval forces. His choice fell on Manus in the Admiralty Islands, a British protectorate; and on the last day of February MacArthur's troops accordingly assaulted that island; but Japanese resistance was very stubborn, and it took a month to clear it entirely of enemies. The Americans then set about creating a base organisation there with all their accustomed energy and originality; and the Royal Navy, when it reappeared in the Pacific in strength at the beginning of 1945, was to make good use of its excellent facilities. While Manus was being developed MacArthur decided to carry out a three-pronged combined operation in the Humboldt Bay area of north-west New Guinea,[1] where the Japanese were trying to establish naval and air bases in the hope of regaining the initiative by striking to the east; and it was to support those assaults that the Fifth Fleet came south in March. On the way Spruance's carrier aircraft attacked the Palaus, where they hoped to catch Koga's main fleet; but it had actually beaten another hasty retreat—this time to Singapore. The chief interest in the attack on the Palaus lies in the fact that it was the only occasion when American carrier-borne aircraft mined an enemy port on a large scale. It is a fact that the Royal Navy exploited the air-laid mine to a far greater extent than its American colleagues, who generally relied on the bomb, and to a lesser extent the torpedo, as their principal offensive weapons. The harbour in the Palaus was at any rate closed by mines for a long

[1] See Map p. 185.

time, with the result that the Japanese Navy—which had quite recently been driven from the Marshalls and the Carolines—was now left with no advanced base in the theatre, except for an ill-protected anchorage in among the islands between Borneo and the Philippines; and it was plain that their fleet would never be able to play its full part in the defence of that group while it had to work from far away Singapore or from ports on the China coast. Henceforth their Combined Fleet laboured under impossible handicaps.

To return to New Guinea, the assaults near Humboldt Bay took place on 22nd April, 1944, and achieved complete surprise. Within four days all the initial objectives had been seized, and MacArthur at once planned his next leap—which was to be a double one to the islands of Wakde and Biak off the north-west coast of New Guinea.[1] Those assaults took place on 17th and 27th May respectively; but the Japanese garrisons resisted as fanatically as ever, and because their high command realised that possession of those islands by the Americans would pierce the ring of airfields defending the Philippines, their Navy reacted more strongly than for many months past. Early in June they made two attempts to reinforce Biak by sea. On both occasions they turned back, however, as soon as a threat developed; and although at the second attempt Admiral Crutchley's Australian-American cruiser and destroyer force pursued them hotly to the north, he did not succeed in bringing them to action. By 21st June MacArthur's men were firmly in possession of Biak; and the following 1st August, by which time South-West Pacific forces had seized other islands in the same area, may be said to mark the conclusion of the New Guinea campaign. MacArthur's next objective was Morotai in the Halmahera group, which lay directly on the path towards the Philippines—on which the General's eyes had been fixed ever since his expulsion from the group in 1942.

While all three American commands were thus making striking progress in the Pacific, Admiral Mountbatten had been planning to take the offensive in the Indian Ocean by launching a combined operation against northern Sumatra; but when it became plain that such an undertaking could not be mounted in the spring of 1944 without prejudicing the invasion of France, he substituted the more modest aim of seizing the Andaman Islands. In December, 1943,

[1] See Map p. 185.

however, almost all the assault shipping which had been so laboriously collected in the Indian Ocean was recalled to the Mediterranean to take part in the Anzio landing;[1] and that forced the Supreme Commander to put aside his hope of making an amphibious assault in the near future. Furthermore, the decision taken at the Cairo conference in November, 1943, that the principal Allied effort against Japan should take place in the Pacific doomed the South-East Asia theatre to playing a secondary role; for it was recognised that the main British fleet would ultimately go to the Pacific. Though Mr. Churchill disagreed with this strategy, and early in 1944 revived the plan to attack Sumatra, the Chiefs of Staff held to the earlier decision. None the less, the Admiralty was by that time able to send substantial reinforcements to Somerville's Eastern Fleet; though they recognised that many of the most modern ships would ultimately go on to Australia, where the fleet which was to work in the Pacific would have to assemble. It thus happened that, although there was still no amphibious force in the theatre, by March, 1944, the Eastern Fleet's strength had reached the point at which its commander could at last strike offensive blows; but he still possessed only one fleet carrier, and to mitigate his weakness in the vital element of carrier air power the Americans agreed to lend him their experienced veteran the *Saratoga*. On 21st March the fleet sailed to meet that welcome reinforcement, and shortly afterwards Somerville was ready to strike. Leaving Trinco-malee with two fleet carriers, three capital ships, six cruisers and fifteen destroyers (among which were units from the American, French and Dutch navies, as well as from the R.A.N. and R.N.Z.N.) he steamed right across the Bay of Bengal to a point close off the northern tip of Sumatra.[2] On 19th April bombers and fighters from the *Illustrious* and *Saratoga* attacked shipping, oil tanks and airfields at Sabang, inflicting considerable damage on the enemy, who was taken completely by surprise. This was an encouraging beginning to the long-deferred offensive in the Indian Ocean; but a more ambitious project had meanwhile been planned by the Supreme Commander, and early in May Somerville therefore took his fleet to Exmouth Gulf on the west coast of Australia. This time the intention was to attack the very important oil refineries at Soerabaya in eastern Java, which produced a large proportion of the aviation fuel needed by

[1] See pp. 332-6.   [2] See Map p. 153.

the Japanese. Not since we had been expelled from the entire Eastern archipelago early in 1942 had White Ensign ships penetrated into those waters. The attack by 85 bombers and fighters took place on 17th May, and was entirely successful. Severe damage was done to the oil refineries and the naval base, and Somerville took his ships back to Ceylon well satisfied with the results of his incursion into the enemy's waters. The *Saratoga* now returned to America, since the *Indomitable* and *Formidable* were both expected to join the Eastern Fleet in the near future. Though it had proved impossible to fulfil the Supreme Commander's hope of carrying out a major combined operation in his theatre, by the middle of 1944 the situation had none the less been transformed. The Japanese Army's offensive into Assam, which in March had looked dangerous, had been halted; on the seas, though the U-boats were still proving a considerable nuisance, and actually provided Dönitz with his best results of the period,[1] we had managed to catch and sink both their supply ships (the *Charlotte Schliemann* and the *Brake*); and that was bound to curtail their operations. Our own submarines were patrolling with rising vigour off the enemy's coasts and on the supply routes to the Burmese ports; and British and American shore-based aircraft had begun to infest the enemy's harbours and estuaries with mines, so impeding still further the flow of supplies to his land forces. But there was another factor which had begun to affect Japanese prospects very seriously—namely, the attrition from which their merchant navy was suffering. The reader will remember that it was not until the autumn of 1943 that they introduced a general convoy system, and began to take measures to conserve their mercantile tonnage.[2] By the beginning of 1944 their total available tonnage had fallen below the five million mark, and in the first five months of that year their losses rose more steeply than ever before. It was mainly the far-ranging American submarines which produced the drastic rise in the rate of attrition; for in that period they sank 212 ships of nearly one million tons. But direct air attacks, such as those on Truk and the Palau Islands described in this chapter, also contributed a quota—as did the shore-based aircraft and submarines of the South-East Asia Command. Moreover, the Allied authorities fully realised that the blockade of Japan could, by cutting her off from her overseas territories, destroy

[1] See pp. 356-7.   [2] See p. 252.

her economy and bring her industries to a stop; and they intended to pursue that purpose with every weapon in their armoury. With maritime control throughout the vast Pacific and South-East Asia theatres slipping rapidly from the grasp of the Japanese, while the Allied land forces were enjoying the inestimable benefits derived from control of the seas, it was plain that the tide of war had already turned.

CHAPTER XIX

SUCCESS IN THE ATLANTIC AND ARCTIC

1st January–31st May, 1944

" The officer who shall have the charge of a convoy entrusted
to him is to consider the protecting of it as his most particular
duty, in the execution of which he is to be very watchful to
prevent it being surprised, and very alert in defending it if
attacked."

Regulations and Instructions Relating to His
Majesty's Service at Sea (1806).

AT THE beginning of 1944 there were about 20 U-boats at sea
in the North Atlantic, and half a score more off the Azores;
but when Dönitz ordered the latter to work against the convoys
on the north-south Gibraltar route in co-operation with Luftwaffe
planes from western France, they quickly lost several of their
number. In the middle of January Dönitz boldly moved the
majority of the North Atlantic boats into the Western Approaches,
hoping to strike hard at the dense traffic moving in and out of the
Irish Sea by the North Channel. Luftwaffe long-range aircraft were
to work with those U-boats as well, and the Germans believed
that they had at last organised efficient sea-air co-operation;
but events were quickly to show that such hopes were ill-founded.
In the first place the Admiralty's Submarine Tracking Room
had, as so often before, given forewarning of the enemy's intention.
Secondly, support groups were quickly moved to the danger zone
to reinforce the convoy escorts; and, thirdly, Coastal Command
switched many of its bombers from the southern bases, whence they
had been patrolling over the Bay of Biscay, to airfields in Northern
Ireland. Within a few days of the U-boats starting to move eastwards a very warm reception had thus been arranged for them. On

28th January Coastal Command aircraft scored two quick successes, and next day Captain Walker's five sloops of the 2nd Escort Group —relentless harbingers of hard times for the U-boats—arrived at the spot where trouble was expected. This time, moreover, the escort carriers *Nairana* and *Activity* were there to help the anti-submarine vessels. The first success came on 31st January, when the *Wild Goose's* Asdic team gained a contact which they handed on to Walker's *Starling* "on a plate," enabling the latter to sink U.592. The group commander then continued his patrol, but it was uneventful until 7th February, when he joined a homeward-bound Gibraltar convoy which we knew to have been reported by enemy aircraft. After dark on the 8th the *Wild Goose* reported another contact, the *Woodpecker* fired a 22 charge barrage, and Walker signalled to her " Come over here and look at the mess you have made." The mess was the remnants of U.762. Early next morning the alert *Wild Goose* picked up an object ten miles away on her radar, closed in to Asdic range, and was soon in contact. The other sloops soon joined in; but this enemy proved very wily. She fired acoustic torpedoes at her tormentors, and managed even to survive several of the dreaded "creeping attacks."[1] Walker and his colleagues were, however, not to be denied. After eight hours of almost continuous attacks, in which they expended 266 depth charges, they finished off U.238. As the threatened convoy had meanwhile gone on its way unharmed, the sloops then renewed their patrol. In the early hours of 11th the *Wild Goose* again reported that she had a submarine contact. She and the *Woodpecker* attacked, and unmistakable evidence of success soon came to the surface. The enemy had been U.424. While these heavy blows were being struck some three hundred miles to the west of Ireland, farther to the north aircraft from the escort carrier *Fencer* had found and destroyed U.666 on the 10th; and that night a Leigh-Light Wellington damaged U.283 so badly that she scuttled herself. There was now a pause, because Dönitz, though he had no idea how serious his losses had been, was growing anxious, and had moved the U-boats farther west. When, however, on the 17th there were signs of a threat developing against two outward convoys, three escort groups were quickly sent to support them. Next afternoon the frigate *Spey* of the 10th Escort Group found and sank U.406, and

[1] See p. 312.

Barracudas attacking the *Tirpitz* in Kaafiord, 3rd April, 1944

The *Tirpitz* in Kaafiord under attack from Fleet Air Arm aircraft, 3rd April, 1944. The smokescreen is just developing

X craft

A chariot under way, March, 1944

on the morning of the 19th the *Woodpecker* and *Starling* blew U.264 to the surface and destroyed her. On the same day the *Spey*, whose group was on its way to support another outward convoy, added U.386 to the score. But that evening the U-boats at last got in a blow against the escort group which had so often outwitted and outfought them; for an acoustic torpedo fired by U.764 blew the *Woodpecker's* stern off. For nearly a week her comrades struggled in heavy seas to tow her in; but on the 27th she capsized off the Scilly Islands. It was the first loss suffered by Walker's ships during four years of almost continuous escort duty. So ended perhaps the most remarkable anti-submarine operation of the war.[1] During the 27 days that the 2nd Escort Group was at sea its five sloops sank six enemies, while other groups and Coastal Command aircrews added five more. Moreover, twelve convoys passed through the Western Approaches during that period, and none of them came to any harm. Captain Walker and his men were given a deservedly rousing welcome when they berthed at Liverpool on 25th February; while Dönitz for his part must have regretted his decision to try and strike in waters which were always one of our most sensitive spots. He was, however, still very far from throwing up the sponge, for at the end of February he made a new attempt to establish a fuelling rendezvous off the Azores, in order to extend his operations in distant theatres. But the American escort carrier groups mentioned earlier were still on patrol there,[2] and it was they who sank no less than five operational boats in March and April, and finally caught the "milch cow" (U.488) herself. These successes greatly weakened the U-boat effort off West Africa and in the Indian Ocean, to which waters some of the destroyed boats had been bound. Nor have we yet reached the end of the losses inflicted on the Atlantic U-boats in the early months of 1944; for when Dönitz switched his main strength into the Western Approaches a number of boats stayed behind, much farther out to sea, with the object of attacking our convoys in mid-ocean. But the Canadian and British escorts were now both strong and well-trained, and they dealt very roughly with any enemies who threatened their charges. In February they sank U.91 and U.358; and the latter success produced the longest

---

[1] The closest parallel to the accomplishments of the 2nd Escort Group on this occasion is probably the sinking of six Japanese submarines to the north of the Solomons in May, 1944, by the American destroyer *England*.

[2] See p. 307.

continuous hunt of the whole war; for four frigates of the 1st Escort Group held contact and attacked for 38 hours before success came to them, and when their victim was *in extremis* she managed to sink the frigate *Gould* with an acoustic torpedo. March produced another very long hunt of 30 hours, before C2 (Canadian) group destroyed U.744 on the 6th, and Dönitz then shifted the survivors of the mid-ocean boats farther north. The attempt to get clear of our searching forces was, however, vain; for two more boats were sunk a few days later, and in the early hours of the 15th Walker's sloops and the aircrews of the escort carrier *Vindex* added U.653 to the score. Dönitz now admitted defeat, and evacuated the central Atlantic, except for a few boats working in very small and widely scattered groups. He cancelled all operations against convoys, and told Hitler that they could not be renewed until the new types of boat had entered service.[1] Between January and March, 1944, 3,360 merchantmen crossed the Atlantic in 105 convoys, losing only three ships in the process; and the price exacted from the enemy for his extremely modest successes was 29 U-boats. Furthermore, in April six of the boats left in widely dispersed positions in the Atlantic were found and destroyed, and Dönitz thereupon cancelled all offensive operations. On 1st May there were only five boats left in the whole northern ocean, and the escorts soon made a virtually clean sweep of them. Such was the decisive nature of the third Allied victory in the Atlantic battle, fought in the waters where the U-boat "aces" had enjoyed their "happy time" in 1940–41.[2]

We must now glance briefly at events in the Bay of Biscay and on the U-boat transit route round the north of Scotland during the period when the sea and air convoy escorts were scoring such striking successes. At the beginning of 1944 the U-boats' new search receivers, which were capable of detecting transmissions from our 10-centimetre radar sets,[3] had gained for them a considerable measure of immunity from our patrolling aircraft, and out of 116 boats which crossed the Bay in January and February Coastal Command aircraft sank only two. The R.A.F. then began to make sweeps very close to the French coast, in the hope that Mosquitos fitted with the new 6-pounder guns might find a chance to use them against surfaced U-boats; but March brought only one such

---

[1] These were the Type XXI and XXIII boats. See p. 303.
[2] See pp. 90-3.   [3] See p. 307.

success. Moreover, in that month Dönitz was told to keep 40 U-boats in western France ready to strike at our shipping in the event of the expected cross-Channel invasion taking place, and that reduced passages across the Bay to a mere trickle. Meanwhile boats from Norway were passing round the north of Scotland submerged, and in consequence the air patrols made few sightings and achieved no successes. In sum it is therefore plain that for the first five months of 1944 the accomplishments of the air patrols on the U-boat transit routes were very disappointing. Early in May, however, the ice in the Baltic thawed, and a stream of U-boats began to move from Germany up the Norwegian coast. We at once switched the northern air patrols in that direction, and between 16th May and 3rd June they sank seven enemies and forced four others to turn back. These were by far the best results ever achieved by the northern transit area patrols, and the only unsatisfactory feature of the period was that all but one of the boats fitted with the new " Schnorkel " breathing-tube got through safely.[1] The month of May, 1944, may be said to mark the end of the so-called " Bay Offensive"; since after that date conditions around the British Isles altered fundamentally. The Biscay air patrols had started, at first in a small way, at the beginning of 1941; but by the following year they were absorbing a very big effort. In all they sank 50 U-boats and damaged 56 more; but no less than 2,425 U-boats passed across the Bay while the offensive was in progress. Further-more, over half the successes were achieved during the brief 94-day period (1st May–2nd August, 1943) when Dönitz ordered the U-boats to stay on the surface by day and fight it out with the aircraft;[2] and the cost of the offensive to Coastal Command was heavy. No fewer than 350 aircraft were lost on such operations. Taking the war as a whole, there is no doubt at all that the convoy air escorts were more effective than the patrols as U-boat killers, and were also less costly; for only 70 convoy air escorts were lost on warlike operations, and their flying hours-per-U-boat-sunk were far the lower. The lessons suggested by the foregoing statistics are important; since it seems that there is in the British services, as in those of some other countries (notably America and Japan) as persistent a tendency to underestimate the beneficial effects of the escort-of-convoy strategy—especially in the matter of actually

[1] See p. 303 regarding the development of this device.   [2] See p. 305.

destroying enemy raiders—as there is to exaggerate the advantages of hunting and patrolling. Mahan's dictum, propounded over half a century ago, that "the result of the convoy system . . . warrants the inference that, when properly systematised and applied, it will have more success than hunting for individual marauders—a process which, even when most thoroughly planned, still resembles looking for a needle in a haystack"[1] thus receives further and full confirmation from both wars of the 20th century—and in particular from the achievements of the sea and air escorts in the second of them.

Early in 1944, while the events already described were taking place in the Western Approaches and far out in the wide wastes of the North Atlantic, Dönitz decided to reinforce his Mediterranean flotillas, which had recently lost a good many of their number.[2] Between January and March nine out of twelve boats successfully passed through the Gibraltar Straits—an accomplishment which, from the Allied point of view, was not to be tolerated. We therefore strengthened our sea and air patrols, and made good use of the new American Magnetic Air Detection (M.A.D.) equipment, by means of which a submerged U-boat could be located from the air; and those measures jointly offset to a considerable extent the consistently poor Asdic conditions experienced in the Straits. In May only one more boat got through, and in face of the rising price which we were exacting Dönitz cancelled the despatch of further reinforcements. Between September, 1941, and May, 1944, he ordered 95 boats to the Mediterranean, and 62 of them reached their new theatre safely; but the good work of the Allied escort forces on the station prevented their operational strength ever rising above 26. Although, as we have already remarked, the Mediterranean U-boats inflicted serious losses in the early days, and were always a far greater menace than the much more numerous Italian submarines, one may doubt whether on balance it was the enemy who benefited from the diversion of so large a proportion of his strength from the vital Atlantic theatre.

As to the distant U-boat operations, at the beginning of 1944 it was only in the Indian Ocean that they were accomplishing any significant results. Between January and March they sank 29 merchantmen (188,000 tons) in that theatre; and that considerable

[1] *The Influence of Sea Power on the French Revolution and Empire* 1793-1812, Vol. II, p. 217.
[2] See pp. 284 and 331.

achievement by a small number of enemies (never more than six Germans and three or four Japanese) caused the Admiralty to press on the C.-in-C., Eastern Fleet, the view that their depredations could be better countered by hunting groups than by sailing as much shipping as possible in convoy—the exact opposite to what all our experience in other theatres had indicated. By May, however, most of the German U-boats had withdrawn to Penang, and the seven survivors of the new group which Dönitz had ordered out had not yet arrived. Thus a short lull followed, and by the middle of the year, with more convoys organised and more sea and air escorts available, Admiral Somerville had the situation well in hand. Three German and two Japanese submarines were destroyed by British ships and aircraft in the vast area stretching from the Cape of Good Hope to the Malacca Straits during the first five months of 1944.

While our sea and air anti-submarine forces were sweeping the U-boats off the waters of the Atlantic the Admiralty and the American Navy Department had been planning to increase the flow of east-bound shipping; since the build-up of American forces in Britain for the invasion of western Europe was now in full swing. The giant liners (*Queen Mary*, *Queen Elizabeth*, etc.[1]) were steadily ferrying to and fro between New York and the Clyde about twice a month, crammed with 15,000 American troops on each eastward journey; but the supplies, vehicles, ammunition and other multifarious stores needed by the fighting men had to be carried across in ordinary convoys. The outcome of the discussions between the two maritime Allies was that in March we reclassified all merchantmen employed on the transatlantic run into three categories according to speed; and in the following month we began to sail Fast, Medium and Slow convoys across the western ocean. Not only did this save tonnage by avoiding the necessity for a ship possessed of a reasonable turn of speed (say 9 knots) sailing in a 7-knot convoy, but it prevented the convoys becoming so large as to be unwieldy. Though we had long since learnt that, given an equal proportionate strength of escorts, large convoys were safer than smaller ones, there was a limit beyond which size could not be carried without risk of confusion at night or in low visibility. In the Atlantic the limit was about 80 ships, and the reorganisation of March, 1944, kept our

[1] See p. 243.

convoys broadly within that figure. It should not, however, be forgotten that our ability to increase the number of convoys and at the same time withdraw many flotilla vessels to prepare for the invasion of Normandy owed everything to the number of new ships which were by this time being delivered from the building yards and factories of Britain and America—and especially to the transfers made to the Royal Navy under the Lend-Lease programme.

We must now review the work of the Home Fleet during the period when the Western Approaches command was gaining the third victory over the Atlantic U-boats. At the beginning of 1944 the strategic situation in the far north had been transformed by the sinking of the *Scharnhorst* and the immobilisation of the *Tirpitz*, and the Commander-in-Chief, Admiral Sir Bruce Fraser, had no serious misgivings about continuing the Arctic convoys. True there were 25-30 U-boats stationed in north Norway; but the Luftwaffe was still weak, and its co-operation with the U-boat arm left a good deal to be desired. Furthermore, the Home Fleet possessed ample strength in flotilla vessels, and escort carriers were at last entering service in such numbers that the convoys could enjoy the great benefit of carrying their own air defences along with them. The first outward convoy of the year sailed in January in two sections known as JW 56A and B, totalling 36 merchantmen. The first section ran into an unusually severe gale even for those normally stormy waters; and U-boats sank three of its number. For the second section the escort was specially reinforced, no merchantman was lost and one U-boat was destroyed. But the flotilla leader *Hardy* was crippled by an acoustic torpedo, and had to be sunk by our own forces. The corresponding homeward convoy RA 56 (of 37 ships) arrived in British ports safely in February.

Admiral Fraser now decided that the conditions justified a return to the earlier practice of sailing large convoys about every five weeks, and JW 57, which sailed on 20th February therefore consisted of 42 merchantmen. The Germans, incensed by their failure against the January convoys, determined to achieve what they called "a grand slam" this time, and threw in all their strength. But it was we who held most of the trump cards, and the enemy only won one trick—by sinking the destroyer *Mahratta*. No merchantman was lost, and the escorts destroyed two U-boats. The next homeward convoy RA 57 (of 31 merchantmen) sailed from Kola Inlet on 2nd March, and had with it the escort carrier *Chaser*, which had come out with JW 57. In spite of very rough weather and violent snowstorms her rocket-firing Swordfish did brilliantly. Three U-boats were sunk during the operation, and only one merchantman was lost. The Admiralty and the C.-in-C. now decided to press home the advantage which they had so plainly gained. Two escort carriers were therefore allocated to the next convoy, and two support groups (one of them Captain Walker's) were sent to reinforce the normal escort; for JW 58, which consisted of 49 merchantmen, was the largest convoy so far sailed on this route. Once again the enemy made a determined onslaught; but the odds against the U-boats were too heavy. Fighter and anti-submarine aircraft from the escort carriers *Activity* and *Tracker* did excellent work—the fighters by shooting down many shadowing aircraft, and the Swordfish A/S planes by co-operating most successfully with the surface escorts. By sinking U-961 Captain Walker raised his personal score to 14 U-boats, and three others met their end at the hands of the sea and air escorts. Once again the deep-laden merchantmen steamed into Kola Inlet quite unscathed, except for one ship which had been damaged by ice early in the voyage and forced to return to Britain. As so often when the U-boats had fired large numbers of acoustic torpedoes, the enemy made fantastic claims of successes—in this case nine destroyers sunk and four probably sunk; but the number of U-boats which did not report after the battle none the less made it plain to their headquarters that the operation had not been a success.

Before JW 58 had sailed our intelligence organisation had reported that the *Tirpitz* had nearly finished repairing the damage inflicted by the midget submarines in the previous September,[1] and the Admiralty therefore decided to strike again at her before she was fully fit for sea. The plan this time was to use the greatest possible strength of carrier-borne bombers, which would attack during the passage of the convoy. On 30th March Admiral Fraser's fleet accordingly left Scapa in two forces, the first consisting of the battleships *Duke of York* (fleet flagship) and *Anson*, the fleet carrier *Victorious*, one cruiser and five destroyers: while the second comprised the old fleet carrier *Furious*, four escort carriers, and three cruisers. The actual attack on the *Tirpitz* was to be conducted by

[1] See pp. 317-8.

Vice-Admiral Sir Henry Moore, second-in-command of the Home Fleet; and for that purpose the two fleet carriers each had on board a strike wing of 21 Barracuda bombers. Forty fighters, some flown from the fleet carriers and others off the escort carriers, were to accompany each of the two striking forces. The essence of the plan was surprise: for we knew that, if the enemy was forewarned, gun and fighter opposition was certain to be strong, and the target might well be completely shrouded in smoke by the time that the bombers arrived. While the fleet was steaming north-east towards the Arctic circle the weather was unusually favourable, and it also became plain that, as the escort of JW 58 was dealing very successfully with the opposition, it would be unnecessary for the main fleet to give it help. Admiral Fraser therefore decided to seize what, in those latitudes, might well prove a fleeting opportunity, and advanced the attack on the *Tirpitz* by 24 hours. This meant that the escort carriers had to do some very hard steaming to reach the rendezvous in time; but by the afternoon of 2nd April both Home Fleet forces had concentrated successfully at the flying-off position 120 miles to seaward of Altenfiord. By 4 a.m. next morning, 3rd April, all was ready; and half an hour later, just as the sun was rising over a calm sea, the first striking force and its fighter escort were winging their way towards the target. The second contingent followed after a short interval, and only two of the 120 aircraft taking part had mechanical failures or came to grief during the fly-off—a fine tribute to the work of the maintenance crews in the difficult conditions of the Arctic. Admiral Bisset, who commanded the *Furious's* force, described the departure of what was up to that time by far the largest number of Royal Navy aircraft to set out on a single operation as "a grand sight." Just before 5.30 a.m. the first wave of bombers dived on the target, while the fighters sprayed the *Tirpitz* and the German shore A-A positions with machine-gun fire. The enemy was taken completely by surprise, and opposition was weak. The bombers' attacks were beautifully co-ordinated, and within a minute all was over. Smoke and flames could be seen pouring from the injured titan, and we now know that she received no less than nine hits (one or two of them with 1,600-pound armour-piercing bombs), as well as one very near miss. The second wave came in about an hour later and, as was to be expected, found the smoke screen a good deal denser and enemy gunfire more intense;

The escort carrier H.M.S. *Emperor* in an Atlantic gale, 1944

The end of a U-boat: U.675 sunk 24th May, 1944
by a Sunderland of 4th Operational Training Unit

Aircraft Carriers : The assault carriers with the invasion convoy approach
the South of France, August, 1944

H.M.S. *Fencer* on escort duty in the Arctic, Spring, 1944

but again the attacks were made in such quick succession that the defences were completely outclassed. Five more hits were obtained. On board the *Tirpitz*, which had actually been about to put to sea, all was chaos, and the crew suffered over 400 casualties; but—partly perhaps because the Barracuda pilots, in their anxiety to score hits, dived rather lower than had been intended—none of the bombs penetrated the main armour belt protecting her vital compartments. The truth was that, with the weapons given to them, it would in any case have been very difficult for the Fleet Air Arm bombers to sink the battleship. They did, however, put her out of action for about three months.

By 8 a.m. all the striking force except two Barracudas, and all their fighter escort except one, had landed safely on the carriers' decks, and Admiral Moore stood out to sea to prepare to repeat the blow next morning. On reconsideration, however, and believing that the *Tirpitz* had been more seriously damaged than was actually the case, he cancelled his intention; and next night the weather broke. By the 6th April the fleet was back in Scapa. The First Sea Lord had meanwhile been pressing the Commander-in-Chief to attack again quickly, even though the carrier aircraft were unlikely to sink the battleship; for Sir Andrew Cunningham was not the man to lose any chance of belabouring an injured enemy, and he considered it a matter of first importance to put the battleship out of action for as long a period as possible. But the C.-in-C. considered that he was unlikely to achieve anything considerable by doing so, because it was highly improbable that he could again catch the enemy by surprise. The interchange of messages between London and the fleet flagship generated some heat, for Admiral Fraser held that this was an issue on which the fleet commander's views should be decisive; but in the end he agreed to repeat the operation—provided that the conditions were favourable. On 21st April Admiral Moore accordingly sailed again with a force similar to that employed on the first occasion; but the weather proved quite unsuitable and, after waiting in the Barents Sea as long as his fuel permitted, he sent his striking forces to attack enemy shipping in the Norwegian " Leads," where they did considerable execution, and then returned to the main base.

Apart from the fact that, as long as the *Tirpitz* remained afloat, the destruction of a few thousand tons of shipping off Norway seemed, on the face of it, a rather secondary matter, there was a great deal to be said for our maritime forces making their presence felt off that steep-cliffed island-studded coast in the spring of 1944; for our strategic deception plan aimed to convince the enemy that we intended to invade Norway, so forcing him to keep as many ships, men and aircraft as possible locked up in that country—far away from the Normandy beaches on which the eyes of the Allied planners had long been focused. Thus, quite apart from the importance of the iron ore traffic from Narvik to Germany, and our desire to stop the shipment of supplies to the German forces in the far north, there were valid strategic reasons for keeping up the pressure in those waters. The offensive was in fact a four-pronged one, and was waged jointly by the Home Fleet's carrier-borne bombers, by the strike aircraft of Coastal Command, by our submarines, and by the motor torpedo-boats (many of them Norwegian-manned) which lay concealed in the fiords and inlets in order to ambush passing convoys. Furthermore, on 14th April, in between the successful attack on the *Tirpitz* and the abortive attempt to repeat the operation, the midget submarine X.24 penetrated right into Bergen harbour, hoping to sink the floating dock that lay there. Though it was a large merchantman, and not the floating dock, which she actually destroyed, her bold attack, like the many acts of sabotage carried out by the Norwegian resistance movement, helped to keep the nerves of the occupation forces on edge. We now know that our very varied offensive off Norway not only inflicted heavy shipping losses, but that the deception plan was more successful than we would have dared to hope at the time; for Hitler himself became obsessed with the idea that an Allied invasion of Norway was imminent, and insisted on keeping large forces in that country—including a group of 30 U-boats stationed at Bergen.

With the successful passage of convoy JW 58 in April the Royal Navy had delivered to Russia the full quantities of weapons and stores promised by the Allied governments, and a pause ensued while the fleet prepared to play its great part in the invasion of Normandy. In May, however, we brought home from Murmansk a large convoy of 45 empty ships, and during its passage the experienced crews of the *Fencer's* Swordfish sank three more U-boats. The third phase of the Arctic convoys thus ended on a note of high success to the escorts; for only four merchantmen out of the 276 which had sailed outward or homeward were lost, and the enemy U-boats and bombers had been very roughly handled, 13 of the former being sunk. In May the Home Fleet carriers made two more attempts on the *Tirpitz*, only to be frustrated each time by bad weather; and then all attention was turned to the narrow waters of the English Channel, where we had to establish as firm a measure of control as possible before the invasion flotillas set out for Normandy.

Our strategic aims in the Channel and its approaches were, as off Norway, entrusted to a wide variety of naval and air forces. While Coastal Command Strike Wings constantly swept along the Dutch and north German coasts in search of enemy shipping, the M.T.B.s and M.G.B.s of our Coastal Force flotillas made night forays over to the other side, and fought many fierce actions with the German E-boats and with the powerful escorts of their coastal convoys; minelayers laid defensive fields off Seine Bay against encroachment by German surface warships into the waters where the assault convoys would anchor; and submarines patrolled off the Biscay bases to catch supply ships sailing to and from northern Spain. We also formed a Western Channel Patrol of destroyers to work, generally with cruiser support, against the German "fleet torpedo-boats"[1] based on Cherbourg and Brest. In the early hours of 26th April such a force engaged in a running fight with three of the German T.B.D.s; and although the Canadian destroyer *Athabaskan* was hit by a torpedo and blew up, one enemy was sunk and another driven ashore to become a total loss.

Though maritime control can never, by its very nature, be complete until final victory is almost won, and the enemy even managed to strike one or two quite hard blows against the dense traffic sailing at this time along our south coast—notably when E-boats sank two L.S.T.s out of a convoy engaged on an invasion rehearsal on 28th April—by the middle of May, 1944, our sea and air forces had established a degree of ascendancy which reduced the risks inherent in the greatest combined operation in history to reasonable proportions. Though everyone involved in the organisa-

---

[1] These were well-armed ships of about 1,300 tons displacement, and would have been classed as destroyers in the Royal Navy. The Germans, however, called them "fleet torpedo-boats" to distinguish them from their very powerful (2,700-ton) Z-class destroyers.

tion and planning of that vast undertaking was too deeply conscious of the dangers involved and of the size of the stake ever to be over-sanguine, as May advanced towards June confidence waxed; and at least the Royal Navy and its comrades of the R.A.F. and of the United States Navy knew that nothing that could contribute to success had been neglected.

CHAPTER XX

NEPTUNE'S TRIDENT

1st June–5th July, 1944

> " Fair stood the wind for France
> When we our sails advance,
> Nor now to prove our chance
> Longer will tarry;
> But putting to the main
> At Caux, the mouth of Seine
> With all his martial train
> Landed King Harry."
>
> Michael Drayton (1563-1631), Agincourt.

IT WAS towards the end of 1941 that the British planners seriously turned their attention to the problems involved in the return of our armies to the continent of Europe—though such a project must then have seemed to belong to the realms of optimistic hopes rather than practical operations of war. None the less a plan (called " Round-up ") for the invasion of Europe in 1943 was then drafted. The entry of the United States into the war, however, altered many considerations fundamentally, and new proposals for building up American forces in Britain (called " Bolero") and subsequently launching the Allied armies in a cross-Channel operation (called " Super Round-up ") were therefore next produced. In the spring of 1942, when the danger of a Russian collapse was considered very serious, the British Chiefs of Staff had an additional plan prepared. This one, called " Sledgehammer," was an emergency undertaking whose object was to seize and hold a bridgehead in France in order to take some of the weight of Germany's military might off Russia. " Sledgehammer " was never intended to be a full-scale invasion, but its preparation is none the less of historical importance —not least because, like " Round-up," it was a British conception, and our American Allies later entertained suspicions that we were not really in favour of making a cross-Channel assault. Two months after the " Sledgehammer" plan had been initiated a body called the " Combined Commanders" was brought into being in Britain in order to place study of the re-entry into Europe on a firm inter-service basis. The naval representative was Vice-Admiral Sir Bertram Ramsay, of Dunkirk fame; and on 18th June, 1942, the Admiralty appointed him " Naval Commander Expeditionary Force" for the invasion of France and the Low Countries. Ramsay's connection with the Combined Commanders was however inter-rupted by his participation in the invasion of North Africa in November, 1942, and in the assault on Sicily in July of the following year; but by October, 1943, he was back in London, and able to devote his great powers of organisation and leadership entirely to the cross-Channel plan. On 26th May the code-word describing the operation was changed to " Overlord," and on 7th September the Admiralty informed all authorities that the naval operation within " Overlord " had been given the apt name of " Neptune." It is with that operation that we are here mainly concerned.

The outline plan for " Overlord " was approved at the Quebec conference in August, 1943. It provided for the landing of three divisions in the assault force, followed up by two more, on a thirty-mile stretch of the Normandy coast between the rivers Orne and Vire.[1] One reason for this choice for the site of the landings was that, because no major port existed on that part of the coast, it was likely to be less well defended than the beaches near to such ports. But that advantage was offset by the need either to capture a good harbour quickly or to provide means for faster unloading than would be possible over beaches; and since the former could not be guaranteed, the planners recommended that two artificial harbours should be constructed off the assault area. Though the creators of the plan recognised that three divisions was an extremely slender force with which to attack a strongly fortified coast, shortage of landing ships and craft seemed at that time to preclude any possibility of increasing the weight of the initial blow. Our American Allies had meanwhile been pressing very hard for the cross-Channel operation to take place as early as possible—and at first they had hoped to launch it in 1942. But they finally yielded to the strong

[1] See Map p. 367.

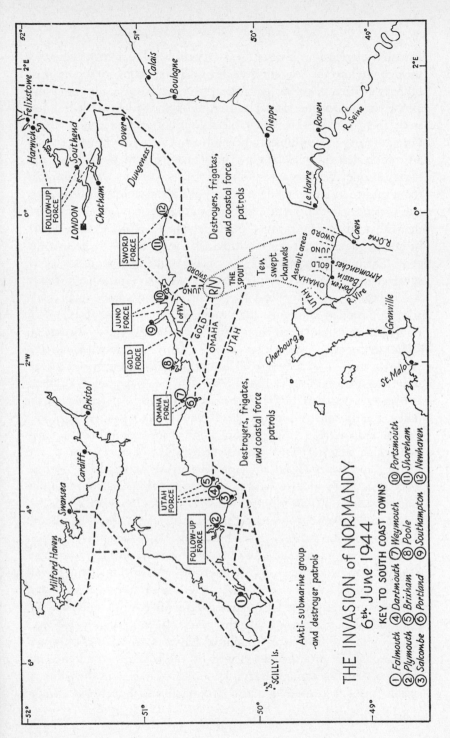

THE INVASION of NORMANDY
6th June 1944

KEY TO SOUTH COAST TOWNS

① Falmouth ④ Dartmouth ⑦ Weymouth ⑩ Portsmouth
② Plymouth ⑤ Brixham   ⑧ Poole   ⑪ Shoreham
③ Salcombe ⑥ Portland   ⑨ Southampton ⑫ Newhaven

British preference for a maritime or "peripheral" strategy, whereby the approach to the western European theatre, and so to the heart of Hitler's Germany, would be made only after a succession of blows aimed at the Mediterranean perimeter had weakened the enemy sufficiently to reduce the inevitable risks involved in a frontal attack. None the less many influential Americans continued to believe that all our strength should be concentrated on the frontal attack, and regarded the Mediterranean operations as "diversions" from the main theatre in France; and we have already seen how it took long and patient negotiations at Casablanca in January, 1943, to convince them that, after clearing the Axis forces from North Africa, Sicily should be the next target.[1] That decision made it inevitable that the cross-Channel undertaking could not be launched before the early summer of 1944; but nothing that has come to light since the war has indicated that, even had the Mediterranean strategy not been adopted, enough combined operations ships and craft, and enough trained men, could have been collected to enable us to mount an assault in north-western France any earlier; for the Americans would certainly not have agreed to starve their Pacific campaigns of ships and men in order to nourish the European project. Indeed, in British eyes it seemed at the time, and still seems, that our American Allies greatly underestimated the difficulties and dangers involved in launching a great combined operation across notoriously stormy, tide-swept waters against the most strongly fortified coast in the world; and had such an attempt been made in 1943, let alone in 1942, it is likely that it would have ended in a repetition of the failure against Dieppe—though on a vastly greater scale.

At the Quebec conference in August, 1943, the British and American representatives agreed that the cross-Channel invasion should take place in May of the following year, and in November the Russians were told of this intention at Teheran. But it was 6th December, 1943, before President Roosevelt nominated General Eisenhower as Supreme Commander for "Overlord," and the long delay in making that appointment produced serious, and one may feel avoidable difficulties for the planners; for as soon as Eisenhower had studied the proposals approved by the Quebec conference he, and also General Montgomery, who was to command the military assault forces, represented that a stronger initial punch on a wider

[1] See p. 285.

front was essential to success. Early in 1944 the decision was therefore taken to increase the assault force to five divisions, and to make additional landings at the base of the Cotentin peninsula with the object of capturing Cherbourg as quickly as possible.[1] But to the Admiralty and the Naval Commander this belated change meant that all the plans had to be revised, and that many more warships, merchantmen and combined operation vessels had to be found; and perhaps worst of all—for we were already suffering from an acute shortage of man-power—crews had to be produced and trained to man the additional ships. In the end the Combined Chiefs of Staff agreed to postpone by a month the landing in southern France, which they had originally intended to launch simultaneously with the invasion of Normandy, so releasing more ships and craft for the northern assault; and the Admiralty paid off large numbers of our older warships in order to release their crews for operation "Neptune." But even these emergency measures could not produce enough ships and men, and an appeal for more help was therefore made to the U.S. Navy. This Admiral E. J. King, the Chief of Naval Operations, at first refused—mainly, it appears, because he considered that we were holding back excessive strength in the Home Fleet. When however in April, 1944, the manifold responsibilities of that fleet in the Arctic and North Sea were fully explained to him, he agreed to send across three battleships, two cruisers and twenty-two destroyers—which was more than we had originally asked for.

In the middle of February Admiral Ramsay issued his outline plan to all the naval authorities, and on 10th April his final plan followed. It comprised a formidable volume of over 700 foolscap pages. After stating that his object was "to secure a lodgment on the continent from which further offensive operations can be developed," he allocated the naval forces required for convoy escort, minesweeping, gun support for the Army, and every other duty which would arise in so vast an undertaking. The actual assault was to be carried out by two big amphibious forces called the Eastern and Western Naval Task Forces. Rear-Admiral Sir Philip Vian was appointed to command the former, which was mainly British and was to land the three divisions of the British Second Army in three sectors (called " Sword," "Juno" and "Gold") on a thirty-mile front to the west of the River Orne; while the Western Task Force, which

[1] See Map p. 367.

was predominantly American, was placed under Rear-Admiral A. G. Kirk, U.S.N., who was to land the American First Army in two sectors (called "Omaha" and "Utah") covering a twenty-mile front to the west of the British assault area.[1] The "Utah" sector was at the base of the Cotentin peninsula, and it was on the success of that assault that the early capture of Cherbourg mainly depended. In order to achieve a rapid build-up two follow-up forces, one British and the other American, were to come in immediately behind the assault forces; and after them would come a steady flow of troop-ships and supply vessels carrying the reinforcements and supplies needed to defeat the inevitable enemy counter-attack, and so enable the Allied armies quickly to take the offensive.

The warships allocated to operation "Neptune" totalled 1,213. They ranged from heavy-gunned battleships and monitors down to midget submarines, and they assembled at the various ports of Britain according to the duties for which they had been nominated. Thus the 107 bombarding ships concentrated at Belfast and in the Clyde, while the 286 destroyers, sloops, frigates and corvettes detailed for escort duty concentrated at the south coast ports from which the convoys would actually set out for France. The combatant warships (excluding combined operations ships and craft) were predominantly British or Canadian (79 per cent); but the U.S. Navy supplied $16\frac{1}{2}$ per cent of the total, and other Allied Navies $4\frac{1}{2}$ per cent. The combined operations vessels included ships and craft of many different designs, and an enormously wide range of functions. There were ships specially fitted to serve as headquarters for the assault force commanders, and proud liners converted to Landing Ships Infantry, with the light assault craft (L.C.A.s) in which the soldiers were to be carried in to the beaches hanging at their davits; there were Landing Ships and Landing Craft Tanks (L.S.T.s and L.C.T.s) to carry land artillery and all types of mechanical vehicles, while others were specially equipped for anti-aircraft defence, or with banks of rockets to fire on to the beaches just before the soldiers leapt ashore; there were special craft for smoke laying, for breaking down concrete obstacles, and for eliminating land mines; there were amphibious tanks capable of swimming themselves ashore, and there were maintenance and repair vessels, and even small floating docks, to help keep the huge fleet in fighting trim. In sum the

[1] See Map p. 367.

functions of the combined operations vessels in "Neptune" represented the result of four years of accumulated British and American experience of amphibious warfare in modern conditions. In all, they numbered no less than 4,126, and although about three-quarters of them flew the White Ensign it should not be forgotten that the majority had been built and armed in America, whence they had been transferred to Britain under the Lend-Lease programme. Nor did the warships and the combined operation vessels comprise by any means the whole of the maritime forces allocated to the operation; for hundreds of merchant ships were requisitioned to undertake duties such as channel marking, salvage work and cable-laying; for towing and attending to the unwieldy components of the artificial harbours; for supplying oil, coal, water and ammunition to the warships which would remain for long periods close off a hostile coast; and for meeting a whole host of other duties—all of which were described and provided for in the Naval Commander's plan. In fact, it is true to say that not only was every type of vessel in the British Merchant Navy—liners, tankers and refrigerator ships, coasters, deep-sea traders and fishing vessels—represented, but all the associated harbour services of Britain also made their contribution; for the tugs, the water carriers, the cargo lighters and the buoy-laying vessels (to name only a few) all provided essential services in "Neptune." No other wartime undertaking can ever have emphasised more clearly the vast ramifications of the maritime services, and how sea power is only effectively wielded when they are all organised by a centralised authority, and inspired by a single commander to achieve one great purpose.

The planners gave much attention to the enemy's probable reaction to the sailing of the invasion fleet. Because the German Navy was by this time very weak in surface ships, and the Allied Air Forces had gained almost complete mastery of the skies, we expected that minelaying and submarine attacks would be the greatest threats; but we knew that about 30 E-boats as well as 10 destroyers or torpedo-boats were based on the Channel coast, and that there were at least 50 U-boats in the Bay of Biscay bases. The organisation to deal with the surface, air and underwater threats was worked out with the utmost care. The Germans would, we considered, regard minelaying, in which they had already displayed great ingenuity, as one of their best defensive weapons;

and we therefore established very elaborate arrangements for sweeping the cross-Channel routes, and for clearing the shallow waters on the other side where our ships would have to anchor. Nearly 300 minesweepers of various types were detailed for this service, which the Royal Navy was to provide for the American as well as the British assault force. To deal with the U-boats four support groups were allocated to the Plymouth command, while six more, reinforced by three escort carriers, would cruise to the west of Land's End, ready to strike whenever a periscope appeared. These ships were, of course, additional to the anti-submarine escorts provided to every convoy. To prevent German E-boats or destroyers molesting the cross-Channel traffic two dozen destroyers and frigates were to patrol on the flanks of the invasion routes; while 22 flotillas of British and American coastal craft (M.T.B.s, M.G.B.s and M.L.s) were allocated to the southern naval commands to protect the heavy traffic moving to and fro along our south coast. To deal with German bombing attacks against the shipping while on passage, and against the vessels crowded in the offshore anchorages, special anti-aircraft ships and craft were included in each assault force; and Fighter Direction Ships fitted with the latest radar sets were provided to control our shore-based fighters.

The towage and placing of the many units needed to form the two artificial harbours (called " Mulberries ") and the five craft shelters ("Gooseberries") associated with them was a major naval undertaking in its own right. The sinking of 55 elderly merchantmen and a few obsolete warships to form one section of the harbour breakwaters was perhaps the simplest part of the project; for towing across and placing the huge concrete caissons (called " Phœnix " units), which displaced up to 6,000 tons each and were to form the rest of the breakwaters, was certainly a very difficult task; while the landing of the many miles of floating pier (called "Whale" units), and their associated pier-heads designed, as Mr. Churchill put it "to go up and down with the tide," presented peculiar problems of their own. In all, the British and American " Mulberries " comprised 400 units of various types, totalling some 1½ million tons; and about 160 tugs were needed to tow them to Seine Bay. When completed the British " Mulberry " was to provide a sheltered anchorage for 7 deep-laden ships of large tonnage, 20 coasters, 400 tugs and auxiliary vessels and 1,000 small craft.

Particular attention was given in the " Neptune " plan to the organisation and training of the heavy bombardment ships; for we had learnt at Dieppe and off Salerno what a vital contribution they could make to success in a combined operation. Each of the five assault forces was given a group of warships for fire support, and the targets initially allocated to them were the 23 heavy German coastal batteries which overlooked the assault area; for it was essential to put them out of action if the first waves of soldiers were to get ashore without suffering heavy losses. Air spotting was arranged for the bombardment ships, as well as ground observation; and as the fighting moved inland they were to be ready instantly to answer any call for fire from the Army—for whom they would act as heavy mobile artillery. The naval support was to continue as long as the battle front was within range of the warships' guns.

In the preparations for " Neptune " no subject was more often debated than the date of " D-Day " and the time of " H-Hour." The avoidance of pilotage errors during the approach to the beaches, the achievement of accurate counter-battery fire by the bombarding ships, and the quick clearance of the underwater obstructions which we knew the Germans were erecting off the assault area were the overriding considerations; and they all pointed to the need to make the first landings in daylight—as the Navy would in any case have preferred. But the clearance of lanes through the beach obstructions by the special teams who would go inshore with the first assault waves was only possible while the tide was fairly low, and that limited still further the choice of D-Day and of H-Hour. It was finally accepted that a moonlight night was essential to ensure navigational accuracy during the invasion fleet's approach, and also to enable the paratroops to be dropped at the chosen points astride the River Orne and at the base of the Cotentin peninsula. Thus the decision was that the actual assault should take place about forty minutes after "nautical twilight" (which begins when the sun is 12 degrees below the horizon) and between 3 and 4 hours before high water. These conditions only coincided on 3 or 4 days in each month; and if bad weather or some other cause necessitated postponement of the operation it would therefore be necessary to wait several weeks before a new opportunity occurred. Plainly such an eventuality might well lead to loss of surprise; but that was a risk which could

not be circumvented. On 8th May General Eisenhower pro-
visionally fixed D-Day for 5th June, and on 23rd the order to prepare
accordingly was passed to all the naval authorities in Britain. This
set in motion the very carefully planned preliminary movements of
warships and merchantmen towards the ports and bases from which
they would actually set out for France. The main focus of assembly
now became the great stretch of sheltered water between the Isle of
Wight and the adjacent mainland—the Solent and Spithead. These
were the anchorages from which our fleets and expeditions had again
and again set out to distant parts of the world, ever since the dawn
of British sea power; and as the month of May, 1944, advanced
towards June they once again became crowded to capacity with
ships wearing the White, Red and Blue Ensigns of the British
maritime services, or the Stars and Stripes of America. If a seaman
of ancient times could have viewed the lines upon lines of ships he
would probably have guessed the broad nature of the enterprise for
which they were destined; but many of the vessels were of such
strange appearance that their functions would have caused him
extreme perplexity. The Solent and Spithead were actually shared
by the British and American task forces; but the plan also provided
for British ships and convoys to use the ports to the east of the Isle
of Wight, and for most of Admiral Kirk's to assemble in the more
westerly harbours. At the executive signal to "carry out operation
Neptune" each convoy or task unit would proceed to sea at its
appointed time, to pass in succession through a sea rendezvous some
fifteen miles to the south-east of the Isle of Wight, and then steam
south towards Seine Bay.

On 25th May, when the Supreme Commander confirmed D-Day
for 5th June, Admiral Ramsay gave the order to all his ships to
open the operation orders; and one can well believe that some of
the young officers in command of the smaller craft must have been
daunted by the size of the document they had to study and digest.
Very severe security restrictions now came into force, and the crews
of all ships were kept virtually cut off from communication with
the land. Because high water occurred forty minutes later as each
day passed H-Hour could not be finally fixed until D-Day had been
irrevocably established; and General Eisenhower still had freedom
to postpone it by twenty-four hours if conditions for 5th June
appeared unfavourable. But a longer postponement would mean

that the whole operation would have to be deferred for several weeks, and the complex " Neptune " machinery which had been so laboriously created, and which was now beginning to turn smoothly like a giant flywheel, would have to be run down and stopped. Though the officers responsible for the operation were well aware that such a possibility existed, they could hardly bear to contemplate the prospect.

On 1st June Admiral Ramsay took over operational command of all the Neptune forces from his " Battle Headquarters" at Southwick House near Portsmouth, and during the next few days the machinery of the naval plan gradually accelerated until, by the morning of the 4th, all the ships and craft were either on the move or ready to sail. That day, however, the weather was so bad that the Supreme Commander took advantage of the option still open to him and postponed the operation for twenty-four hours. By the evening all the convoys which had sailed had re-anchored except one, which missed the postponement signal and had to be turned back by pursuing ships and aircraft. Late on the 4th the meteorologists forecast an improvement in the weather; and General Eisenhower then decided irrevocably that the assault would take place on the 6th. H-Hour was now fixed at 6.30 a.m. for the "Omaha" and "Utah" sectors, and at 7.25 to 7.45 a.m. for the three British assaults. After the commanders had met again very early on the 5th to confirm the decision, Ramsay laconically noted in his diary that "the invasion of France would take place the following day."

Before the 5th June was far advanced a steady stream of ships and craft was heading out to sea from the Solent and Spithead, and from the other assembly ports on the Channel coast. The wind was blowing freshly from the west, and the flat-bottomed landing craft were soon labouring in a choppy sea; but they pressed steadily ahead towards the rendezvous off the Isle of Wight, where they turned south to enter the channels which the minesweepers ahead of them had already cleared and marked.[1] The sweepers carried on to within sight of the French coast; but the enemy's suspicions were not aroused, and as the daylight hours went by the anxious watchers at Battle Headquarters realised that, incredible though it seemed, we really were going to achieve tactical as well as strategic surprise.

[1] See Map p. 367.

Though our deceptive operations off Norway, and the diversionary movements now taking place farther to the east in the Dover Straits, helped to keep the enemy guessing where the blow would fall, it is likely that it was the high degree of command of the air established by the Allied Air Forces which contributed most to this astonishing accomplishment; but on the critical night the German Naval Group Command West had withdrawn its normal patrols because of the weather—believing that, in the prevailing conditions, the invasion fleet would not put to sea. It is thus true to say that, as in the invasion of Sicily,[1] the training of the Allied landing craft crews in the ancient art of seamanship played a vital part in gaining the initial advantage of surprise. Losses attributable to the enemy during the passage across-Channel were insignificant; but a number of the smaller craft succumbed to the weather. None the less, the crucial night of 5th-6th June passed without any developments which might have endangered the operation.

As dawn broke on D-Day the assault convoys were approaching their allotted sectors of the Normandy coast, and at 5 a.m. the heavy bombers of the R.A.F. and U.S.A.A.F. opened the onslaught on the German coastal batteries; but low cloud vitiated the accuracy of the attacks, and many of the bombs fell far inland of the targets. Shortly before the arrival of the assault waves medium bombers and fighters smothered the actual beach defences with lighter bombs and cannon fire. Meanwhile, the heavy bombarding ships were taking up their stations off the coast, and soon after 5.30 a.m. all along the fifty-mile front they opened up on the German batteries with the heaviest rain of shells so far fired at land targets from the sea.[2] The assault convoys had meanwhile anchored in their " lowering positions " seven miles offshore (eleven miles in the case of the American convoys), and had hoisted out their landing craft. At 5 a.m. green lights shone out from the "Juno" and "Sword" beaches, where two midget submarines which were acting as navigation beacons had been patiently waiting for three days. Thus guided the landing craft, which had already formed up in their various groups, moved steadily inshore towards their appointed beaches. Destroyers steamed close on the flanks of each assault force, engaging the beach defences, while the

[1] See pp. 290-1.
[2] Some of the preliminary bombardments by the U.S. Navy in the later stages of the Pacific War were heavier than in " Neptune."

The Invasion of Normandy, June, 1944

The Invasion of Normandy, June, 1944
The blockships and Phœnix caissons of the breakwater

The assault on Walcheren, November, 1944.
Royal Marines disembarking from a tank landing craft

The Invasion of Normandy, June, 1944.
A general view of the pierhead of Mulberry Harbour

gun and rocket craft, and the Army's self-propelled artillery embarked in landing craft, added the weight of their fire during the
approach.

In the British assault area the enemy's reaction was at first slight,
but the rough sea and the beach obstacles caused a good deal of
trouble; for the tide was higher than we had expected, and the
clearance teams could not blast passages through the obstructions in
time to give the landing craft a clear run to the beaches. The whole
"Sword" assault force none the less got ashore almost exactly on
time, and although severe fighting developed on the beaches, which
soon became strewn with wrecked or damaged landing craft, the
soldiers quickly gained a firm hold. Because the "Sword" assault
force's eastern flank was exposed to the fire of the most numerous
German coastal batteries, and was also open to attack by warships
coming out from the mouth of the Seine, it had been given the
strongest covering and bombardment squadron; and throughout the
landings the 15-inch guns of battleships and monitors, and the lighter
weapons of cruisers and destroyers fired incessantly on the German
defences. The "Juno" force next to the west suffered some delays
while on passage, and H-Hour, which was to have been 10–20
minutes later than in the "Sword" and "Gold" sectors, was
accordingly postponed for another ten minutes. Inevitably this
meant that the tide was higher, and that the beach obstacles were
covered by more water than we had hoped; and the result was
that the landing craft grounded among the obstacles instead of short
of them. The Royal Marine's No. 48 Commando on the right
suffered particularly heavily; but all the beaches were quickly
secured, the reserve groups followed in hard on the heels of the
assault brigades, and in the afternoon the first of the follow-up
forces arrived as intended. In the "Gold" sector on the right of
the British assault the beach obstacles were denser than anywhere
else; for the Germans had erected no less than 2,500 of them on
that 3¼-mile stretch of coast, and in consequence many landing craft
were wrecked or damaged. Here another Royal Marine Commando
(No. 47) greatly distinguished itself; for in spite of losing nearly
all its craft and being totally cut off from the rest of the assault
force, the marines managed to capture and hold the little harbour of
Port-en-Bessin, to which we attached considerable importance. For
all the difficulties encountered, by dusk on D-Day all the British

assault forces had gained a firm grip on their beach-heads, and men and vehicles were pouring ashore.

In the American assault area H-Hour was at 6.30 a.m., about an hour earlier than the times selected for the three British assaults; and Admiral Kirk's bombarding ships did not open fire until fifty minutes before touch-down, compared with two hours on the British front. This did not give enough time to neutralise all the coast defences. Furthermore, because the American assault convoys' lowering positions were four miles farther to seaward than the corresponding British positions, the landing craft had to make very long passages inshore. Though the " Utah " force, supported by British as well as American bombarding ships, met only light opposition on the beaches and made rapid progress inland, in the adjacent " Omaha " sector serious difficulties were encountered. Those beaches were strongly held and well defended, and heavy surf was breaking on them. Moreover, the bombing and bombardments had not neutralised the coast defence guns, and in consequence the landing craft suffered severe losses on the way in, and the groups lost cohesion. The underwater obstacles thus were not cleared before the assault waves arrived, and a good deal of confusion arose in the approaches to the beaches. For some hours the situation was difficult; but order was restored, and in the afternoon the defenders began to give way. Before nightfall a satisfactory beachhead had been won by the " Omaha " force.

As D-Day drew to a close it became plain to those who had been watching and waiting in understandable anxiety at headquarters that the success of the assault had surpassed our most sanguine hopes. Though losses of landing craft had been heavy, the rest of the invasion fleet had suffered little; 132,715 men and many thousands of vehicles had been landed; and the casualties suffered by the Army (about 4,200 British and 6,600 American) had been astonishingly light. In retrospect it is clear that the very careful planning and training, and the achievement of surprise, were the chief factors which brought success; but the gun support given to the assault forces by the large and small warships undoubtedly contributed enormously to the breaching of Hitler's vaunted Atlantic Wall at such small cost. It now remained to be seen whether we could build up the strength of the invasion army quickly enough to defeat the expected counter-attack.

The next phase opened well for the Allies; for the night dispositions made for the protection of the shipping in the crowded waters of Seine Bay frustrated the German E-boats and the Luftwaffe's air attacks. Mines soon became our chief anxiety; for it was now that the enemy began to lay the pressure-operated "oyster" mine, against which no effective counter-measure had yet been devised. It was the American task force that at first suffered the more heavily from those weapons; but later in June the greatest difficulties arose in the British sector, where a considerable number of ships were sunk or damaged by mines.

While the assault brigades were establishing themselves on shore and expanding their beach-heads the follow-up convoys were already moving down-Channel from the east or up-Channel from the more westerly British ports. Some started out from the Thames estuary, and the passage of large troopships through the Dover Straits emphasised the extent to which we had regained control of those long-disputed narrows. On D-plus-one Day no less than eight such convoys arrived in Seine Bay, exactly at the times laid down in the plans; but the choppy sea caused delays and difficulties in unloading —and continued to do so for many days. None the less, by the middle of June half a million Allied soldiers and 77,000 vehicles had been landed, and the strength of the British and American Armies had reached a point where they could take the offensive with confidence.

Throughout the days following the assault one of the most urgent needs was to press ahead with the artificial harbours and craft shelters; for the speed of unloading on the beaches depended chiefly on the ferry craft not being delayed by unfavourable weather. By 10th June all the blockships had been sunk in place to form the first section of the breakwater for the British " Mulberry," and the long and clumsy tows of " Phœnix " caissons and " Whale " pier units were beginning to arrive. A week later both the artificial harbours were taking shape, the small ports of Courseulles and Port-en-Bessin were in use, and unloading had been speeded up by ordering L.S.T.s and coasters to beach themselves and remain high and dry when the tide went out—thus eliminating the need to transfer their cargoes to ferry craft. Meanwhile, the special force (called " Pluto "), which had been organised to lay pipelines from the anchorages to enable tankers to pump their fuel supplies directly ashore, was making good progress; but the scheme for laying such lines right across the Channel encountered many difficulties, and did not prove its worth during the assault phase.

Though the weather encountered during the first period of operation " Neptune " was never really favourable, and the choppy sea and the surf breaking on the beaches continued to tax the smaller vessels severely, by the middle of June there seemed to be no doubt that the Allied Navies would successfully meet the requirements of the vitally important build-up; but the gods who rule wind and weather decided to put the sea services to a very severe test before yielding to their resolution and ingenuity.

A violent storm in the English Channel in June is a rare occurrence, but by daylight on the 19th it was plain to all the " Neptune " forces that they were to be treated to one. For more than three days the wind blew strongly from the north-east, with gusts rising to gale force. Heavy seas swept over the half-constructed breakwaters to crash on shore with devastating strength. Ships dragged their anchors all over the place, landing craft were swept helplessly towards the rocks and on to the beaches, where they piled up—sometimes on top of each other—in utter confusion. Unloading came to a standstill, and the crews of the warships and merchantmen could only struggle to save their ships. When the wind finally eased on the 22nd the whole assault area was strewn with a vast flotsam of wreckage; for over 800 landing craft had been driven ashore. Admiral Ramsay at once took emergency steps to restore the situation; but the storm had deprived the Allied armies of 105,000 tons of stores and 20,000 vehicles, and the deficiencies could not be fully made up for another month. Furthermore, the American " Mulberry " was so badly wrecked that it was decided not to attempt repair, but to concentrate all the remaining material on completing the less damaged British harbour. This important task was accomplished on 19th July, by which time the three piers and their associated floating roadways were all being used to disembark stores and vehicles directly on shore; but, largely because of the storm, completion of the artificial harbour took twice as long as we had planned.

We must now retrace our steps to D-Day in order to see how the German naval command in western France reacted to the invasion of Normandy. At the time when the assault convoys crossed the

Channel the special groups of U-boats which had, on Hitler's orders, been held in the Biscay ports and in Norway were all in harbour; but as soon as the enemy realised that the expected invasion really had been launched the Biscay U-boats, and also the three destroyers which were lying in the Gironde estuary, were ordered to proceed to the scene of the landings. Our air patrols however quickly reported the enemy's movements, and the German destroyers, which had been severely harried from the air, accordingly put into Brest. Late on the 8th, having collected one reinforcement, they put to sea again, and in the early hours of the following morning they were brought to action by the 10th Destroyer Flotilla to the west of Cherbourg. After a sharp running fight one enemy (ZH.1) was sunk, and another (Z.32) was driven ashore to become a total loss. The other two regained Brest, but one of them (Z.24) had suffered such severe damage that she was out of action for a long time. Thus was the German destroyer threat quickly eliminated. Meanwhile Coastal Command's air patrols were dealing with the Biscay U-boats very firmly, and between the 6th and the 10th they sank no less than six of them and damaged many others. Though U-boats sank two British frigates in the Channel on the 15th, it was not until then—nine days after the invasion had been launched—that one solitary boat reached its intended patrol position off the assault area; and she did no more than sink one L.S.T. Some of the Norway boats had meanwhile left for the Channel by the long route round the north of Scotland; but, as with the Biscay boats, their movements did not escape the attention of Coastal Command's watchful air patrols, which sank six of them in the North Sea before the end of June. These severe losses did not however at once deter the U-boat command, and during the latter part of the month we became aware that half a dozen enemies were slowly creeping up-Channel towards the convoy routes. The Admiralty at once shifted our sea and air patrols farther to the east, and before the end of the month they accounted for three more enemies. The only unsatisfactory feature of the period was that almost all the sunk boats were not fitted with the " Schnorkel " breathing-tube;[1] and we found that those which were so fitted had gained a high degree of immunity from the searching radars of our anti-U-boat aircraft. The realisation that our short-wave airborne radar, which had hitherto served us so

[1] See p. 303.

outstandingly well, had lost a good deal of its effectiveness was a matter for serious concern; for when U.984 torpedoed four ships in a Channel convoy in quick succession on 29th June she showed what might happen if a considerable number of " Schnorkel " boats penetrated to our shipping routes. Fortunately this proved an isolated success to the enemy, and taken as a whole the U-boats' effort had little impact on the build-up of the invasion armies.

As to the German E-boats, though they continued to prove elusive targets, a number of them were sunk in the many night encounters which took place between them and our patrols and escorts; but it was the R.A.F.'s heavy bombing attacks on their bases at Havre and Boulogne on 14th and 15th June which did most to eliminate their threat. Lastly, the Luftwaffe's bombing attacks on the ships crowded in the assault anchorages, though often a nuisance, never came near to disrupting the operation. Right to the end the pressure-operated mine remained the most dangerous of the enemy's weapons.

Throughout June some of the heavy bombarding ships remained off the French coast to answer calls for fire support from the Army; and their shooting proved extremely effective against enemy concentrations of men and vehicles. To give only one example, on the 30th the *Rodney* astonished the Germans by planting her 16-inch shells squarely on tanks which were massing for a counter-attack 17 miles inland from the " Gold " beaches. Again and again did such ships earn the warm appreciation of the soldiers, and the frequent lamentations of the German army commanders also testify to the effectiveness of the naval gunfire.

Towards the end of June conditions in the assault area became sufficiently stabilised to enable the sea-going naval commands to be replaced by a Flag Officer, British Assault Area, on shore at Courseulles; and on 30th June and 3rd July Admirals Vian and Kirk therefore returned to Britain with the knowledge that their tasks had been magnificently accomplished. Meanwhile, the American Army was closing in on Cherbourg, and a special bombardment force of British and American warships was formed to neutralise the powerful batteries defending the approaches to the port. In fact, this bombardment proved one of the less successful of such undertakings, and most of the ships suffered damage without doing appreciable harm to the German guns. Cherbourg however fell to the land forces on 26th June, and the British and American navies at once set about restoring the shattered port facilities, and clearing the hundreds of mines which the Germans had laid in the harbour; but the destruction wrought by the enemy was so widespread, and the mines were so densely sown, that it was mid-July before any deep-draught ships could enter in safety. Thereafter the port of Cherbourg and the artificial harbour at Arromanches jointly met the needs of the invasion armies until they had broken out of the original perimeter.

The good progress made on land in June enabled the naval forces employed in "Neptune" gradually to be reduced, and by the beginning of July some gun support ships and large numbers of combined operation vessels were withdrawn for further service in the Mediterranean, where preparations for the assault on southern France were in train. On 5th July the millionth Allied soldier stepped ashore in France, and that day may be taken as the end of the assault phase of operation "Neptune." As Admiral Ramsay said in his report, the landings were carried out in all essentials "exactly as planned"; but a great measure of the success achieved can confidently be attributed to the superb organisation created by him and his staff, and to the very careful training programme which the soldiers and sailors of each assault force underwent before a single craft set out for France. It is perhaps as a feat of organisation rather than as a fighting victory that "Neptune" will be remembered; for the weakness of the enemy at sea and in the air, and the vast superiority enjoyed by the Allies in both elements, actually saved the Allied navies from having to do a great deal of fighting in order to establish and maintain firm command of the Channel. But it was of course our control of the oceans across which so many of the men and so much of their equipment had firstly been carried, and then our control of the narrow seas, which made the entire undertaking possible. As so often in the past, it was sea power wisely deployed and energetically wielded that brought victory to the land forces sent to attack the enemy in a theatre of our own choice.

CHAPTER XXI

THE ADVANCE INTO EUROPE

6th July–31st December, 1944

" The fleet and army acting in concert seem to be the natural
bulwark of these Kingdoms."

Thomas More Molyneux, *Conjunct Expeditions* (1759).

ALTHOUGH at the Cairo conference in November, 1943, the
Combined Chiefs of Staff had agreed that a landing (called
operation " Anvil ") should be made in southern France to coincide
as nearly as possible with the Normandy assault, such a strategy had
never had much appeal to the British representatives; and when it
became plain that, because the capture of Rome had been so long
delayed, the armies in Italy would not have advanced nearly as far
as we had hoped by the time that the new operation was to be
mounted, the British Chiefs of Staff urged that it should be
abandoned. Their view was that by concentrating enough strength
on the Italian campaign we could not only win an important victory
in the Lombardy plains, but would draw away from Normandy
just as large enemy forces as might be diverted to counter a landing
in southern France. The debate on these issues was long-drawn;
but the Americans would not yield, and as they were to provide by
far the largest share of the forces, it was inevitable that they should
have the decisive say regarding the use to which they were to be
put. On 1st July, 1944, the Prime Minister therefore gave way "in
the broadest interests of Anglo-American co-operation," and later
in that month the code word for the operation was changed to
" Dragoon "—a word chosen by Mr. Churchill which, whether
intentionally or not, aptly described his feelings over the pressure
to which he had been subjected. We will return to the planning
and execution of the new undertaking shortly.

384

After the fall of Rome on 4th June the Fifth and Eighth Armies advanced rapidly up Italy as far as the "Gothic Line," which the Germans had constructed between Pisa on the west coast and Pesaro on the Adriatic,[1] while the Allied navies continued their arduous but unspectacular work of opening up captured ports, keeping the land forces supplied, and supporting their flanks where they came down to the sea. While the long Anzio stalemate was still in progress we had become aware of the value of the island of Elba to the enemy, and had originally intended to seize it by assault from the sea towards the end of May; but sufficient trained forces could not be collected in time. After the capture of Rome and the advance northwards to the Gothic Line the theatre commanders decided to go ahead with the seizure of the island, even though its importance had been greatly reduced; and in the middle of June British and American landing craft accordingly embarked French troops in Corsica. The naval forces were commanded by Rear-Admiral T. Troubridge, who had recently carried out the northern assault at Anzio, and early on the 17th June, after British mine-sweepers had cleared the approaches, landings were made at several points. German resistance was stubborn and, as so often before, we found that the sacrifice of preliminary bombardments in the interests of surprise was a mistake. Furthermore, because of the danger from mines the naval commander was not given any heavy bombarding ships for this operation; and the small gun vessels and support landing craft could not deal effectively with the German batteries which engaged the assault forces as they approached the beaches. Not until heavy bombers had been called up did German resistance weaken, but on 19th the garrison surrendered. One interesting sidelight on the assault on Elba is that it was the first time since Gallipoli that mules were landed to provide transport for the troops' supplies; and as the rocky tracks leading from the beaches were ill-suited to vehicles they proved their value.

Meanwhile the plan for operation "Dragoon" was being prepared at Allied Forces Headquarters near Naples, and 15th August had been named as D-Day. Though this was much later than had at first been intended, and with the lapse of about nine weeks since the Normandy landings the original strategic purpose of the operation was no longer valid, the landing craft and bombard-

[1] See Map pp. 112-13.

ment ships could not be assembled any sooner. Sir John Cunningham, the naval C.-in-C., placed the responsibility for the naval side
of the assault in the hands of Vice-Admiral H. K. Hewitt, U.S.N.,
and he proceeded to apply all the accumulated experience of the
previous combined operations in which he had taken part. Thus
the assault was to be made in full daylight after the heaviest possible
preliminary bombardments; and a special force of seven British
and two American escort carriers was given to Rear-Admiral
Troubridge in order that its 200 naval fighters should be instantly
available to provide cover for the invasion fleet and close air support
for the troops. The assault forces were to consist of three American
divisions and a few French Commandos, all of whom would
embark at Naples, while a French armoured brigade was to be
carried to the scene of the landing from Oran. The follow-up forces
comprised seven French infantry divisions, and as two of them as
well as the three American assault divisions came from General
Alexander's command in Italy it was inevitable that "Dragoon"
should bring his campaign to a temporary halt. The main landings
were to take place in three sectors on a 45-mile stretch of coast to
the east of Marseilles, while a fourth assault force was to seize certain
outlying islands which we believed the enemy to have fortified.[1]
Each assault force was given a bombardment group of British,
French or American warships, some of which had come straight
from taking part in operation "Neptune"; while about 140
British and American minesweepers were to clear the approaches
and the inshore waters. The landing ships and craft were predominantly American, but the Royal Navy was represented in
almost every one of the many different categories. In all 881
warships and some 1,370 smaller craft were allocated to the operation; and of the former 65 per cent were American and 33 per cent
British—a reversal of the proportions supplied by the two main
Allies for the Normandy operation.

Convoys for all the assault and follow-up forces were organised
on the principles which had by this time become well established,
and between 9th and 13th August the main groups sailed from
Naples and Taranto. The gun support ships assembled at Naples,
Palermo, Malta and Taranto, and concentrated at sea with the
assault forces to which they had been allocated; while Admiral

[1] See Map pp. 112-13.

Troubridge's escort carriers sailed from Malta on 12th August to reach their flying-off position at dawn on D-Day. H-Hour was at 8 a.m. on the 15th, and after nearly two hours of heavy bombing and bombardments the assault troops encountered only feeble resistance. Losses were extremely light (on the naval side less than a dozen ships, most of which were small), and by the evening of 17th 87,000 men, 12,500 vehicles and 46,000 tons of stores had been put ashore. The advance inland was rapid, and quickly took the main American force beyond the range of the warships' guns; but the French Army, which quickly swung westwards towards the great ports of Toulon and Marseilles, still had need of their support. Enemy air opposition was so slight that the carrier air crews were not severely tested; but they did excellent work in spotting for the bombardment ships, in giving close support to the troops, and in harrying the retreating enemy columns. So ended the assault phase of operation "Dragoon." Though superbly organised and executed, it is difficult not to feel that in it we took a sledge hammer to crack a nut.

When the French Army approached Toulon some of the bombarding ships were switched to the duty of neutralising the powerful batteries defending the naval base; but, as at Cherbourg, the well-sited guns proved very hard to put out of action.[1] On 27th August, however, Toulon fell to the French land forces, which captured Marseilles on the following day. In both cases the mine-sweepers at once cleared the approaches to the ports, neither of which was severely damaged. As we had also seized Port de Bouc, twenty miles west of Marseilles, to provide an unloading port for fuel supplies, by the beginning of September ample capacity to handle all the armies' needs had been secured. On 25th September Admiral Hewitt's command came to an end, but a reduced force of warships remained off the French coast to give support to the troops advancing eastwards towards the Italian frontier.

At the time of the "Dragoon" landings the German Navy possessed very little strength in the western Mediterranean, and its reaction was feeble. Early in September they did, however, attempt to use their special assault craft, collectively known as "Small Battle Units," against the invasion shipping. We had already encountered such weapons as the human torpedoes (*Marders*),

[1] See p. 382.

one-man submarines (*Molch*) and explosive motor-boats (*Linsen*) at Anzio and off the Normandy beaches;[1] and we had found that, provided our patrol craft were alert, we had little to fear from them. In " Dragoon " they suffered heavy losses without accomplishing anything significant.

In July and August, 1944, the U-boats based on Toulon suffered heavily from American bombing attacks, and the last survivors were scuttled shortly before the port fell. So ended the U-boat campaign in the western Mediterranean; while the capture of the airfields in southern France put an end to the troublesome bombing attacks against our convoys moving along the north African coast. With the two chief threats against our shipping simultaneously eliminated we were now able to begin sailing merchantmen independently— so releasing more escort vessels to the Eastern Fleet, where there was still important work for them to do. Because there were now few targets for the Mediterranean submarine flotillas they too were reorganised at this time, and in September the famous 10th Flotilla, which had achieved so much and endured such heavy losses at the time of Malta's ordeal, was disbanded. Between 1st June, 1940, when Italy entered the war, and the end of 1944 our submarines sank 286 enemy supply ships totalling over a million tons in the Mediterranean, as well as four cruisers and 17 destroyers or torpedo-boats; but perhaps their most important accomplishment was the destruction of no less than 21 enemy submarines (16 Italian and 5 German); which showed that as an anti-submarine vessel the submarine had great possibilities—a view which experience in other theatres fully confirmed. The campaign did, however, cost the submarine service a heavy price; since 45 British boats and 5 Allied boats working under our control did not return from Mediterranean patrols.

In the Adriatic excellent progress was made in August and September, 1944, when we made many small landings on the Dalmatian islands in conjunction with the Yugoslav partisans, and our coastal craft repeatedly harried the convoys in which the Germans were trying to withdraw their garrisons. With our hold on the offshore waters constantly being tightened and extended, the condition of all the German forces in Yugoslavia, Albania and western Greece became increasingly precarious; for not only was

[1] See pp. 334 and 391-2.

it becoming impossible to keep them supplied, but their best line of retreat to the north was now imperilled. During the autumn months our destroyers and coastal craft reached ever farther up the Adriatic, and fought a series of sharp actions with the German light warships and convoy escorts, which they generally worsted. The minesweepers also worked steadily up the coast, clearing the approaches to each captured port and so enabling supplies for the starving civilian population to be rushed in. In September Split and Zara were both captured, and British cruisers at once arrived to organise relief work. By the end of the year the German hold was reduced to the Istrian Peninsula; but our light warships were very active in the approaches to Trieste, Fiume and Pola,[1] and were gradually bringing the enemy's supply traffic to a complete stop. All the rest of the Dalmatian coast was securely in Allied hands.

Across the Adriatic in Italy Allied purposes had not, however, prospered equally. In September an attempt by the weakened Fifth Army to breach the Gothic Line and open the way into the Po valley failed to reach the key city of Bologna, and in the following month the winter weather put a stop to all major offensive operations. Thus was a decision in Italy deferred for another six months and more.

Early in September the Germans began to withdraw their garrisons from southern Greece, Crete and the Ægean islands, and we at once formed a striking force of escort carriers, cruisers and destroyers under Rear-Admiral Troubridge to put a stop to the movements by sea. In the middle of the month that force worked for the first time to the north of Crete—the waters in which the Royal Navy had suffered so grievously in May, 1941.[2] Now the roles were reversed; for it was our ships which had ample air cover, and it was the enemy who was trying to carry out evacuations. On 19th September Troubridge's destroyers located and sank U.407 off Crete, and five days later American bombers attacked Salamis and destroyed the last U-boats in the whole theatre. The total cost of the Mediterranean campaign to the Germans was 68 U-boats;[3] but they sank 95 Allied merchantmen totalling nearly 450,000 tons,

---

[1] See Map pp. 112-13.   [2] See pp. 160-1 and 163-5.
[3] This figure includes 6 boats bound for the Mediterranean which were sunk in the Western approaches to Gibraltar.

as well as the battleship *Barham*, the carriers *Ark Royal* and *Eagle*, four cruisers and 12 destroyers. In sum therefore it seems true to say that the price paid by the U-boat arm for its successes was not unreasonable; for the Mediterranean boats undoubtedly helped to prop up a tottering Italy in 1941, and caused us considerable embarrassment throughout the succeeding three years.

After Admiral Troubridge's first operation to the north of Crete he swept up into the Ægean, where his carrier aircrews and surface ships attacked many shore targets and sank scores of small craft engaged on evacuating the island garrisons; but the Germans persisted and, to their credit, succeeded in removing some 37,000 men to temporary safety on the Greek mainland, largely in transport aircraft working by night. October saw the virtually complete elimination of enemy sea power from the long-contested waters of the Ægean, and the final withdrawal of the Germans from southern Greece. British minesweepers moved into Piræus, the port of Athens, and other harbours hard on the heels of the retreating enemy, and on 15th October the relief force which we had organised (called operation " Manna ") began to arrive. Unfortunately the German withdrawal was followed by an attempt by the Communists to seize power in Greece, and virulent civil strife soon broke out. On the Prime Minister's authority a British division was at once carried from Italy to Athens; but for many weeks the situation was critical, and our troops and warships were involved in severe fighting. The British policy was that a new government of Greece should be elected by constitutional processes; but it was not until the middle of January 1945 that we were in control of all Attica, and the Communist attempt to seize power had been finally defeated. Though the troubles in Greece were a tragic experience, especially to the Royal Navy warships which were sent to hold the ring in all the country's ports throughout those anxious weeks, we may be thankful for the resolution with which the British Government acted—though with scant sympathy from our American Allies; for it undoubtedly forestalled a situation which would have been fraught with danger for post-war Europe. We may also remark that, as so often in the past, it was our maritime power which enabled the British policy to be put into effect with such promptitude and firmness.

By the end of 1944 Allied maritime control had thus been fully reasserted throughout the whole Mediterranean, except for small areas in the north Ligurian Sea and at the head of the Adriatic; and German merchant shipping had been virtually eliminated from the whole theatre. During the last seven months of the year enemy losses of merchant shipping amounted to 378 ships of nearly 700,000 tons; and in addition our sea and air forces sank a very large number of small craft and auxiliary warships employed on supply duties. The contrast between the enemy's prospects and our own cannot be better demonstrated than by the fact that we, with a vastly greater traffic to defend, lost no more than five ships (7,000 tons) in the same period. In such circumstances it was certain that, whereas the Allied land forces would continue to gain strength from the steady stream of seaborne supplies and reinforcements reaching them, the Axis armies would suffer from slow strangulation.

The great change in the strategic situation which came about in the Mediterranean as 1944 drew to a close enabled us to make a major redistribution of our naval forces. Many of the larger warships passed straight to the Indian Ocean by way of the Suez Canal; since plans to build up a new fleet to join hands with our American Allies in the Pacific were now far advanced. A considerable number of escort vessels had however to be brought home; for the " Schnorkel " U-boats were causing us a good deal of trouble in our inshore waters. It is therefore to the Home theatre that we must next turn, to review the events which had taken place since our invasion army had gained a firm hold on the Normandy beach-heads.

Throughout July the Royal Navy's heavy bombarding ships, which were now meeting the needs of the American Army as well as those of the British land forces, were constantly answering calls for long-range gun support; while stores and reinforcements continued to pour ashore through the British " Mulberry " or over the beaches. German minelaying, generally done at night by aircraft, was still the chief cause of trouble; but the E-boats now reappeared in some strength, and the enemy also sent a large variety of his " Small Battle Units " to attack our offshore shipping. To deal with these craft, and also provide the British Army with close gun support on its exposed eastern flank, Admiral Ramsay formed a special squadron of small gun vessels. By day the squadron closed the shore to answer calls for fire; but after nightfall its craft patrolled around the anchorage to intercept any enemies who might attempt to penetrate into it. This " Support Squadron Eastern Flank " fought many close-range actions with E-boats and Small Battle Units at this time, and nearly always frustrated their purposes. To give only one example, on the night of 2nd-3rd August the Germans sent out twenty explosive motor-boats (*Linsen*), about five dozen human torpedoes (*Marders*) and a number of E-boats equipped with a new long-running circling torpedo (*Dackel*). Their arrival in the small hours of the morning gave the defenders a lively time; but few of the German special craft survived, and the damage that they inflicted was totally out of proportion to the effort made.

Early in July, for all that the first attempts by the U-boats to penetrate into the Channel had proved disastrous, the enemy sent reinforcements from Brest. Though they were all Schnorkel-fitted, and so enjoyed a considerable degree of immunity from our air patrols, they fared very badly at the hands of our convoy escorts and support groups. Between 1st July and 4th August no less than nine U-boats were destroyed in the Channel—all but two of them at the hands of our warships; and in return for those heavy losses they inflicted little damage. U.763 did, however, have a remarkable experience at this time, and lived to tell the tale; for after being heavily attacked she lost all accuracy of navigation, and un-intentionally penetrated well inside the closely guarded waters of Spithead! Moreover, she extricated herself from what must have seemed a highly precarious situation, and got safely back to Brest.

On 3rd July the Americans struck westwards from the base of the Brittany peninsula with the object of capturing Brest, which we badly needed as an additional entry for supplies and reinforcements. British warships came across to give support with their heavy guns, while landing craft put ashore reinforcements in small ports close up to the front; but German resistance was very stubborn, and progress was slow. The threat to Brest did, however, cause the U-boat command to shift its forces firstly to the more southerly Biscay ports (La Pallice and Bordeaux) and then, in the middle of August, to Norway. We, however, anticipated that the Germans would attempt to save as much as possible from the trap which was now closing on their bases in western France, and so started a com-bined sea and air offensive to assert our control of the long-contested waters of the Bay of Biscay. Home Fleet cruisers and destroyers therefore came south to work from Plymouth, while the R.A.F.'s Bomber Command attacked the bases themselves, and Coastal Command aircraft swept the inshore waters in strength. The offensive lasted for three weeks during which 12 U-boats, nearly 60,000 tons of merchant shipping, two destroyers and a great many smaller warships were sunk. By 27th August the German naval forces on the Biscay coast had almost ceased to exist. The only unsatisfactory feature of the period was that the enemy managed successfully to transfer no less than 31 U-boats to Norway. In part this arose because, being Schnorkel-fitted, they eluded our air patrols, and in part because a clever diversion of some boats to the Channel, where in August they did better than in any previous month, kept our attention away from the movements then in progress farther to the west. None the less by the end of that month four more U-boats had been sunk in the narrow seas. As the surviving Channel boats also then began to withdraw to Norway it can be said that the closing days of August, 1944, mark the end of the U-boat campaign against our invasion traffic. Though they had caused us to deploy a very large sea and air effort, they never came near to inflicting such losses as would imperil the build-up of our armies; and the attempt to interfere with our convoys was very costly to the enemy.

The land assault on Brest itself opened on 25th August with strong naval support, including the 15-inch guns of the famous *Warspite*; but it was 18th September before Allied troops entered the town. The capture of the Brittany base did, however, mark an important stage in the restoration of our control over the Western Approaches to the British Isles. Ever since June, 1940, it had been the German surface warships, submarines and aircraft working from western France which had constituted the chief threat against our Atlantic shipping; and together they had forced us to bring in all our convoys round the north of Ireland, and to send our north-south traffic by circuitous routes far out into the Atlantic. Now the Admiralty was able to route convoys through the South-Western Approaches, so shortening the journeys and enabling our mercantile tonnage to be used more economically. At the end of August the combined South Atlantic and Gibraltar homeward convoys SL 167/MKS 58 therefore sailed north close to the Portuguese coast, and approached British ports by way of the South-Western Approaches; and thereafter that became the normal practice for outward as well as homeward convoys. Thus did a success on land bring relief and aid to those responsible for the conduct of the war at sea.

Meanwhile important developments had taken place on the Normandy front; for after substantial German forces had been trapped in a pocket around Falaise the Germans began a headlong retreat towards the Seine and, on 20th August, the British Second Army struck eastwards along the Channel coast. Havre was at first by-passed, but Dieppe was captured on 1st September, and Ostend a week later. Moreover on the 4th British forces entered Antwerp, to find the great port virtually undamaged. To the Navy it seemed obvious that the first need was to clear the Germans from the banks of the Scheldt, and then to seize the island of Walcheren at the mouth of that river;[1] for until those two purposes had been accomplished we could make no use whatsoever of Antwerp. Indeed, the advance across France and Belgium had been so rapid that the Army had far outrun its supplies, and was almost immobilised until such time as we could land replenishments much closer to the new front than the Normandy ports. But in fact no such strategy was adopted. In the first place substantial forces remained behind to besiege the French Channel ports. Havre was assaulted from the sea, land and air early in September and surrendered on the 12th; but it was 22nd before Boulogne fell, and 1st October before Calais was captured. In each case naval parties moved in quickly; but the ports had been so thoroughly wrecked, obstructed and mined that it was obvious that some weeks would elapse before any substantial quantity of supplies could be unloaded in them. These events marked the end of the build-up phase of operation "Neptune," and on 7th September the last beaches ("Juno") were closed and the Flag Officer, British Assault Area (Admiral Rivett-Carnac), moved his headquarters from Arromanches to Rouen. Since the end of the assault phase we had landed over 350,000 men, 152,000 vehicles and nearly 1½ million tons of stores—mostly through the original assault area; the defending warships had fought 28 actions with enemy surface ships, and had swept over 600 mines; while the large and small bombarding ships had engaged hundreds of targets at the Army's

[1] See Map p. 74.

request. Now the beaches which had hummed with activity for over three months gradually returned to their pre-"Neptune" state of quiet; and the warships formerly engaged in guarding the anchorages moved eastwards up-Channel to prepare for new duties.

The capture of Antwerp brought to a head the divergent views of Field-Marshal Montgomery and General Eisenhower regarding the strategy to be adopted on land; for while the former wished to strike north-east into the heart of Germany on a "narrow front" the latter preferred to advance to the Rhine and beyond on a broader front. On 17th September the airborne assault was launched at Arnhem, but narrowly failed to gain a bridgehead over the lower Rhine. Nor did Montgomery's first attempt to strike north-east from Antwerp prosper; and in the meanwhile no progress was being made with the eviction of the enemy from the banks of the Scheldt. At this critical juncture the Combined Chiefs of Staff were in session at Quebec, and on 10th September they urged on General Eisenhower the need to gain the use of Antwerp as soon as possible. Admiral Ramsay was, of course, greatly concerned at the delay in opening the Scheldt, and on 5th October he vigorously disputed Montgomery's assertion that he "could take the Ruhr without Antwerp." It was, however, the middle of the month before the 21st Army Group commander concentrated his efforts on getting the river opened.

Meanwhile plans were being made to carry out a seaborne assault on the key island of Walcheren simultaneously with an attack from the landward side; but in the execution of the former purpose we were handicapped by the fact that the Royal Marine Special Service Brigade, which was trained for amphibious warfare, had been employed as infantry ever since the Normandy landings, and had recently been engaged in besieging Dunkirk. Not until 27th September was the brigade withdrawn from that static role and brought forward to Ostend; and even then, as Army type landing vehicles were to be used against Walcheren, some retraining was plainly desirable. It was thus late October before the assault force was ready. Admiral Ramsay had meanwhile nominated Captain A. F. Pugsley to take command of the naval side, and early on 1st November his 181 landing craft started out from Ostend to assault the heavily fortified island, while heavy bombarding ships came across from England to give their support. Meanwhile the Canadians on the south bank of the Scheldt had at last captured Breskens, on the opposite shore to Walcheren, and their comrades were slowly fighting their way across very difficult country, much of which was flooded, along the north bank of the river towards the key island. It was from Breskens that a Commando was carried across the Scheldt early on 1st November, and successfully captured Flushing. At 9.45 a.m. that morning, although the weather was so unfavourable that our bombers were grounded and the bombarding ships were severely handicapped, Brigadier B. W. Leicester led the Marines in to assault on either side of a gap which the bombers had blasted earlier in the island's protective dyke at Westkapelle; but the enemy was fully alert, large and small guns poured a heavy fire on to the assault craft, and when the Marines got ashore furious fighting developed on the dyke. None the less they made steady progress and, with the Canadians advancing on to Walcheren from the landward side, the fate of the German garrison was plainly sealed. On 8th November the German commander of the island and 29,000 of his troops surrendered. British casualties were heavy, especially among the Royal Marine assault force and Captain Pugsley's support vessels and troop-carrying craft. But in the assault on Walcheren, where the opposition was little if at all less strong than in the Dieppe raid, the Royal Marines added another glorious chapter to their long history.

The sweeping of the seventy miles of estuary and river leading to Antwerp started on 4th November, before Walcheren had actually surrendered. No less than ten flotillas were employed, and they swept a great many mines; but progress was so rapid that on 26th the first merchantman passed safely up-river. Thereafter a steady stream of convoys sailed between the Thames and Antwerp, and although the enemy did his utmost with E-boats and Small Battle Units to interrupt the traffic, our escort forces sank many of them, and losses among the merchantmen were few. Thus, nearly twelve weeks after the capture of Antwerp, were we at last able to use it as the main entry for the Army's supplies and reinforcements.

It is, of course, impossible to prove that if we had concentrated on opening the river Scheldt early in September, 1944, we could have restored the Army's mobility in time for it to strike into Germany while the enemy was still off-balance and regrouping his forces; but what seems undeniable is, firstly, that without the use of Antwerp the Allied land forces could not undertake a large scale new offensive and, secondly, that the river banks could have been cleared very much sooner. Had we merely "masked" the German garrisons in the Channel ports, which in any case were so badly wrecked that they could not handle any appreciable quantity of supplies for many weeks, and driven ahead for Breskens early in September, we could surely have gained control of the south bank more quickly—for all that the country was intersected by many easily defended canals, and large areas were under water; and the capture of Breskens, besides getting half-way towards opening the river, would have trapped the large numbers of the German Fifteenth Army which, retreating from the Seine valley, actually managed to cross the Scheldt and reform to the north of the river. But the Supreme Commander gave no strategic directions to accomplish such a purpose. One may also feel that our forces around Antwerp were fully adequate to clearing the north bank of the river soon after the port itself was captured; but the Army Group commander's eyes were at the time turned to the north-east—in the direction in which he desired to thrust into Germany. Though it is a tradition of the Royal Navy that, once the Army has been landed, all its own interests should be subordinated to those of the soldiers, it is difficult not to feel that in the case of Antwerp that tradition was carried too far; and that may have contributed to the committal of a strategic error of some magnitude. Again and again, from the time of the Spanish Armada, throughout the Dutch wars of the 17th century and those against France in the 18th, down to the despatch of the Naval Brigade to Antwerp in 1914, has control of the Scheldt played a vital part in British strategy. It may be therefore that it was to the Naval Staff and the Admiralty that we should have looked for a full appreciation of its importance in 1944. Yet no joint plans had been prepared in advance to take immediate advantage of the capture of the historic port; and the rapid preparation of such plans was probably handicapped by the wide separation of the Supreme Commander's headquarters from those of the 21st Army Group and the Naval C.-in-C. in September–October, 1944.[1] Lastly, it does

[1] Admiral Ramsay's headquarters moved from Southwick House, Portsmouth, to Granville on the west coast of the Cotentin Peninsula between 8th and 10th September, 1944, just after the capture of Antwerp. General Eisenhower's headquarters were also at Granville at that time, but moved to Versailles, with a forward command post outside Rheims, on

seem difficult to understand why the pressure exerted by the Combined Chiefs of Staff, by the Supreme Commander, and by Admiral Ramsay to get the Scheldt opened was so long in producing the desired action by Field-Marshal Montgomery.

20th September. Field-Marshal Montgomery's main headquarters were near Bayeux in Normandy until the break-through at the end of the August. They then moved forward to Brussels in two steps, but were not fully established there until early in October.

CHAPTER XXII

ATLANTIC AND ARCTIC

1st June–31st December, 1944

"The Battle of the Atlantic was the dominating factor all through the war. Never for one moment could we forget that everything happening elsewhere . . . depended ultimately on its outcome."

W. S. Churchill, *The Second World War*,
Vol. V, p. 6 (Cassell, 1952).

WHEN THE invasion of Normandy was launched the Home Fleet was carrying out diversionary operations off the Norwegian coast, and keeping a watchful eye on the German bases in case their major warships should be sent on a foray into the Channel. Though we believed at the time that the *Scheer, Lützow, Hipper, Prinz Eugen*, four light cruisers and a number of destroyers and torpedo-boats were fit for sea, we now know that contemporary estimates of the effective strength of the German surface fleet were far too high, and that in fact very few of the big ships were in fighting condition. On 14th June Admiral Sir Henry Moore, second-in-command of the Home Fleet, took over as C.-in-C. from Sir Bruce Fraser, who was to command the British Pacific Fleet, soon to form in the Indian Ocean; and the new C.-in-C.'s first problem was to restart the Arctic convoys, which had been suspended since the previous March because of the need to devote all our resources to ensuring the success of operation "Neptune." We were, however, aware that the *Tirpitz*, which was still in Altenfiord, had nearly completed repairing the damage inflicted by the Fleet Air Arm on the previous 3rd April;[1] and Admiral Moore therefore considered it essential to neutralise her again before the traffic to and from North Russia was restarted.

[1] See pp. 360-1.

He accordingly sailed from Scapa on 14th July with his main force, and three days later 45 Barracuda torpedo-bombers escorted by 50 fighters took off at first light from the *Formidable*, *Indefatigable* and *Furious*. Unfortunately the enemy gained warning of the approach of the striking force, and by the time it reached the target the smoke screen was so dense that bombing had to be carried out blind. No hits were obtained, and fog frustrated a second attempt. The chief lesson to be derived from this disappointing result was that much faster aircraft were needed if we were to have a good chance of surprising the enemy battleship; but the Fleet Air Arm possessed no such aircraft, and the R.A.F.'s Mosquitos, which could have met the need, were all employed escorting the strategic bombers on raids into Germany—a duty from which General Eisenhower refused to release them.

The Germans sent out a group of U-boats to catch the Home Fleet carriers as they were returning from the abortive attack on the *Tirpitz*; but we located their patrol line, and Coastal Command's far-ranging aircraft sank three of the group and damaged several others between 17th and 19th July. But those successes, though very welcome, did not eliminate the need to provide the new convoys with strong escort and covering forces; for we were aware that there were still about 30 U-boats in the far north, and the battleship in Altenfiord could not be ignored. Thus when convoy JW 59, of 33 merchantmen, sailed on 15th August it was given a powerful escort of 18 flotilla vessels and two escort carriers; and Admiral Moore took the main fleet to sea with the double object of covering the convoy and launching another strike at the *Tirpitz*. Low cloud frustrated the first attempt by the carrier aircrews on the 22nd; but two days later they tried again, and that time the striking force did achieve a measure of surprise. Unfortunately the one heavy bomb which hit the battleship in an ideal position, penetrating through eight decks into her vitals, failed to explode. The *Indefatigable* and *Formidable* waited off the coast in alternating fog and gales for five more days, and on 29th their aircrews made another attempt—only to find the target completely shrouded in smoke. Once again blind bombing produced no hits. The poor results obtained in this whole series of attacks on the *Tirpitz* was intensely disappointing to the naval aircrews—the more so as they almost always had to contend with very difficult conditions of sea and weather; but the plain truth was that the Barracuda torpedo-bomber was not a good enough aircraft for such a difficult undertaking.

While the carrier air attacks on the *Tirpitz* were in progress, convoy JW 59 and the homeward-bound RA 59 were actually enjoying fairly easy passages, and both arrived at their destinations intact. Though the *Kite*, formerly one of the sloops of Captain Walker's 2nd Escort Group,[1] was sunk by a U-boat while escorting the east-bound convoy, the destruction of three such enemies during the double operation more than avenged her loss. Towards the end of September the next outward convoy, JW 60 of 30 ships, also arrived safely; and all that the U-boats had so far to show for their efforts against the new series of convoys was the sinking of two empty merchantmen in RA 60.

The Chiefs of Staff had meanwhile been considering ways and means of resolving the deadlock caused by the inability of the Fleet Air Arm to put the *Tirpitz* out of action, so necessitating our keeping at home two large carriers which were urgently needed in the Far East; and they had decided that the Lancaster bombers of the R.A.F., which could carry 12,000 pound bombs, should try their hand. On 11th September, 39 of the heavy bombers accordingly flew to a Russian airfield near Archangel; but conditions there were so primitive that six of the bombers were damaged beyond repair on landing, and refuelling proved a very slow process. Not until 15th were 28 of the striking force serviceable; but that morning they attacked and, in spite of some interference from smoke, obtained one hit and two near misses. The damage done to the *Tirpitz* could not be repaired in Norway, and the Germans therefore moved her to Tromsö, where she was to act as a floating battery against the invasion fleet which they had so long expected us to send against that country. Thus was the *Tirpitz* at last driven from the commanding strategic position on the flank of the convoy route to Murmansk; and soon afterwards the *Formidable* and *Indefatigable* left for the Far East by way of the Mediterranean.

Meanwhile the offensive against enemy shipping moving up and down the Norwegian coast had been greatly increased; for we fully realised that it was only by that route that the Germans could supply their considerable land forces in northern Finland and bring back

[1] Captain Walker died suddenly on 9th July, 1944, probably as a result of the immense strain he had borne during nearly five years of almost continuous anti-submarine operations.

the iron ore from Narvik. Moreover, the importance of the iron ore shipments had been enhanced by the increasing reluctance of the Swedes to allow their ships to carry it from the Gulf of Bothnia to German ports. Fleet Air Arm strike and minelaying aircraft, Coastal Command bombers, Home Fleet submarines and the Norwegian-manned M.T.B. flotillas all joined in this offensive. At first it was the carrier-borne aircraft and the submarines which achieved the best results, but in September and October the reinforced Strike Wings of Coastal Command overtook the other arms. By way of adding still further variety to the offensive, on 11th September the midget submarine X 24, which had been towed across the North Sea, penetrated into Bergen harbour, sank the large floating dock, and withdrew undetected to meet her parent submarine and return home in safety.

In November pressure against the enemy's coastal traffic was further intensified by a cruiser and destroyer striking force from the Home Fleet raiding the inshore waters off Lister Light, where in a sharp night action they sank two of a four-ship convoy as well as five of its six escorts. By the end of the year, though traffic had not been entirely stopped, the enemy's losses had risen so sharply that his withdrawal from Finland was being gravely jeopardised, his forces in north Norway were not getting their supplies, and the iron ore reaching Germany from Narvik was dwindling.

On 20th October convoy JW 61, of 29 merchantmen, left for North Russia, and about ten days later the corresponding homeward convoy sailed in two sections from the White Sea and Kola Inlet. This time two support groups and three escort carriers, additional to the normal close escort, accompanied the convoys. The U-boats, many of which now lay in wait close off the entrance to Kola Inlet, were brushed out of the convoys' paths, and all the merchantmen arrived safely at their destinations. The failure to destroy any U-boats on this occasion was undoubtedly attributable to the very bad Asdic conditions which commonly prevailed in those waters. The next outward convoy (JW 61A) consisted only of two large liners carrying home 11,000 Russian ex-prisoners of war whom our armies had released during their recent advance across western Europe; and they too arrived safely.

Meanwhile Bomber Command was planning to complete the destruction of the *Tirpitz*; but the next attempt, made by 38

Lancasters which flew from British bases on 29th October, produced only one near miss, and for the following fortnight bad weather prevented any repetition of the operation. On 12th November, however, conditions had improved and 32 Lancasters took off. They not only found clear weather over the target but, by what the German naval C.-in-C., Norway, called "a whole series of unhappy coincidences and failures," they arrived before the smoke screen was effective, and also caught the defending fighters on the wrong foot. Conditions for bomb aiming were thus almost ideal, three hits with 12,000-pound bombs and several near misses were obtained, and the battleship turned turtle with nearly 1,000 of her crew trapped inside her. It cannot be denied that there was considerable chagrin in the Royal Navy over the fact that it was the sister service that firstly drove the *Tirpitz* away from Altenfiord, and then achieved her final destruction; but the failure of its own air arm to accomplish those purposes stemmed basically from the pre-war neglect of naval aviation—and for that misjudgment the Royal Navy itself cannot escape a share of the responsibility. Though the German battleship only fired her big guns once at an enemy target,[1] the influence which she so long exerted on our maritime strategy and dispositions has been made clear earlier in this narrative; and we may conclude the story of her career by remarking that between January, 1942, when she arrived in Norway, and her destruction nearly three years later she was attacked eight times by naval aircrews, once by midget submarines and seven times by R.A.F. bombers.

Soon after the destruction of the *Tirpitz* the last pair of Arctic convoys of 1944 (JW and RA 62, of 32 and 28 merchantmen respectively) set out on their long journeys. Rather paradoxically they encountered stronger opposition than any of their predecessors of this period; for the Luftwaffe's torpedo-bombers had returned to North Norway in some strength. The escort was, however, amply strong enough to deal with the air as well as the U-boat threat, no merchantmen were lost and two U-boats were sunk. So ended a very successful phase on the Arctic route. During the latter half of 1944 all the 159 merchantmen sent to Russia arrived safely to deliver a huge quantity of war stores to our Ally, while only two of the 100 ships in the homeward convoys were sunk; and the cost to the enemy of his attempts to interfere with the movements was

[1] In the bombardment of Spitzbergen on 18th September, 1943. See p. 317.

nine U-boats sunk and many others damaged. These experiences confirmed what had become plain long previously in the Atlantic battle—namely, that well-disciplined convoys escorted by a powerful combination of flotilla vessels and small aircraft carriers provided a high degree of protection to the merchantmen, and also produced excellent opportunities to strike back hard at any enemies which endeavoured to molest them.

We have already seen how from early June until nearly the end of August, 1944, the main effort of the U-boats was directed against our cross-Channel invasion traffic, though with little success. But it would have been contrary to Dönitz's very persistently applied strategy to have entirely neglected the more remote waters at such a time, and in June there were actually a few boats on patrol off eastern Canada, off West Africa and in the Caribbean; while four of the large " U-cruisers " were outward-bound to the Indian Ocean with the last surviving "milch cow" (U.490) to act as their supply ship. All U-boats passing through the central Atlantic had, however, to run the gauntlet of the roving American escort carrier groups, which we have already encountered in this narrative;[1] and, acting on the excellent intelligence which we were now able to give our anti-submarine forces, they struck very hard at these enemies. Between June and September they sank seven German and one Japanese U-boat; and included in the former was one of the U-cruisers and also the precious "milch cow." These highly gratifying results, taken with earlier successes achieved by the American escort carriers, led however to a misconception regarding anti-submarine strategy which has proved very long-lasting; for whereas the American Navy claimed that the " Hunter-Killer Groups" (as it called the roving carrier forces) were more effective as U-boat killers than the sea and air convoy escorts, the truth was that their accomplishments were only made possible by the very accurate intelligence which we were able to give them. Without that benefit the escort carrier groups of 1944 would, almost certainly, have been no more effective than the hunting groups on which we ourselves had wasted a considerable effort four years earlier. Taking the war as a whole there is no doubt at all that the sea and air escort forces, and the supporting ships and aircraft sent to reinforce

[1] See p. 307.

threatened convoys, were by far the most effective U-boat killers.[1]

Between June and August, 1944, the only theatre where the distant U-boats achieved significant results was the Indian Ocean. There the four or five German and two Japanese boats generally on patrol sank 17 merchantmen of over 100,000 tons; and we destroyed only two enemies (one German and one Japanese) in return. These unsatisfactory results stemmed basically from the same causes as before—namely, that the Eastern Fleet still did not possess enough escort vessels to give the merchantmen adequate protection, and that it was difficult to organise convoys throughout the whole of that vast theatre. In the autumn, however, enemy successes declined sharply, largely because of the losses inflicted on the reinforcements sent out from Germany while they were on passage in the Atlantic; and the sinking of the last "milch cow," already mentioned, finally crippled the Indian Ocean U-boat forays. In October the Germans ordered all the surviving boats which could be made fit for a long sea passage to leave for Europe not later than January, 1945; but four of them were sunk on the way. Three arrived safely, and the last four in the Far East were turned over to the Japanese. So ended a campaign in which a small number of enemy submarines caused us substantial losses and considerable dislocation—especially in the autumn of 1942 and the early months of 1944.[2] The chief interest of the U-boat operations in the Indian Ocean lies in the fact that they show how very vulnerable our shipping is to sporadic attacks by enemies working singly in a remote theatre where the organisation of properly escorted convoys is difficult. Elsewhere the distant U-boats caused us little trouble during the latter part of 1944; but in the autumn Schnorkel-fitted boats appeared in the Gulf of St. Lawrence and off Halifax, sank a few ships and evaded the searching Canadian and American warships and aircraft. But it was by that time impossible for the enemy to maintain boats far overseas for long periods; and even though their occasional appearances forced

---

[1] The relevant figures are:

Warship and air escorts and supports	339
Warship, submarine and air patrols	242
Mines	26
Bombing raids and other air strikes	85
Other and unknown causes (including 7 by forces of U.S.S.R.)	93
Total	785

[2] See pp. 227 and 356-7.

us to continue to sail all Atlantic shipping in convoy, and our inability to eliminate them was irritating, the truth was that the U-boats' lunges to remote waters had been defeated.

We saw earlier how between August and October, 1944, the Germans successfully transferred their Biscay-based boats to Norway.[1] After those movements had been completed there was a short lull while they were reorganising their Norwegian bases; but in the autumn a steady stream of boats began to move from the North Sea round the north of Scotland, to take up patrol positions in our inshore waters; for the enemy had decided that, having been driven from the Atlantic and the Western Approaches, his only hope lay in exploiting the immunity obtained from the Schnorkel by trying to ambush ships close off our coasts. We strengthened our air patrols over the northern transit area; but the U-boats nearly always made their journeys submerged, and the aircraft very rarely located any of them. Thus in October 49 U-boats passed in or out by the northern route, and all we managed was to damage one of them; while in December, when fifty were on passage, none was even sighted. The enormous amount of flying done at this time by Coastal Command aircraft for very little result led to the aircrews reporting spouting whales or the small waterspouts frequently encountered in those waters (called "willy-waws" by seamen) as smoke from Schnorkel funnels; and many depth charge attacks were made on such false targets. We now know that every air report of Schnorkelling U-boats made between September, 1944, and the end of the war must be regarded as suspect, and that comparatively few genuine enemies were sighted, let alone attacked from the air in that period.[2] In September one solitary enemy was sunk by an aircraft off Bergen, and in the following month the only success was achieved by a frigate sent to co-operate with the northern air patrols. Nor did the last two months of the year produce better results. Happily the very fact that the U-boats had adopted the tactics of staying submerged as much as possible deprived them of so much mobility that, compared with the surface-operating "wolf-packs" of the earlier phases of the Atlantic battle, they were extremely poor destroyers of merchant ships; but that was only a very partial

[1] See p. 393.
[2] Post-war research has revealed that only 88 of the 216 aircraft "sightings" reported in that period were on genuine U-boats.

consolation for our inability to find and sink them. Moreover, the enemy did occasionally score some unpleasant successes right on our front door-step, as when U.482 sank a corvette and four large merchantmen, all of them in convoy, close off the northern coast of Ireland in late August and early September, 1944, and evaded all our searching forces. We were particularly sensitive about U-boats penetrating into the Irish Sea, where traffic was very heavy; and in October the Admiralty therefore had a deep minefield laid across the southern entrance to those waters; but no U-boat was caught in it in 1944. Next we tried attacking the U-boat shelters in Bergen from the air; and on 4th October four U-boats were destroyed or damaged beyond repair in one R.A.F. raid. But the shelters themselves, and the boats actually inside them, suffered little. It thus came about that at the close of 1944 something like a state of stalemate had arisen in our home waters. Although we lost only 14 merchantmen during the last four months of the year, and safely convoyed over 12,000 ships in and out of our home ports, the whole of our anti-U-boat effort in the theatre only achieved the destruction of twenty enemies. Plainly the Admiralty had good grounds for feeling anxious about the future; for with the new boats (Types XXI and XXIII[1]), which were capable of much higher speed underwater, completing in some numbers it was not by any means impossible that the enemy would at last regain the initiative of which we had deprived him as long ago as May, 1943. And if that happened the whole Allied campaign in western Europe might be imperilled.

[1] See p. 303.

CHAPTER XXIII

VICTORY IN THE WEST

1st January–8th May, 1945

" There must be a beginning of any great matter, but the
continuing unto the end until it be thoroughly finished yields
the true glory."

Sir Francis Drake to Lord Walsingham,
17th May, 1587.

AT THE time when the British fighting services saw the passing
of what was for them the sixth New Year of the war the
Mediterranean Fleet's chief responsibility was to keep the Allied
armies in Italy supplied, mainly through the ports of Leghorn on
the west coast and Ancona on the Adriatic; but a cruiser and
destroyer squadron, known as " Flank Force," was continuously
employed in support of the soldiers who were fighting their way
along the south coast of France towards the Italian frontier; our
coastal craft and destroyers were very active in the northern Adriatic
and the Ligurian Sea, where the enemy was still trying to keep his
inshore traffic moving; and a considerable number of warships were
still in Greek ports, where their presence helped to preserve the
precarious political truce which had just been arranged. Lastly, the
sweeping of mines, our own as well as the enemy's, was a constant
commitment on which dozens of British flotillas were continuously
engaged.

In February, 1945, Turkey, Egypt and certain of the Levant
states declared war on Germany, and that action, if somewhat
belated, enabled us to establish virtually complete control over the
whole of the eastern Mediterranean. The minesweepers could now
clear the waters right up to the Dardanelles, and that enabled us to
send convoys straight through to Odessa. Thus was a far easier
and shorter supply route to Russia opened up; but, as we shall see

408

shortly, this did not relieve us of the need to continue sending supplies for our Ally's northern armies by the Arctic route. In the same month the Mediterranean Fleet had to carry large numbers of Allied fighting men with their equipment from Italy to southern France, in accordance with a decision of the Combined Chiefs of Staff to reinforce our armies and air forces in western Europe at the expense of those in Italy. The switch was accomplished smoothly and without loss, using troop transports, which sailed in escorted convoys, while a shuttle service of L.S.T.s, L.C.I.s and store ships transported the equipment.

On 17th March a German-manned destroyer and two torpedo-boats made a night sortie from Genoa to lay mines off our bases in Corsica. Shore radar stations, however, gave warning of their approach, and in the early hours of 18th they were intercepted by two British destroyers, which sank both the torpedo-boats after a running fight. This was the last of the many destroyer actions fought in the Mediterranean.

On 9th April the Eighth Army opened a new offensive in Italy with the object of breaking into the Lombardy plains. Success depended to a considerable extent on turning the strong defensive position guarding the approaches to the Po valley on the Adriatic flank. The Navy therefore embarked troops in L.V.T.s (Landing Vehicles Tracked) and other assault craft, and landed them in the enemy's rear, while larger warships supported the main offensive with their guns. The result was that the Germans gave way along the whole front, our troops followed up fast, and on 27th they crossed the Adige. Meanwhile to the west the Fifth Army's new offensive had also prospered, on the 24th the Americans entered Spezia and three days later the great port of Genoa also fell to them. During this advance the " Flank Force," already mentioned, was kept very busy bombarding the enemy's coastal communications, while naval parties at once set about clearing and reopening each of the captured ports. These successes on land put an end to the forays by German assault craft and "small battle units," which had been a constant feature of the fighting in the Ligurian Sea and Adriatic during the preceding months. Though the Germans put a big effort into the production of those craft, and persevered with them almost to the end, they never accomplished anything significant in the Mediterranean, and themselves suffered heavy losses on almost every sortie. While one may admire the gallantry of the small battle units' crews, who again and again set out on hopeless missions, the conclusion that they could not act as effective substitutes for the more conventional instruments of maritime power is inescapable. None the less it remains true that resolutely manned special assault craft can, in the hands of a power possessed of reasonably well-balanced maritime forces, sometimes achieve important results—as was shown by the Italian underwater swimmers' attack on the British battleships in Alexandria in December, 1941, and by our own successes against the *Tirpitz* and other important targets using midget submarines or the British version of the " human torpedo."[1]

By the end of April our light craft commanded the whole of the northern Adriatic, and had gained undisputed control of the last of the enemy's coastal waters in the Ligurian Sea. German seaborne traffic had been brought to a complete standstill, and very few of their merchantmen or warships remained afloat. Taking the war as a whole, our various arms and services sank 3,082 Axis merchantmen totalling over four million tons in the Mediterranean; and it is certain that the steady attrition of the enemy's cargo tonnage contributed enormously to the defeat of their offensive purposes in Africa, and finally reduced their armies in Italy, the Balkans and southern France to a hopeless condition. On 29th April, 1945, the instrument whereby the whole of the Axis forces in Italy surrendered unconditionally was signed at Allied Headquarters. It came into force on 2nd May.

Thus did the steady pressure of our Mediterranean strategy ultimately bring a great victory in the theatre. If it was our maritime power which made that victory possible, the campaign had, from the very beginning, been a joint one in which all three services were indispensable each to the other; for if the Army depended on the sea services for transport, support and supply, the fortunes of the Navy always ebbed and flowed as the balance on land swung to and fro; and neither of the older service's affairs could have prospered without the constant co-operation and collaboration of the Air Forces. Because the strategy was British-conceived it was natural that we should have supplied the largest share of the forces required; but

[1] See pp. 173 and 317-8. The most successful operation by the British version of the human torpedo (known as "Chariots") was the sinking of the Italian cruiser *Ulpio Traiano* in Palermo harbour on 3rd January, 1943.

after the autumn of 1942 the assistance of our American Allies was very great—especially on land and in the air. At sea the Royal Navy carried virtually the whole burden from June, 1940, until operation " Torch " was launched in November, 1942; and thereafter by far the largest share fell on the same service, with the solitary exception of the forces deployed for the " Dragoon " landings in southern France in August, 1944. If the Mediterranean victory was a triumphant proof that modern developments had in no way vitiated the traditional benefits to be derived from a maritime strategy, especially in surprising the enemy by landing in theatres of our own choice, the campaign which preceded it provided ample evidence that the basic requirements for success in assaults from the sea remained unchanged; for it was by applying modern techniques to that ancient science that we finally reaped the reward for all that we had endured in the early years. Posterity will surely judge that in the Mediterranean campaign of 1940-45, and especially during the first long period of Admiral Sir Andrew Cunningham's command, the Royal Navy added to its long history a new chapter as glorious as any previously written in it.

In the Home theatre at the beginning of 1945 the main fleet's chief responsibilities were to fight the Arctic convoys through to Murmansk and Archangel and to strike at the German coastal traffic off Norway; while the Western Approaches command and all the other shore naval authorities in Britain were grappling with the problems involved in the appearance of large numbers of U-boats in our coastal waters, and with the enemy's vigorous attempts to interfere with the heavy traffic now running between the Thames ports and Antwerp.

On 2nd January the Allied cause sustained a severe loss when Admiral Sir Bertram Ramsay was killed in an aircraft accident in France; for we have already seen how the entire naval side of the campaign in western Europe was planned, organised and controlled by him. Though it is true that the triumphant success of operation " Neptune " had set the seal on the great work to which he first set his hand in the evacuation from Dunkirk in 1940, and had continued in the invasions of North Africa and Sicily, his unrivalled experience of amphibious warfare, and the respect in which he was held by the senior officers of the other services—American as well as British— were still of inestimable value. His deputy, Vice-Admiral A. G.

Kirk, U.S.N., took over his responsibilities temporarily, and on 19th January Vice-Admiral Sir Harold Burrough, lately in command at Gibraltar, became Allied Naval Commander, Expeditionary Force, in his place.

At the turn of the year west Holland was still a German stronghold, and about forty E-boats as well as large numbers of "small battle units" worked from bases on that coast against our Thames-Scheldt, east coast and Channel convoys. It was now that the German midget submarines called *Seehunde* entered the fray, and they proved far more successful than all the many varieties of human torpedo and explosive craft which the enemy had been employing off Normandy and in the Mediterranean. In the shallow waters off our east coast and in the approaches to the Scheldt, where the traffic was very dense, mines were the greatest menace; and in the first two months of the year those laid by E-boats and aircraft caused us the loss of fifteen ships totalling some 36,000 tons. Fortunately for us the Luftwaffe stopped minelaying towards the end of January, and the Germans probably thereby lost the best opportunity of disrupting our traffic. E-boat and midget submarine forays however continued, and at times they reached as far up the east coast as Yarmouth and as far down-Channel as Dungeness; but it was the mines rather than torpedo attacks which caused us the most trouble and the heaviest losses. We kept a strong force of frigates and coastal craft, as well as many aircraft, on patrol off the Belgian coast and in the Scheldt approaches, while others continuously swept and searched for these enemies in our coastal waters; but we still found that they were elusive targets, and it was not until we had developed really close co-operation between our sea and air forces that we gained the upper hand. The tactics which we now developed against the E-boats were basically the same as had proved so effective against U-boats crossing the Bay of Biscay transit routes and in the Mediterranean "swamp" operations;[1] namely, that an aircraft which sighted an enemy would "home" the nearest surface warships to the scene by wireless, whilst herself maintaining contact with the enemy. It is indeed interesting to find that only by the joint employment of well-trained sea and air forces could patrolling for either E-boats or U-boats be made really effective.

On the night of 8th-9th March we received a sharp reminder

[1] See pp. 284 and 336.

that there was still a powerful German garrison in the Channel Islands, when a raiding force attacked and surprised the nearby port of Granville on the mainland, inflicted considerable damage and got away safely with one small British collier as prize. Though the raid had no strategic significance it was a blow to Anglo-American pride —the more so as the headquarters of both General Eisenhower and Admiral Ramsay had until recently been at Granville. Three nights later the German naval forces in western Holland made a determined foray into the Scheldt, using all the various types of special assault craft which they had collected; but the defences were very alert and destroyed no less than 22 human torpedoes (*Biber* and *Molch*) and 16 explosive motor boats (*Linsen*). On the Allied side not a single ship was even damaged. In spite of the very heavy losses which the "small battle units" were suffering, and the appalling weather they generally encountered, the Germans continued to send reinforcements to the Dutch bases almost to the end of the war. In March we lost 16 merchantmen of some 42,000 tons in the coastal waters, and again it was the mines laid by E-boats which did most of the damage.

Meanwhile Bomber Command's long-range aircraft were steadily infesting the western Baltic with mines, while Coastal Command's Strike Wings of Beaufighters were constantly sweeping the north German coast for shipping, and reaching out as far as the Kattegat. In January our air-laid mines forced the enemy to shift his U-boat training from the favourite waters off Danzig to Oslo fiord, and by March the intensity of our minelaying and the constant air attacks were threatening to bring about a complete collapse of the German minesweeping service—which had so far served them extremely well. Harbours and swept channels were constantly closed, and their losses rose steeply to 26 ships (nearly 70,000 tons) sunk by mines during the month. By the end of March the training of the crews of new U-boats was being severely hampered, and the whole of the enemy's coastal traffic in the Baltic, the southern North Sea and off Norway was grinding to a halt. But before we consider the events of the final five weeks of the war we must return to the beginning of the year to review the main campaign against the U-boats.

Surprising though it may seem, the early months of 1945 were an anxious period for the British naval authorities; for we knew that new U-boats were still taking the water far faster than we were sinking them, we were expecting the greatly improved Type XXI and XXIII boats to enter service in some numbers, and we knew that since the arrival of the " Schnorkel " our radar-fitted aircraft had lost much of their effectiveness. Thus there were grounds for believing that, unless we could reverse the unfavourable trends, the enemy might regain the initiative sufficiently to renew the campaign against our North Atlantic convoys in strength; and heavy losses in that theatre might, so the Admiralty considered, jeopardise the whole land campaign in western Europe. As we now know that the German U-boat strength actually reached the peak figure of 463 boats in March, 1945, and that during the first two months of that year large numbers of escort vessels and maritime aircraft which had to be deployed at home to cope with the four or five dozen U-boats which were working in our coastal waters, it is plain that the Admiralty's anxieties were by no means ill-founded.[1] Energetic steps were taken to improve the situation. The Chiefs of Staff approved that some 300 escort vessels due to leave shortly for the Far East should be held back, and directed Bomber Command to devote more of its effort to U-boat bases and building yards: the Admiralty at once started to lay deep minefields in the English Channel and Irish Sea, and new tactics were introduced for the sea and air forces engaged in this phase of the battle. The real difficulty lay in the fact that until a U-boat committed a hostile act, we found them extraordinarily hard to locate. Support groups were therefore sent to trail along in the wake of the convoys, ready to pounce instantly on any enemy that revealed its presence; while the transit route from Norway round the north of Scotland was intensively patrolled by aircraft and flotilla vessels. In January there were 39 U-boats in our coastal waters, and six of them penetrated into the Irish Sea—which was one of our most sensitive spots. Though they sank no more than seven ships during the month the efforts of all our warships destroyed only six enemies; and our aircraft had no successes at all. In February the number of U-boats off our coasts rose to 51; but they sank only a few more ships than in the preceding month, and their

[1] On 1st January, 1945, there were 426 escort vessels at home, and 37 groups were working in the Western Approaches Command alone. Coastal Command then had 420 aircraft based in Britain and Iceland.

own losses rose to twelve—three-quarters of which were accounted for by our surface warships. During the month the four frigates of Commander P. W. Burnett's 10th Escort Group carried out a very successful patrol on the transit route to the north of the Shetlands. Between 3rd and 17th February they sank three U-boats, all of them with the new ahead-throwing weapons.[1]

In March our anti-submarine forces did better still. Though the number of enemies around our coasts rose to 53, and they sank ten merchantmen (45,000 tons) as well as three escort vessels, we accounted for 15 of them—11 of which were sunk by warships and four by aircraft. Three of the successes were achieved by the 21st Escort Group's frigates when, during the latter part of the month, they conducted an intensive search in the waters known as the Minches—the narrow passage between the west coast of Scotland and the Hebrides. Meanwhile Dönitz was still sending small numbers of U-boats to remote positions overseas, in order to force us to divert some of our strength from the inshore campaign. These boats sank a few ships in the Gulf of St. Lawrence, off the east coast of America and in the approaches to Gibraltar; but they were no more than a nuisance. Moreover, when the U-boat command tried the old group tactics in March, and sent six large boats to work off the Azores, they were quickly located by the roving American escort carrier groups which were still patrolling those waters, and four of them were sunk in a few days.

We now know that it was actually in March, 1945, that all the trends in the long struggle against the U-boats at last began to move decisively in the Allied favour. Our bombing raids were causing serious dislocation in the building and assembly yards, and also destroyed a number of completed U-boats; our successes were rising fast both in the inshore waters and overseas; the enemy's total strength showed a decline; and, best of all, though the first Type XXI boat (U.2511) became operational in that month and two of the smaller Type XXIII were already at sea, the new boats were not entering service nearly as fast as the Germans had hoped and we had feared.

While the Western Approaches Command and the authorities

[1] These were known as "Hedgehog" and "Squid," and possessed a great advantage over depth charges; for whereas in a depth charge attack the ship was bound to lose Asdic contact during the last stage of the approach, so giving the enemy a chance to take avoiding action undetected, the ahead-throwing weapons could be fired while still in Asdic contact.

at Plymouth, Portsmouth, Chatham and Rosyth were all fully engaged in the inshore campaign against the U-boats Admiral Sir Henry Moore's Home Fleet was conducting the Arctic convoys and the offensive off the Norwegian coast. In big ships the fleet was now very weak, for almost all had gone either to the Indian Ocean or the Pacific; and as Admiral Moore had no fleet carrier the Admiralty allocated half a dozen escort carriers to him by way of substitutes. Though well suited to the work of defending the Arctic convoys they were too slow, and their aircraft complements were too small, to enable them to strike really telling blows off Norway. This was the more regrettable because the Germans were now withdrawing from northern Finland to Narvik, whence they were shipping large numbers of men and considerable quantities of equipment southwards.

The " cycle" for the Arctic convoys (i.e. the period between the start of successive movements) was at this time shortened from five weeks to thirty days, which meant that the same ships often had to take part in consecutive operations. They were conducted alternately by Rear-Admiral R. R. McGrigor, commander of the 1st Cruiser Squadron, and Vice-Admiral Sir F. Dalrymple-Hamilton of the 10th Cruiser Squadron. In January the latter took out the 35 ships of JW 63 without loss; but the corresponding homeward convoy was struck by an exceptionally violent gale. Though all the merchantmen finally arrived safely it was the weather rather than the enemy that produced the worst troubles. While this double operation was in progress Home Fleet M.T.B.s penetrated into the Norwegian "Leads," and between 6th and 8th January sank three large ships heavily laden with iron ore; and a few nights later a cruiser-destroyer force under Admiral McGrigor encountered a strongly escorted convoy near Egersund. Two German merchantmen and one of their escorts were sunk; but the endeavour to catch three large destroyers which left Narvik for the Baltic on 26th January was less successful. Having no destroyers available Admiral Moore sent two cruisers across to try and intercept them near Bergen —which they accomplished in the early hours of 28th. But the German ships were faster than the British cruisers and, although two of them were damaged, they managed to find safety under the guns of the shore defences. Though attacked later from the air they all finally reached the Baltic safely, as did the fourth and last destroyer

from Narvik a short time later. It had always been difficult to
intercept fast enemy warships off a coast where the weather was very
fickle and there were innumerable fiords in which they could seek
shelter if hard pressed; but there is no denying that the escape of
the four destroyers was disappointing. Their return to Germany did
however mark the final end of the enemy's attempt to maintain a
powerful naval force in north Norway, where it could threaten both
the Arctic convoys and the traffic crossing the North Atlantic.

Convoy JW 64 of 26 ships, left the Clyde on 3rd February
accompanied by two escort carriers, a cruiser and 17 flotilla vessels;
and it encountered stronger opposition than had been experienced
for some time. Not only did the Germans deploy a powerful U-boat
force across its track, but the Luftwaffe's torpedo-bombers re-
entered the fray. In their first sortie they never found the convoy;
but on 10th February some thirty of them made a determined
attempt to penetrate the defences. The carrier-borne fighters and
A-A gunners were however alert and well trained, and they
accounted for several of the attackers. Though the Germans claimed
great successes, in fact not a ship in the convoy was even damaged.
The only loss suffered was the torpedoing of one of the frigates of
the escort by a U-boat just outside Kola Inlet. The corresponding
homeward convoy (RA 64 of 34 ships) had a difficult time. Because
his U-boat patrol lines in the Barents Sea had repeatedly failed to
catch our convoys, the enemy was now concentrating most of the
boats in the shallow waters close off the Murmansk coast, where
Asdic conditions were always very difficult. Moreover, we had to
depend to a considerable extent on the Russian Navy and Air Force
to clear these enemies off their own front doorstep—or at any rate
to keep them submerged while the convoys were passing: but
although they did their best within the limits of their somewhat
rudimentary conception of anti-submarine warfare, their efforts
were singularly unproductive. When two large merchantmen
coming in from the White Sea to join convoy RA 64 were sunk
just inside Murmansk Admiral McGrigor took the matter into his
own hands, and sent all his flotilla vessels to sea to sweep the
approaches vigorously before the convoy sailed. They sank one of
the U-boats lying in ambush; but the convoy was slow in getting
to sea, and that gave the other enemies the chance to put their heads
up again. A frigate and a merchantman were torpedoed and badly

damaged just outside, and at the end of an anxious day the corvette *Bluebell* was hit and blew up. Only one of her crew survived. Then the convoy was struck and scattered by a violent gale, and on 20th, before it had reformed properly, the torpedo-bombers from north Norway attacked. Somehow the escort carrier *Nairana* managed to get her fighters off the heaving flight deck, and they and the A-A gunners again defended the merchantmen with remarkable success. Not a ship was hit in the main attack, but three days later a straggler was sunk astern of the convoy. Next another gale struck, and blew with unabated fury for two days, scattering the labouring merchantmen far and wide. Escorts could not be refuelled at sea, and Admiral Moore had therefore to send fresh ships out to relieve them: many merchantmen suffered breakdowns and damage, and it was a much-battered convoy that finally turned down the west coast of Scotland. One ship struggled into harbour after nothing had been heard of her for a week, and it seems miraculous that none of them foundered.

A fortnight after the end of RA 64's long ordeal the next outward convoy (JW 65 of 24 ships) sailed from the Clyde. All went well until it was within sight of its destination, when an unlucky snow storm put a stop to flying at a critical moment. The U-boats lying in wait seized their chance, and sank the sloop *Lapwing* and two merchantmen. The Admiralty now decided that the constant losses suffered right off Kola Inlet could be tolerated no longer, and arranged to send out indicator nets to catch the U-boats, and the fast minelayer *Apollo* to lay a deep field protecting the convoy route. Meanwhile the Russians had been persuaded to sweep a new passage through the German minefields, and by sending the next convoy (RA 65) that way, what time warships put up a pyrotechnic display on the old route, it slipped through the trap unharmed, and arrived in British ports intact.

In March and April Home Fleet carrier aircraft, destroyers and M.T.B.s continued their offensive sweeps off Norway; but they scored no very important successes—partly because enemy traffic had now declined. On 16th April the 22 ships of Convoy JW 66, the last outward Arctic convoy of the war, left Britain under Rear-Admiral A. E. M. B. Cunninghame-Graham, who had taken over the 10th Cruiser Squadron from Admiral Dalrymple-Hamilton. A support group went ahead to punch a hole through the U-boat patrol line in the Barents Sea and clear away the dozen enemies lurking off Kola; and these measures were so successful that not a ship was lost. Before RA 66, the corresponding homeward convoy, sailed on 29th April the escorts again swept the approaches to Kola Inlet, and that time they caught and sank two U-boats. Though one of the escorting frigates was torpedoed and sunk soon after the convoy put to sea, all the merchantmen reached home unscathed.

One more Arctic convoy sailed in each direction, though with reduced escorts, shortly after the surrender of Germany; and the famous series ended quietly when RA 67 steamed into the Clyde on 31st May with lights burning. In forty outward convoys we had sent 811 ships to north Russia, and the 720 which arrived safely delivered about four million tons of cargo, 5,000 tanks and over 7,000 aircraft.[1] The total cost to us of the homeward as well as the outward convoys was 92 merchantmen and 18 warships; but as we sank the *Scharnhorst*, three enemy destroyers and 38 U-boats during the operations the balance of success plainly lay with the Allies. As the Admiralty organised and controlled all the Arctic convoys, and the Home Fleet provided nearly all the escorts, the Royal Navy and the Merchant Navies of Britain and America may jointly share in the pride with which posterity will surely look back on a remarkable accomplishment.

The month of March, 1945, produced important developments in western Europe; for Field-Marshal Montgomery's men then forced a passage across the Rhine south of the Dutch frontier, and swung north to cut off all the German forces in Holland. The E-boats and special assault craft in Dutch bases were now in a grave predicament, since fuel and other replenishments could only be run in by sea; but their attacks on our convoys and their minelaying forays into the Scheldt estuary continued until the middle of April, though with declining success and rising losses to our ever-active sea and air escorts and patrols. Early in April five E-boats were sunk in quick succession, and the last of the many night clashes between them and our frigates and coastal craft took place off the Scheldt in the early hours of 13th. In 1945 the E-boats sank 31 merchantmen (89,000 tons), the great majority of which fell victims to the mines that they laid rather than to their torpedo attacks: the midget submarines (*Seehunde*) sank nine ships (18,000 tons), but the

---

[1] Thirty-three ships in outward convoys turned back during the voyage, due to having suffered ice damage or breakdown of machinery.

other types of "small battle units" caused us hardly any losses, and themselves suffered very heavily indeed. The same period also saw the final operations in the Bay of Biscay, where French and British warships under French command carried out a series of bombardments and small landings in support of the resistance forces which were containing the German garrisons of La Rochelle, La Pallice, Lorient and Nantes. On 20th April the River Gironde was opened to Allied shipping,[1] and early in May the last German forces on that coast surrendered.

The campaign against German merchant shipping was meanwhile moving to a climax, with the strike aircraft of Coastal Command, the carrier-borne aircraft and light forces of the Home Fleet, and Bomber Command's minelayers all joining in. Together they inflicted very heavy losses in April and early May, especially in the Skagerrak, the Kattegat and the western Baltic; and by 7th May, when the Admiralty ordered all attacks to cease, German mercantile traffic had been brought to a standstill. Taking the war in the Home Theatre as a whole it was the mines laid by our ships and aircraft which caused the heaviest enemy losses (604 ships totalling more than 660,000 tons); and second to the mines came the direct air attacks on shipping with 289 ships (574,000 tons). The Royal Navy's surface warships, which accounted for 86 ships (303,000 tons), achieved their best results early in the war, and it was of course their steady pressure which then swept German shipping off all the seas and oceans of the world; but the same service's submarines, with 104 ships of 318,000 tons to their credit, exacted a steady toll from 1940 (when restrictions on attacks on merchant ships were lifted) to the end of the war. Indeed, study of the campaign as a whole shows that the virtually complete destruction of the German Merchant Navy was the result of the combined endeavours of all the various arms of the Royal Navy and Royal Air Force.

We must now turn to the struggle against the U-boats during April, when no less than 44 of them sailed outward-bound from Norway, mostly to take up patrol billets in our inshore waters. They were now submerging on leaving their bases, and remaining

---

[1] The town of Bordeaux had been captured by French resistance forces as early as 31st August, 1944; but as the Germans held the mouth of the river Gironde until April, 1945, we had been unable to make any use of the port.

submerged, using their "Schnorkels" skilfully, throughout almost the whole of their patrols—in one case (U.1199) for as long as fifty days. Though we were still finding them difficult to locate unless and until they attacked a merchantman, once they had revealed their presence they rarely got away unscathed. The scene of greatest activity in April was off our north-east coast, where several of the Type XXIII, none of which did we ever manage to sink, were working. Elsewhere, and especially in the western approaches to the Channel and Irish Sea, we did a good deal better. During the last five weeks of the war the U-boats sank ten merchantmen (52,000 tons) close off our coasts, and two small warships: but their own losses amounted to 23 boats, of which ten were sunk by surface warships, six by aircraft and the remainder were either shared between the sea and air forces or destroyed by mines, grounding or accident. Between 1st January and 8th May, 1945, the inshore U-boats sank 38 merchantmen (156,000 tons), and we accounted for 32 of them. Though we cannot claim to have defeated them decisively enough to force them to withdraw, and our inability to deal with the new types gave grounds for anxiety, they had certainly been severely checked.

In late April and early May, because the Russian armies were threatening their Baltic bases, the Germans began to move all their surviving U-boats, including those which were not yet fully operational, to Norway; and the Royal Air Force's Beaufighters, Mosquitos, rocket-firing Typhoons, and anti-submarine Liberators at once opened a very vigorous offensive over the Kattegat. In all 27 U-boats fell victim to our air patrols during the last five weeks, and 18 more were destroyed in bombing attacks on their bases. It is worth remembering that it was only during those final weeks, when the German fighter and A-A defences were collapsing, that the heavy bombers succeeded in destroying a substantial number of U-boats in their home bases; but the constant raids on building and assembly yards, and attacks on vital communications such as the Dortmund-Ems canal, did unquestionably contribute a lot to delaying the entry into service of the new types of U-boat.

On the afternoon of 4th May Dönitz broadcast to his U-boats to cease operations and return to base. There were at the time, 33 on passage inwards or outwards, and a dozen in our inshore waters; and we may note that twelve of the new Type

XXI had by that time completed working-up, while 91 others were doing trials or training their crews. Thus the margin by which we had been saved from having to deal with a large number of those dangerous enemies was very narrow. It was the victory on land which forestalled a renewal of the campaign in what might well have proved a highly dangerous form.

By noon on 8th May, when the Admiralty signalled to all ships and authorities that the U-boats at sea had been ordered to surface, report their positions, and then proceed to certain British bases flying a large black flag, few of them had obeyed Dönitz's order of 4th, and some were still proceeding outward-bound submerged. Only very slowly and reluctantly did the U-boat commanders comply with the Admiralty's instructions, and a few ignored them altogether. On 9th we sent a special escort force to Loch Erribol on the south side of the Pentland Firth to receive the surrendered U-boats, and within the next six days 18 came in. Meanwhile, British warships had gone across to Norway to take charge of all boats which could be made fit for sea, and by 6th June 97 (including 17 Type XXIII and one Type XXI) had been inspected in the British reception bases and routed onwards with the White Ensign flying above the Nazi's crooked cross. In all 156 U-boats surrendered, but 221 others scuttled themselves, mostly in German or Norwegian ports, rather than submit to that indignity. The last two reached Argentine waters in late July and early August, only to be interned.

So ended the second German attempt to bring Britain to her knees by striking at her merchant shipping. Between 1939 and 1945 they completed 1,162 U-boats of which 785 were destroyed by one means or another. The total sunk at sea was 632, of which no less than 500 were accounted for by British ships and aircraft. Those figures provide eloquent proof of the extent to which the Atlantic Battle was mainly a struggle between the U-boats and the British Navy and Air Force; and those two services actually shared as equally in the successes achieved as they had shared the burden of the long struggle. Enemy submarines (Italian and Japanese as well as German) sank 2,828 Allied and neutral merchant ships totalling 14,687,231 tons during the war, and damaged many hundreds of others; and by far the largest share of the sunk mercantile tonnage (nearly 11½ million tons) fell on the British

Merchant Navy.[1] In addition the German U-boats sank 175 Allied warships, of which the great majority were British. Our Merchant Navy lost 30,248 men through enemy action, while Royal Navy casualties amounted to 51,578 killed or missing—a large proportion of which must be attributable to the U-boats. We British are notoriously slow to give vent to the passion of hatred; but there is no doubt that the ruthlessness and cunning of the U-boats ultimately aroused feelings of intense loathing in the minds of our seamen. To them the U-boats were always the chief enemy, and they knew beyond doubt that until the seas and oceans had been cleansed of the last of them innocent ships would never be able to move about the world on "their lawful occasions."

While the U-boats were reluctantly hoisting the black flag of surrender, or endeavouring to find some more acceptable solution to the problems posed by the utter defeat of their country, cruisers and destroyers of the Home Fleet had gone to Copenhagen to accept the surrender of the German surface warships; while other warships carried the King of Norway and his government back to their country, and British vessels of all types rushed in relief supplies for the long-suffering people of the countries recently released from the Nazi yoke. The German cruisers *Prinz Eugen* and *Nürnberg* were the only major warships immediately fit for sea, and on 24th May they were escorted by British destroyers from Copenhagen to Wilhelmshaven. The *Scheer*, *Lützow*, *Köln* and *Emden* had all been destroyed in bombing attacks; the *Seydlitz* and *Hipper* were scuttled or wrecked by their own crews; the *Leipzig*, damaged in collision, passed into British hands, while the wrecks of the *Gneisenau* and of the uncompleted *Graf Zeppelin* were taken over by the Russians at Stettin and Gydnia respectively. Thus was the once proud German Navy, built to challenge Britain's sea supremacy, extinguished for the second time within thirty years.

[1] In 1939 the British Merchant Navy possessed 9,488 ships of all types totalling 21,215,261 Gross Register tons. Thus war losses were more than half of our original tonnage.

CHAPTER XXIV

THE WHITE ENSIGN RETURNS TO THE PACIFIC

1st June, 1944–8th August, 1945

" Not by rambling operations, or naval duels, are wars decided but by force massed and handled in skilful combination."

A. T. Mahan, *Sea Power in its Relation to the War of* 1812.

B Y THE beginning of June, 1944, Admiral Nimitz's Central Pacific forces were ready for their next leap westwards, which aimed to seize the key islands of the Mariana group. Once again he organised two large attack forces starting out from widely separated bases, and on 8th June they sailed from the Solomon Islands and Pearl Harbour with the object of assaulting Saipan, Tinian and Guam.[1] After very heavy attacks by the 900 aircraft of Admiral Mitscher's Fast Carrier Task Force, and prolonged bombardments by heavy-gunned warships of Admiral Spruance's Fifth Fleet the U.S. Marines landed on Saipan on 15th. But the Japanese realised that the loss of the Marianas would not only remove the last major obstacle from the sea road leading to the Philippines, but would lay their homeland open to attack by heavy bombers based on the airfields in the group; and their Navy therefore reacted more strongly than at any time since the end of the Solomons campaign. The commander of the Japanese fleet, Admiral Ozawa, laid a clever plan to lure the dreaded American carriers within reach of shore-based aircraft while keeping his own ships outside their range; but the annihilation of Japanese air power in the Marianas by Mitscher's aircrews destroyed its prospects. Moreover, the American submarines which had been trailing his fleet since it set

[1] See Map p. 431.

The assault on Walcheren, 1st November, 1944.
Picking up survivors from a landing craft

Surrendered U-boats at Lisahally near Londonderry

course to the east from the Philippines sank two of his precious carriers (the *Taiho* and *Shokaku*) on 19th June, just when he was ready to launch his striking forces against the Fifth Fleet. The Japanese naval airmen did actually get in the first blows, as Ozawa had intended; but so strong were the American fighter defences that they inflicted no damage at all, and themselves suffered heavy losses. Throughout the preliminary Japanese movements Admiral Spruance was much concerned for the safety of the Saipan invasion force, and he therefore declined to be drawn too far to the west. Not until late on 20th did his reconnaissance aircraft locate Ozawa's main force; but an air attack at extreme range, just as darkness was descending, succeeded in sinking another fleet carrier (the *Hiyo*), and severely damaged many other important enemy ships. Recovery of the American strike aircraft in darkness—a risk which Admiral Mitscher accepted with his eyes open—proved, however, expensive; and about 100 aircraft were lost. Though the " Battle of the Philippine Sea" thus fell short of a decisive victory, and some writers have suggested that Spruance should have pursued his adversary more vigorously, there is no doubt about two points. Firstly, the Japanese attempt to interfere with the invasion of the Marianas was utterly defeated; and secondly, their naval aircrews suffered such heavy losses that thenceforth they never had enough trained pilots to man their surviving carriers. On 9th July the stubborn resistance of the Saipan garrison was finally quelled, and early in the following month Guam and Tinian were also both secured by the Americans.

Meanwhile in the South-West Pacific theatre General MacArthur had tightened his hold on the whole north coast of New Guinea by seizing certain offshore islands, and was planning his next leap. This was aimed to the north, against the Halmahera group, which lay directly on the road towards the Philippines; and the assault was timed to coincide with the attack on the Palau group and the western Caroline islands,[1] which were the next objectives of the Central Pacific forces after the capture of the Marianas. This double blow had as its purpose the seizure of Morotai in the Halmaheras and Ulithi in the western Carolines, which were needed as advanced bases for the invasion of the Philippines.

It was 15th September, only about six weeks after the end of the fighting in the Marianas, that the Americans struck again. Morotai

[1] See Map p. 341.

and Ulithi were easily won, and although the Japanese contested Pelelieu, the key island in the Palau group, for more than two months they failed to prevent General MacArthur's and Admiral Nimitz's forces joining hands in the Philippine Sea. The period June to September, 1944, thus saw the fruition of the strategic plan to which the Americans had been working ever since the first landings in the Solomons in August, 1942, and the assault on the Gilbert Islands in November of the following year. Rarely, if ever before in history has maritime power been more skilfully and successfully employed than in the successive leaps across thousands of miles of ocean which distinguished the Pacific campaigns. If it was mainly the Fast Carrier Striking Force which established the command at sea on which the strategy utterly depended, it was the highly trained Amphibious Forces which again and again exploited the benefits thereby gained; and without the attention which the Americans gave to " logistics "—the science of supply and replenishment—the prolonged operations of their naval forces would never have been possible.

While the Central and South-West Pacific forces were closing in on the Philippines with masterly confidence, Admiral Somerville had at last been able to assume the offensive in the Indian Ocean in a modest way; for reinforcements had gradually been reaching the Eastern Fleet from the Mediterranean and Home theatres. But the South-East Asia Command still did not possess the specially trained amphibious forces which would have enabled the Supreme Commander, Admiral Mountbatten, to mount a major combined operation across the Bay of Bengal, such as he had proposed a year earlier;[1] for almost all the combined operation vessels sent to him had been recalled to Europe to take part in the Anzio assault, and the growing realisation that we were unlikely to achieve the downfall of Germany in 1944 had postponed their return to the Indian Ocean indefinitely. Furthermore, all the South-East Asia Command's purposes were, as so often, bedevilled by disagreements between Britain and America on the grand strategy to be adopted against Japan; for whereas we wished the greater part of our fleet to play a part in the Pacific theatre, the Americans attached importance to the support of General Chiang Kai-Shek's Chinese forces, and desired us at all costs to keep open their supply route from India.

[1] See pp. 342 and 347-8.

We were, moreover, inclined to the belief that our Ally's strategic views were coloured by their lack of enthusiasm for the return of the White Ensign ships to the main Pacific theatre; for when we first offered them the British fleet they stated that they preferred us to form an Empire task force to work under General MacArthur's South-West Pacific Command, rather than join hands with Admiral Nimitz. The issue was not resolved until the second Quebec conference in September, 1944, when President Roosevelt replied to Mr. Churchill's proposal that the British fleet should be used in the main theatre that "it was no sooner offered than accepted"; but even then Admiral E. J. King, U.S.N. (the Chief of Naval Operations) gave the British representatives at the conference the clear impression that the President's decision was little to his liking. In retrospect the American view of the importance of the contribution which the Chinese could make to the defeat of Japan seems to have been considerably exaggerated. Though they were certainly containing large numbers of Japanese soldiers, it would have been impossible in any case for those enemy forces to be moved to the key points in the Pacific—for the simple reason that Japanese maritime power was by this time too far gone in defeat. Thus the fate of all the Japanese armies in China depended—not on supplying Chiang Kai-Shek, but on command of the seas; and as long as the enemy could not regain such command his forces on the Asian mainland were in fact wasting assets. Indeed the American emphasis on the importance of the land campaigns in China appears to be a surprising, though not a unique example of their occasional hankering after a continental as opposed to a maritime strategy; and the fact that such views found expression at the very time when American sea power was reaping such abundant rewards in the Pacific makes the emphasis they placed on operations on the Asian mainland the more puzzling. We may also here note that when, in the autumn of 1944, the U.S. Navy expressed a strong preference for striking from the Philippines across to the coast of China, it was General MacArthur, a soldier, who insisted that the proper strategy was to continue the advance by sea up the island road towards the Japanese mainland.

The first offensive operation by the reconstituted Eastern Fleet was a carrier air attack on the Andaman Islands on 21st June; but in the following month Admiral Somerville was able to execute a more ambitious project, and on 25th July naval aircrews took off from the *Victorious* and *Illustrious* to strike at Sabang on the northern tip of Sumatra[1] simultaneously with a heavy bombardment of the port installations by battleships, cruisers and destroyers. The air and naval bombardments together inflicted considerable damage on enemy airfields, oil tanks and port facilities. This was the last operation directed by Admiral Somerville, who was relieved by Admiral Sir Bruce Fraser, lately C.-in-C., Home Fleet, on 23rd August. It was, perhaps, a little unjust that the change should take place just when the offensive prospects, which had been denied to Somerville throughout the whole of his 29 months of command, had so greatly improved; but the change of appointments was part of the larger readjustments then in train, and Admiral Fraser was soon to take the greater part of the Eastern Fleet to the Pacific.

Late in August and early in September the Eastern Fleet's carrier aircrews again attacked Japanese installations in northern Sumatra, and in mid-October the whole fleet sailed to strike at the Nicobars once more. This operation was planned to divert Japanese attention from the Philippines, where the Americans landed on 20th of that month, and our ships therefore remained in the Bay of Bengal for several days, during which air strikes and bombardments were frequently repeated; but it is doubtful whether the diversionary plan had any effect on Japanese naval dispositions. On 22nd November Admiral Fraser formally assumed the title of C.-in-C., British Pacific Fleet, and his former command (now renamed the East Indies Fleet) was taken over by Vice-Admiral Sir Arthur Power. One more carrier air attack took place in the Bay of Bengal before the end of the year; but bad weather frustrated the attempt to put the oil refinery at Belawan Deli in Sumatra out of action on 20th December.

While the aircraft carriers and other surface ships were thus increasing their pressure and re-establishing our control of the Bay of Bengal, our submarines, of which 26 were based on Ceylon, were intensifying their patrols in the Malacca Straits and off Japanese bases from southern Burma to far away Java. They not only sank 16 merchantmen (35,000 tons) during the last six months of 1944, but also accounted for two German and one Japanese submarine. In September, however, the 8th Submarine Flotilla moved to

[1] See Map p. 153.

Western Australia, and thereafter its boats came under the American Seventh Fleet, which was responsible for the South-West Pacific theatre.

By the end of 1944 the sweeps and air attacks by the East Indies Fleet, the patrols in offshore waters by our submarines, and the minelaying by Allied aircraft had so far deprived the Japanese of control of the Bay of Bengal that only a dribble of supplies was getting through by sea to their armies in Burma and Siam. Large ships now stood little chance of survival on the route between Singapore and Rangoon, and the small coasting craft which they had to employ as substitutes could not possibly meet the needs of their land forces. There now remained to them only the long overland route from the ports on the South China coast right across Siam; and that too was soon to be imperilled. It was indeed in this period that all the Japanese forces in South-East Asia began to experience an acute shortage of supplies, and that was bound to have a decisive influence on the land campaigns. But our renascent maritime power was having yet wider effects than the strangulation of the enemy armies in the theatre; for our submarines, bombers and mines were jointly taking such a heavy toll from the ships running between Japan proper and the conquests that she had gained so easily in 1942 that her whole economy was beginning to suffer, and the Allies' blockade was affecting all their plans and purposes very drastically. The British land forces in the South-East Asia theatre were, on the other hand, being steadily nourished by a great flow of seaborne supplies, and in consequence by June, 1944, the Fourteenth Army in Burma had taken the offensive and was forcing its way eastwards towards the Irrawaddy valley. In October, after the end of the monsoon season, we therefore prepared to assist the land operations by gaining full control of the strip of deeply indented, jungle-clad coast known as the Arakan, which stretches some 300 miles to the north-east from the Irrawaddy estuary.[1] Our plan had been to seize firstly the key port of Akyab by assault from the sea in February, 1945; but when we learnt that the Japanese were withdrawing from it a Royal Marine Commando brigade was quickly embarked and carried there. On 2nd January Akyab was won without serious opposition, and our combined operations flotillas and light naval craft then prepared to extend our hold over

[1] See Map p. 153.

the whole of that long-disputed stretch of coast by a series of landings, reaching south-west towards Rangoon.

While these promising developments were taking place on the Burma coast, the British Pacific Fleet was beginning to form in Ceylon, and on 4th December Admiral Fraser flew to Australia, where its main base was to be established at Sydney, and then on to Pearl Harbour for discussions with Admiral Nimitz on the employment of his ships. But before telling the story of the return of the White Ensign to the Pacific we must briefly review the events which took place in that theatre in October and November, 1944, while we were building up our strength and taking the offensive in the Indian Ocean.

The Americans were so encouraged by the great successes claimed in the carrier air attacks on the Philippine bases in September (which were actually considerably exaggerated) that they advanced the date of their assault on those islands from 15th November to 20th October. As in previous large combined operations two assault forces, one coming from Hollandia in New Guinea and the other from Hawaii via Manus in the Admiralty Islands,[1] were to be employed for the initial landings, which were to take place in Leyte Gulf. The naval side was made the responsibility of Admiral Kinkaid's Seventh Fleet, which was specially reinforced for the purpose. Serving under his command were the Australian cruisers and smaller warships which had worked with the Seventh Fleet since its inception, but the enterprise was otherwise entirely an American one. While the plans were being completed Admiral Halsey's Third Fleet[2] struck repeatedly at the enemy bases in the Philippines themselves, in Formosa and the islands of the Nansei Shoto which they used as staging points for reinforcements moving south from their homeland.[3] So effective were these blows that when the assault forces landed at Leyte on 20th October they encountered little initial resistance. It was now that the Japanese first employed suicide tactics by sending "Kamikaze"[4] pilots in bomb-laden planes to immolate themselves on the decks of Allied

[1] See Map p. 185.
[2] The Third and Fifth Fleets consisted in general of the same ships, the title being altered according to whether Admiral Halsey or Spruance was in command.
[3] See Map p. 431.
[4] The name "Kamikaze," meaning "Divine Wind," given to the Japanese "Special Naval Attack Force," derives from the salvation of their country in 1281, when a timely typhoon destroyed a Mongol invasion fleet.

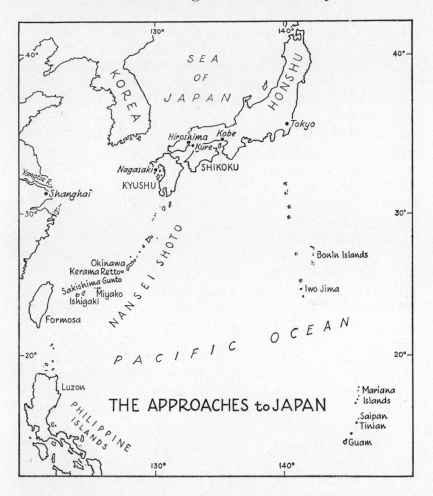

THE APPROACHES to JAPAN

warships, and on the day after the landings the cruiser *Australia* was the first ship to suffer in that way. During the succeeding weeks such attacks became an almost daily occurrence; but although many ships were damaged few were lost, and the new tactics never looked like imperilling the assault on the Philippines. What did come very near to accomplishing such a purpose was the sortie by the Japanese Navy which started on 22nd October. Their plan was to lure Halsey's very powerful fleet away from its chief function of covering the landings by sending south from Japan a decoy force, which would include all their surviving carriers—even though very few

431

aircraft or aircrews could be provided for them. While the Third Fleet was attending to the decoy force two strong squadrons of battleships, cruisers and destroyers were to emerge into the Philippine Sea by way of the San Bernardino and Surigao Straits north and south of Leyte Gulf, to join hands in an attack on the invasion shipping in the early hours of 25th October.[1] The southern Japanese force was however intercepted and almost annihilated by Kinkaid's Seventh Fleet in the Surigao Straits on the night of 24th-25th; but Halsey had meanwhile swallowed the bait of the decoy force from Japan, and had set off in hot pursuit of it with his entire strength— leaving the San Bernardino Strait wide open to the centre Japanese force. The result was that when its commander, Admiral Kurita, emerged into the Philippine Sea early on 25th with four battleships, eight cruisers and eleven destroyers he found nothing except a few American escort carriers and destroyers to bar his way into Leyte Gulf. Happily he failed to seize the golden opportunity which Halsey's impetuosity, and a misunderstanding between him and Kinkaid about whether the exit from the San Bernardino Strait was guarded, had thrown at his feet. He engaged the escort carriers in a somewhat desultory manner, probably taking them to be far more powerful units; and after they and their few accompanying destroyers had counter-attacked most gallantly, he withdrew by the way he had come. In response to urgent appeals from Kinkaid two of the carrier groups of the Third Fleet had meanwhile been detached to support the slender forces covering the invasion shipping; but they arrived too late to do more than harry the retreating Kurita. Halsey's other two groups did ultimately succeed in sinking all four carriers of the Japanese decoy force; but although its commander, Admiral Ozawa, had carried out his part of the plan to perfection he could not know that Kurita's hesitancy had already made vain the sacrifice of his ships. In spite of the escape of the greater part of Kurita's force the losses suffered by the Japanese Navy in the three battles collectively known as Leyte Gulf were so heavy that never again was it able to send out anything resembling a balanced fleet, or interfere effectively with the development of the Allies' offensive strategy. Though all thus ended well on 25th October, 1944, and in any case our preponderance at sea was so great that a setback would in all probability have been only tem-

[1] See Map p. 341.

porary, there is no doubt that Kurita's irresolution at a critical moment rescued the American command from a very awkward predicament. It seems that the chief lesson to be drawn from the narrowness of the escape is that in a big combined operation unification of command is essential; for had the Seventh Fleet not been under MacArthur and the Third Fleet under Nimitz the misunderstandings between Kinkaid and Halsey would surely have been unlikely to arise.

After the Battle of Leyte Gulf, Allied operations in the Philippines prospered. As always General MacArthur used his maritime power most skilfully; and by a succession of subsidiary assaults from the sea he extended his hold on the group so rapidly that, by the early days of 1945, he was ready to tackle the main island of Luzon, where lay the capital city of Manila, from which he had been expelled in defeat in 1942 and on which his eyes had ever since been focused.

At the beginning of 1945 the British Pacific Fleet was still in the Indian Ocean, where the carriers were re-equipping and training their aircrews; for we were well aware that the Americans had far outstripped us in the science of naval air operations, and especially in working scores of aircraft from several carriers simultaneously and for a single purpose. Our backwardness had arisen from the fact that the European theatres had given us little scope to develop those arts, while the expansion of the Fleet Air Arm had been so rapid that it had constantly threatened to outstrip our capacity to train new aircrews; and we had no illusions regarding the superiority of American aircraft, such as the Avenger bomber, over our own corresponding types. The Royal Navy was however determined that on its return to the Pacific its American comrades should find no cause to regard its operational efficiency as inferior to their own very high standard.

On 4th January Rear-Admiral Sir Philip Vian attacked the oil refineries at Belawan Deli in Sumatra with aircraft from the *Indomitable*, *Victorious* and *Indefatigable*; and this time he was much more successful than on the previous occasion, when bad weather had frustrated the striking force's attempts to reach the primary

---

[1] Japanese losses amounted in all to three battleships, four aircraft carriers, ten cruisers and nine destroyers. The Americans lost only two escort carriers, three destroyers and a submarine.

target.[1] But this operation was really only a preliminary to the heavier blow which we intended to strike while the fleet was on its way to Australia. On 16th January Admiral Vian accordingly left Ceylon with four carriers, one battleship, three cruisers and ten destroyers to attack the two big refineries at Palembang in eastern Sumatra, which were capable between them of meeting the greater part of Japan's needs of aviation fuel.[2] On 24th and 29th January, with a refuelling period in between, about 50 Avengers from the four carriers, escorted by some 80 fighters, devastated the refineries and inflicted heavy losses on the Japanese aircraft caught on the nearby airfields. These were by far the most successful attacks so far made in the Indian Ocean, and on 4th February the fleet arrived at Fremantle full of confidence in the future—though still quite unaware of what it held. At Fremantle Vice-Admiral Sir Bernard Rawlings hoisted his flag in the *King George V* as second-in-command, British Pacific Fleet, while Rear-Admiral Vian continued in command of the First Aircraft Carrier Squadron. Then the whole fleet pushed on to Sydney, where it arrived on 11th and 12th February and was met by Admiral Fraser, the C.-in-C., who had established his headquarters ashore at that base.

Long before the fighting fleet moved to its new theatre the Admiralty had begun to prepare the floating supply organisation which it would need; for we had accepted the principle that in all important respects the British Pacific Fleet would be self-supporting, and we were well aware that without a "Fleet Train" on the American model it would be impossible for it to carry out protracted operations far from any permanent base. Unfortunately, the Admiralty found it extraordinarily difficult to acquire ships which were well suited to such work, since most of our best merchantmen were needed to sustain the already much reduced programme of imports into Britain and to supply our armies overseas. The consequence was that the Admiralty had to do the best it could with a heterogeneous collection of ships drawn from a wide variety of sources. Some were commissioned into the Navy and wore the White Ensign; others, principally tankers, wore the Blue Ensign of the Royal Fleet Auxiliaries; some were ordinary merchantmen flying the Red Ensign, and a few came from the merchant navies of our European Allies and worked under their national colours.

[1] The attack on 20th December, 1944. See p. 428.   [2] See Map p. 153.

Moreover, their crews were as mixed in origins as the ships themselves: and that was bound to produce administrative complications. In spite of all the difficulties inherent in creating a large new supply organisation some 12,000 miles from home, we did finally assemble about 60 ships for the Fleet Train, and a Flag Officer was specially appointed to command them; but we were never able to provide enough fast tankers, and the lack of them was to prove a serious handicap to the fighting ships. In December, 1944, the Americans had agreed that we should use Manus in the Admiralty Islands as an "intermediate base" until such time as a more advanced base could be set up in the Philippines, and the Fleet Train ships accordingly now began to carry supplies there from Australia.

Although by the end of February, 1945, most of the warships had arrived on their new station, and the arrangements for their supply while on active operations were well advanced, the actual employment of the British fleet had not yet been settled. Whereas General MacArthur wanted to use it at once in the Philippine operations, and then to liberate Borneo, Admiral Nimitz wished to include Fraser's ships in the covering forces for the invasion of Okinawa. Not until mid-March, and after a good deal of pressure from London, did Nimitz's view prevail, and on the 15th Admiral Rawlings accordingly signalled to the C.-in-C. Pacific from the *King George V* at Manus reporting the fleet's readiness for service. Admiral Nimitz replied on behalf of the United States Navy with a warm welcome for the British contingent which, he said, "will greatly add to our power to strike the enemy." Thus did the British Government fulfil its promise that we would not rest until the last enemy had been defeated.

To return to the Indian Ocean, the departure of the British Pacific Fleet for Australia left Admiral Power with two capital ships, nine cruisers, four escort carriers and about two dozen destroyers with which to carry on the offensive; but as he had in addition some 70 flotilla vessels for escort-of-convoy duty he was no longer plagued, as his predecessor had been, by having to divert his fleet destroyers to such duties. Moreover, the German and Japanese submarine campaign in this theatre was now virtually over; for the last of the U-boats (apart from four which remained behind and were finally turned over to the Japanese) were withdrawing towards the Cape of Good Hope on their way back to Europe.[1]

Meanwhile, with the Fourteenth Army making good progress down the Irrawaddy, the prospect of capturing Rangoon in the near future appeared excellent, and a plan to achieve that purpose by an assault from the sea was therefore prepared. Operation "Dracula," as it was called, was, however, bound up with the question whether the Army would reach Rangoon before the monsoon broke in May; and to give General Slim's men every chance of winning the race against the weather, transport aircraft were organised to fly in supplies for them from the recently captured bases on the Arakan coast. The success of this policy was such that the seaborne assault on Rangoon appeared likely to prove redundant, and towards the end of February the Supreme Commander therefore decided that it should be dropped. However, the strong American desire to use their transport aircraft to supply General Chiang Kai-Shek's armies, whose operations in China they regarded as more important than any purpose in South-East Asia, led to the decision to withdraw them on 1st June; and that made it doubtful whether the Fourteenth Army would capture Rangoon before the monsoon broke. Admiral Mountbatten now had no alternative but to remount the seaborne assault, and D-Day was fixed for 2nd May. The naval assault forces assembled at Ramree on the Arakan coast, which we had captured in the previous January, and between 27th and 30th April six convoys set out for the scene of the landings. Meanwhile, the main East Indies fleet under Vice-Admiral H. T. C. Walker covered their progress, carried out diversionary bombardments of the Andaman and Nicobar Islands, and then swept into the Gulf of Martaban to catch any Japanese ships attempting to escape from Rangoon.[2] On the night of 1st-2nd May minesweepers cleared the approaches to the river estuary, and the troopships then cautiously approached the coast. The navigational hazards were so serious that the "lowering positions" of the transports had been placed no less than 25 miles offshore, which meant that the landing craft had to make very long passages to reach their beaches. None the less, the first waves touched down on time—only to find that the Japanese had already evacuated the whole area. Most of the troops therefore re-embarked in their landing craft, and after the sweepers had cleared the mines from the twenty miles of river, they were carried up to Rangoon

[1] See p. 405.   [2] See Map p. 153.

by water. Though the seaborne expedition thus beat the Fourteenth Army by a short head, there is no doubt that the credit for the recapture of the great port belongs mainly to the soldiers who had fought their way down the Irrawaddy valley.

On 9th May, just after the main fleet had returned to Ceylon from covering the Rangoon expedition, one of our submarines on patrol in the Malacca Straits reported the Japanese heavy cruiser *Haguro* and a few smaller warships steering towards the Andaman Islands, whose garrison they actually intended to evacuate. The fleet at once left Trincomalee; but on 11th it was sighted from the air, whereupon the *Haguro* and her consorts reversed course. Admiral Walker, however, expected the enemy to make a second attempt and therefore steamed well clear to the south to avoid being re-sighted. On the night of 14th-15th he detached his escort carriers and the 26th Destroyer Flotilla (five ships under Captain M. L. Power) to search the waters north of Sumatra. His guess was quickly proved correct, and late on the following evening one of the destroyers picked up the enemy by radar at 34 miles' range. Captain Power now closed at high speed, with his ships formed to catch the cruiser whichever way she turned. A close-range mêlée followed, but many of the British destroyers' torpedoes found their mark, and at 2 a.m. on 16th the *Haguro* was sent to the bottom about 45 miles off Penang. It was a heartening success for the East Indies fleet at last to sink a major Japanese warship, and the action in the Malacca Straits left us in virtually undisputed control of the whole Indian Ocean. The Supreme Commander could now go ahead confidently with his plan to carry out large-scale landings on the east coast of Malaya; but before we tell the story of the last phase in South-East Asia we must return once more to the Pacific.

On 19th February, a week after Admiral Rawlings's ships reached Sydney, the U.S. Marines assaulted Iwo Jima in the Bonin Islands,[1] whose importance lay in the fact that they were only some 650 miles from Tokyo, and by gaining use of the airfields which the Japanese had built on them the American heavy bombers could be given fighter escorts right through to their targets. The Japanese, however, defended Iwo Jima most stubbornly, and it was 16th March before all resistance had been quelled. But the Americans did not wait until that tiny island (it measured only 4½ miles long and 2½ wide)

[1] See Map p. 431.

was cleared of enemies before going ahead with their next plan, which was to be a much bigger seaborne assault on Okinawa, the key island in the Nansei Shoto; and in the execution of that purpose the British fleet was to play a part for, as we have seen, Nimitz's proposal to use our ships on the northern operation had been preferred to MacArthur's plan to employ them in the Philippines and against Borneo.

The Okinawa expedition was one of the biggest of the Pacific war, and Admiral Spruance's Fifth Fleet (of which the British contingent formed a part) totalled over 1,200 ships. Two Attack Forces, one from the Solomons and the other from Leyte, sailed on 8th and 21st March respectively, and while they were steaming towards the objective, Mitscher's carrier aircrews struck repeated blows at the airfields and naval bases on the Japanese mainland. On 23rd he switched to the defences of Okinawa itself, and three days later the first landings took place on the Kerama Retto, where the Americans planned to set up an emergency repair base. That same day, 26th March, Admiral Rawlings, who had with him the battleship *King George V*, the fleet carriers *Indomitable*, *Victorious*, *Indefatigable* and *Illustrious*, five cruisers and eleven destroyers, took up his station off the Sakishima Gunto,[1] with the object of preventing the Japanese using the six airfields of that group as staging points for reinforcements flying from Formosa to Okinawa. The principal striking power of our fleet consisted of the 218 bombers and fighters embarked in the carriers, and on 26th and 27th they made their first attacks on the targets allocated to them. The general plan was to strike on two or three successive days, and then refuel at sea from the tankers of the Fleet Train. Meanwhile, the main American attack groups were approaching Okinawa, and after very heavy preliminary bombardments from the sea and air the assault waves touched down at 8.30 a.m. on 1st April.

The most dangerous Japanese reaction to the assault on Okinawa was the massed attacks by " Kamikaze " suicide planes against the offshore warships, and on 6th April the *Indefatigable* was hit by one such attacker; but her armoured flight deck saved her from serious damage. That evening a Japanese squadron consisting of the giant battleship *Yamato*, one cruiser and eight destroyers came south from the Inland Sea to attack the Allied invasion fleet; but the sortie was

[1] See Map p. 431.

a very forlorn hope, and early next morning Mitscher unleashed his carrier aircrews, who soon sent the whole force except a few of the destroyers to the bottom. The " Battle of the East China Sea" of 7th April, 1945, was the last attempt to challenge Allied control of the sea approaches to Japan.

On 9th April Spruance switched the British carriers to the airfields in northern Formosa, from which enemy bombers had been setting out to attack the invasion shipping off Okinawa; and on 12th and 13th they accordingly struck at those new targets. Admiral Rawlings's force should then have returned to Leyte, but a revival of enemy activity in the Sakishima group caused him to suggest that he should first neutralise those airfields once again. The offer was readily accepted, and three more heavy attacks accomplished the purpose satisfactorily. On 20th, by which time the B.P.F. had been working continuously off the enemy's coasts for a month, Admiral Rawlings took his ships back to Leyte to replenish.

Meanwhile on Okinawa the assault forces had been encountering very stubborn resistance, and repeated attacks by Kamikazes were causing a good deal of damage to the offshore shipping; but American ingenuity in devising counter-measures, and the resolution with which the fighter aircraft and ships' gunners met the menace of the suicide bombers, prevented them ever inflicting such losses as might have forced the fleet to withdraw.

On 1st May the British fleet was ready to re-enter the fray, and sailed north from Leyte in much the same strength as before. Three days later Admiral Rawlings reopened his attack on the Sakishima Gunto with a battleship and cruiser bombardment of the airfields, and it was now that the British ships came in for their full share of suicide attacks. On the 4th the *Formidable* and *Indomitable* were both hit, but were able to carry on working their aircraft; five days later the *Formidable* was hit again, and another Kamikaze crashed aboard the *Victorious*. Though many aircraft parked on the carriers' flight decks were destroyed, the strikes at the enemy airfields continued until 25th, on which day the fleet set course for Manus. During its first two months of active service in the Fifth Fleet (26th March–25th May) the British carrier aircrews flew 5,335 sorties in which they dropped nearly 1,000 tons of bombs on enemy airfields and port installations. Aircraft losses had totalled 160, but about a third of them arose from deck landing accidents—to which the flimsy

Seafire fighters (which were converted R.A.F. Spitfires) were especially prone.

The struggle on Okinawa did not end until 21st June, and proved one of the costliest campaigns of the Pacific war; but it gained for the Allies excellent airfields within easy striking reach of the Japanese mainland.

Meanwhile, General McArthur's forces, having regained the whole Philippine group, were conducting a series of combined operations in Borneo, chiefly with the object of recovering the oil-fields in that island. The campaign, in which Australian troops and warships played a part, opened with an attack on Tarakan on 1st May and ended with the seizure of the oil centre of Balikpapan in the Dutch part of the island on 1st July.[1] Though the combined operations were beautifully planned and executed, it is difficult not to conclude that, taking account of the stage the war had reached, the destruction which they involved was hardly justifiable; for the Japanese garrisons were already so completely cut off that their ultimate surrender was certain.

One part of the British Pacific Fleet, including the newly arrived carrier *Implacable*, left Manus on 10th June to attack the Japanese naval base at Truk in the Carolines—which the Americans had by-passed in their great drive westwards across the central Pacific; and on 28th the main body sailed from Sydney to resume duty with the Third Fleet.[2] When Admiral Rawlings met Admiral Halsey off Japan in mid-July they discussed the manner in which the British task force should be fitted into the Third Fleet's organisation, and how it should be employed during the next phase of the offensive. This was to consist of carrier air attacks and heavy gun bombard-ments of the Japanese mainland, preparatory to the final invasion which the Allied leaders planned to launch in November; and Admiral Rawlings unhesitatingly accepted that his ships should serve as an additional group of the American Fast Carrier Task Force. On 17th July his ships accordingly went into action against targets on the Japanese mainland, and that operation set the pattern for the succeeding weeks. Admiral Halsey was, however, determined that the Royal Navy should have no share in the destruction of the last

[1] See Map p. 341.

[2] Admiral W. F. Halsey had relieved Admiral Spruance in command of the main American sea-going force on 28th May, and in consequence its title changed from Fifth to Third Fleet.

German supply ship in the Ægean, attacked and later sunk by Beaufighters, February, 1944

Raid on Soerabaya by aircraft of the East Indies Fleet, 17th May, 1944

U.S. Marines approach the beach at Bougainville in the Northern Solomon Islands, 1st November, 1943. (*Official U.S. Coast Guard Photograph*)

H.M.S. *Formidable* after an attack by Japanese suicide planes, May, 1945. The carrier was fully operational again within two hours

remnants of the Japanese Navy, most of which were lying in their base at Kure. When therefore he switched his carrier air power on to those targets towards the end of July Rawlings's ships were given other duties. After three days of sustained onslaught on Kure the Japanese ships had nearly all been sunk at their moorings, American honour had been satisfied, and Pearl Harbour had been avenged.

While the onslaught on Japan's towns, dockyards, airfields and industries was in progress, far to the south we carried out a whole series of penetrations into enemy waters using the latest type of midget submarine (XE-craft). On 30th July XE.1 and XE.3, which had been towed from Borneo by parent submarines, planted their charges under the heavy cruiser *Takao*, which was lying off the Singapore naval base, and damaged her so severely that she sank on to the seabed. At about the same time other XE-craft cut the telegraph cables off Saigon and Hong Kong. Though these "attacks at source" came too late to influence the progress of the war, the gallantry with which they were carried out makes them worthy of remembrance; and they confirmed what we had learnt in the attacks made on specially important targets (such as the *Tirpitz*[1]) in the European theatres—namely, that in the hands of skilled and determined crews the midget submarines were excellently suited to the purpose for which they had been designed.

While the Third Fleet was prosecuting its offensive against targets on the Japanese mainland with ever-rising vigour the blockade of that country was being tightened to a stranglehold. In 1944 the Japanese Merchant Navy's losses shot up to over two million tons, and by the end of that year, when the Allies had established themselves firmly in the Philippines, Japan was virtually cut off from her overseas possessions. Her merchant ships were, however, still able to move between the homeland and the ports of North China, Korea and Manchuria, and considerable quantities of supplies were being drawn from those sources. The final stage of the blockade consisted therefore of sealing off Japan from the mainland of Asia; and in March, 1945, the American Army Air Force therefore opened a very intensive minelaying campaign with that purpose. It lasted 142 days, during which 12,000 mines were laid in ports and channels around the Japanese coast. By the end of July enemy shipping

[1] See pp. 317-8.

movements had come almost completely to a standstill, Japanese industries were in chaos, her economy was breaking down, and her people were starving. The blockade had in fact been far more successful than we realised at the time; and the pattern was exactly the same in South-East Asia as in the Pacific. In both theatres the steady attrition suffered by the Japanese merchant navy reduced to impotence the numerous land forces which they had locked up in remote territories. Finally, we may remark how the strategy by which Germany had hoped to bring Britain to her knees, and which failed only narrowly to accomplish its object, was applied by the Allies with complete success against Japan; and that the same instruments of war—the submarine, the bomber and the mine— were used in both campaigns. The difference between failure in the one case and success in the other lay chiefly in the fact that whereas Britain was from the very beginning fully conscious of the value of her mercantile tonnage, and strove her utmost to protect and conserve it, the Japanese squandered their assets with reckless prodigality. Of the $8\frac{1}{2}$ million tons of Japanese merchant shipping which were sunk or destroyed during the whole war, about 57 per cent was accounted for by Allied submarines, 29 per cent by aircraft and 7 per cent by mines; but the mines had an important additional influence through the long delays they imposed on enemy shipping movements by closing ports and channels.

When the American carrier aircraft had destroyed the last enemy warships in Kure the Third Fleet, including the British contingent, moved north-east up the Japanese coast and continued its air attacks and bombardments against shore targets. After each series of strikes the fighting ships withdrew to their fuelling rendezvous, and in spite of frequent storms (for the typhoon season was now at its height), and the chronic handicap imposed by the small and slow tankers of the Fleet Train, Admiral Rawlings managed to keep up with his American colleagues. It was while the fleet was striking at airfields in Honshu on 6th August that the news of the explosion of the first atomic bomb over Hiroshima was received; but the naval operations continued until the 11th, when Japan accepted the terms of the " Potsdam Declaration ". In the final phase hundreds of aircraft were destroyed on the Japanese mainland, heavy gun bombardments pulverised dockyards and factories along the coast, and a virtually clean sweep was made of enemy shipping. It is now plain that, no matter what other measures had been taken by the Allies, the surrender of Japan could not have been long deferred; for she had been totally defeated at sea, and the blockade of the homeland had encompassed her final ruin.

Given a free choice the men of the B.P.F. would probably all have wished to remain off the Japanese coast to witness the last scenes; but plans had been made much earlier for the fleet to return to Sydney after the series of strikes just described, and in consequence no fresh tankers had been sent up to them. The result was that on 12th August the greater part of Admiral Rawlings's force regretfully set course to the south, leaving only his flagship the *King George V*, the carrier *Indefatigable* and certain smaller units, including a few from the Australian and New Zealand Navies, to represent the British Empire at the surrender ceremonies, which took place on board Halsey's flagship, the *Missouri*, on 2nd September. It was from the quarterdeck of the *King George V* that, after she had anchored in Tokyo Bay, the British sailors watched the sun set with highly appropriate symbolism behind the snow-capped cone of Japan's sacred mountain Fujiyama.

Meanwhile, in the Indian Ocean Admiral Mountbatten had ordered that the combined operation against the west coast of Malaya, which had reached an advanced stage of planning, should go ahead; and the whole East Indies Fleet therefore set out across the Bay of Bengal with the object of occupying Penang and then sweeping the approaches to Singapore. But on 19th August General MacArthur, in his capacity of Supreme Commander, Allied Powers, ordered that no landings were to be made until the instrument of surrender had been signed: and this somewhat unnecessary insistence on formality dislocated all the purposes of the South-East Asia theatre. The fleet and the troop transports had to hang about in very uncomfortable circumstances, in monsoon weather and short of supplies, off the Nicobars; and it was 28th August before they reached Penang. On 2nd September we landed forces there and also at Sabang in Sumatra, what time the sweepers were clearing the waters to the south. Next day the Commander-in-Chief, East Indies Fleet, arrived at Singapore. His warships were soon followed by the troop transports, and on 12th September Admiral Mountbatten accepted the surrender of all the Japanese forces in his theatre at a ceremony in the Singapore Municipal Buildings. The re-occupation of Hong Kong presented peculiar political difficulties: for the Americans would not concern themselves in any way with a British colony, and we had to take account of General Chiang Kai-Shek's susceptibilities as well; but on 30th August Rear-Admiral C. H. J. Harcourt arrived there with a strong naval force, and another surrender ceremony was enacted on 16th September. Lastly, Admiral Fraser sent a squadron to Rabaul, to receive the surrender of the 140,000 Japanese troops who had been cut off in New Britain and the adjacent islands for over a year, while other British warships and troop transports arrived in the Dutch East Indies with the object of establishing order and starting the flow of relief supplies for the civil population.

In the final phase of the war against Japan the ships of the British Pacific and East Indies Fleets and the Fleet Train were all employed on urgent humanitarian tasks. Prisoners-of-war, who had languished in appalling conditions for over three years, had to be rescued and succoured: food and medical supplies had to be carried to the starving people of South-East Asia: and order had to be maintained over a vast area. Many months thus elapsed before the White Ensign ships had completed those duties, and their own crews could return " to enjoy the blessings of the land and the fruits of their labours."

APPENDIX

SELECTED STATISTICS CONCERNING THE WAR AT SEA

3rd September, 1939–15th August, 1945

MERCHANT SHIPPING LOSSES CAUSED BY ENEMY ACTION

5,150 ships totalling 21,570,720 Gross Registered tons were sunk. Of this total 2,714 ships of 11,455,906 tons were British, and the remainder were Allied and neutral. In 1939 the British Merchant Navy consisted of 9,488 ships of 21,215,261 tons. Thus 28·6 per cent of the original total of ships and 54·4 per cent of the original tonnage were sunk. Of the total Allied losses:

2828	ships	of	14,687,231	tons were sunk	by	submarine
820	„	„	2,889,883	„	„	„	aircraft
534	„	„	1,406,037	„	„	„	mine
104	„	„	498,447	„	„	„	warship raider
133	„	„	829,644	„	„	„	merchant raider
99	„	„	229,676	„	„	„	E-boat
632	„	„	1,029,802	„	„	„	other cause, scuttling, capture, unknown etc.

The biggest annual loss was in 1942 when 1,664 ships of 7,790,697 tons were sunk, of which total U-boats accounted for 1,160 ships of 6,266,215 tons.

The theatre of greatest loss was the North Atlantic, where 2,232 ships of 11,899,732 tons were sunk. Second to the North Atlantic were the waters around the United Kingdom (including the Arctic) where 1,431 ships of 3,768,599 tons were sunk.

The months of greatest loss were March, 1942, when 273 ships of 834,164 tons were lost, of which 95 ships of 534,064 tons were sunk in the North Atlantic and 98 ships of 183,773 in the Far East; and June, 1942, when 173 ships of 834,196 tons were lost, of which U-boats accounted for 144 ships of 700,235 tons, all but 20 of them (76,690 tons) being sunk in the North Atlantic.

In addition to losses caused by enemy action about 1,600 ships of over 3,000,000 tons were lost through "marine causes" (i.e. grounding, collision, etc.) during the war.

GERMAN U-BOAT LOSSES

Of the 1,162 U-boats built and commissioned during the war, 785 (U.31 was sunk twice) were lost through one cause or another, 156 surrendered and the remainder were scuttled at the end of the war.

Appendix

Of the 785 sunk U-boats, the instruments which brought about their destruction were as follows:

Surface ships	246
Shore based aircraft (excluding bombing raids) .	245
Ship borne aircraft	43
Shared between surface ships and aircraft . .	50
Submarines	21
Bombing raids	61
Mines . . . , ...	26
Accidents, marine causes, scuttling . . .	57
Russian action	7
Unknown causes	29

British forces (including those of the Commonwealth and Allied forces operating under British control) sank 514, United States forces sank 166, and 12 were shared between British and United States forces.

CASUALTIES

Royal Navy casualties amounted to 50,758 killed, 820 missing, 14,663 wounded. The Women's Royal Naval Service had 102 killed and 22 wounded. The British Merchant Navy lost 30,248 men through enemy action.

Appendix

MAJOR WARSHIP LOSSES OF THE NAVIES OF THE BRITISH COMMONWEALTH

	R.N.	R.A.N.	R.C.N.	R.I.N.	BRITISH SHIPS MANNED BY ALLIED NAVIES
Battleships	3	—	—	—	—
Battle cruisers	2	—	—	—	—
Aircraft carriers	5	—	—	—	—
Escort carriers	3	—	—	—	—
Cruisers	28	3	—	—	1
Destroyers	132	4	6	—	7
Submarines	74	—	—	—	3
Monitors	1	—	—	—	—
Sloops	10	2	—	1	—
Cutters	3	—	—	—	—
Frigates	10	—	1	—	—
Corvettes	22	—	10	1	5
Fleet minesweepers	32	3	4	—	—
Fast minelayers	3	—	—	—	—
Other minelayers	5	—	—	—	—
Armed merchant cruisers	15	—	—	—	—
Anti-aircraft ships	6	—	—	—	—
Fighter-catapult ships	2	—	—	—	—
Submarine and destroyer depot ships	2	—	—	—	—

In addition 1,035 auxiliary and minor war vessels of the Royal Navy, including those on loan to the Commonwealth and Allied navies, were lost.

Appendix

PRINCIPAL WARSHIP LOSSES OF THE GERMAN AND ITALIAN NAVIES

	GERMAN NAVY (including ex-Italian and ex-French ships taken into service)	ITALIAN NAVY (including ex-French and ex-Yugoslav ships taken into service)
Battleships	2	I
Battle cruisers	2	—
Pocket battleships	3	—
Old battleships	2	—
Aircraft carrier (never completed)	I	—
Cruisers	8	14
Destroyers and torpedo-boats	101	85
Armed merchant cruisers ..	7	—
Minelayers	23	3
Submarines	785	84
Corvettes and escort vessels ..	25	5
Minesweepers (M-boats and R-boats)	282	35
Sperrbrecher (mine destructor ships) ..	64	—
S-boats (M.T.B.s, called E-boats by British)	146	about 50
Miscellaneous craft	860	about 72
Naval Ferry barges	500-600	about 60

NOTE.—The Italian losses have been calculated from 10th June, 1940–8th September, 1943.

Appendix

CONVOYS

A total of 2,889 escorted trade convoys were run to and from the United Kingdom. Out of 85,775 ships that sailed in them, 654 were sunk, a loss rate of only 0.7 per cent.

U.K. COASTAL CONVOYS

A total of 7,944 convoys were run. Out of 175,608 ships that sailed in them 248 ships were sunk, a loss rate of 0·14 per cent.

ARCTIC CONVOYS (*August*, 1941–*May*, 1945)

811 ships sailed in convoy to North Russia. 720 completed their voyage, 33 turned back for various reasons and 58 (7·2 per cent) were sunk.

717 ships sailed in convoy from North Russia, of which 29 (4 per cent) were lost.

The total tonnage of war stores despatched to Russia by the Arctic route was approximately 4,000,000 tons, of which about 300,000 tons were lost en route. The war stores included 5,000 tanks and over 7,000 aircraft.

TRANS–ATLANTIC TROOP MOVEMENTS

1st January, 1942–*31st December*, 1943
175 "Operational Convoys" (i.e. Monster Liners generally sailing singly) carried:

Eastwards 907,954 and Westwards 185,578 fighting men of all services.

1st January, 1944–*8th May*, 1945
All troopships, including Monster Liners carried:
Eastwards 2,093,791 and Westwards 675,319 fighting men.

Summarising the foregoing 3,862,642 Allied fighting men crossed the North Atlantic in one or the other direction between 1st January, 1942, when the movements started on a big scale, and the end of the war. But, in addition to these figures, a very large number of men, the total of which has never been computed, were carried across the Atlantic before 1st January, 1942, to and from the Middle East, between Australia or New Zealand and the Middle East, to and from Malaya, India, Burma and Ceylon, from Britain to North Africa, and on many other routes. It is probably no exaggeration to say that, entirely excluding the work of American troop transports in the Pacific, ten million voyages were made by soldiers to and from the predominantly British theatres of war in British or British controlled ships.

INDEX

INDEX

ABDA Command, formation of, 180; naval operations, 182-4; disintegration of, 184

Acasta, H.M.S., loss of, 69; 95

Achates, H.M.S., loss of, 268-9

Achilles, H.M.N.Z.S., in Battle of the River Plate, 52-6; damaged, 257

Activity, H.M.S., anti-U-boat operations, 352; Arctic convoy escort, 359

Addu Atoll, naval base at, 186-7

Admiralty, organisation and responsibilities of, 30-2; war plans and policy of in '39, 33-9; pre-war precautions for defence of merchant shipping, 44; hastens installation of radar, 52; attention focused on Norway in early April '40, 59-61; action taken on German invasion of Norway, 63-5; preparations in case of invasion of the Low Countries, 72; organises withdrawal from Dunkirk, 73-80; anti-invasion plans, 86-7; recasts convoy organisation on fall of France, 89; changes ciphers, 98; reinforces Mediterranean fleet, 107; action taken against French squadron making for Dakar, 108; orders Board of Inquiry after action off C. Spartivento, 115; develops defences of merchant shipping against air attack, 118; dispositions against enemy surface raiders, 122-4; introduces continuous escort to N. Atlantic convoys, 126; dispositions against *Bismarck*, 124; 133-6; pressure on to release Coastal Command aircraft, 141; introduces " checkmate " system for suspicious ships, 142; seriously considers withdrawing to Suez Canal area, 173; strategy in S.E. Asia in Oct. '41, 175-7; 189; concern at sinkings in western Atlantic, 194; calls for Coastal Command to be strengthened, 195-6; responsibility for control of Atlantic convoys July '42, 196; presses for air attacks on warships in Brest, 197; precautionary orders against German Brest squadron, 197-8; plans raid on St. Nazaire, 203-4; concern at running Arctic convoys in summer, 204; intervention in passage of PQ17, 206-8; expects renewal of pack attacks in the Atlantic, 222; anticipates U-boats move to Cape of Good Hope, 227; preparations for operation " Torch," 241-2; sends *Victorious* to the Pacific, 254; Operational Research Department, 264; concern at sufficiency of naval forces for " Avalanche," 297; efficiency of intelligence organisation, 304; prepared to deal with acoustic torpedoes, 309; disbands minelaying squadron and releases A.M.C.s, 314; development of midget submarines, 316; investigation by in escape of *Lützow* to Baltic, 320; difficulties over naval command set up in S.E. Asia, 342-3; offer to form a " British Pacific Ocean Force," 344-5; in planning for " Neptune," 366-72; concern at introduction of new types of U-boats, 407; 414; orders attacks on enemy shipping to cease, 420; formation of Fleet Train for B.P.F., 434-5

Admiralty Islands, captured, 346; use as intermediate base for B.P.F., 435